THE CHARTERED INSTITUTE OF MARKETING

Chartered Postgraduate Diploma in Marketing

STUDY TEXT

Marketing Leadership and Planning

Valid for assessments up to September 2013

The Chartered
Institute of Marketing

BPP
LEARNING MEDIA

First edition July 2012

ISBN 9781 4453 9151 9

e-ISBN 9781 4453 7624 0

British Library Cataloguing-in-Publication Data
A catalogue record for this book
is available from the British Library

Published by

BPP Learning Media Ltd
Aldine House, Aldine Place
142-144 Uxbridge Road
London W12 8AA

www.bpp.com/learningmedia

Printed in the United Kingdom by Polestar Wheatons

Hennock Road
Marsh Barton Industrial Estate
Exeter, Devon
EX2 8RP

Your learning materials, published by BPP Learning
Media Ltd, are printed on paper obtained from
traceable sustainable sources.

We are grateful to The Chartered Institute of Marketing for
permission to reproduce in this text the unit syllabus.

Lead Author: Yasmin Sekhon

Contents

1 Studying for The Chartered Institute of Marketing (CIM) qualifications

There are a few key points to remember as you study for your CIM qualification:

(a) You are studying for a **professional** qualification. This means that you are required to use professional language and adopt a business approach in your work.

(b) You are expected to show that you have 'read widely'. Make sure that you read the quality press (and don't skip the business pages), read *Marketing, The Marketer, Research and Marketing Week* avidly.

(c) Become aware of the marketing initiatives you come across on a daily basis, for example, when you go shopping look around and think about why the store layout is as it is; consider the messages, channel choice and timings of ads when you are watching TV. It is surprising how much you will learn just by taking an interest in the marketing world around you.

(d) Get to know the way CIM write their exam papers and assignments. They use a specific approach (the Magic Formula) which is to ensure a consistent approach when designing assessment materials. Make sure you are fully aware of this as it will help you interpret what the examiner is looking for (a full description of the Magic Formula appears later).

(e) Learn how to use Harvard referencing. This is explained in detail in our CIM Chartered Postgraduate Diploma Assessment Workbook.

(f) Ensure that you read very carefully all assessment details sent to you from CIM. There are strict deadlines to meet, as well as paperwork to complete for any assignment or project you do. You also need to make sure have your CIM membership card with you at the exam. Failing to meet any assessment entry deadlines or completing written work on time will mean that you will have to wait for the next round of assessment dates and will need to pay the relevant assessment fees again.

2 The Chartered Postgraduate Diploma Syllabus

The Chartered Postgraduate Diploma in Marketing is aimed at Brand Managers, Strategic Marketing Managers, Business Development Managers and middle to senior Marketing Managers. If you are a graduate, you will be expected to have covered a minimum of half your credits in marketing subjects. You are therefore expected at this level of the qualification to demonstrate the ability to manage marketing resources and contribute to business decisions from a marketing perspective and pass the diagnostic entry test to level 7.

The aim of the qualification is to provide the knowledge and skills for you to develop an 'ability to do' in relation to strategic marketing planning and leading its implementation. CIM qualifications concentrate on applied marketing within real work-places.

The complete Chartered Postgraduate qualification is split into two stages. Stage 1 comprises 4 units. Stage 2 is a work-based project that should enable those who pass it, with the relevant experience and continuing professional development, to become Chartered Marketers.

The Stage 1 qualification contains four units:

- Unit 1 Emerging Themes
- Unit 2 Analysis and Decision
- **Unit 3 Marketing Leadership and Planning**
- Unit 4 Managing Corporate Reputation

The syllabus, as provided by CIM, can be found below with reference to our coverage within this Study Text.

Unit characteristics – Marketing Leadership and Planning

The purpose of this unit is to enable students to develop effective high level strategic marketing strategies relating to an organisation's corporate and business strategic intent in the short-, medium- and long-terms. Students should be able to analyse the corporate strategy, determine a range of high level marketing and relationship strategies, and demonstrate how these strategies will deliver an organisation's desire for growth and expansion, its changing stance on CSR, ethics and key strategic decisions.

The focus of this unit is on developing and delivering strategic marketing plans to support the delivery of an organisation's value proposition (not just the marketing function).

In order to deliver effective, innovative and creative marketing plans, students must recognise the need to deliver sophisticated change management programmes, designed to enable an organisation to be increasingly flexible and responsive in meeting the changing requirements of the market place, balanced against the requirements of the corporate strategy. This will require students to consider the reasons for change and the types of change management plans that should be put in place.

This unit is designed to provide a detailed understanding of the major issues in developing a relevant, agile and flexible market-oriented organisation, which can respond to a dynamic and changeable market environment. Students should demonstrate a detailed understanding of the issues concerning the degree of influential leadership required to execute such change within an organisation, both from the top down and from the bottom up. This will require a thorough understanding of the resources required to implement change within an organisation and to establish the level of competence and capability required to deliver an organisation's value proposition to its key stakeholders and markets.

Overarching learning outcomes

By the end of this unit students should be able to:

- Critically evaluate the links from the corporate strategy to the marketing strategy and ways of delivering an organisation's corporate mission and vision effectively

- Develop marketing strategies to establish an organisation's competitive and sustainable marketing and relationship strategies to achieve the organisation's strategic intent and deliver its value proposition

- Develop strategic but operational marketing plans at organisational level (not just functional) using synergistic planning processes, taking account of different planning frameworks (cross-functional and board level contribution) and ensuring they are within the resource capabilities of an organisation

- Determine the most appropriate organisational structures for market-oriented organisations and changing organisations, while evaluating the resource implications and requirements

- Develop sustainable competitive advantage through suitable approaches to leadership and innovation

- Assess the link between change programmes, marketing activities and shareholder value, show how these can contribute to an organisation's ongoing success, and evaluate the concepts of power, trust and commitment in the context of negotiating change with key stakeholders

Part 1 – Delivering marketing strategies

SECTION 1 – Developing and delivering an organisation's vision and mission (weighting 30%)

		Covered in chapter(s)
1.1.1	Critically analyse how to create a clear, simple, reality-based vision for an organisation and its stakeholders: ■ Identifying strategic intent ■ Creating a unique image of the organisation for the future ■ The balance of inspiration versus capability and capacity ■ Enlisting stakeholders in future possibilities ■ Balancing internal and external constraints on the vision for the future ■ Organisation's aspirations and purpose	1
1.1.2	Critically evaluate the importance of mission statements in communicating an organisation's strategic vision and identity, including: ■ Purpose, feelings and direction ■ Basis of objectives ■ Basis for strategy ■ Focal point for stakeholders ■ Values of the organisation, including moral, ethical and sustainability positioning	1
1.1.3	Identify distinctive competences of the organisation and how they can be leveraged to achieve an organisation's mission: ■ Distinctive essence of the organisation ■ Market and business definition ■ Intended positioning in the marketplace ■ Role of contribution and identification of future intent	1
1.1.4	Examine the different approaches to the strategic process: ■ Emergent, Logical incrementalism (Mintzberg/Quinn) ■ Deliberate (Kotler, Wilson and Gilligan, McDonald)	2

SECTION 2 – Developing marketing strategies and value proposition (weighting 70%)

		Covered in chapter(s)
1.2.1	Determine an organisation's value proposition through analysis of an organisation's vision, mission and corporate objectives: ■ Market definition ■ Setting strategic objectives ■ Price/value and proposition	3
1.2.2	Utilising the strategic audit, develop and present corporate strategies that are creative, customer-focused, innovative and competitive for a variety of contexts, incorporating relevant investment decisions and business cases which meet corporate objectives: ■ Product/market strategies ■ Growth strategies ■ Competitive strategies ■ Global and channel strategies ■ Brand and positioning strategies ■ CRM strategies	3
1.2.3	Critically evaluate the marketing strategy process, utilising the three key areas/levels in marketing strategy development: ■ Core strategy ■ Creation of competitive positioning (market targets, differential advantage and cost leadership) ■ Control	3
1.2.4	Determine a series of measures that enable an estimation of desired results for an organisation: ■ Marketing metrics ■ Relative perceived quality ■ Loyalty retention ■ Customer satisfaction ■ Relative price (market share/volume) ■ Market share (volume/value) ■ Perceived quality/esteem	6

The Chartered Institute of Marketing

Part 2 – Strategic marketing planning

SECTION 1 – Strategic marketing plans (weighting 30%)

		Covered in chapter(s)
2.1.1	Critically evaluate the concept of strategic marketing planning as a tool to deliver an organisation's value proposition: ■ Efficacy of formalised marketing planning ■ The specification of sustainable competitive advantage and marketing planning and its contribution to commercial success and to delivering the organisation's value proposition ■ Preparedness to meet change and implement market-focused orientation across the organisation ■ Contextualisation of marketing planning in a corporate framework (McDonald, 2007)	4
2.1.2	Analyse the corporate objectives and translate into overarching marketing objectives to support giving direction to a marketing plan: ■ The interactive process – balancing an organisation's ambitions with knowledge from individual business units ■ Relevant marketing objectives to enhance the attainment of the firm's ability to satisfy customers and foster innovation ■ From corporate objectives to setting a balanced array of marketing objectives that cover marketing and financial aspects	4

2.1.3	Assess the variables facing an organisation in order to assess the impact of the future corporate and marketing objectives against its current competences, resource capacity and financial positioning:
	
	■ Analyse key areas within an organisation:
	  – Market share
	  – Innovation
	  – Resource
	  – Productivity
	  – Social aspects and profit
	  – Alternative measures of success eg, for NFP
	
	■ Core competences:
	  – Potential access
	  – Significant contribution
	  – Difficulty for competitors to copy
	
	■ Auditing resources:
	  – Technical resources
	  – Financial standing
	  – Managerial skills
	  – Information systems
	
	■ Ansoff matrix and Gap Analysis
		4

2.1.4	Make clear recommendations that determine either changes in the strategy or further resource requirements to support the delivery of the strategic marketing plan: ■ Resource audit ■ Core competences for the attainment of a successful marketing plan ■ Marketing audit to underpin the marketing plan	4

		Covered in chapter(s)
2.1.5	Develop marketing plans utilising corporate planning frameworks to deliver an organisation's strategies and meet corporate objectives: ■ Planning typologies ■ Marketing design and implementation of planning systems ■ Integration of the marketing planning process with organisation's overall strategy and objective (to include: corporate and strategic issues, competition, industry, SWOT, business environment [PEST], marketing objectives, strategy, monitoring evaluation)	4
2.1.6	Critically evaluate why marketing plans can fail: ■ Design and implementation issues ■ Gaining management support ■ Separation of operational planning from strategic planning ■ Integration of marketing planning into a total corporate planning system	4

The Chartered Institute of Marketing

SECTION 2 – Assessing and utilising organisational resources and assets (weighting 40%)

		Covered in chapter(s)
2.2.1	Assess an organisation's structure and critically evaluate its appropriateness to align and deliver its strategy and fulfil its vision: ■ Centralisation versus decentralisation ■ Lines of authority and communications ■ Committees, teams, taskforces required ■ Organisational life phases	5
2.2.2	Critically evaluate existing systems and processes and identify future needs in line with an organisation's strategy requirements: ■ Budget setting ■ Planning systems ■ Accounting systems ■ Information management and flows	5
2.2.3	Assess the competency of an organisation's workforce in order to establish future capability and capacity requirements: ■ Skills, knowledge and expertise ■ Quality and fit ■ Employee expectations ■ Attitudes	5
2.2.4	Ascertain where the new marketing strategy will impact and how it will fit into the broader organisation: ■ Impact on other organisational strategies ■ Fit with systems and culture ■ Required organisational changes ■ Communication strategies	5
2.2.5	Establish a clear funding framework in order to deliver the marketing strategy effectively and ensure sufficient and realistic financial resource is available: ■ Bid for funding at board level ■ Sufficient funds for implementation and delivery of the strategy ■ Full measuring, control and evaluation frameworks in place	5

SECTION 3 – Monitoring and measuring marketing (weighting 30%)

		Covered in chapter(s)
2.3.1	Critically evaluate the concepts of adaptability, efficiency and effectiveness as means of measuring the success or otherwise of marketing strategies for a range of organisational sectors: • Efficiency/effectiveness matrix in measuring longevity of marketing strategies (McDonald, 2007) • Tactical versus strategic orientation	6
2.3.2	Critically evaluate and use quantitative techniques for evaluating business and marketing performance and delivery of the marketing strategy, including: • Brand equity and brand value • Shareholder value analysis • Benchmarking analysis • Comparative assessments with previous strategies and budgetary control techniques	6
2.3.3	Measure financial returns achieved as a result of specific investment decisions and compare them to the original investment appraisal or business case: • Historic decisions informing current decision-making • Short-term versus long-term • Linkages between strategic and financial appraisal from manager's own perspective (in a strategic management context – Grundy and Johnson, 1993 BJM)	6
2.3.4	Propose and critically evaluate the development of sustainable marketing strategies and ethics, and analyse the value generated by these strategies to the organisation's overall strategy: • Investment in sustainable marketing strategies • Developing appropriate messages to stakeholders and shareholders • Sustainable product development strategies and communication methods to influence consumer behaviour in a long-term sustainable context	6
2.3.5	Assess the value that the marketing proposition has generated and how it can contribute to shareholder value: • Value-based planning models • Creation of additional value • Role of marketing due diligence	6

Part 3 – Market-led strategic change

SECTION 1 – Leading and inspiring an organisation (weighting 40%)

		Covered in chapter(s)
3.1.1	Critically evaluate and identify the methods for measuring successful and effective leadership strategies in determining and defining an organisation's strategic focus and intent: ■ Different leadership theories in achieving strategic focus: 　– Trait approach/Behaviour approach 　– Power/influence approach 　– Situational approach 　– Integrative approach	7
3.1.2	Critically evaluate a range of approaches to successful leadership of the organisation and of the marketing function: ■ Characteristics of a successful leader ■ Characteristics of followers ■ Characteristics of the situation ■ Relating and integrating the primary types of leadership approaches in order to ensure successful and effective leadership strategies ■ Ethics of leaders	7
3.1.3	Critically evaluate and analyse the dominant leadership paradigms: ■ Classical/Visionary/Transactional/Organic ■ Organisational considerations according to different leadership paradigms	7
3.1.4	Critically evaluate the concept of power and influence in promoting a coherent philosophy regarding sources of power and how it can be exercised in the organisation: ■ Influence processes (Kelman proposed three different types of influence processes – instrumental compliance, internalisation and personal identification) ■ Different types of power according to their source (French and Raven, 1959) ■ Control over information power ■ Dichotomy between position power and personal power (Bass 1960, Etzioni 1961)	7
3.1.5	Critically evaluate the concept of bi-cultural leadership in developing capabilities effectively within new sub-cultures and across boundaries: ■ Examine how leaders create an organisational climate that encourages a healthy balance between collaboration and competition ■ Which encourages risk-taking and risk assessment and which is boundary-less	8
3.1.6	Explore ways of developing thought leadership within the organisation to assist in the development of a culture of innovation and learning, including: ■ Keeping stakeholders connected ■ Engaging and expediting learning ■ Developing a learning organisation ■ Investing in knowledge capital through knowledge management ■ Maintaining knowledge of innovation and passing it on	8
3.1.7	Utilise the management team, internal resources and networks to develop tools to access key stakeholders, including: ■ Setting up steering committees ■ Establishing formal links with strategic planners and leaders ■ Establishing communities and networks with business leaders ■ Continuously seeking internal and external customer information	8

			Covered in chapter(s)
3.1.8	Assess your own leadership style and recommend how it can be improved and maximised to aid business thinking, working with colleagues, inspiring people and achieving goals: <ul><li>Leadership styles (Transitional, Transformational, Traditional)</li><li>Group dynamics/team motivation</li><li>Reflective thinking and feedback</li><li>Different methods of measuring leadership effectiveness</li><li>Difficulties of measuring effectiveness of a leader</li></ul>		8

The Chartered Institute of Marketing

SECTION 2 – Developing a market-oriented culture (weighting 30%)

		Covered in chapter(s)
3.2.1	Critically evaluate the concept of a market-oriented culture and consider the implications for an organisation in achieving it, including: ■ Customer orientation ■ Cross and inter-functional orientation ■ Competitor orientation ■ Profit orientation	9
3.2.2	Assess the different characteristics of culture in a broad context and evaluate the need for change to achieve true market orientation, including: ■ Values, beliefs and assumptions ■ Symbols ■ Heroes ■ Rituals ■ Culture and strategic implications ■ Organisational climate	9
3.2.3	Explore ways in which the organisation can go about creating and shaping a market-oriented culture: ■ Working towards common goals ■ Collective identity ■ Embracing differences and diversity ■ Common goals ■ Fostering support ■ Focus on innovation ■ Focus on performance ■ Focus on learning and development	9
3.2.4	Critically evaluate the concept of shared values and show how they can be effectively communicated in a market-oriented organisation: ■ Organisational values, eg CSR, sustainability ■ Cultural values ■ Ethical values ■ Economic values	9
3.2.5	Determine measures for success in transforming an organisation's culture to one of true market orientation: ■ Externally focused organisation ■ Market orientation matrix (Heiens, 2000) ■ Customer/Competitor focused – toward an integrated approach (Slater and Narver, 1994) ■ Market orientation and business performance	9

SECTION 3 – Developing and delivering organisational strategies for change (weighting 30%)

		Covered in chapter(s)
3.3.1	Assess the key drivers and pressures on organisations to change in today's dynamic marketing environment: ■ Environmental audit ■ Contemporary issues ■ Global challenges	10
3.3.2	Critically evaluate barriers to organisational change, making recommendations of how best to overcome them: ■ Cultural barriers to change ■ Competency inadequacies ■ Community barriers ■ Personal barriers	10
3.3.3	Critically evaluate why organisations often avoid corporate led change, including: ■ Public scrutiny of large corporate organisations ■ Political/legislative reasons ■ Union intervention ■ Prior strategic commitments ■ Inertia	10
3.3.4	Critically evaluate the different methods of change available to organisations: ■ Incremental ■ Discontinuous ■ Re-engineering	10
3.3.5	Design a process for change, to provide insight into the level of involvement and interaction stakeholders will have in the transformation of an organisation and its market orientation, including consideration of constraints and contingencies: ■ Surface/profound change management ■ Organisation wide change – strategic change management ■ Stakeholder mapping – power versus support or resistance ■ Stakeholder personal analysis (getting inside an individual's head) ■ The nature of opposition (knowing your 'enemies' in change) ■ The nature of support (knowing your allies in change) ■ Measuring the impact of change	10
3.3.6	Prepare a change plan for an organisation, taking into account the need for appropriate resources, capabilities, skills and motivations for its execution: ■ HR policy – recruitment, training, job definition and roles, rewards and incentives, relationships and hierarchies ■ Customer/competitor relations ■ Cross-function and inter-departmental relations ■ Innovation ■ Integrating internal and external pressures ■ Monitoring and measuring success	10

The Chartered Institute of Marketing

3 Assessment

The assessment for *Marketing Leadership and Planning* is an integrated work-based project with a number of compulsory tasks for completion.

In order to help you prepare for the project, we have also written a Chartered Postgraduate Diploma in Marketing Assessment Workbook, which is available either through your usual book retailer or our website: http://www.bpp.com/learningmedia

4 The Magic Formula

The Magic Formula is a tool used by CIM to help both examiners write exam and assignment questions, and you, to more easily interpret what you are being asked to write about. It is useful for helping you to check that you are using an appropriate balance between theory and practice for your particular level of qualification.

Contrary to the title, there is nothing mystical about the Magic Formula and simply by knowing it (or even mentioning it in an assessment) will not automatically secure a pass. What it does do, however, is to help you to check that you are presenting your answers in an appropriate format, including enough marketing theory and applying it to a real marketing context or issue.

The Magic Formula for the Chartered Postgraduate Diploma in Marketing is shown below:

Figure A   The Magic Formula for the Chartered Postgraduate Diploma in Marketing

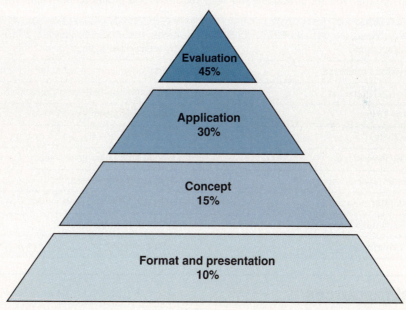

You can see from the pyramid that for the Chartered Postgraduate Diploma marks are awarded in the following proportions:

- **Presentation and format – 10%**

   You are expected to present your work professionally which means that assignments and projects should **always** be typed. Even in an exam situation attention should be paid to making your work look as visually appealing as possible. CIM will also stipulate the format that you should present your work in. The assessment formats you will be given will be varied and can include things like reports to write, slides to prepare, press releases, discussion documents, briefing papers, agendas and newsletters.

- **Concept – 15%**

  Concept refers to your ability to state, recall and describe marketing theory.

- **Application – 30%**

  Application based marks are given for your ability to apply marketing theories to real life marketing situations. For example, a question may ask you to discuss the definition of marketing and how it is applied within your own organisation. Here you are not only using the definition but are applying it in order to consider the market orientation of the company.

- **Evaluation – 45%**

  Evaluation is the ability to asses the value or worth of something, sometimes through careful consideration of related advantages and disadvantages, or weighing up of alternatives. Results from your evaluation should enable you to discuss the importance of an issue using evidence to justify your opinions.

  For example, if you were asked to evaluate whether or not your organisation adopts a marketing approach you should provide reasons and specific examples of why you think they might take this approach, as well as considering why they may not take this approach, before coming to a final conclusion.

5 A guide to the features of the Study Text

Each of the chapter features (see below) will help you to break down the content into manageable chunks and ensure that you are developing the skills required for a professional qualification.

Chapter feature	Relevance and how you should use it
Introduction	Shows why topics need to be studied and is a route guide through the chapter
Syllabus reference	Outlines the syllabus learning outcomes covered in the chapter
Chapter topic list	Study the list, each numbered topic denotes a numbered section in the chapter
Key Term	Highlights the core vocabulary you need to learn
Activity	An application-based activity for you to complete
The Real World	A short case study to illustrate marketing practice
Exam tip/Assessment tip	Key advice based on the assessment
Chapter roundups	Use this to review what you have learnt
Quick quiz	Use this to check your learning
Further reading	Further reading will give you a wider perspective on the subjects you're covering

6 Additional resources

To help you pass Stage 1 of the Chartered Postgraduate Diploma in Marketing we have created a complete study package. The **Chartered Postgraduate Diploma Assessment Workbook** covers three units of the Chartered Postgraduate Diploma level: Analysis and Decision, Marketing Leadership and Planning and Managing Corporate Reputation. Practice questions and answers and tips on tackling assignments are included to help you succeed in your assessments. The **Emerging Themes Study Support Text** is a support text written by the CIM Emerging Themes examiner and is designed to guide you through the Emerging Themes unit. It includes guidance on researching themes for different sectors, illustrative examples, publication protocols and best practice on how to present your assessment.

The Chartered Institute of Marketing

Our A6 set of spiral bound **Passcards** are handy revision cards and are ideal to reinforce key topics for the Analysis and Decision exam.

7 Your personal study plan

Preparing a study plan (and sticking to it) is one of the key elements to learning success.

Think about the number of hours you should dedicate to your studies. Guided learning hours will include time spent in lesson, working on fully prepared distance learning materials, formal workshops and work set by your tutor. We also know that to be successful, students should spend **approximately three times** the amount of time spent working through guided learning conducting self study. This means that for the entire qualification with four units you should spend time working in a tutor guided manner and three times that completing recommended reading, working on assignments, and revising for exams. This Study Text will help you to organise this portion of self study time.

Now think about the exact amount of time you have (don't forget you will still need some leisure time!) and complete the following tables to help you keep to a schedule.

	Date	Duration in weeks
Course start		
Course finish		Total weeks of course:
Project received	Submission date	Total weeks to complete:

Content chapter coverage plan

Chapter	To be completed by	Considered in relation to project?
1 Creating an organisational vision and mission		
2 Formulating corporate and marketing strategies		
3 Developing corporate strategy and value proposition		
4 The concept of strategic marketing planning		
5 Assessing resource requirements		
6 Measuring and evaluating marketing strategies		
7 Leadership theories and strategies		
8 Leadership and the organisation		
9 Developing a marketing-oriented culture		
10 Organisational strategies for change		

Marketing Leadership and Planning

The Chartered
Institute of Marketing

CHAPTER 1

Creating an organisational vision and mission

Introduction

Steven Covey (1989) implored us to 'begin with the end in mind'. If we do not know where we want to get to, what the purpose of the journey is then we will not be able to create a clear and coherent strategy or course of action for the organisation.

The most successful organisations and the most successful leaders have a clear vision and mission. Lack of attention in this area will lead to strategic thinking that is confused, muddled and often misunderstood. Close attention in this area will ensure that leaders are able to clearly communicate their organisation's purpose to all of their stakeholders and ensure that objectives are both coherent and congruent.

Those missions that are most successful are those that are developed with the consideration of the organisation's stakeholders. To be delivered effectively all stakeholders need to feel that they play an important role in its delivery.

Topic list

The importance of the vision and mission .... (1)

Perspectives on organisational purpose .... (2)

Involving stakeholders in future possibilities .... (3)

Developing an effective mission statement .... (4)

Core competences of the organisation .... (5)

1.1.1	Critically analyse how to create a clear, simple, reality-based vision for an organisation and its stakeholders:
	■ Identifying strategic intent
	■ Creating a unique image of the organisation for the future
	■ The balance of inspiration versus capability and capacity
	■ Enlisting stakeholders in future possibilities
	■ Balancing internal and external constraints on the vision for the future
	■ Organisation's aspirations and purpose
1.1.2	Critically evaluate the importance of mission statements in communicating an organisation's strategic vision and identity, including:
	■ Purpose, feelings and direction
	■ Basis of objectives
	■ Basis for strategy
	■ Focal point for stakeholders
	■ Values of the organisation, including moral, ethical and sustainability positioning
1.1.3	Identify distinctive competences of the organisation and how they can be leveraged to achieve an organisation's mission:
	■ Distinctive essence of the organisation
	■ Market and business definition
	■ Intended positioning in the marketplace
	■ Role of contribution and identification of future intent

1 The importance of the vision and mission

> ▶ **Key terms**
>
> De Wit and Meyer (2005) make a distinction between '**Vision**' and '**Mission**'. While the corporate 'mission' outlines the fundamental principles guiding strategic choices a 'strategic vision' outlines the desired future at which the organisation hopes to arrive. In other words vision provides a business aim while mission provides business principles.

Managers must constantly make choices and seek solutions based on an understanding of what their organisation is intended to achieve. They are confronted every day with many different claimants who believe that the organisation exists to serve their interests. Many of us will have to make tough choices and often we are forced to weigh up the interests of different stakeholders and decide which take priority on certain matters.

> ▶ **Assessment tip**
>
> In March 2010, the main focus of the assignment was on 'the corporate mission and vision. Candidates were given strategic responsibility to review their organisation's marketing strategy and recommend the changes required to enable the organisation to deliver its corporate vision and mission in the context of the economic challenges and the current economic climate.'
>
> More recently in June 2011, candidates were given strategic responsibility for raising stakeholder value in the organisation. Part of this meant undertaking a strategic audit and making recommendations for improvements to the organisation's value proposition in the context of its vision and mission.

Where managers have a clear understanding of the organisation's vision and mission this can provide strong guidance during processes of strategic thinking, strategy formation and strategic change. The vision and mission can act as a guiding light, a fundamental principle against which strategic options can be evaluated and decided upon.

Vision and mission statements should be more than mere statements. They have many roles and functions, from being inspirational to clearly and concisely conveying the strategic direction of the organisation. Arguably

they can motivate teams and lead individuals through organisational change, while realising a common goal for the whole organisation.

1.1 Key issues of organisational visions and missions

> ▶ **Key terms**
>
> **Vision** outlines what the organisation wants to be and what it aspires to be in the longer term. The vision should help to inspire, energise and motivate key stakeholders within the organisation.
>
> The vision and mission statements should complement each other. The vision needs to identify the organisation's strategic intent and create a unique image of the organisation for the future. This can be based on its current situation but needs to take the organisation into the future. The need for it to energise, motivate and inspire is fundamental; however, there needs to be a balance of inspiration versus capability and capacity. In addition, the vision must also balance internal and external constraints; it may be tempting to include a truly inspirational vision, but if it is completely unachievable or has little context the chances are it will fail to inspire in the first instance.
>
> **Mission** comes from the Latin word mittere which means 'to send'.
>
> A mission is a **task, duty or purpose** that sends some on their way. Hence corporate mission can be understood as the basic drivers sending the corporation along its way and consists of the fundamental principles that mobilise and propel the firm in a particular direction. The mission statement needs to focus on the company's current state, while the vision focuses on the future. However, there can be overlap as the mission statement will need to take into account the purpose, feelings and direction of the organisation. It needs to consider its objectives and general strategic direction. In essence, it has to be able to communicate the strategic vision and identity of the organisation. The values of the organisation, whether moral, ethical and sustainability positioning also need to be appropriately considered when writing the mission statement.

The concept of organisational visions and missions can be an elusive concept. To many people they are merely lists of principles that, while they may have potential PR value, have little if any bearing on the actual business, let alone the process of strategy choice, formulation and implementation. Often they are included in the organisation's documentation but their relevance lacks context and meaning to key stakeholders.

However, clear visions and missions can be very concrete and play a critical role in determining strategic decision making and action. They need to be catalysts for action; they need to be meaningful. Lists of words together that are not appropriately understood by the organisation's stakeholders or noticed can mean they are ignored and never play a strategic role within the organisation.

THE REAL WORLD

Innocent Drinks

'Staying true to our purpose will give us the best shot at achieving our vision of innocent becoming:

The earth's favourite little food company

A company that makes delicious, healthy, natural, ethical food universally available for all. It's a big task – to do so we're up against the biggest food and drinks companies in the world who have billions of pounds of resources at their disposal. But never underestimate the power of a group of people who believe in what we're doing.'

This highlights an organisation that has written a simple yet powerful vision. It not only encompasses the long term goal of being the favourite company, but also highlights its humble beginnings, so in essence the root of its success is not forgotten. The vision is explained further using key words such as 'delicious', 'healthy', 'natural' and 'ethical' so that the central focus of the company is not forgotten. The vision is short enough to inspire and relevant enough to have an impact. It also explains how the company is up against big names, the fact that it is competing in such a competitive industry adds to its strengths. This highlights its capabilities while acknowledging the potential external constraints that could impact its success. All in all it is aspirational and able to convey the purpose of the organisation, making it explicit and well contextualised.

Strategic planning and leadership are interlinked especially when considering the organisation's vision. The organisation needs to clearly understand what business the company is in, what it wants to represent, what its image is and what strategic direction it would like to go in the future. Before a vision can be written there needs to be consideration of the key target groups, the industry/market the organisation is operating in, the changes and developments within that industry as well as internal competences ie integrating both the internal and external context.

This will then allow the organisation to develop a vision that encompasses the many different aspects of the environment (internal and external) within which the organisation operates. This will also help the organisation to communicate the vision and mission in a way that is clear and succinct as well as inspiring and exciting. It is also the foundation on which the strategic direction of the organisation can be developed, revised or evolves to take into account the long-term future vision.

Examples of some popular mission statements:

- Google's mission is to organise the world's information and make it universally accessible and useful
  (www.google.co.uk)

- Microsoft's mission is to enable people and businesses throughout the world to realise their full potential
  (www.microsoft.com)

- Dell's mission is to be the most successful computer company in the world at delivering the best customer experience in markets we serve
  (www.dell.co.uk)

- Facebook's mission is to give people the power to share and make the world more open and connected
  (www.facebook.com/facebook/info)

Each of these statements builds on the organisation's core competences, as well as giving a sense of purpose and direction to the organisation. They also focus on what the organisation feels matters to them, whether this is accessibility (in Google's case) or the customer experience (Dell) or getting people connected (Facebook). The mission statement also needs to have a close link to the strategy rather than sitting separately from it, without a connection.

To understand how a mission impacts on strategy, two areas require closer attention:

- **First**, it is necessary to know what types of fundamental principles actually make up a corporate mission

- **Second**, it needs to be examined what types of roles are played by a corporate mission in the strategy formation process

The successful direction of the organisation is as a result of the effective interaction between management and the board of directors. The board of directors must be coherent in their view and implementation of the organisational mission. Their activities, described as **'corporate governance'**, govern the strategic choices and action of the management of the organisation. The task of corporate governance is to shape, articulate and communicate the fundamental principles that will drive the organisation's activities. Fundamentally, it involves the set of relationships between the organisation and its stakeholders.

A well written and powerful mission statement will help to attract different stakeholders, from volunteers, donors to other key community members with whom the organisation requires engagement.

1.2 Elements of organisation mission

Organisational purpose can be defined as the reason why an organisation exists. The perception that managers have of their own organisation's purpose gives direction to the strategic process and will include the strategic choices and the way it is ultimately implemented.

More often than not a manager's view of the organisation's purpose will be part of a broader set of business principles that steers strategic thinking.

The Chartered
Institute of Marketing

It is this set of principles that firms the base of an organisation's identity and guides its strategic decision making that is often referred to as the organisational (or corporate) mission.

A good mission statement needs to be in language that helps to discriminate one organisation from another; differentiate itself from its competitors and demonstrate how it is distinctive. This could include what advantages it offers to clients in contrast to services offered by competitors, or any specific added value that it needs to communicate to its stakeholders. In short, how is this organisation really different and better for clients than others with which it competes? Often a badly written mission statement that lacks focus, direction and content can reflect the general state of the organisation and its leadership team.

De Wit and Meyer (2005) identify three components of a corporate mission as follows:

- **Organisational beliefs:** to work in unison a common understanding is needed amongst all organisational stakeholders. The stronger the set of beliefs subscribed to by the stakeholders the easier communication and decision making will become and the more confident, cohesive and driven the group will be. If people do not share the same beliefs joint decision making will be protracted and conflict will arise.

- **Organisational values:** each person in an organisation can have their own set of values. Yet, when an organisation's stakeholders share a common set of values this can have a strong impact on the strategic direction. Widely held values contribute to a clear sense of organisational identity which will attract some individuals and dispel others. To be of most use and influence such values must be embodied in the organisation's culture.

- **Business definition:** most firms have a clear identity from being active in a particular sector or industry. For such organisations, having a delimiting definition of the business they want to be in strongly focuses the direction in which they develop. Their business definition functions as a strong guiding principle and helps to distinguish opportunities from diversions. Here while a clear business definition can focus the organisation's efforts it can also lead to short-sightedness and missing new business developments and opportunities.

The strength of the mission will depend on whether and how effectively these three elements as outlined above fit together and are mutually, reinforcing Campbell and Yeung (1991).

When a consistent and compelling mission is formed this can ignite the organisation with a sense of purpose and create an emotional bond as well as a rational reason for developing the members' work in a manner consistent with the mission. Omitting to have a clear mission statement that is well written or communicated in another form and fails to identify the key components of the organisation can imply an organisational strategic drift and lack of purpose; therefore, it sends out potentially negative messages to the organisation's key stakeholders.

1.3 Functions of organisational mission

While a corporate mission can be articulated by means of a mission statement, in practice not everything that is called a mission statement meets the above criteria. Organisations can have a mission statement, even if it has not been explicitly written down. Non-written statements however do risk divergent interpretations and could lead to a dilution of the mission being implemented and acted upon.

There are a number of benefits of a clear, coherent and well communicated mission:

- **Direction:** a mission can point the organisation in a certain direction, by defining the boundaries within which strategic choices and actions must be taken.

- **Legitimisation:** a mission conveys to all stakeholders inside and outside the organisation what activities it is pursuing and on what basis. Through specifying the business philosophy that will guide the company the chances are increased that stakeholders will accept, support and trust the organisation.

- **Motivation:** a mission can inspire individuals to work together in a particular way, with the power to motivate people over a prolonged period of time.

- **Strategic change:** a mission statement, articulated in an inspiring and thought provoking way can enable a change of attitude within an organisation which can lead an organisation in a new direction.

The importance of mission statements for the organisation can be far reaching. From communicating the purpose of the organisation, to engaging stakeholders and demonstrating the strengths of the organisation in comparison to its competitors. It is also evidence that the organisation wishes to communicate with its stakeholders, motivating them to engage, understand and appreciate the organisation's purpose in a way that captures the true identity of the organisation.

THE REAL WORLD

An example of a mission statement that engendered change is that of BMW, where the board of directors proclaimed the motto 'enterprise mobility'. From the external viewpoint this does not focus attention on the product 'cars' but on the mobility as a specific customer need. From the internal standpoint 'enterprise mobility' challenges every single employee and organisational unit in their behaviour. This visionary battle cry is supported by a number of 'action maxims' that form the mission statement. Here values, norms and behavioural patterns are anchored, as well as the employees' ability to formulate and accept positive criticism.

BMW's current mission statement is 'The BMW Group is the world's leading provider of premium products and premium services for individual mobility' (http://www.bmw.co.uk). The statement is clear; it identifies its key market (premium) and builds on its key core values of mobility and being the leading provider of products as well as services. There is also a clear focus on its core values rather than including generic statements that lack the necessary context.

1.4 Strategy development

The leadership team needs to understand the external and internal factors that will impact the company's strategy and its operations. External factors can include the economic environment, interest rates, governmental changes and social factors. The external factors as well as internal organisational factors such as its financial performance, its distinctive competences, and its product portfolio amongst others need to be considered in the context of the mission and vision. A number of analysis tools including SWOT, PESTLE and BGM can be analysed to develop the vision and mission.

The development of the vision needs to be underpinned using appropriate analysis, this will allow it to become an enhanced vision, rather than a statement that is often ignored.

2 Perspectives on organisational purpose

Organisations increasingly face two competing pressures:

(a)   They require a certain amount of **economic profitability** to survive; and

(b)   They need to exhibit a certain amount of **social responsibility** if they are to retain the trust and support of key stakeholders.

In this section we explore two perspectives. At one end of the debate are those people who argue that corporations exist to serve the purpose of their owners. This point of view is commonly referred to as the 'shareholder value **perspective**'.

At the other end of the spectrum are those people who argue that corporations should be seen as joint ventures between a number of parties. This is referred to as the 'stakeholder value **perspective**'.

The Chartered Institute of Marketing

Table 1.1   Shareholder/stakeholder value perspective

The shareholder value perspective	The stakeholder value perspective
Corporations are instruments whose purpose is to create economic value on behalf of those who invest risk-taking capital in the enterprise and should drive the purpose whether they are privately or publicly held	Corporations are a coalition between various resource suppliers, with the intention of increasing their common wealth. An organisation should be regarded as a joint venture in which all participate to achieve economic success
Many people making this argument feel that the well being of the shareholder is best served if the strategy of the company leads to higher share prices and/or higher dividends	The emphasis shareholders place on share price appreciation and dividends must be balanced against the legitimate demands of the other partners. Demands are both quantitative and qualitative in nature
Supporters of this perspective state that it is challenging for management to pursue shareholders' interests where ownership and managerial control have become separated	Managers must recognise their responsibility towards all constituents since maximising shareholder value to the detriment of other stakeholders is unjust. Managers have a moral obligation to consider the interests and values of all joint venture partners
Emphasis on profitability not responsibility. Objective of the corporation is to maximise shareholder value within the boundaries of what is permissible. There is no moral obligation to treat stakeholders well	Managing stakeholder demands is an end in itself. It is easier to work as a motivated team where all interests are served and there is a greater sense of partnership, ownership and trust

In establishing the organisation's mission managers need to determine their own view on as to the purpose of the organisation. The key issue is whether behaviour should be guided by profitability, responsibility or both. The purpose of the organisation will be influenced by expectations, what the expectations are of the industry, if they feel that stakeholders cannot be ignored or if they feel that only shareholders matter. Another key consideration is what the overall vision and direction is of the organisation. This will often impact the decisions they make and the view point they take on the above perspectives.

ACTIVITY 1.1

Talk with managers in your organisation and identify what behaviours determine their view of the organisation and what they believe the purpose of the organisation should be. Compare and contrast their responses. What does this tell you about the ability to create a mission statement that will be universally accepted?

ACTIVITY 1.2

Critically evaluate a mission statement for an organisation of your choice. Compare it to its vision and highlight the differences.

It is possible to search for ways to achieve the best of both worlds – high profitability and high responsibility at the same time. Commentators such as Steven Covey (1992) advocate a principle-centred approach to leadership and the development of a universal mission which seeks 'win-win' for the organisation and its stakeholders.

2.1 Shareholders and stakeholders: A new perspective on corporate governance

If stakeholders are to be engaged in the development of corporate strategy and the organisational mission it is useful to define exactly what a stakeholder is and where the term emanates from.

Freeman and Reed (1983) proposed two definitions of stakeholder:

- **The wide sense of stakeholder:** any identifiable group who can affect the achievement of an organisation's objectives or who is affected by the achievement of an organisation's objectives

- **The narrow sense of stakeholder:** any identifiable group or individual on which the organisation is dependent for its continued survival.

They made the point that strategies need to account for those groups who can affect the achievement of the firm's objectives.

Stakeholders' level of interest and power (see Table 1.2) is also a consideration, as well as the levels of risk involved. Kangas (2011) discussed that, organisation failure can often be a result of overlooking stakeholders with the most influence in the long term.

Friedman and Miles (2006) state that the organisation itself should be thought of as a grouping of stakeholders and the purpose of the organisation should be to manage their interests, needs and viewpoints. A key theme that runs through the discussions of stakeholders is survival and success. Stakeholders are regarded as integral in ensuring the survival and success of the organisation.

There are a number of differing theoretical concepts when analysing stakeholders. This includes descriptive, instrumental and normative stakeholder theory.

The following key principles apply to each:

- **Descriptive**: the aim is to understand how managers deal with stakeholders and how they represent their interests when making key strategic decisions. The organisation is viewed as a constellation of interests, sometimes competitive and sometimes co-operative; the context will determine what the focus is. It is recognised that stakeholders have a number of different interests and points of focus and they all need to be accounted for by the organisation.

- **Instrumental approach**: corporate governance needs and goals are focused on in this approach. The different consequences of taking into account stakeholders needs in managing stakeholders as well as the achievement of various corporate governance goals is fundamental to the instrumental approach.

- **Normative**: the more moral philosophical aspects of the organisation and the industry within which it operates are considered and are linked to the activities as well as the management of the organisations. Normative theory is linked to stakeholder theory and so takes into account the moral and philosophical considerations of the stakeholders, going beyond just shareholder interest.

THE REAL WORLD

Primark – fast fashion clothing

In recent years Primark has been subject to much media attention not only for its success but also for its business practices. Primark is a key player in the textile manufacture and clothing distribution industry. The industry itself has seen dramatic changes in recent years. Consumers have an array of competitors to choose from. Moreover, consumers have high expectations, wanting fashionable clothing at affordable prices.

Primark has sourced clothes from a number of countries namely China, Bangladesh, India and Vietnam where materials and labour costs are lower. Primark is a prime example of an organisation that has a number of stakeholders, both nationally and internationally, but also one that has to respond to varying needs: from that of the consumer, wanting 'fast fashion', affordable prices and up-to-date styles, to suppliers offering low cost labour and goods, to interested parties concentrating on business ethics and ensuring that the business provides western audiences with fair trade goods that do not exploit any individual.

The Chartered
Institute of Marketing

Primark has used a number of different initiatives to facilitate engagement with its key stakeholders, however diverse these may be. A key factor is that through this communication they are able to ensure there is a continuous dialogue with the key stakeholders. Primark has used initiatives such as the community engagement programme it has in India. A key challenge is that the organisation needs to keep its focus on market and industry changes, as well as fulfilling the demanding and ever evolving needs of its customers against the backdrop of stakeholder expectations.

2.2 Use of stakeholder concepts in strategy formulation

- **Stakeholder strategy process** is a systematic method for analysing the relative importance of stakeholders, their co-operative potential (how they can help the corporation achieve its objectives) and their competitive threat (how they can prevent the corporation from achieving its objectives).

- **Stakeholder audit process** is a systematic method for identifying stakeholders and assessing the effectiveness of current organisational strategies.

Each process analyses the stakeholder environment from the standpoint of the organisational mission and seeks to formulate strategies for meeting stakeholder needs and concerns.

One analytical device – a stakeholder power matrix, illustrated below – depicts an organisation's stakeholders. The first dimension is one of 'interest' and 'stake'. The second dimension is its 'power', which ranges from the formal power of shareholders, to the economic power of customers, to the political power of special interest groups.

Table 1.2   Stakeholder power

	Formal or voting power	Economic power	Political power
Equity stake	<ul><li>Shareholders</li><li>Directors</li><li>Minority interests</li></ul>		
Economic stake		<ul><li>Customers</li><li>Competitors</li><li>Suppliers</li></ul> <ul><li>Debt holders</li><li>Unions</li></ul>	<ul><li>Foreign governments</li></ul>
Influencers			<ul><li>Consumer groups</li><li>Government</li><li>Trade associations</li></ul>

3 Involving stakeholders in future possibilities

Often it is said that if people do not feel involved they will not be committed. Involvement is the key to implementing new practices increasing commitment to new ideas and preventing resistence to change. People tend to hold on to old views, old ways, old habits and make these hard to change.

Increasing involvement is a fundamental part of stakeholder management. Fostering involvement, and therefore commitment, acts as a catalyst in the change process. Stakeholder involvement is also enhanced by stakeholders understanding what is happening, which is dependent on effective communication by the organisation.

The downside of involvement is risk. Whenever you involve people in the 'problem' you risk losing control. It seems safer to simply tell them, direct them, or advise them. Many unexperienced managers hesitate to involve people in decision-making for fear of opening up other options or compromising their position.

Most managers learn that the effectiveness of their decisions depends on their quality and commitment from others, and that commitment comes through involvement. Managers are then willing to assume the risks and to develop the skills of involving people appropriately. Involvement also requires leadership, engagement,

understanding strategic decisions. Contextualising these decisions is fundamental to the success of the organisation. Engagement needs to take place at all levels, both internally and externally with stakeholders.

3.1 Driving and restraining forces

The research of Lewin (1951) contributed to understanding the change process. His Forces Model is discussed further in Chapter 10; when people become involved in a problem they become significantly and sincerely committed to coming up with solutions. Once people feel involved they become responsible for results. Enlightened leaders understand that when people are meaningfully involved they willingly commit. The vision and mission statements are designed to engage various stakeholders and should embrace future possibilities. However, their success and relevance is dependent on the leadership of the organisation. This is linked to the organisation's strategy; if there is a lack of integration and linkage, disjointed messages will be sent out to key stakeholders and the credibility of the company to deliver the future it promises will be compromised.

4 Developing an effective mission statement

There are no hard and fast rules about how to create an effective mission statement but here are some issues that you should bear in mind:

- **Ask yourself the right questions**. To begin, ask yourself these kinds of questions: What business are you in? Why are you in this business? What do you want for yourself, your employees, and your customers?

- **Say it clearly**. Your mission statement needs to clearly state business goals and objectives. It should explain what the business is, what special niche it inhabits in the marketplace, and how it will make a difference in the lives of customers and clients.

- **Decide what makes your organisation different**. Never forget that you are pursuing the same customers as your competitors. How is it that you stand out from those other companies? Ask yourself if it is because you do something better, cheaper, or faster than others. Identify any underlying philosophies or values that guide your company.

- **Build your brand**. Use your mission statement to build your unique brand. Make sure to communicate your business's key value to the customer or client segment that you are serving.

- **Keep it short and sweet**. A strong mission statement shouldn't ramble on endlessly. Ideally, you should be able to summarise your company's mission in a few sentences. Consider it your 'elevator pitch' — you, your board of directors, your managers and your other employees should be able to state your company's mission succinctly in the time it takes to ride an elevator from the ground floor to the top floor.

- **Be honest**. Make sure that when you read your own mission statement, it reflects what you truly believe. Too much pomp and self-congratulatory language will turn off those who read it, so avoid saying that your company is the 'best' at this and the 'world leader' at that.

- **Make it a joint effort**. Even if you are the sole proprietor of your business, don't write your mission statement in a vacuum. It's incredibly helpful to get the input of others, both inside and outside the company. Collaborators can help you to better see the strengths and weaknesses of your mission statement. Ask for the input, including external stakeholders such as your key clients, suppliers and partners with whom you may have a very close professional relationship.

- **Polish the language**. Your mission statement should be error-free, eloquent, and precise. It should be dynamic and inspirational.

- **Spread the word**. Once your mission statement is complete, start sharing it by posting it appropriately. It should be prominently displayed on the company's website, as well as in brochures and other marketing material. You could consider adding it to the bottom of company emails if it's brief enough or sending it out as a press release. Be creative in getting the word out.

 The Chartered Institute of Marketing

- **Revise as needed**. Your mission statement should not be set in stone. As the business grows and changes, so too might its company's mission. Revisit your mission statement on a regular basis to evaluate whether it should be revised or updated. However, the values are unlikely to change significantly if they are effectively communicated from the start.

It is vital when developing the organisation's mission statement to understand the strategic focus of the organisation. What is the focus? How does it link to the organisation's strategy as well as the marketing strategy? The mission statement should be a focal point to develop further communications strategies for the organisation, both within the organisation and externally.

When critically evaluating mission statements, bear in mind the overlaps in the discussions. Key areas such as mission, vision, values, core competences and identity inter-relate, making it more challenging for leaders, management and organisational teams to differentiate (Khalifa, (2011). However, they should all successfully integrate in order to send out an effective consistent and powerful marketing identity to the world.

5 Core competences of the organisation

5.1 Identifying core competences

> ▸ **Key term**
>
> **Core competences** are the collective learning in the organisation, especially how to co-ordinate diverse production skills and integrate multiple streams of technologies and organising work and the delivery of value.

The most powerful way to prevail in global competition and particularly in challenging and uncertain times is to be clear about the source of your competitive advantage. The organisations to emulate are those that are adept at reinventing themselves, identifying new markets, quickly entering emerging markets and dramatically shifting purchasing patterns in established markets. Core competences of an organisation should enable them to build and sustain their competitive advantage when their competitors cannot do so, making it more difficult for competitors to imitate products or services.

This might seem easy to achieve but it is deceptively difficult. Often it requires radical change in the management of organisations. If an organisation is in decline it is important that the senior management team assume responsibility.

In the short term an organisation's competitiveness derives from the price/performance attributes of the current range of products or services. In the long run competitiveness is derived from an ability to build, at lower total cost and more speedily than competitors, the core competences that spawn unanticipated products.

The real sources of competitive advantage are found in management's ability to consolidate organisation-wide technologies, production skills, knowledge and learning into competences that enable the organisation to adapt quickly to emerging opportunities and fulfil its mission.

Key core competences are communication, involvement and a deep commitment to working across organisational boundaries. Large organisations may involve many levels of staff across a wide variety of functions who together have the means and legitimacy to blend their own expertise with those of others in new and interesting ways.

Unlike physical assets which deteriorate over time, competences are enhanced as they are applied and shared. Competences need to be nurtured and protected.

Hamel and Prahalad (1994) describe competences as 'the glue that binds existing businesses' and 'the engine of new business development'. Patterns of diversification are guided by competences, not just by the attractiveness of markets. It is important to remember that the core competence can take on a number of forms; it can be the development of products, levels of innovation, distribution, customer services and beyond.

BPP
LEARNING MEDIA

However at a strategic level it is how the actual organisation manages this and sustains it for its long term competitive advantage.

5.2 Identifying core competences – and losing them

How do you identify a core competence? The following explains the most important characteristics.

A core competence:

(a)   Provides potential access to a wide variety of markets. GPS of France developed a core competence in 'one-hour' processing, enabling it to process films and build reading glasses in one hour.

(b)   Should make a significant contribution to the benefits perceived by the customer of the end product it contributes significantly to the value enjoyed by the customer. For example, for GPS, the waiting time restriction was very important.

(c)   Should be difficult for competitors to imitate – and it will be difficult if it is a complex harmonisation of individual technologies and production skills. This will be the case if it is technically complex, involves specialised processes, involves complex interrelationships between different people in the organisation or is hard to define.

Few organisations are likely to build world leadership in more than five or six fundamental competences. If a company compiles a list of 20 to 30 capabilities then they have probably not got a grasp of their core competences. However, creating a long list is a good start to help identify and bundle similar capabilities together.

ACTIVITY 1.3

Using the above guidelines create a full list of the competences for your own organisation. Shortlist this to five or six core competences. Critically evaluate the list and consider the contribution of these core competences for the future direction of the organisation.

Organisations that ignore identifying and building on their core competences do so at some risk. Organisations that judge their own and their competitors' competitiveness primarily in terms of price/performance are encouraging the erosion of core competences – or are making too little effort to enhance them.

While it is possible for such organisations to have a competitive product, when the fundamental technologies, environmental conditions or business models change as a result of external forces the organisation could be vulnerable.

While activities like outsourcing provide a shortcut to building a more competitive product this is often done at the risk of losing the people-oriented skills required inside the organisation to sustain product leadership.

If an organisation chooses to pursue alliances, partnerships and joint ventures in order to achieve and maintain competitive advantage, this can only be done once it has decided where to build its core competences.

Another reason for losing competences is to forego opportunities to establish competences that are evolving in existing businesses. In divesting of businesses too early, organisations run the risk of closing the door on future opportunities.

The Chartered Institute of Marketing

Zappos – tapping into the billion pound market

Zappos, the online shoe company is a prime example of using its core competences to its advantage and to position itself above its competitors and so gain high market share. In 2009 it agreed to sell ownership to Amazon. However prior to selling it had almost perfected its business to ensure loyal, repeat and committed customers. The company was not convinced by a decision to outsource its call centre. It believed that it could never truly capture the information it needed about customers if it did not take calls by its own employees. Also managing inventory through outsourcing was not producing the results it required. In other words, the company firmly believed that to take care of its customers its operations needed to be done in house.

A call centre was opened in San Francisco at a cost; however, its core competences certainly strengthened the organisation to become what it is today. How were they able to do this?

- Offering customers a 365-day returns policy

- Encouraging feedback from customers, having the telephone number featured prominently on the web to make interaction easy

- No 'average handling time' for call representatives, giving time to customers rather than hurrying customers unnecessarily

- 'Sticking to the knitting', rather than using other media. They thought in most cases customers prefer the telephone to other forms of communication as it is direct and meets their needs

- Surprise gestures for customers, faster delivery times, upgrades on delivery

Zappos is a prime example of a company deciding to focus on its core competences and then use them to their advantage, to the point that they differentiate them from their competitors. This needed time, money, commitment and resources. However, there was a long term dedication and vision to be an outstanding retailer and by identifying and using these core competences to their advantage, they were able to do this.

Aligned with competences are the resources that an organisation needs to enable it to participate and complete in its chosen markets.

Threshold resources are those resources that an organisation needs to enable it to participate in essence without these resources it would be difficult for an organisation to survive.

Unique resources are those that are unique to the organisation in comparison to its competitors; these can be a source of competitive advantage. An example of a unique resource may be the ownership of a particular raw material, or a geographical location that only the organisation has access to.

Core competences are activities, process or the organisation's ability to meet its critical success factors to gain competitive advantage in the market place. Threshold competences are the minimum capabilities required for the organisation to survive and compete, while core competences are required to gain competitive advantage, making it difficult, if not impossible, for competitors to copy the offering or take over market share. It is important to note that threshold levels evolve and change over time with the change in market dynamics; this may require tradeoffs to be made for certain markets as well as different customer bases.

5.2.1 From core competences to core products

The link between core competences and the end product or service is termed the core product. Core products are the physical embodiment of one or more core competences.

5.2.2 The role of core competences in a diversified organisation

Diversified organisations have a portfolio of products and a portfolio of businesses. Such organisations also have a portfolio of competences. Senior management must possess the skills, capabilities and vision to build these

competences across the organisation and administrate the means for assembling resources spread across multiple businesses.

There are a number of risks to establishing sustainable core competences if senior management perceive the organisation as a multiplicity of separate business units:

(a) **Under-investment in developing core competences and core products**. No single business may feel responsible for maintaining a viable position in core products or be able to justify the investment required to build world leadership in some core competence. Managers of such business units will tend to under-invest with an holistic view imposed by senior management. It may also result in the organisation's mission being diluted – the business unit may actually choose to work outside the mission statement or create its own.

(b) **Imprisoned resources**. As a business unit evolves it develops its own set of competences. Typically, the people who embody this competence are seen as the sole property of the business in which they live and grow up. Managers of such 'competence carriers' are not only unwilling to lend their talented people to others but may actually hide talent to prevent its redeployment in the pursuit of new opportunities. When competences become imprisoned the people who carry the competences do not get assigned to the most exciting opportunities; they become demotivated and their skills begin to atrophy. Senior management are seldom able to look four or five levels down into the organisation, identify the people who embody critical competences, and move them across organisational boundaries.

(c) **Bounded innovation**. If core competences are not recognised the business units will only pursue those innovation opportunities close at hand. Hybrid opportunities like laptops, notebooks and iPods will not emerge. Recognition of core competences and cross-SBU-thinking is required. Conceiving of the organisation in terms of core competences widens the domain of innovation.

Table 1.3   Two concepts of corporation

	Business unit	Core competence
Basis for competition	Competitiveness of today's products	Inter-firm competition to build competences
Corporate structure	Portfolio of businesses related in product-market terms	Portfolio of competences, core products and businesses
Status of the business unit	Autonomy is sacrosanct; the business unit 'owns' all resources other than cash	Business unit is a potential reservoir of core competences
Resource allocation	Discrete businesses are the unit of analysis; capital is allocated by business	Businesses and competences are the unit of analysis; top management allocates capital and talent
Value added of top management	Optimising corporate returns through capital allocation trade-offs among businesses	Enunciating strategic architecture and building competences to secure the future

(De Wit and Meyer, 2005)

5.3 Redeploying to exploit competences

In order for an organisation to maximise the ability for its core competences to fulfil its organisational mission and ensure business units share competences in the common good its senior management can implement a number of measures:

(a) With the help of stakeholders within the organisation, in particular business unit managers, identify organisational-wide competences and ask managers to identify the projects and people associated with them.

(b) This sends an important message to middle management – core competences are corporate resources and may be reallocated by corporate management on products and projects that enable the fulfilment of the corporate mission. This can be further underlined if each year during the strategic planning or budgetary process, business unit managers must justify their hold on the people who carry the organisation's core competences.

(c) The positive contribution of the business unit managers should be made visible across the organisation. Such co-operative managers should be celebrated as team players.

(d) 'Competence carriers' should be regularly brought together from across the organisation to trade notes, ideas and share best practice. This will help build a strong sense of community.

From core competences new business opportunities are born and developed. Only if core competences are known, nurtured and developed can an organisation ensure the successful fulfilment and development of its organisational mission and be best prepared for the future.

5.4 Strategy as the exploitation of competences

Strategic opportunities must be related to the firm's resources. A strategic approach involves identifying a firm's **competences**. The **distinctive competence** of an organisation is what it does well, uniquely, or better than rivals. These competences may come about in a variety of ways:

- **Experience** in making and marketing a product or service

- The talents and potential of **individuals** in the organisation

- The **quality of co-ordination**

- Competences are a kind of resource and the idea of strategy as being based on competences is one aspect of the resource-based view promoted by Hamel and Prahalad (1990)

Core competences critically underpin the organisation's competitive advantage (Johnson & Scholes (2001)).

According to Johnson & Scholes (2001) an organisation must achieve at least a **threshold** level of competence in **everything** it does. The organisation's **core competences** are those where it **outperforms competitors** and that are **difficult to imitate**.

Competitiveness depends on **unique resources** or core competences. The organisation's level of performance in its core competences may be judged in three ways:

(a) Comparison with past results
(b) Comparison with industry norms
(c) Benchmarking

In many cases, a company might choose to combine competences.

Bear in mind that **relying on a competence is no substitute for a strategy**. However, a core competence can form a basis for a strategy.

CHAPTER ROUNDUP

- A mission statement is made up of organisational beliefs, and organisational values, it is how the business defines itself.

- There are a number of functions of organisational mission: to give direction, legitimisation, motivation, and inspire strategic change where appropriate.

- Stakeholders are a key part of the strategy formulation.

- Stakeholders need to be involved in the strategy development process.

- The mission statement creates the key context for the overall strategic direction of the organisation, but some can be very ambiguous. There will be a number of stakeholders' needs to fulfil and it must say something useful to the key stakeholders, from a financial, social and business perspective.

- When developing a mission statement a number of factors need to be considered that will vary dependent on the organisation, the product, the service and the industry.

- The core competence of the organisation is its collective learning especially how to co-ordinate diverse production skills, integrate multiple streams of technologies, organising work and the delivering of value.

- Identifying the organisation's core competences is a key part of the strategy development process.

FURTHER READING

Bartkus, B and Glassman, M. (2008) Do firms practise what they preach? The relationship between mission statements and stakeholder management. *Journal of Business Ethics*. Dec, Vol83 Issue 2, pp207-216.

Brown T. (2001) *Turning mission statements in action*. Harvard Business Publishing Newsletters.

Ebrahim, G., Fatemeh, N. and Golpar B. (2011) A survey of the relationship between the characteristics of mission statement and organizational performance. *Research Journal of Business Management*, Jul-Sep, Vol5 Issue 3, pp117-124.

Kaplan, Norton and Barrows. (2008) *Formulating (and revising) the strategy*. Harvard Business Publishing Newsletters.

Wang Y. and Lin J. (2011) Empirical research on the influence of mission statements on the performance of non-profit organizations, 2nd International Conference on Challenges in Environmental Science and Computer Engineering (CESCE 2011), Procedia Environmental Sciences. 2011 11 Part A:328-333 Part A Language: English. DOI: 10.1016/j.proenv.2011.12.052.

The Chartered Institute of Marketing

http://www.bmw.co.uk [Accessed March 2012]

Andrews, K. (1987) *The Concept of Corporate Strategy*. Irwin, Homwood. IL.

Campbell A. and Yeung S. (1991) Creating a sense of mission. *Long Range Planning*, Vol24, No 4, August, pp 10-20.

Covey, S. (1992) *Principle centred leadership*. London, Simon and Schuster.

De Wit, B. and Meyer, R. (2005*) Strategy synthesis: resolving strategy paradoxes to create competitive advantage*. 2nd edition. Stanford, Cengage.

Dibb, S. and Simkin, L. (2009) *Marketing essentials*. 1st edition. Stanford, Cengage.

Doyle, P. and Stern, P. (2006) *Marketing management and strategy.* 4th edition. Harlow, FT Prentice Hall.

Freeman, E. and Reed, D. (1983) Stockholders and stakeholders: a new perspective on corporate governance. In Huizinga (ed) *Corporate governance: a definitive exploration of the issues*. Los Angeles, CA, UCLA Extension Press.

Friedman, L. and Miles, S. (2006) Stakeholders theory and practice. Oxford, Oxford University Press.

Hamel, G. and Prahalad, C.K. (1994) Competing for the future. Boston, MA, Harvard Business Review Press.

Hooley, G., Saunders, J., Piercy, N. and Nicouloud, B. (2007) *Marketing strategy and competitive positioning*. 4th edition. Harlow, FT Prentice Hall.

Johnson, G. and Scholes, K. (2001) *Exploring public sector strategy*. Harlow, Prentice Hall.

Kangas, P.J. (2011) Stakeholder Management Quality Press.com http://asq.org/quality-progress/2011/03/back-to-basics/stakeholder-management-101html [Accessed 07.06.12]

Khalifa, A.S. (2011) Three Fs for the mission statement: what's next? *Journal of Strategy and Management*, Vol 4 Issue 1, pp25–43.

Lewin, K. (1951) *Field theory in social science: selected theoretical papers.* New York, Harper.

QUICK QUIZ

1   What do De Wit and Meyer say the differences are between a vision and a mission?

2   De Wit and Meyer identify three significant components of a corporate mission. What are they?

3   What are the benefits of a clear, coherent and well communicated mission?

4   What did Freeman and Reed (1983) propose as two potential definitions of a stakeholder?

5   List the key factors to consider in creating an effective mission statement.

6   How could you describe core competences?

7   How can organisations enable core competences to be sustained and nurtured?

8   Identify two organisations that have used core competences to their advantage.

Activity 1.1

You will find that intuitively managers will fall into two categories: holding the shareholder value perspective or the stakeholder value perspective. This will be based in part on their own attitudes, values and behaviours, past experiences and future aspirations. Do their answers surprise you? An organisation must strive to recruit people that will be positively inclined to fulfil the organisation's mission. If there are major differences in the responses you receive, question why this is happening. Perhaps senior management has not worked hard enough at communicating its mission. Perhaps people have been misrecruited. How can you ensure that the organisation creates a mission that is as widely understood and accepted as possible?

Activity 1.3

The idea of core competence was introduced into management literature in 1990 by C K Prahalad and Gary Hamel. They outlined three tests to be applied to determine whether something is a core competence. First, a core competence provides potential access to a wide variety of markets. Second, a core competence makes a significant contribution to the perceived customer benefits of the end product. Third, a core competence is difficult for competitors to imitate because it is a complex harmonisation of individual technologies and production skills. The core competence idea is useful to managers not only for focusing them on the essentials, but also for identifying those things that are 'not at the core'. Think about the strengths of the organisation. Does it define and provide a perceived customer benefit? Does it benefit the customer better than the competition? Does it enable your organisation to be truly different? Is it difficult for the competition to copy?

QUICK QUIZ ANSWERS

1   De Wit and Meyer make a distinction between vision and mission. While the corporate mission outlines the fundamental principles guiding strategic choices a strategic vision outlines the desired future at which the organisation hopes to arrive. In other words vision provides a business aim while mission provides business principles.

2   De Wit and Meyer identify three other components of a corporate mission as follows:

–   Organisational beliefs: to work in unison a common understanding is needed amongst all organisational stakeholders. The stronger the set of beliefs subscribed to by the stakeholders the easier communication and decision making will become and the more confident, cohesive and driven the group will be. If people do not share the same beliefs joint decision making will be protracted and conflicting.

–   Organisational values: each person in an organisation can have their own set of values. Yet, when an organisation's stakeholders share a common set of values this can have a strong impact on the strategic direction. Widely held values contribute to a clear sense of organisational identity which will attract some individuals and dispel others. To be of most use and influence such values must be embodied in the organisation's culture.

–   Business definition: most firms have a clear identity from being active in a particular sector or industry. For such organisations, having a delimiting definition of the business they want to be in strongly focuses the direction in which they develop. Their business definition functions as a strong guiding principle and helps to distinguish opportunities from diversions. Here while a clear

business definition can focus the organisation's efforts it can also lead to short-sightedness and missing new business developments and opportunities.

3   There are a number of benefits of a clear, coherent and well communicated mission:

- Direction: a mission can point the organisation in a certain direction, by defining the boundaries within which strategic choices and actions must be taken.

- Legitimisation: a mission conveys to all stakeholders inside and outside the organisation what activities it is pursuing and on what basis. Through specifying the business philosophy that will guide the company the chances are increased that stakeholders will accept support and trust the organisation.

- Motivation: a mission can inspire individuals to work together in a particular way, with the power to motivate people over a prolonged period of time.

- Strategic change: a mission statement, articulated in an inspiring and thought provoking way can enable a change of attitude within an organisation which can lead an organisation in a new direction.

4   Freeman and Reed (1983) proposed two definitions of a stakeholder:

- The wide sense of stakeholder: any identifiable group which can affect the achievement of an organisation's objectives or which is affected by the achievement of an organisation's objectives

- The narrow sense of stakeholder: any identifiable group or individual on which the organisation is dependent for its continued survival

5   There are no hard and fast rules about how to create an effective mission statement but here are some issues that you should bear in mind:

- Ask yourself the right questions
- Say it clearly
- Decide what makes your organisation different
- Build your brand
- Keep it short and sweet
- Make it a joint effort
- Polish the language
- Spread the word
- Revise as needed

6   Core competences can be defined as the collective learning in the organisation, especially how to co-ordinate diverse production skills, integrate multiple streams of technologies, organise work and deliver value.

- A core competence provides potential access to a wide variety of markets

- A core competence should make a significant contribution to the perceived customer benefits of the end product

- A core competence should be difficult for competitors to imitate – and it will be difficult if it is a complex harmonisation of individual technologies and production skills

7   With the help of stakeholders within the organisation:

- The positive contribution of the business unit manager should be made visible across the organisation. Co-operative managers should be celebrated as team players.

- Competence carriers should be regularly brought together from across the organisation to trade notes, ideas and share best practice. This will help build a strong sense of community.

8   Coca Cola, Oxfam, and Virgin Atlantic are examples amongst others.

CHAPTER 2

Formulating corporate and marketing strategies

Introduction

In this chapter we discuss ways in which strategy is made in organisations. There are many approaches, each with something to offer. We start by reviewing the rational model. This is the classic approach; it has its weaknesses, but its great strength is its thoroughness. As a result, this method forms a good checklist of the things that what strategists should consider, if only briefly. The rest of this chapter is about other approaches to strategy. Generally speaking, these are, generally speaking, descriptive rather than prescriptive; that is to say, they are based on observation of what real world organisations actually do when making their strategies. We explore the thought process in developing strategy and stress the importance of understanding the wider environmental forces at work in developing a successful strategy. Finally, we look at the importance of strategy in smaller organisations.

Strategies are formed differently in different organisations; some plan, while others prefer to react to events; for others there is strategic drift where they are not proactively developing the organisation's strategy at all.

Mintzberg and Waters (1985) stated that strategy is formed in organisations through a pattern in a stream of decisions made.

Topic list

The rational model	1
Evaluation of a formal system of strategic planning	2
Deliberate and emergent strategies	3
Strategy and managerial intent – deliberate strategies	4
Strategic thinking	5
Strategic decisions in smaller organisations (SMEs)	6

1 The rational model

1.1 An outline of the model

▶ **Key term**

Planning: 'the establishment of objectives and the formulation, evaluation and selection of the policies, strategies, tactics and actions required to achieve these objectives. Planning comprises long-term/strategic planning, and short-term operations planning'.

The rational model is a formal approach to achieving a stated objective. In this chapter we discuss different approaches to making strategies. First, we outline the rational model. This is the traditional form of strategic management. It is characterised by being all encompassing, imposed from the top and sometimes unwieldy. The rational model is a formal and planned approached to developing strategy.

There are a number of aspects to a planned strategy. In the main the organisation has precise intentions as to what it would like to achieve, where it would like to be; this is analysed by taking into account both internal and external factors impacting the organisation.

The central leadership of the organisation writes and facilitates the plan. There is very much a central control to ensure that any decisions made relating to the plan are developed by central leadership, so maintaining control and minimising risk.

Planned strategies are generally developed in the context of a controllable and predictable environment. It is important to understand when examining different approaches to the strategic process how decisions have been made and what information has been accounted for when making decisions. How does the strategic intent of the organisation fit in with the organisation's overall vision and mission (see Chapter 1)? To what extent is the strategy able to achieve the overall objectives of the organisation? These objectives can range from achieving market orientation, innovation or entrepreneurial–related objectives.

THE REAL WORLD

Ciba-Geigy

Goold and Quinn, in their text *Strategic control* (1990), cite Ciba-Geigy, a Swiss-based global firm with chemicals and pharmaceuticals businesses, as an example of formal strategic control and planning processes.

(a) Strategic planning starts with the identification of strategic business sectors, in other words, areas of activity where there are identifiable markets and where profit, management and resources are largely independent of the other sectors.

(b) Strategic plans are drawn up, based on a comprehensive analysis of market attractiveness, competitors and so on.

There are three important aspects to these plans:

(i) Long-term objectives
(ii) Key strategies
(iii) Resources requirements

1.2 Models of strategic management

Characteristics of strategic plans using the rational model:

- Documented (written down)

- The result of a formal, systematised process with a start and end point

- Determined or endorsed by senior managers, with little direct involvement from operational managers, although they may be consulted

Figure 2.1   Strategic planning

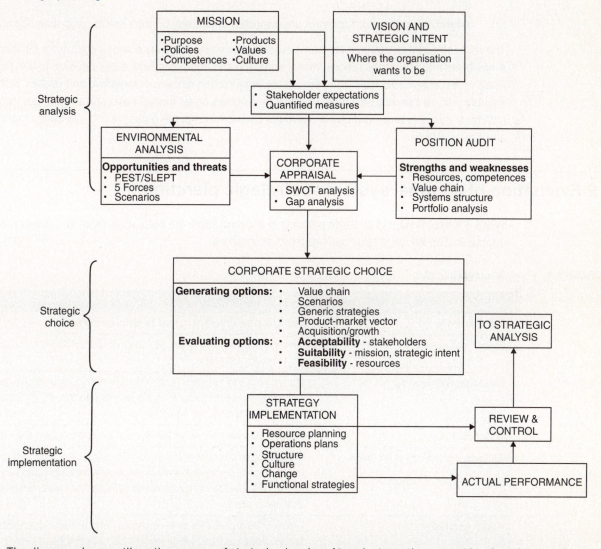

The diagram above outlines the process of strategic planning. At each stage, the process involves the use of various techniques, tools and models to make sense of the situation.

The rational model of strategic planning moves from the theoretical to the practical; from thinking about what the organisation exists for to doing something concrete about it. It is also an iterative process: it is not done once and for all.

In large organisations there may be a planning department which produces a revised plan at regular intervals; work will continue on some or all of the processes at all times. It is a process of refinement, of **adaptation to the environment**.

1.3 Assessing the rational model

1.3.1 Assumptions of the rational model

(a) **Top-down**. Senior managers, or planning departments, 'think great thoughts'. The results of their deliberations are documented in a plan, and are refined into greater and greater detail.

(b) **Corporate first**. Strategies for the organisation as a whole are developed prior to strategies for individual business units or functions.

(c) **Breakdown**. Strategic planning can be broken down into its subcomponents, in the same way as manual work can be.

(d) **Objective evaluation**. Strategies are evaluated objectively on their merits, unclouded by bias.

The rational model is less popular than it was. It is possible to advance strong arguments for it and against it. It has been argued that the rational model approach can stifle creativity, delay decision making as well as limit levels of responsiveness required to ensure the organisation remains competitive and evolves with the environment. It can also be argued that planning occurs on an annual basis and often it can focus on individual business units, rather than having a central focus to the organisation's planning process. (Mankins and Steele, 2006).

2 Evaluation of a formal system of strategic planning

When a formal system of strategic planning is adopted, there are both advantages and disadvantages to this approach. The following table outlines these alternatives.

Table 2.1   Strategic planning

Advantages	Comment
Identifies risks	Strategic planning helps in managing these risks.
Forces managers to think	Strategic planning can encourage creativity and initiative by tapping the ideas of the management team.
Forces decision making	Companies cannot remain static – they have to cope with changes in the environment. A strategic plan draws attention to the need to change and adapt, not just to 'stand still' and survive.
Better control	Management control can be better exercised if targets are explicit.
Enforces consistency at all levels	Long-term, medium-term and short-term objectives, plans and controls can be made consistent with one another. Otherwise, strategies can be rendered ineffective by budgeting systems and performance measures which have no strategic content.
Public knowledge	Drucker has argued that an entrepreneur who builds a long-lasting business has a 'theory of the business' which informs his or her business decisions. In large organisations, the theory of the business has to become public knowledge, as decisions cannot be taken only by one person.
Time horizon	Some plans are needed for the long term.
Co-ordinated	Activities of different business functions need to be directed towards a common goal.

The Chartered Institute of Marketing

Advantages	Comment
Clarifies objectives	Managers are forced to define what they want to achieve.
Allocates responsibility	A plan shows people where they fit in.

2.1 Criticism of the rational model in practice

Criticisms of the rational model concern how it has worked in **practice**, and more fundamental problems of **theory**. Mintzberg (1994) is prominent among the critics.

Table 2.2   Criticism of the rational model in practice

Problems	Comment
Practical failure	Empirical studies have not proved that **formal planning** processes ('the delineation of steps, the application of checklists and techniques') contribute to success.
Routine and regular	Strategic planning occurs often in an **annual cycle**. But a firm 'cannot allow itself to wait every year for the month of February to address its problems'.
Reduces initiative	Formal planning discourages **strategic thinking**. Once a plan is locked in place, people are unwilling to question it. Obsession with particular performance indicators mean that managers focus on fulfilling the plan rather than concentrating on developments in the environment.
Internal politics	The assumption of **objectivity** in evaluation ignores political battles between different managers and departments.
Exaggerates power	**Managers are not all-knowing**, and there are **limits** to the extent to which they can control the behaviour of the organisation.

2.2 Criticism of the rational model in theory

Table 2.3   Criticism of the rational model in theory

Criticism	Comment
Formalisation	'We have no evidence that any of the strategic planning systems – no matter how elaborate – succeeded in capturing (let alone improving on) the messy informal processes by which strategies really do get developed'.
Detachment: divorcing planning from operations	This implies that managers do not really need day-to-day knowledge of the product or market. But strategic thinking is necessary to detect the strategic messages within the nitty gritty of operations (eg like finding gold dust in a stream).
Formulation precedes implementation	A strategy is planned – then it is implemented. But defining strengths and weaknesses is actually very difficult in advance of testing them. 'The detached assessment of strengths and weaknesses may be unreliable, all bound up with aspirations, wishes and hopes.' Discovering strengths and weaknesses is a learning process. Implementing a strategy is necessary for learning – to see if it works.
Predetermination	Planning assumes that the environment can be forecast, and that its future behaviours can be controlled, by a strategy planned in advanced and delivered on schedule. In conditions of stability, forecasting and extrapolation make sense, but forecasting cannot cope with discontinuities (eg the change from mainframe computing to PCs).
The military analogy (John Kay)	An army's objective is to beat the enemy; the strategy describes how. This analogy is easy to grasp, but it may not be particularly relevant to business organisations. Their objectives are more complex and perhaps more ill defined than an army's. They compete with other organisations for customers. They are less able to command resources than an army. Their employees want the organisation (and their jobs in it) to remain in permanent existence.

(Mintzberg, 1994; Kay, 1993)

2.3 Where do we go from here?

Mintzberg's (1994) critique has not been fully accepted. Although the idea that planning is the only means by which strategies can be made is flawed, planning does have many uses. These are supporting roles; they cannot fully account for the making of strategy itself.

- It can force people to **think**.
- It can **publicise** strategic decisions.
- It can help **direct** activities in some cases.
- It can **focus debate**.

The great thing about the rational model is that it is **comprehensive**. Even if it is unrealistic to think of a given organisation moving with stately deliberation through an annual planning cycle, the rational model does give us a checklist that can be used to identify areas in which a company's strategy making may be capable of improvement.

Johnson, Scholes and Whittington (2007) presented four views (lenses) from which strategy can be developed:

1. Strategy as design

By analysing the firm's industry, environment and available resources, the ideal strategy and clear direction can be determined. This process follows an analysis-selection-implementation process. This tends to be a top-management driven.

2. Strategy as experience

Strategy as experience would argue that the design lens is inaccurate as top management may be too distant from the day-to-day development of the organisation. Strategic development needs to adaptive and can be divided into intended, realised and emergent strategies. There is continuous development of strategies based on experiences.

3. Strategy as ideas

This view regards strategy as a process that comes from from within an organisation and is influenced by the environment around it. This approach is a 'bottom up' that requires an organisational culture that encourages employees to discuss and share their ideas, differing from strategy as a design approach.

4. Strategy as discourse

This view focuses on making choices based on different possibilities and then inspiring confidence for the choice taken. This view is very high on legitimacy and lower on actual rationality and innovation. Managers are able to gain influence, power and establish their legitimacy as strategists over time and through the choices they make.

ACTIVITY 2.1

Apply the rational model to your own organisation. Critically evaluate the model and outline its strengths and weaknesses in the context of your own organisation. Consider whether it helps to achieve the long term strategic goal of your organisation or hinders it, giving examples to support the statements you make.

▶ Assessment tip

You may well find applying the rational model a useful source of ideas. It can also be the basis to identify the organisation's core competences, the strategic goal of the organisation, as well as breaking down the vision and mission and critically evaluating their relevance to the organisation.

The Chartered Institute of Marketing

2.4 The need for new strategic models

The Real World example below illustrates a radically different approach to marketing strategy.

THE REAL WORLD

Honda

Honda is now one of the leading manufacturers of motorbikes. The company is credited with identifying and targeting an untapped market for small 50cc bikes in the US, which enabled it to expand, compete in the European market and severely damage indigenous US bike manufacturers. By 1965, Honda had 63% of the US market, but this occurred by accident. On entering the US market, Honda's **planned strategy** was to compete with the larger European and US bikes of 250ccs and over. These bikes had a defined market, and were sold through dedicated motorbike dealerships. Disaster struck when Honda's larger machines developed faults – they had not been designed for the hard wear and tear imposed by US motorcyclists. Honda had to recall the larger machines. Honda had made little effort to sell its small 50cc motorbikes – its staff rode them on errands around Los Angeles. Sports goods shops and ordinary bicycle and department stores had expressed an interest, but Honda did not want to confuse its image in its target market of men who bought the larger bikes. The faults in Honda's larger machines meant that reluctantly, Honda had no alternative but to sell the small 50cc bikes just to raise money. They proved very popular with people who would never have bought motorbikes before. Eventually the company adopted this new market with enthusiasm with the slogan: 'You meet the nicest people on a Honda'. The strategy had emerged, against managers' conscious intentions, but they eventually responded to the new situation.

2.5 Strategies as patterns of management decisions

According to Andrews (1987) strategy is a **pattern of senior management decisions**. Andrews does not separate **objectives** from the **strategies** designed to achieve them, as strategy arises out of the **general management process** whereby **senior** managers direct and control the business. This general management process generates **consistent** decisions. For example, a firm's managers may prefer certain types of market opportunities (eg low risk) than others.

For Andrews (1987), **corporate strategy** is: 'the **pattern** of decisions in a company that determines and reveals its objectives, purposes, or goals, that produces the principal policies and plans for achieving those goals, and defines the range of business the company is to pursue, the kind of economic and human organisation it is or intends to be, and the nature of the economic and non-economic contribution it intends to make to its shareholders, employees, customers and communities'.

Porter (1996) stated that operational effectiveness is not a strategy; while it is necessary it is not sufficient for long term sustainability. A key aspect of a successful strategy is undertaking activities or making decisions that are different to rivals' and outperforming what they do. Strategies may also have to be revised according to industry changes; however, any new positioning must be appropriately sustained into a competitive advantage.

2.5.1 Freewheeling opportunism

Freewheeling opportunism is a pattern of strategy that displays little apparent coherence or forethought.

It is common among highly entrepreneurial individuals who are prepared to seize opportunities and back hunches. It can be present in larger, highly innovatory businesses, but is a high risk approach, depending for its success on a combination of experience, talent and market awareness.

Emergent strategies do not arise out of conscious strategic planning, but from a number of *ad hoc* choices, perhaps made lower down the hierarchy. They may not initially be recognised as being of strategic importance. Emergent strategies develop out of **patterns of behaviour**, in contrast to planned strategies or senior management decisions which are imposed from above.

3 Deliberate and emergent strategies

No realised strategy will be wholly deliberate or wholly emergent. The line between deliberate and emergent elements within each strategy will be in part influenced by organisation structure and culture. It is important to realise that there are two distinct approaches to strategy development from analysis, deliberation and planning to experiential, adjustment and a gradually crafted strategy. The strategic implications to leaders, managers, planners and stakeholders varies; however, both need to be critically analysed, evaluated and understood to fully appreciate their applicability to the organisation.

The diagram below should help explain the point.

Figure 2.2   Deliberate and emergent strategies

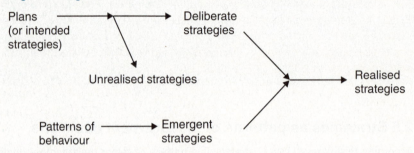

The task of **strategic management** is to control and shape these emergent strategies as they develop.

3.1 Implicit or explicit strategies

We already mentioned the fact that entrepreneurs have a theory of the business which they may or may not document.

- Implicit strategies may exist only in the chief executive's head.
- Explicit strategies are properly documented.

Some plans are more explicit than others.

ACTIVITY 2.2

Identify and critically evaluate the implicit and explicit strategies that have taken place in your own organisation. What do you feel are the advantages and disadvantages of each type of strategy?

3.2 Emergent strategies and how to craft them

The rational approach fails to identify **emergent strategies**, or allow for them, according to Mintzberg. Operations level can be where strategic change starts. Emergent strategies arise out of **patterns of behaviour**. They are not the result of the conscious intentions of senior managers. They have to be shaped or **crafted**.

Realised strategies include intended and emergent strategies.

The Honda Real World example, referred to the planned strategy of selling large bikes giving way to a strategy which had emerged almost by accident. Mintzberg develops this theme further.

Managers cannot simply let emerging strategies take over. Why?

- **Direction**. The emergent strategy may be **inappropriate** for the long-term direction of the organisation and may have to be corrected.

- **Resources**. It may have future implications for **resource use** elsewhere: in most organisations, different parts of the business compete for resources.

- Managers might wish to build on the strategy by **actively devoting more resources** to it.

Mintzberg (1994) uses the metaphor of **crafting strategy** to help understand the idea. Strategies are shaped as they develop, with managers giving help and guidance, devoting more resources to some, exploiting new opportunities and **responding** to developments. For example, Honda's management reacted to the emergent strategy, eventually, and shaped its development.

Separating 'thinking' and 'doing' has the following result:

(a) A purely deliberate strategy hampers rapid learning from experience (once the formulators have stopped formulating). For example, it is hard with deliberate strategies to stumble by accident into strategic growth.

(b) A **purely emergent strategy defies control**. It may in fact be a bad strategy, dysfunctional for the organisation's future health.

Deliberate strategies introduce strategic change as a sort of quantum leap in some organisations. In this case, a firm undergoes only a few strategic changes in a short period but these are very dramatic.

In other organisations, however, strategic change can be **haphazard**. Mintzberg (1994) mentions the example of the Canadian National Film Board. This used to make short documentaries but ended up with a feature film by chance. This forced it to learn the marketing of such films, and so it eventually became much more involved in feature length productions than before – strategy by accident.

Another example of this was the personal digital assistant (PDA) market. While Apple invested heavily in this market, its competitors failed to do so; Sony, Hewlett-Packard and Motorola did not recognise a demand for this product, failing to create a category for it. Eventually it was Palm Inc that got the share of the market.

The strategist must be able to **recognise** patterns and to manage the process by which emergent strategies are created. In other words, the strategist must be able to **find strategies** as well as **invent them**.

Mintzberg (1994) lists these activities in crafting strategy, summarised in the following table.

Table 2.4   Crafting strategy

Activity	Comment
Manage stability	Most of the time, managers should be implementing the strategies, not planning them. Obsessions with change are dysfunctional. Knowing when to change is more important. Formal planning is the detailed working out of the agreed strategy.
Detect discontinuity	Environments do not change regularly, nor are they always turbulent, though managers should be on the lookout for changes. Some small environmental changes are more significant for the long term than others, though guessing which these are is a problem.
Know the business	An intimate feel for the business has to include an awareness and understanding of operations.
Manage patterns	Detect emerging patterns and help them take shape. Some emergent strategies must be uprooted; others nurtured.
Reconciling change and continuity	'Crafting strategy requires a natural synthesis of the future, present and past'. Obsessions with change and/or continuity can be counterproductive.

3.3 Bounded rationality

In practice, managers are limited by time, by the information they have and by their own skills, habits and reflexes.

- Strategic managers do **not** evaluate all the possible options open to them in a given situation, but choose from a small number of possibilities.

- Strategy making necessitates compromises with interested groups through political bargaining. This is called **partisan mutual adjustment**.

- The manager **does not optimise** (ie get the best possible solution).

- Instead the **manager satisfices**. The manager carries on searching until he or she finds an option which appears tolerably satisfactory, and adopts it, even though it may be less than perfect. This approach Herbert Simon (1991) characterised as **bounded rationality**.

3.4 Incrementalism

Lindblom (1991) described another approach. **Incrementalism** involves **small scale extensions** of past practices. For example, supermarket retailers in the UK such as Tesco, Asda and Sainsbury's did not move from their original position of selling groceries only to being the entire 'one stop' stores they are today. They increased the number of non-grocery items sold gradually (or incrementally) over a long period. By the time these retailers had diversified into offering banking products, the notion of them selling more than just food was not in the slightest way unusual to their stakeholders.

The benefits of incrementalism are that:

- It avoids major errors.

- It is more likely to be acceptable, because consultation, compromise and accommodation are built into the process.

3.4.1 Disadvantages of incrementalism

- Incrementalism does not work where radical new approaches are needed, and it has a built-in conservative bias. Forward planning does have a role.

- Even as a descriptive model of the public sector, it does not always fit. Some changes do not seem incremental, but involve dramatic shifts.

- Incrementalism ignores the influence of corporate culture, as it filters out unacceptable choices. It might only apply to a stable environment.

3.5 A middle way? Logical incrementalism

Logical incrementalism: managers have a general idea of where the organisation should go, but strategies should be tested in small steps, simply because there is too much uncertainty about actual outcomes.

Strategy is best described as a **learning process**. Logical incrementalism has the best of both worlds.

- The broad outlines of a strategy are developed by an in-depth review.

- There is still practical scope for day-to-day incremental decision making.

3.5.1 Contrasts

The implications of rationality and incrementalism can be expressed in diagrammatic form here as Figures 2.3 and 2.4.

Figure 2.3   Rational planning model

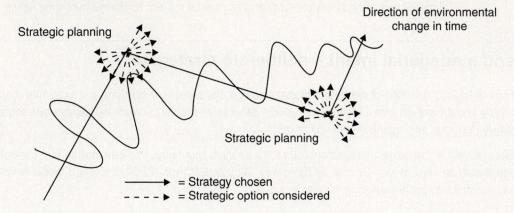

Figure 2.4   Incremental model

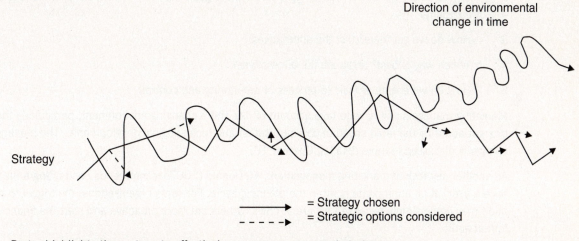

Porter highlights three steps to effectively manage an emergent strategy:

Step 1   Identify critical areas of uncertainty

Analyse the key aspects of the organisation, parts that are doing well, not so well and can be improved. From there think about what might be good opportunities for the organisation as well as what these opportunities can bring to the organisation, what positive impact this will have on the organisation. Also it is important to double check any assumptions that have been made by the organisation. For example when Disney decided to open in Europe it made a lot of assumptions that were very much related to the US, from duration of holidays for Europeans, food consumption at theme parks, employment hours to the money spent on merchandise.

Step 2   Execute smart experiences

Think about best practice within the industry. Also undertake secondary research to find out more about the environment so that this can underpin key decisions. The secondary research should be included in the audits within the organisation. Also, there needs to be consideration of external benchmarking as well as business modelling to help develop thoughts and ideas.

Step 3   Adjust and redirect based on the results of the experiments

It may be that as a result of internal analysis and experiments the strategy may need to be revised or developed in a different direction; at times this can be difficult as there are individuals or groups of individuals that have been following a previous strategy and may not want change.

The development of a new strategy will still require more experiments, audits and analysis of the internal and external environment and so may be subject to change over time again.

4 Strategy and managerial intent – deliberate strategies

Kotler's (2006) definition of **marketing management** is 'the process of planning and executing the conception, pricing and promotion, and distribution of goods, services and ideas to create exchanges with target groups that satisfy customer and organisational objectives'.

Most models of marketing management follow the **analysis, planning, implementation and control model** (that you should be familiar with by now) in some way. Gilligan & Wilson (2004) present a model which uses five key questions to guide marketing managers:

1   Where are we now? (competitive position, product range, market share, financial resources)

2   Where do we want to be? (strategy is formulated, goals are set – this involves all managers in the company)

3   How do we get there? (list the alternatives)

4   Which way is best? (evaluate the alternatives)

5   How do we ensure arrival? (a process of monitoring and control)

Marketing managers will have to take account of risk and a changing environment, particularly those changes brought about by the rapid speed of communication and technological developments. The management of change is discussed in more detail in Chapter 10.

As another key task of marketing management, McDonald (2007) recommends conducting a marketing audit once a year, at an appropriate point in the planning cycle. For some organisations, the trigger to perform an audit may come simply because they are in crisis. Others are more proactive and start the financial year with a formal audit.

In order to exercise proper strategic control, a marketing audit should satisfy four requirements:

(a)   It should take a **comprehensive** look at every product, market, distribution channel and ingredient in the marketing mix.

(b)   It should **not be restricted** to areas of apparent ineffectiveness such as an unprofitable product, a troublesome distribution channel, or low efficiency on direct selling.

(c)   It should be carried out according to a set of **predetermined, specified procedures**.

(d)   It should be conducted **regularly**. The auditors should be independent of particular job and organisational interests.

Each manager tasked with performing an audit on their area of responsibility should avoid making forecasts from previous performance and will need to use data from the marketing information system, sales data and other valid sources. Checklists can be issued to each manager who needs to contribute to the process.
A hierarchy of audits may be created by various managers with detail varying from level to level, business unit to business unit within the organisation group. The top level audit would look at issues globally from a strategic level.

McDonald breaks down the key information required into the external and internal audit.

The external audit should cover:

- **Business and economic environment:** economic, political, fiscal, legal, social, cultural, technological

- **The market:** total market, size, growth and trends

- **Market characteristics:** developments and trends: products, prices, physical distribution, channels, customers, consumers, communication and industry practices

- **Competition:** major competitors, size, market share/coverage, market standing and reputation, production capabilities, distribution policies, marketing methods, extent of diversification, personnel issues, international links, profitability, key strengths and weaknesses

The internal audit should cover the organisation and look at:

- Sales – total, by geographical location, by industrial type, by customer, by product.
- Market shares
- Profit margins and costs
- Marketing information/research
- Marketing mix variables – product management, price, distribution, promotion, operations and resources

Johnson and Scholes (1988) suggest an approach which follows a similar outline to the rational model, but which accounts for the political and cultural influences on managers. Johnson and Scholes (1988) discuss two other ways in which strategy can arise through deliberate management intent rather than simply emerging. These are discussed below.

4.1 The command view

Here strategy develops through the direction of an individual or group, but not necessarily through formal planning. In this model there is a person or group with acknowledged strategic power and responsibility.

The mechanisms by which this authority arises are reminiscent of Weber's analysis of legitimate authority into legal-rational, charismatic and traditional. Johnson and Scholes (1988) mention the autocratic leader; the charismatic leader whose reputation or personality gives control of strategic direction; and the making of economic and social strategy in the public sector by elected politicians.

4.1.1 Paradigm and politics

(a) The word **paradigm** may be used to signify the basic assumptions and beliefs that an organisation's decision-makers hold in common. Note that this is a slightly different concept from **culture**. The paradigm represents **collective experience** and is used to make sense of a given situation; it is therefore essentially conservative and inhibiting to innovation, while an innovative **culture** is entirely feasible.

(b) The **politics** of the organisation may also influence strategy. 'The political view of strategy development is that strategies develop as the outcome of processes of bargaining and negotiation among powerful internal or external interest groups (or stakeholders).'

Johnson and Scholes (1988) describe the processes by which paradigm and politics influence the process of strategy development:

(a) **Issue awareness**. Internal results, customer responses or environmental changes can make **individuals** aware of a problem. A **trigger** alerts the **formal** information system to the problem, so that organisational activity takes over from the individual's consideration of the problem.

(b) **Issue formulation**. Managers try to analyse and get to the root of the problem. Information may be used to rationalise, rather than challenge, management's existing view of the situation. **Formal analysis** in practice plays a small role.

(c) **Solution development**. Some possible solutions are developed and one is selected. **Memory search:** solutions which worked in the past. **Passive search:** wait for a solution to suggest itself. Solutions begin with a vague idea, which is further refined and explored by internal discussion.

(d) **Solution selection. Eliminate unacceptable plans**. This screening process involves bargaining, diplomacy and judgement rather than formal evaluation according to the business case. ('Unacceptable' might mean unacceptable in terms of organisational politics, rather than in terms of business sense.)

(e)   **Endorsements**. Many strategic decisions **originate from management subsystems**, which senior managers authorise. Junior managers might filter strategic information, or ignore certain options, to protect themselves.

A strategy audit involves assessing the actual direction of a business and comparing that course to the direction required to succeed in a changing environment. A company's actual direction is the sum of what it does and does not do; the direction of the organisation needs to be linked to the organisation's vision and mission statement. If there is a lack of alignment then the chances are that communication to key stakeholders may become confusing and so impact the credibility of the organisation. The strategy also needs to be compared to the external market, market forces and competitor and financial realities. Both the internal assessment and the external or environmental assessment of the organisation are key parts of the strategic audit.

The ever evolving and changing organisation's business environment needs to be considered when developing the audit. What is viewed as uniqueness or distinctiveness today can soon become commonplace tomorrow as new entrants and competitors enter the industry or change the environment by modifying the dynamics of the industry as well as expectations of the industry and the consumer. Hence a critically reviewed and developed strategy can envisage changes in the environment and react to them accordingly. A clear understanding of the audit findings that are then integrated into the development of the strategy is fundamental to the evolvement and success of the strategy. Successful companies do more than simply understand their environments but are also key in helping to develop the industry and its environment.

It is important to note that an audit is only as good as its application and usage; an audit that is not referred to appropriately and its implications considered can in effect be no help at all.

ACTIVITY 2.3

Undertake a strategic audit for your organisation; using the findings from the audit think of how you could potentially change/revise the organisation's marketing strategy to make it more competitive and sustainable in the long term.

THE REAL WORLD

Enron

Enron is now notorious for its unethical practices. However, its collapse is traceable to a failure of strategic control. In the early 1990s, Enron was extremely successful as a market maker in the supply of gas and electricity. Its strategy was 'asset light': it did not produce gas, or very much electricity, but it used its financial expertise and its control of gas pipelines and electricity grids to make large profits from the integration of supply and demand. Unfortunately, early success bred hubris and quite junior executives were allowed to make major investments in industries whose characteristics were totally different from the homogeneity of product and ease of distribution of gas and electricity. In each case, the strategies failed because they made large demands for capital and low utilisation of Enron's core trading competences. Johnson and Scholes (1988) are less averse to planning than Mintzberg (1994), but instead of assuming a rational objectivity, they anchor plans in the behaviour of the organisation and the people in it.

5 Strategic thinking

Ohmae (1982) argues that successful strategic thinking involves a creative and intuitive approach to the business, not just logic.

 The Chartered Institute of Marketing

5.1 Strategic thinking as an intuitive process

Kenichi Ohmae (1982) (in his book *The Mind of the Strategist*) argues that **formal strategic planning processes have withered strategic thinking**. Strategy is essentially a creative process:

- **Successful strategists** 'have an idiosyncratic **mode of thinking** in which company, customers and competition merge in a dynamic interaction out of which a comprehensive set of objectives and plans for action eventually crystallises'.

- 'Successful business strategies result not from rigorous analysis but from a **particular state of mind**'.

For Ohmae (1982), the challenge to strategic management is to try to reproduce this ability in organisational structures, forms and cultures. A strategist should be able to see beyond the present. There are several aspects to **strategic thinking:**

- Flexible thinking (what if? questions).

- Avoiding wrongly-focused perfectionism.

- Keeping details in perspective (especially **uncertain details**).

- Focusing on key factors and the essentials (or **distinctive competences**) of a business.

5.2 How successful strategic thinking operates

(a)   **Ask the right questions**. Find a **solution to a problem** rather than a **remedy to a symptom**. (Analogy: painkillers reduce a headache; they do not go to the underlying problem which may be poorly made spectacles or bad lighting.

(b)   **Observe the problems**.

(c)   **Group problems together** by a process of abstraction (eg brainstorming) to see what they have in common (the key factors).

Ohmae (1982) gives an example from an organisation's personnel system:

Figure 2.5   An example of an organisation's personnel system

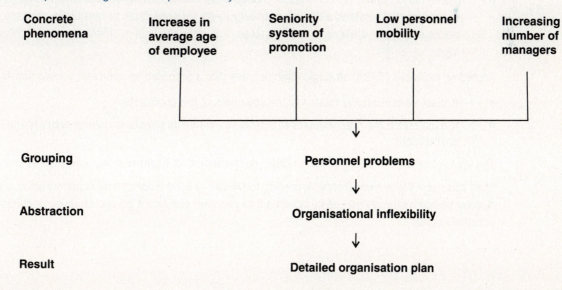

5.3 The environment and competition

> **▶ Key term**
>
> **Competitive strategy** is 'the taking of offensive or defensive actions to create a defendable position within an industry ... and ... a superior return on investment'.

The environment cannot be ignored. Strategy can be seen as a response to environmental forces.

Porter and Ohmae see business strategy in competitive terms. Competitive advantage is always relative to competitors. Possible future conditions must also be considered. The competitor analysis needs to address key issues in a critical manner. A mere description of the competition or the environment is not enough to underpin strategic development, potentially market orientation and long term sustainability. The following need to be considered (Porter, 1980):

- Competitor's objectives
- Competitor's assumptions
- Competitor's strategy
- Competitor's capabilities

This information may not be readily available, hence it may be secondary information that is the main source; the critical analysis of this data will be critical to the valuable nature of the information.

For Hofer and Schendel (1978) a strategy secures a fit with the environment. Success flows from this fit:

(a) The environment is a key factor in the behaviour of any organisation as organisations derive their **inputs** from it and distribute their **outputs** to it.

(b) **Fit or suitability** suggests that 'organisations are successful when they intentionally achieve internal harmony and external adaptation to their environment. Managers should use analytical techniques to identify the relationship between the organisation's internal capability and competences, and the external outputs. In very basic terms, the need for the fit is identified by the SWOT analysis and strategies are undertaken to secure the fit.'

(c) Hofer and Schendel (1978) suggest that strategy is a mediating force between the organisation and the environment. Therefore, although a strategy might be acceptable or feasible in principle, this does not necessarily make it the right one to choose. Arguably, the choice of strategy should follow a strategic logic.

According to Stacey (1993) **strategic logic** requires that a proposed sequence of actions satisfy two conditions:

- It must be consistently related to the objectives of the organisation
- It must match the organisation's capability (including its structure, control systems and culture) to its environment

The idea is that all the pieces of the strategic puzzle should fit together in a predetermined manner.

Most businesses face competitors. According to Ohmae (1982) what counts is performance in **relative terms**. 'A good business strategy' is 'one by which a firm can gain significant ground on its competitors at an acceptable cost'.

The Chartered Institute of Marketing

Table 2.5 Strategic approaches

Method	Comment
Re-adjust current resources	Identify the key factors for success (or distinctive competence) and concentrate resources on these activities.
Relative superiority	A relative advantage can still be achieved by exploiting the competitors' actual or potential weaknesses.
Challenge assumptions	Challenge the accepted assumptions of doing business in a particular market (eg telephone banking challenges the need for branch networks in banks).
Degrees of freedom	Finding new ways of exploiting markets (eg by segmentation, product/service differentiation etc).

In all cases, direct competition on the competitors' own turf is avoided. Successful strategy is the interplay of three Cs: **customers**, **competitors** and the **corporation**. Ohmae (1982) calls this the **strategic triangle**.

Porter (1980) highlights the importance of taking a competitive viewpoint. Porter suggests that over the past 20 years, firms have been learning to play to a new set of rules: benchmarking, outsourcing and the nurture of a few basic core competences.

The assumption is that rivals can easily copy any position, and so many companies are competing destructively with each other in a state of **hyper-competition**. As Porter says, 'the root of the problem is the **failure to distinguish operational effectiveness and strategy**'.

Table 2.6 Strategy and operational effectiveness

Task	Comment
Operational effectiveness is not the same as strategy	Operational effectiveness involves doing the same things better than other firms. Improvements here can be imitated.
Strategy rests on unique activities	Competitive strategy is about being different … choosing to perform activities differently or to perform different activities than rivals.
A sustainable strategic position requires trade-offs	Trade-offs limit what a company does. Trade-offs occur in three ways: ■ When activities are not compatible (eg an airline can offer a cheap no meals service, or offer meals; doing both results in inefficiencies) ■ Where there will be inconsistencies in image and reputation ■ Where an activity is over- or under-designed for its use (eg overqualified staff in menial positions)
Strategy is about combining activities	This is hard to imitate. (Operational effectiveness is about being good at *individual* activities).
Strategy is about choices, not blindly imitating competitors	Many firms operate inefficiently, and so can benefit by improving operational effectiveness, but industry leaders at the productivity frontier need to make choices and trade-offs.

Ohmae and Porter make three assumptions:

■ The survival of a business is impossible without a competitive strategy.
■ The actual strategy chosen will be unique to the organisation.
■ The marketplace is sometimes like a battlefield.

5.4 Competitive advantage

Competitive advantage is ensuring you are able to do things that potentially your competitors may not be able to do or would find hard to achieve. However, the strength of the value depends on how quickly if at all the competitors can catch up. Creating a long term strategic competitive advantage involves a number of considerations. In the first instance, the organisation needs to have a culture that allows for innovation and a culture of learning. It is more than just having knowledge but is also about managing the knowledge within the

organisation, to ensure people have the appropriate knowledge in all contexts. Creating such a culture doesn't happen overnight but may be part of the longer term strategy.

The core competences of the organisation also need to be recognised and developed (see Chapter 1).

Also becoming a low cost producer can potentially stop future competitors and their entry into the marketplace.

There is a need to develop key relationships within the industry, with customers, potential and actual stakeholders to ensure that there is dyadic communication and from this communication the information can be used accordingly to create relevant knowledge to underpin key decisions made at a strategic and corporate level.

5.5 The future orientation

There are two approaches to the future:

(a)   The future will change incrementally (eg global warning, demographic trends).

(b)   The future will be radically different (we do not know which inventions will succeed).

Obviously, both approaches are relevant and should be run in parallel.

Hamel and Prahalad (1994) make two suggestions:

(a)   The future is not just something that happens to organisations.

(b)   Organisations can create the future.

THE REAL WORLD

Coca-Cola

In the 1980s, Coca-Cola decided to change its flavour to compete with Pepsi. Market research, taster tests and so forth elicited favourable responses to the change, and so the new formulation was introduced. A small group of consumers vociferously opposed the change, and this opposition spread suddenly and rapidly like an epidemic, forcing Coca-Cola to re-introduce the old formula. It was hard to detect the reasons for this, but if some consumers perceived Coke to symbolise American values, then changing the formula appeared to be an assault on them.

This Real World example illustrates four issues:

(a)   The limitations of planning.

(b)   The seemingly unpredictable behaviour of the environment (as it became fashionable not to drink the new formula).

(c)   Small causes (a few disaffected Coke-drinkers) can generate major consequences, by amplification, almost.

(d)   The limitations to organisational gathering of information.

Consumers, who had initially favoured the product, turned against it, for reasons that could not be predicted by market researchers.

Stacey (1992) outlines a very different view:

(a)   **The environment is not always predictable**. The environment is a **feedback system**, in which some effects can be amplified such as the rapidly expanding boycott of new Coke.

(b)   Organisations can **shape their environment** (eg by moulding customer expectations) rather than just responding to it.

(c)   Too much of a good thing can lead to failure.

- Successful firms embody incremental and revolutionary change.

- Companies do not exist in a state of equilibrium, but instead exist between stability and instability, and it is this creative tension that enables innovation.

(d) Managers' attempts to plan or impose a vision do not always shape up to the reality of emergent strategies. But too much emergent strategy leads to anarchy.

5.6 Learning-based strategy

Learning-based strategy-making recognises the need to exploit the input of the knowledge worker. The flow of fresh ideas challenges the **paradigm**.

There has been considerable theoretical attention paid to the concept of a **learning organisation**, but as yet there is no single coherent model available. In this section we shall attempt to draw together some of the ideas related to strategy.

The idea of strategy as the exploitation of unique core competences inevitably implies that there must be a continuing and effective process of organisational learning in order to maintain competitive edge.

Competences must be kept up-to-date and new ones must be developed and exploited. Similarly, if competitive advantage is based on identifying opportunities in the environment, the company must keep up a constant scanning of existing and potential markets so that profitable segments may be identified.

Learning based on this process of environmental scanning may be termed **signal learning**, since it is largely a process of monitoring and considering the signals that emerge from the business environment.

We mentioned the **paradigm** concept earlier in this chapter.

A strong paradigm is developed as a result of success; if circumstances change, a strong paradigm may be a recipe for failure. Companies must be prepared to respond creatively to developments in the environment generally and particularly in their marketplaces.

5.7 Knowledge as a resource

With the transformation of advanced economies away from manufacturing and towards ever more complex service industries, there has been a growing awareness of the importance of the **knowledge worker**, whose input is based on a high degree of skill and learning, and of the **knowledge-intensive firm**, which employs large numbers of such workers. A firm of accountants is a good example of a knowledge-based firm.

There is an obvious requirement for such firms and workers to maintain, develop and exploit their knowledge, collectively and individually. With this requirement comes recognition of the human resource as a source of competitive advantage.

Nonaka (1994) identifies two types of knowledge:

(a) **Tacit** knowledge may be compared to individual skills. It is personal and rooted in a specific context.

(b) **Explicit** knowledge is formal, systematised and easily shared. An example would be the specification for a technical process.

5.8 Knowledge creation

The exploitation of knowledge requires that its acquisition or creation is organised in a rational fashion.

Argyris (1976) was one of the early exponents of the need for business learning. He used the term **double loop learning** to describe this process. The term is derived from **control theory**, in which a feedback control system that incorporates the option of changing the target is called a double loop system.

In double loop learning, knowledge is not only acquired, organised, stored and retrieved, but the purposes for which this is done are constantly reviewed. This involves regular examination of the organisation's purpose and

objectives in the light of the knowledge already acquired. Double loop learning may also be referred to as **3R learning**, since it incorporates processes of **reflection**, **re-evaluation** and **response** in order to bring about necessary development and change within the organisation.

5.9 The learning organisation

Lynch (2000) quotes Garvin's definition:

'An organisation skilled at creating, acquiring and transferring knowledge, and at modifying its behaviour to reflect new knowledge and insights'.

This clearly reflects Argyris's double loop approach. Senge (1990) has proposed that strategy development should be seen as a learning process. The essential nature of organisational learning in this sense is **active creativity**. Senge suggests that this is best undertaken by co-operative groups.

Implications for strategy. The learning organisation will generate a flow of fresh ideas and insights.

This will promote renewal and prevent stagnation. Increased openness to the environment will enhance the quality of response to events. However, none of this will happen if there is a rigid, prescriptive, **top-down** approach to the strategy-making process. There must be a **wide range of inputs** and a commitment to **discussion and debate**. There must also be mechanisms for effective **knowledge sharing**.

IT systems can be very useful in this process, but the essential precursor is an open-minded commitment to effective learning, led from the top.

The potential advantages of the learning approach must not be allowed to seduce the organisation into endless, unfocused debate. Senior management must guide the process in order to keep it on track. They must also be prepared to take decisions without consultation when circumstances require them to do so.

ACTIVITY 2.4

Thinking about your own organisation, would you describe it as a learning organisation? What factors do you feel are important in creating such an organisation?

6 Strategic decisions in smaller organisations (SMEs)

The characteristics of **smaller organisations** and their limited resources tend to produce a particular pattern of strategic decision making. Generally, this will be rather informal, entrepreneurial and customer-oriented.

Regardless of size smaller organisations must still look for new sources of sustainable competitive advantage that are unique over time (Arnold, 2000). This will mean identifying capabilities, competences and key skills within the organisation. The resources and capabilities of these organisations must be difficult to imitate, but equally not easily substituted. In turn the value created from this needs to be passed on to the customer; this can be done readily by smaller organisations as they are able to potentially know the customer personally, provide a service that is unique, develop relationships that cannot be readily imitated by competitors and so create longer term loyalty and sustainability. However, the initial critical analysis must be undertaken to ensure key areas are identified and appropriately developed.

6.1 The strategic decision process

It is likely that a large company will be influenced by the rational model approach, since it is likely to have the resources to undertake more complex planning. Therefore, the main responsibility for the strategic marketing decisions lies with the top management.

The Chartered
Institute of Marketing

The implementation and the management of the strategy are seen as operational decisions that are carried out by the lower levels of management.

However, in a smaller company the process may be much closer to the emergent approach, with strategic decisions being made as part of an iterative learning process.

A small company would not have the same depth of information as a large company to carry out the same high level of detailed planning. It will not have the resources to employ specialist expertise and gather extensive information before a strategic marketing decision is made.

It is more likely that the smaller company will initially make basic decisions about strategy and then, as learning progresses, further decisions will be made as seems appropriate.

Strategic management needs to regarded as something beyond mere processes, it should used to help an organisation better plan, analyse and develop its capabilities. Strategic management also needs to consider the fundamental decisions and actions that need to be undertaken to shape and guide the organisation both now and in the future. This is relevant not only for profit-making organisations but also for the not-for-profit sectors. It is important to realise that not-for-profit organisations still need to consider their long-term strategies as many organisations in this sector are running their organisations as businesses. As part of the strategic management planning process there needs to be a consideration of the organisation's environment both now and in the future, as well as a match of the internal factors and competences of the organisation.

6.2 The virtual organisation

The concept of the virtual organisation provides an alternative approach for small organisations to overcome their lack of internal expertise and other strategic resources.

Such an organisation is generally defined as being geographically dispersed and therefore dependent on electronic links to complete its production process. Using the concept more loosely, we can say that small organisations may develop a network of partnership relationships with other organisations in order to gain access to information and expertise that can provide benevolent influence on their strategic decisions.

This approach produces what is also known as a network organisation.

The future of planning will also need to include the digital marketing aspect. For example, pull digital marketing will see consumers seeking marketing content from various web searches or consumers giving permission to receive further product and organisation information through email, text messages and also various web sources. The use of blogs, audio and video media is on the increase and so will need to be included in the actual organisation's strategic development and planning process. The use of push digital marketing, technologies are also increasing with organisations sending communications without the consumers' consent, there are a number of media forms, from text messaging, emails to advertising on various webstes. This immediate form of communication is instant, however it needs to be targeted appropriately to ensure consumers respond and react to it, without becoming annoyed by it.

6.3 The B2B buying process

Another difference arises from the difference in the buying behaviour of B2B clients and the differing responses by large and small firms.

Where large customers are spending on major projects, they are likely to put contracts out to tender. It is the larger firms that will tender for these directly; smaller firms will not have the resources to do this, so they will sub-contract to the larger firm winning the contract.

Therefore, the marketing decisions of the smaller company may be dependent on their relationships with the larger companies serving the same market and the amount of outsourcing they do. The smaller firm will aim to form close relationships with the larger contractors so that they are well positioned for subcontracting opportunities.

6.4 Entrepreneurial v bureaucratic decision making

The smaller firm, because it is not subject to the strictures of formal planning processes, is much more able to be entrepreneurial in its decision-making. This means it is more likely to be innovative and quicker to respond than its larger rivals.

It also means the smaller firm is more able to be flexible in the decisions it makes and respond more easily to market changes. Having less formal procedures makes it more able to take rapid customer-focused decisions.

Also, it may well have a different perception of risk and be more willing to take risks based on hunches and soundings in the market than the larger firm.

The smaller company, as already noted, has only limited resources. Often, it may be that the entire decision making process has to be carried out by one person.

▶ **Assessment tip**

When examining the different approaches to the strategic process more often than not the candidates are asked to critically evaluate or analyse their existing marketing strategy and then make recommendations for change. It is important that the key ingredients of the strategy are appropriately analysed from an understanding of the core competences, strengths and weaknesses, as well as an understanding of what competitors are doing. This also needs to be linked back to the strategic direction of the organisation. This analysis should form the basis of developing the approach used to develop the strategy and the strategic thinking of the organisation.

A fundamental part of the process is to understand the central role of auditing when making decisions. The information in the audit should be used to underpin key decisions and needs to be an integral part of the process; the critical evaluation of the audit should help candidates to make recommendations that are appropriately evaluated, developed and help to underpin key strategic decisions, and that are able to analyse complex, potentially incomplete or contradictory areas of knowledge, developing valid, incisive and reliable conclusions as a result.

A recent assignment asked candidates to assess the organisation's marketing strategy and provide recommendations as to how it could be improved to bring about increase in stakeholder value; this required the audit to be used to make key decisions as well as to have a clear understanding of the long term strategic direction of the organisation after the appropriate analysis had been undertaken. The changes required needed to be critically analysed to produce incisive and critical answers relevant to the organisation rather than mere description lacking the appropriate rationale, evaluation and critical thought.

The Chartered Institute of Marketing

CHAPTER ROUNDUP

- The rational model is a formal approach to achieving a stated objective; there are a number of assumptions to the rational model.

- There are a number of criticisms and limitations of the rational model in practice.

- Intended strategies are plans; plans or aspects of plans which are actually realised are called deliberate strategies.

- Emergent strategies are those that develop out of patterns of behaviour.

- A marketing audit should satisfy at least four requirements:

  - It should take a comprehensive look at every product, market, distribution channel and ingredient in the marketing mix.

  - It should not be restricted to areas of ineffectiveness but needs to also focus on good practice.

  - It should be carried out according to a set of predetermined, specified procedures.

  - It should be conducted regularly.

- The external audit should cover the business and economic environment, the market, market characteristics and competition. The focus may vary depending on the industry, product, market or country.

- A competitive strategy is 'the taking of offensive or defensive actions to create a defendable position within an industry…and…a superior stance on investment'.

- Strategic decision making in a smaller organisation (SME) usually follows a particular pattern of strategic decision making; in the main it is informal, entrepreneurial and customer oriented.

FURTHER READING

Collins, J. and Porras J.L. (1991) Built to Last: Successful Habits of Visionary Companies. Harper Collins

Mintzberg, H. (1994) The fall and rise of strategic planning. *Harvard Business Review*, Jan-Feb, Vol72(1), pp107-114.

Stratis, G. and Powers T. (2001) The impact of multiple strategic marketing processes on financial performance. *Journal of Strategic Marketing*, Vol 9(3), pp165-191.

REFERENCES

Andrews, K. (1987) *The concept of corporate strategy*. Irwin, Homwood, IL.

Argyris, C.(1976) Single-loop and double-loop models in research in decision making. *Administrative Science Quarterly*, 21, pp 363–375.

Bowman, C. and Faulkner, D (1996) *Competitive and Corporate Strategy*. Irwin, London.

De Wit, B. and Meyer, R. (2005) *Strategy synthesis: resolving strategy paradoxes to create competitive advantage*. 2nd edition. London, Cengage.

Doyle, P. and Stern, P. (2006) *Marketing management and strategy*. 4th edition. Harlow, FT Prentice Hall.

Gilligan, C and Wilson, R. (2004) *Strategic marketing management*. 3rd edition. Butterworth, Burlington, MA Heinemann.

Goold, M. and Quinn, J.J. (1990) *Strategic control: milestones for long term performance*. London, Hutchnison.

Hamal, G. and Prahalad, C.K. (1994) *Competing for Future*. Boston, Harvard Business School Press.

Hamel, G. and Prahalad, C.K. (1989) *Strategic intent. Harvard Business Review*, May-June, pp63–67.

Herbert, S (1991) *Bounded Rationality and Organizational Learning*. Organization Science 2(1) pp125–134

Hofer, C. and Schendel, D. (1978) *Strategy formulation: analytical concepts*. St. Paul, West.

Johnson, G. and Scholes K. (1988), *Exploring Corporate Strategy*. 2nd edition. Prentice Hall, UK Ltd.

Johnson, G., Scholes K. and Whittington, R. (2007), *Exploring Corporate Strategy*. 8th edition. Harlow, FT Prentice Hall.

Kay, J. (1993) *Foundations of corporate success: how business strategies add value*. Oxford, Oxford University Press.

Kotler, P. and Keller, K. (2006) *Marketing management*. 12th edition. Harlow, FT Prentice Hall.

Lindblom, C.E. (1959) The science of muddling through. *Public Administration Review*, 19, pp78–88.

Lynch, R. (2000) *Corporate strategy*. 3rd edition. London, Pitman Publishing.

Mankins, M.C. and Steele (2006) Stop making plans; start making decisions. *Harvard Business Review*. Jan.

McDonald, M. (2007) *Marketing plans – how to prepare them, how to use them*. 6th edition. Oxford, Butterworth-Heinemann.

Mintzberg, H. (1994) *The rise and fall of strategic planning*. 8th edition. New York, NY Free Press.

Mintzberg, H. and Waters, J.A. (1985) *Of Strategies, deliberate and emergent*. Vol. 6, Issue 3, pp 257–272. July/September.

Nonaka I (1994) *A Dynamic Theory of Organizational Knowledge Creation*. Organizational Science. Vol 5 No. 1. Feb pp 14-37.

Ohme, K. (1982) *The mind of the strategist: the art of Japanese business*. New York, McGraw-Hill.

Porter, M.E. (1980) *Competitive Strategy*. New York, Free Press.

Porter, M.E. (1985) *Competitive advantage: creating and sustaining superior performance*. New York, Free Press.

Porter, M.E. (1996) What is a strategy? *Harvard Business Review*, Nov-Dec.

Senge, P. (1990) *The Fifth Discipline: The art and practice of the learning organisation*. New York Doubleday

Stacey, R. (1992) "Managing Chaos" Dynamic Business Strategies in Unpredicted World. London, Kogan Page.

Stacey, R. (1993) *Strategic management and organisational dynamics*. London, Pitman.

QUICK QUIZ

1   What are the three stages of strategic planning?

2   What five principle criticisms did Mintzberg raise against the rational model in practice?

3   What are emergent strategies?

The Chartered Institute of Marketing

4   What is the difference between implicit and explicit strategies?

5   What are the disadvantages of incrementalism?

6   Highlight the three steps to effectively manage the emergent strategy process.

7   When analysing the competitive advantage of an organisation highlight what the key considerations are.

8   What are the few processes described by Johnson and Scholes by which paradigms and politics influence the process of strategy development?

ACTIVITY DEBRIEFS

Activity 2.1

The rational model may be right for some organisations and not for others. It works best in an industry and environment which is stable and where there is little change expected from year to year. It is seen as a top-down management model and highly formal. The question is how relevant such a model is in today's challenging and uncertain economic environment and, if organisations are wedded to this approach, how it might hinder the organisation's ability to adapt to and survive in the face of environmental uncertainty.

Activity 2.2

Entrepreneurs have a theory of the business which they may or may not document. Implicit strategies may exist only in the chief executive's head. Explicit strategies are properly documented. Clearly some plans are more explicit than others. What has been the impact on you, your team and on the organisation of the execution of each type of strategy? Implicit strategies may cause confusion and instability, particularly if they have little or no regard to the overall vision and mission of the organisation. Then again, they demonstrate nimble thinking which can outwit the competition. Explicit strategies have typically been discussed, consulted and agreed upon with due regard to the organisation and its stakeholders.

Activity 2.3

Strategic audits should be used to analyse the organisation's current situation as well as help to plan future activities. It is important the audit underpins key strategic decisions and helps to make and justify decisions.

Activity 2.4

Learning is a systems-level phenomenon because it stays within the organisation, even if individuals change. While companies do not usually regard learning as a function of production, research on successful firms indicates that three learning-related factors are important for their success:

(a)   Well-developed core competences that serve as launch points for new products and services. (Canon has made significant investments over time in developing knowledge in eight core competences applied in the creation of more than 30 products.)

(b)   An attitude that supports continuous improvement in the business's value-added chain. (Wal-Mart conducts ongoing experiments in its stores.)

(c)   The ability to fundamentally renew or revitalise. (Motorola has a long history of renewing itself through its products by periodically exiting old lines and entering new ones.)

These factors identify some of the qualities of an effective learning organisation that diligently pursues a constantly enhanced knowledge base. This knowledge allows for the development of competences and incremental or transformational change. In these instances, there is assimilation and utilisation of knowledge

and some kind of integrated learning system to support such 'actionable learning'. Indeed, an organisation's ability to survive and grow is based on advantages that stem from core competences that represent collective learning.

QUICK QUIZ ANSWERS

1   Strategic analysis
    Strategic choice
    Strategic implementation

2   ■   There is no proof that formal planning processes contribute to success.

    ■   Strategic planning is routine and regular. It often occurs in an annual cycle. Organisations may not be able to wait several months to be able to address problems.

    ■   It reduces initiative.

    ■   The assumption of objectivity in evaluation ignores internal politics.

    ■   It exaggerates the power of management to control the behaviour of the organisation.

3   **Emergent strategies** do not arise out of conscious strategic planning, but from a number of ad hoc choices, perhaps made lower down the hierarchy. They may not initially be recognised as being of strategic importance. Emergent strategies develop out of **patterns of behaviour**, in contrast to planned strategies or senior management decisions which are imposed from above.

4   Implicit strategies may exist only in the chief executive's head.

    Explicit strategies are properly documented.

5   ■   Incrementalism does not work where radical new approaches are needed, and it has a built-in conservative bias. Forward planning does have a role.

    ■   Even as a descriptive model of the public sector, it does not always fit. Some changes do not seem incremental, but involve dramatic shifts.

    ■   Incrementalism ignores the influence of corporate culture, as it filters out unacceptable choices. It might only apply to a stable environment.

6   ■   Identify critical areas of uncertainty.

    ■   Execute smart experiences.

    ■   Adjust and redirect based on the results of the experiments.

7   ■   Competitor's objectives

    ■   Competitor's assumptions

    ■   Competitor's strategy

    ■   Competitor's capabilities

8   ■   Issue awareness

    ■   Issue formulation

    ■   Solution development

The Chartered
Institute of Marketing

CHAPTER 3

Developing corporate strategy and value proposition

Introduction

Strategic choices are made in the context of an approach to strategic management. We have already discussed several possible approaches to marketing strategy. In this chapter we look in more detail at ways in which strategic advantage may be created. An overview is provided on the importance of linking the marketing strategy to the organisational mission and vision followed by a detailed exploration of the marketing strategy process and the strategic choices to consider in developing a value proposition. Note that these ideas are equally applicable to any basic strategic method, though they are most likely to be used in a more or less deliberate approach.

Topic list

Developing a corporate strategy that meets the needs of the mission	1
Elements of the marketing strategy	2
Competitive strategy: how to compete	3
Positioning strategies	4
Products and markets	5
Channel strategies	6
Growth strategies	7
Hostile and declining markets	8

1.2.1	Determine an organisation's value proposition through analysis of an organisation's vision, mission and corporate objectives:
	■ Market definition
	■ Setting strategic objectives
	■ Price/value and proposition
1.2.2	Utilising the strategic audit, develop and present corporate strategies that are creative, customer-focused, innovative and competitive for a variety of contexts, incorporating relevant investment decisions and business cases which meet corporate objectives:
	■ Product/market strategies
	■ Growth strategies
	■ Competitive strategies
	■ Global and channel strategies
	■ Brand and positioning strategies
	■ CRM strategies
1.2.3	Critically evaluate the marketing strategy process, utilising the three key areas/levels in marketing strategy development:
	■ Core strategy
	■ Creation of competitive positioning (market targets, differential advantage and cost leadership)
	■ Control

1 Developing a corporate strategy that meets the needs of the mission

Having determined the organisation's current position and the desired position through identifying core competences and any gaps (sometimes referred to as gap analysis which you will study in Chapter 4), we can now turn our attention to the strategies needed to reach the intended position. The important point to recognise is that there will almost always be **alternatives**. Identifying these alternatives and carefully evaluating the options is an essential part of the planning process.

In previous chapters we have identified three categories of strategic choice:

(a)   The competitive strategies are the strategies an organisation will pursue for competitive advantage (a condition which is proof against 'erosion by competitor behaviour or industry evolution'). They determine **how you compete**.

(b)   Product-market strategies (which markets you should enter or leave, which products you should sell) determine **where you compete** and the direction of growth.

(c)   **Institutional strategies** (ie relationships with other organisations) determine the **method of growth**.

The diagram below represents these three core strategic choices, along with the models commonly used to explain them.

Figure 3.1   Core strategic choices

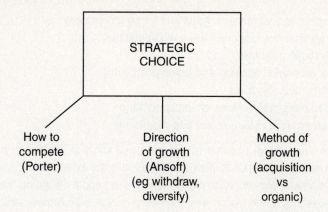

In some instances you might find it difficult to distinguish between **corporate strategy** and **marketing strategy**.

(a)   **Corporate strategy** will ultimately involve decisions and direction for all functions of the operation. Corporate strategy focuses on the corporate objectives and has an organisation wide impact. It is the over arching strategy and is determined before functional strategies.

(b)   **Marketing strategy** incorporates decisions relating to the positioning of the marketing mix to exploit and develop product/market opportunities. The focus is on the marketing objectives and in the main impacts marketing but will also impact to a greater or lesser extent other functions. It feeds into and needs to be linked to the corporate strategy.

ACTIVITY 3.1

Critically evaluate your organisation's corporate strategy and then the marketing strategy, highlighting their fit with one another.

2 Elements of the marketing strategy

The marketing strategy requires clear objectives and a focus in line with the organisation's mission and goals. When a company decides on its mission it is essentially answering two questions:

(a)   What **is** the company's core business/area of activity?
(b)   What **should** this be?

The development of the mission statement was the subject of Chapter 1.

The right customers must be targeted more effectively than they are by its competitors, and associated marketing mixes should be developed into marketing programmes that successfully implement the marketing strategy. It is important that the marketing strategy follows on from the mission statement; there needs to be a strategic fit, so that any marketing communication as a result is consistent.

▶ **Assessment tip**

On the December 2009/March 2010 assignment, Task Two concentrated upon a critical evaluation of the organisation's existing marketing strategy in terms of its competitiveness, with recommendations for change.

The June 2011 assignment asked candidates to assess how the organisation's marketing strategy could be improved to bring about an increase in stakeholder value and a more competitive, innovative and customer-focused value proposition.

The seven components of a marketing plan are:

(a) Organisational mission, goals and corporate strategy

(b) Organisational opportunities and capabilities

(c) Strategic objectives

(d) Target market strategy and brand positioning

(e) Marketing objectives

(f) Marketing programmes for implementation

(g) Performance measurement and monitoring

The marketing strategy must reflect the aims and ethos of the overall corporate plan. Those responsible for the development of the corporate plan should tap into the expertise and knowledge of the marketing function. Marketers should communicate closely with those people designing the wider corporate strategy. McDonald (2007) says this is one reason why marketing needs to be represented at board level. There are key questions (see below) that need to be asked to ensure that the strategy developed is appropriate, well written, relevant and fits in with the organisation's overall vision and mission, as well as engaging with the stakeholders:

- What are the needs of my customers?

- How are their needs changing and developing? How does this impact what they expect from our organisation?

- Which customers are key customers?

- What relationships do we need to develop with them to gather more information and ensure the products and service experience is developed properly?

- How should I target my niche market?

- What will be the relevant forms of communication?

- What are the emerging opportunities in the business environment? What are the threats?

- How can I improve my customer service in order to improve my profit?

- What changes can I bring about in my products or services to increase the profit?

- At a corporate level what needs to be my key considerations?

- Which would be the most competitive strategy based on external and internal factors?

- What are the best means of distributing and selling my products or services?

A key part of strategic management and strategic planning is to understand that that the vision and mission are linked to the corporate objectives, they will impact and influence each other. The market within which the organisation operates influences the development of the vision and the mission, in particular it will influence the development and direction of the marketing strategic objectives, these then filter and impact the overall marketing mix decisions.

The Chartered Institute of Marketing

Figure 3.2   Bowman's strategy clock

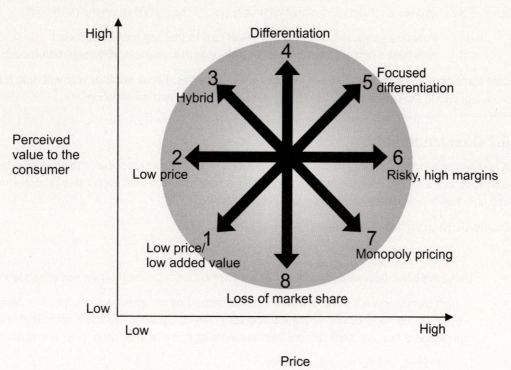

(Bowman C. and Faulkner D., 1996)

Bowman considers competitive advantage in relation to cost advantage or differentiation advantage. There are six core strategic options that are presented, that will impact the strategic decisions made with regards to price and value, from low price to high perceived added value. This analysis can help organisations make strategic level decisions, as well as considering the internal and external factors impacting the organisation to allow them to make competitive strategic decisions.

3 Competitive strategy: how to compete

> ▶ **Key term**
>
> **Competitive strategies** require actions to create a defendable position. They include cost leadership, differentiation and focus.
>
> Competitive advantage is anything which gives one organisation an edge over its rivals in the products it sells or the services it offers.
>
> A firm should adopt a **competitive strategy** to secure **a competitive advantage**.

Competitive strategy means 'taking offensive or defensive actions to create a defendable position in an industry, to cope successfully with...competitive forces and thereby yield a superior return on investment for the firm. Firms have discovered many different approaches to this end, and the best strategy for a given firm is ultimately a unique construction reflecting its particular circumstances' (Porter, 1980).

Having evaluated the overall corporate mission, those responsible for devising the marketing strategy must assess the most promising directions for their business and marketing activity. This will determine the strategic direction, considered in the remainder of this chapter.

3.1 The choice of competitive strategy

Porter (1998) suggests there are **three** generic strategies for competitive advantage:

(a)   **Cost leadership** means being the lowest-cost producer in the industry as a whole.

(b)   Differentiation is the exploitation of a product or service which the **industry as a whole** believes to be unique.

(c)   Focus involves a restriction of activities to only part of the market (a segment) through:

    (i)   Providing goods and/or services at lower cost to that segment (**cost-focus**)

    (ii)   Providing a differentiated product or service to that segment (**differentiation-focus**)

Cost leadership and differentiation are industry-wide strategies. **Focus involves segmentation** but involves pursuing, **within the segment only**, a strategy of cost leadership or differentiation.

3.2 Cost leadership

A cost leadership strategy seeks to achieve the position of lowest-cost producer in the **industry as a whole**. By producing at the lowest cost, the manufacturer can compete on price with every other producer in the industry, and earn higher unit profits, if the manufacturer so chooses.

Cost leadership can be achieved by:

- Setting up production facilities to obtain economies of scale

- Using the latest technology to reduce costs and/or enhance productivity (or use cheap labour if available)

- In high technology industries, and in industries depending on labour skills for product design and production methods, exploiting the learning curve effect. By producing more items than any other competitor, a firm can benefit more from the learning curve, and achieve lower average costs

- Concentrating on improving productivity

- Minimising overhead costs

- Getting favourable access to sources of supply

- Relocating to cheaper areas

THE REAL WORLD

easyJet

E-commerce plays a vital part in the easyJet business plan, and is critical to its ongoing success. As a low-cost operation, controlling the cost of doing business is crucial to the airline's ability to offer low fares. Because the internet provides the most cost-effective distribution channel, easyJet has aggressively pursued its strategy of encouraging passengers to book their seats online, ensuring that 98% of its seats are now sold over the internet. Some of the ways in which easyJet incentivises people to book their cheap flights online are as follows:

- Customers booking online receive a discount of £7.50 for each leg of a journey. easyJet first pioneered the concept of offering a **discount to internet customers** ensuring the cheapest flights are always available online, an initiative that has been widely copied by competitors.

- The **online flight search** not only allows customers to view fares by the date requested, but also allows them to see the cheapest flights over a two-week period.

- easyJet was the first low-cost airline to offer passengers the opportunity to **view their bookings online**, make flight transfers and name changes online for a discounted transfer fee, and request duplicate confirmation e-mails via the internet.

- An additional online feature to offer maximum convenience to the airline's passengers is the possibility to **reschedule flight bookings** during disruption from the comfort of their own home, taking away the need to be at the airport at such times.

- easyJet was the first low fares airline to offer **online check-in** allowing people to print their boarding pass before setting out for the airport, taking away the need to stand in the check-in queue.

- Adding **Speedy Boarding** during the online flight booking process gives passengers the opportunity to be among the first to board the flight, ahead of the regular boarding groups.

- Any easyJet **promotions are exclusive to the internet**, so that customers must be online if they wish to take advantage of special discounted sales fares.

It is important to note that a distinctive feature of companies that follow a cost leadership strategy is to ensure that the savings in cost are passed on to the consumer. Comparing easyJet to other companies it is clearly evident that it does not provide certain services that are expected by customers, eg arranging bookings for you or providing meals on the flight; however, the benefit of these cost savings are passed on to the customers.

easyJet does follow the cost leadership strategy by focusing on reducing costs; however, it needs to be careful that it is not at the expense of other vital factors, and that cost saving becomes so dominant that the company loses vision of why it embarked on such a strategy in the first place.

3.3 Differentiation

A differentiation strategy assumes that competitive advantage can be gained through **particular characteristics** of a firm's products.

Products may be categorised as:

(a) **Breakthrough products** offering a radical performance advantage over competition, perhaps at a drastically lower price or a higher premium price.

(b) **Improved products** which are not radically different from their competition but are obviously superior in terms of better performance for a similar price.

(c) **Competitive products** which derive their appeal from a particular compromise of cost and performance. For example, cars are not all sold at rock-bottom prices, nor do they all provide immaculate comfort and performance. They compete with each other by trying to offer a more attractive compromise than rival models.

3.3.1 There are three key ways to differentiate:

- Build up a brand image
- Give the product special features to make it stand out
- Exploit other activities of the value chain

THE REAL WORLD

We all know about branding and product modification in food. Organic food is increasing in popularity, as it is differentiated on the basis of:

- Possible health benefits (disputed by some nutritionists)

- Kindness to the environment (and to animals)

The end product may be the same (eg pasta) but the ingredients and process by which it is made are a source of differentiation. Retailers and manufacturers of branded goods charge more for organic variants of standard products.

Pret A Manger is a UK-based fast food chain with a twist: sandwiches and salads are made in house throughout each day using natural, preservative-free ingredients. In an industry full of big sandwich factories, and bland, highly processed foods, Pret's unique formula is redefining the traditional wisdom on fast food – and its success is turning more than a few heads in the business world. The first Pret A Manger restaurant opened in London in 1986, with college friends Sinclair Beecham and Julian Metcalfe creating the sort of food they craved but couldn't find anywhere else. By 1992, the friends had expanded their

operations to three sandwich shops, and their business formula was beginning to click. Today, Pret operates 225 shops, with nearly 4,000 employees, and turns over close to 200 million sterling each year. (www.pret.com)

Ultimately this is about differentiating a commodity – in short, decommodifying it. The advantage for retailers is that, with tens of thousands of new food products introduced to US supermarkets each year, the right agricultural pedigree provides further differentiation.

The differentiating factor for Pret A Manger is the fresh nature of their products. This is linked in with their brand values, providing the customers with fresh fast food products on a daily basis. This differentiates them from competitors and so gives them competitive advantage. The other advantage it has is its portfolio of products that is offered to customers from sandwiches and crisps to popcorn, muffins and sushi.

As the operations manager stated: 'Our customers want to be able to purchase a variety of different products, so to keep our menu exciting and innovative, we're constantly introducing new products and flavours. Even though probably only one idea in every 20 makes it through our testing process, on average a new product goes on sale in our UK shops every four days. Existing products are continually being improved. For example, the recipe for the chocolate brownie has been improved 33 times over the last few years. Each change is miniscule but detectable.'

It is important to note that differentiation can take a number of forms, from superior customer service to better product performance. This can mean that the company incurs extra cost, which could be on different communications methods to promote the differentiating factors or through developing brand values and communicating those brand values.

3.4 Focus (or niche) strategy

In a focus strategy, a firm concentrates its attention on one or more particular segments or niches of the market, and does not try to serve the entire market with a single product.

(a) A cost-focus strategy: aim to be a cost leader for a particular segment. This type of strategy is often found in the printing, clothes manufacture and car repair industries.

(b) A differentiation-focus strategy: pursue differentiation for a chosen segment. Luxury goods are the prime example of such a strategy.

The advantages of a focus strategy are:

- A niche is more secure and a firm can insulate itself from competition.
- The firm does not spread itself too thinly.

The drawbacks of a focus strategy are:

(a) The firm **sacrifices economies of scale** which would be gained by serving a wider market.

(b) **Competitors can move into the segment** with increased resources (eg the Japanese moved into the US luxury car market, to compete with Mercedes and BMW).

(c) The **segment's needs may eventually become less distinct** from the main market.

A differentiation focus strategy gives the organisation the possibility to charge a premium price for superior quality or offer a low price product to a small and specialised group of buyers through a cost focus strategy. Examples of this are the Ferrari and Range Rover. The Evoque is another classic example of a niche player in the automobile industry. Aimed at a certain market the Evoque was part designed by Victoria Beckham and is aimed at the discerning consumer who is interested in design as well as the quality of the car. The potential downside of the focus strategy, however, is that characteristically the niche is small and may not be significant or large enough to justify a company's attention.

The Chartered Institute of Marketing

Wagamama – positive energy and positive living

The essence of Wagamama is a no-nonsense combination: simple, high quality yet inexpensive food served up in a sleek, minimalist canteen-style setting, with bench seats and no reservations, alongside an open-plan kitchen. Together these all contribute to the noisy, vibrant buzz of the restaurants. This carefully balanced formula was an instant hit when the first restaurant opened on Streatham Street, near the British Museum in London's Bloomsbury district. Thirteen additional Wagamama restaurants have since opened in London, and the brand has also expanded nationally. It now has around 70 branches in the UK. In addition, the first Wagamama branch outside the UK opened in Dublin in 1998, Amsterdam followed in 2000 and May 2002 saw Wagamama going Down Under with the opening of a restaurant in Sydney. With more international branches in the pipeline, Wagamama is simply following its customers' demands. Much can be learned about Wagamama by examining the meaning of the name itself. Translated literally from Japanese, wagamama means 'wilful/selfish child'. But a broader interpretation would explain the selfishness in terms of looking after oneself, in terms of positive eating and positive living. A single-minded belief in the strength of its own formula, and letting the quality of its product speak for itself has built Wagamama into an extremely strong and much admired brand, as well as enhancing its cool credentials. The personality of Wagamama is also very apparent in its uncomplicated advertising. An image that is frequently used in its ads, amongst other communications, is that of an eager diner with a large bowl completely covering her face as she slurps up what is left in the bottom. Shot in black and white, the image gives an air of being both innocent and childlike but confident and wilful at the same time.

(www.wagamama.com)

3.5 Which strategy is best?

Although there is a risk with any of the generic strategies, Porter argues that a firm **must** pursue one of them. A **stuck-in-the-middle** strategy is almost certain to make only low profits. 'This firm lacks the market share, capital investment and resolve to play the low-cost game, the industry-wide differentiation necessary to obviate the need for a low-cost position, or the focus to create differentiation or a low-cost position in a more limited sphere.'

In practice, it is rarely simple to draw hard and fast distinctions between the generic strategies as there are conceptual problems underlying them.

3.6 Problems with the cost leadership concept

- **Internal focus**. Cost refers to internal measures, rather than the market demand. It can be used to gain market share, but it is the **market share which is important**, not cost leadership as such.

- **Only one firm**. If cost leadership applies across the whole industry, only one firm will pursue this strategy successfully.

- **Higher margins can be used for differentiation**. Having low costs does **not** mean you have to charge lower prices or compete on price. A cost leader can choose to 'invest higher margins in R & D or marketing'. Being a cost leader arguably gives producers more freedom to choose other competitive strategies.

3.7 Problems with the differentiation concept

Porter assumes that a differentiated product will always be sold at a **higher price**.

- However, a **differentiated product** may be sold at the same price as competing products in order to **increase market share**.

- **Choice of competitor**. Differentiation from whom? Who are the competitors? Do they serve other market segments? Do they compete on the same basis?

- **Source of differentiation**. This can include **all** aspects of the firm's offer, not only the product. Restaurants aim to create an atmosphere or 'ambience', as well as serving food of good quality.

Focus probably has fewer conceptual difficulties, as it ties in very neatly with ideas of market segmentation. In practice, most companies pursue this strategy to some extent, by designing products/services to meet the needs of particular target markets.

'Stuck-in-the-middle' is therefore what many companies actually pursue quite successfully. Any number of strategies can be pursued, with different approaches to **price** and the **perceived added value** (ie the differentiation factor) in the eyes of the customer.

Toyota and Benetton are prime examples of organisations which have adopted more than one generic strategy. Both these companies used the generic strategies of differentiation and low cost simultaneously, which led to the success of these companies.

3.8 Strategic decision-making

Bowman's strategy clock can be used to make strategic decisions, as well as considering Porter's generic strategy. These can be the starting points in the analysis process, however other internal and external factors also need to be considered to make an informed decision.

Table 3.1   Industry wide strategies

Advantages	Cost leadership	Differentiation
New entrants	Economies of scale raise entry barriers	Brand loyalty and perceived uniqueness are entry barriers
Substitutes	Firm is not so vulnerable as its less cost effective competitors to the threat of substitutes	Customer loyalty is a weapon against substitutes
Customers	Customers cannot drive down prices further than the next most efficient competitor	Customers have no comparable alternative
Suppliers	Flexibility to deal with cost increases	Higher margins can offset vulnerability to supplier price rises
Industry rivalry	Firm remains profitable when rivals go under through excessive price competition	Brand loyalty should lower price sensitivity

Disadvantages	Cost leadership	Differentiation
New entrants	Technological change will require capital investment, or make production cheaper for competitors	New entrants can differentiate too
Substitutes	Substitutes with improved features or marketing may 'undercut' even a cost leadership strategy if customers use them as better products, making the strategy redundant (and expensive)	Sooner or later, customers become price sensitive
Customers	Cost concerns ignore product design or marketing issues	Customers may not value the differentiating factor
Suppliers	Increase in input costs can reduce price advantages	Differentiation might require specialist inputs
Industry rivalry	Competitors can benchmark their processes or cut costs	Competitors can copy

The Chartered Institute of Marketing

3.9 Competitive positions

Firms can choose a variety of strategies to attack or defend their position. Different strategies are appropriate to challengers, followers, leaders and nichers.

The broad generic strategies outlined above have some flaws, as we have seen. We suggested a number of approaches to price and value. In this section we describe how marketing activities can be used against competitors.

Considering strategic options from a competitor rather than customer orientation is referred to as competitive marketing strategy. Kotler and Singh (1981) identified five offensive and six defensive competitive strategies named after military strategies:

(a) **Offensive warfare**

Offensive strategies can be used by all companies. In order to ensure success, a company must be able to gain an advantage over the competition in the segment or area of attack. In the main, an offensive strategy is often undertaken by organisations that are potentially number 2 or even number 3 in the market. Although it could be that the leader is far too strong to challenge at all, in these cases generally a flanking or a guerrilla strategy is used.

Kotler describes the following attack strategies:

(i) **Frontal attack**

– This is the direct, head-on attack meeting competitors with the same product line, price, promotion and so on. Because the attacker is attacking the enemy's strengths rather than its weaknesses, it is generally considered the riskiest and least advised of strategies.

An attack is called a frontal attack when the opponent's strength is challenged head on. In marketing, the fight is done on all fronts in market segments and areas where the opponent is currently strong. The general idea is that to win in a frontal attack, the challenger requires three times the fire power of the opposite side. What is fire power in marketing? Price of the product, quality of the product, sales effort, advertising effort, and service effort etc are the various types of fire power in marketing. The challenger must be able to deploy superior fire power in the markets he is challenging.

(ii) **Flanking attack**

– The aim is to engage competitors in those product markets where they are weak or have no presence at all. Its overreaching goal is to build a position from which to launch an attack on the major battlefield later without waking 'sleeping giants'.

This allows the organisation to position itself where competitors are not necessarily strong or equally lack presence; however, when critically evaluating this option it is important to question why this strategy has not been undertaken by the competitor themselves. Equally once this has been launched there is nothing stopping a competitor from also launching a similar product or following a similar positioning strategy.

(iii) **Encirclement attack**

– Multi-pronged attack aimed at diluting the defender's ability to retaliate in strength. The attacker stands ready to block the competitor no matter which way he turns in the product market.

– An attacker can encircle by product proliferation as Seiko did in the watch market, supplying 400 watch types in the UK out of 2,300 models world-wide.

– Market encirclement consists of expanding the products into all segments and distribution channels.

(iv) **Bypass attack**

– This is the most indirect form of competitive strategy as it avoids confrontation by moving into new and as yet uncontested fields. Three types of bypass are possible: develop new products, diversify into unrelated products or diversify into new geographical markets.

(v) **Guerrilla warfare**

– Less ambitious in scope, this involves making small attacks in different locations while remaining mobile. Such attacks take several forms: law suits, poaching personnel, interfering with supply networks and so on. The overriding aim is to destabilise by products rather than blows.

(b) **Defensive warfare**

It is generally agreed that only a market leader should play defence in an attempt to hold on to its existing markets in the face of competitive attack.

(i) **Position defence**

– Static defence of a current position, retaining current product-markets by consolidating resources within existing areas. **Exclusive reliance** on a position defence effectively means that a business is a **sitting target** for competition.

(ii) **Mobile defence**

– A high degree of **mobility prevents the attacker's chances of localising defence** and accumulating its forces for a decisive battle. A business should seek market development, product development and diversification to create a stronger base.

(iii) **Pre-emptive defence**

– Attack is the best form of defence. Pre-emptive defence is launched in a segment where an attack is anticipated instead of a move into related or new segments.

(iv) **Flank position defence**

– This is used to occupy a position of **potential** future importance in order to deny that position to the opponent. Leaders need to develop and hold secondary markets to prevent competitors using them as a spring board into the primary market. (For example, Japanese manufacturers used the upper-end executive and coupe market to break into the volume car sector in the US.)

(v) **Counter-offensive defence**

– This is attacking where one is being attacked. This requires **immediate response** to any competitor entering a segment or initiating new moves. Examples are price wars, where firms try to undercut each other.

(vi) **Strategic withdrawal**

– May be a last resort, but 'cutting your losses' can be the best option in the long run. Management resistance to what is seen as a drastic step is likely to be the biggest barrier.

The five attacking strategies for challenging market leaders and the six defensive strategies used to fight off challenges are not mutually exclusive. As contingent factors change, a successful company will reconsider and revise its core strategies.

A commonly cited example of a defensive strategy is that of Johnson & Johnson's Tylenol brand of analgesics, which had a dominant position with regards to the over-the-counter market for pain relief.

Its position had been gained through the product benefits of being an effective pain killer with very low side effects. The perception in the marketplace was that it was gentler than other products. However in the mid

The Chartered Institute of Marketing

1980s, the ingredient ibuprofen became available to all manufacturers for over-the-counter use. This was a threat to Tylenol's current positioning in the marketplace.

In this situation there are key factors and questions to consider:

- Should an organisation continue to emphasise its strengths and what it is known for in the marketplace?

- Should the organisation respond with an aggressive marketing campaign including any one of the following: sales promotion, advertising, in-store promotions, trade deals, B2B business relationship development?

- Should the organisation lower its price to defend its share or increase its price to cover its marketing costs? This will also impact consumers' perception of the product.

- Should the organisation also extend its product lines to include the newly launched product range by its competitors?

- Should the organisation re-assess its distribution strategy?

- These are all key considerations that would need to be assessed when developing a defensive strategy.

4 Positioning strategies

Central to achieving the organisational vision and mission is the need to build up a loyal customer base of satisfied customers.

Taking time to objectively group a market's customers into meaningful market segments is an important discipline. The most successful brands base their marketing strategies on carefully honed market segmentation analyses. Shrewd targeting of certain segments and the development of a clear brand positioning are part and parcel of the market segmentation process and are the foundation of an effective marketing strategy.

Once determined the business must then strive to emphasise to those targeted customers the relevance and applicability of its product and marketing mix proposition. This is primarily achieved through developing a distinctive, plausible and memorable brand positioning.

We can apply these strategies to firms with different positions in the market:

- Pioneers
- Challengers
- Followers
- Nichers

4.1 Strategies for pioneers

- Position defence
- Mobile defence
- Flanking defence
- Contraction defence (withdrawal)
- Pre-emptive defence
- Counter-offence

4.2 Strategies for challengers

Challengers can either attack, accept the status quo, or try and win market share from other smaller companies in the market.

- Frontal attack
- Bypass attack
- Flank attack
- Guerrilla attack
- Encirclement attack

Market challenger strategies:

- Define strategic objective and opponents
- Choose an attack strategy
- Challenge the leader
- Challenge similar companies with weaknesses
- Challenge smaller/localised companies

4.3 Market leader strategies

Grow total market: New users / new uses / more uses
Defend market share: Decide where to defend / innovation / CRM / position defence
Expand market share: Acquisiton / joint venture / partnerships / marketing

4.4 Strategies for followers

Many firms succeed by imitating the leaders. This is common in financial services markets where the basic functionality of a product is similar. Given that there are controls over monopoly status, most markets will have at least two players. Followers can follow:

- **Closely**, by imitating the marketing mix, and targeting similar segments

- **At a distance**, with more differentiating factors

- **Selectively** to avoid direct competition

Kotler (2006) makes the important point that 'followership is not the same as being passive or a carbon copy of the leader'. The follower has to define a path that does not invite competitive retaliation. He identifies three broad followership strategies:

(a) **Cloner**. This is a parasite that lives off the investment made by the leader in the marketing mix (such as in products or distribution). The **counterfeiter** is an extreme version of the cloner, who produces fakes of the original (eg fake Rolex watches for sale in the Far East).

(b) **Imitator**. This strategy copies some elements but differentiates on others (such as packaging).

(c) **Adapter**. This involves taking the leader's products and adapting or even improving them. The adapter may grow to challenge the leader.

4.5 Strategies for market nichers

This is associated with a **focus** strategy and relies partly on segmentation, and partly on specialising. There are several specialist roles open to market nichers:

(a) **End-user specialist**, specialising in one type of customer
(b) **Vertical level specialist**, specialising at one particular point of the production/distribution chain
(c) **Specific customer specialist**, limiting selling to one or just a few customers
(d) **Geographic specialist,** selling to one locality
(e) **Product or service specialist**, offering specialised services not available from other firms
(f) **Quality/price specialist,** operating at the low- or high-end of the market
(g) **Channel specialist**, concentrating on just one channel of distribution

4.6 Brand and positioning strategies

The brand can be used to differentiate from competitors, this is based on the specific characteristics or benefits offered. It is important to remember that a product can be positioned on more than one product benefit, especially if there are a number of strengths of the brand.

5 Products and markets

Product-market strategy includes market penetration, market development, product development and diversification. Ansoff (1965) drew up a **growth vector matrix**, describing a combination of a firm's activities in current and new markets, with existing and new products.

Product-market mix is a short-hand term for the products/services a firm sells (or a service which a public sector organisation provides) and the markets it sells them to.

Figure 3.3   Ansoft's product-market growth matrix

	Existing products	New products
Existing markets	**Market penetration strategy** 1 More purchasing and usage from existing customers 2 Gain customers from competitors 3 Convert non-users into users (where both are in same market segment)	**Product development strategy** 1 Product modification via new features 2 Different quality levels 3 'New' product
New markets	**Market development strategy** 1 New market segments 2 New distribution channels 3 New geographic areas eg exports	**Diversification strategy** 1 Organic growth 2 Joint ventures 3 Mergers 4 Acquisition/take-over

Ansoff's product market growth matrix presents four options. Staying with your existing product in your existing market is low risk, however moving into a new market with an existing product increases the risks, as does a new product in an existing market. The greatest risk is with a new market and product.

5.1 Current products and current markets: market penetration

The firm seeks to:

(a)   Maintain or to increase its share of current markets with current products, eg through competitive pricing, advertising, sales promotion

(b)   Secure dominance of growth markets

(c)   Restructure a mature market by driving out competitors

(d)   Increase usage by existing customers eg air miles, loyalty cards

Good examples of strategies for market penetration are air miles and 'frequent flier' services. A decision to fly with an airline gives the customer air miles, which can be redeemed on later flights, and which will encourage the customer to fly again.

5.2 Present products and new markets: market development

Market development is when the firm seeks new markets for its **current** products or services. It is appropriate when its products are strengths which can be matched by opportunities in new markets.

Ways of developing markets include:

(a)   **New geographical areas** and export markets (eg a radio station building a new transmitter to reach a new audience).

(b)   **Different package sizes** for food and other domestic items so that both those who buy in bulk and those who buy in small quantities are catered for.

(c)   **New distribution channels** to attract new customers (eg organic food sold in supermarkets not just specialist shops).

(d)   **Differential pricing policies** to attract different types of customer and create **new market segments**. For example, travel companies have developed a market for cheap long-stay winter breaks in warmer countries for retired couples.

5.3 New products and present markets: product development

Product development is the launch of new products to existing markets.

(a)   **Advantages**

- Product development forces competitors to innovate.

- Newcomers to the market might be discouraged.

- Market already well understood and market research may have indicated opportunities for new product development

(b)   The **disadvantages** include the expense and the risk.

5.4 New products: new markets (diversification)

Diversification occurs when a company decides to make **new products for new markets**. It should have a clear idea about what it expects to gain from diversification. There are two types of diversification, related and unrelated diversification:

(a)   **Growth**. New products and new markets should be selected which offer prospects for growth which the existing product-market mix does not.

(b)   **Investing surplus** funds not required for other expansion needs, but the funds could be returned to shareholders.

(c)   The firm's strengths match the opportunity if:

(i)   Outstanding new products have been developed by the firm's research and development department.

(ii)   The profit opportunities from diversification are high.

Any recommendation made whether market or product related will call for increased management skills to ensure changes are appropriately managed and teams and individuals lead accordingly. At a time of change, increasing importance will be placed on the manager's ability to communicate rapidly and intelligibly, gain acceptance and support for change and innovation, and motivate and lead people in new and varying directions. This requires an assessment of the current leadership skills within the organisation and an understanding of the skill gaps so that personal development plans can be put in place.

The Chartered
Institute of Marketing

Kellogg's

Kellogg's is the world's leading producer of cereal products and convenience foods, such as cookies, crackers and frozen waffles. Its brands include Corn Flakes, Nutri-Grain and Rice Krispies. Kellogg's is a global organisation operating in nearly 200 countries. A key strategy for Kellogg's is ensuring its products are market leaders or hold a strong second position in the market. It has developed products from its core offerings of traditional cereals to breakfast bars and various cereal related snacks.

Kellogg's has been able to extend its product range and a prime example of this was by introducing Special K, which has been one of its successful products for a number of years. A key consideration for Kellogg's is whether to improve further its product range, differentiate its current product range or target new segments.

Key issues for Kellogg's to consider in its current product portfolio are:

- What are consumers currently expecting from cereal providers? How have their lifestyles changed, for example they may be time poor and so rush and do not have a lot of time for breakfast?

- What other external factors may impact the business, eg technology?

- What might the future trends be?

- What might be the future trends?

- What do consumers expect from the Kellogg's brand and how can Kellogg's ensure these expectations are met?

All the above and more would have to be considered before it could make any informed decision. It is clear that currently Kellogg's has been able to respond, react and meet consumers' expectations by offering Special K cereal and Special K bars.

Kellogg's has come to realise that the potential for growth in the Special K brand was strong and so it was rolled out in Europe and in the UK; relevant product adaptations were made for the UK market and so led to a successful launch. While the manufacturing and logistics had to be developed accordingly, this is an example of product and market development. Kellogg's has been able to successfully retain its core brand values, diversify and develop products according to the ever-changing market requirements.

5.5 Related diversification

Related diversification is 'development beyond the present product market, but still within the broad confines of the industry...[it]...therefore builds on the assets or activities which the firm has developed' (Johnson and Scholes, 2007). It takes the form of vertical or horizontal integration.

Horizontal integration refers to development into activities which are competitive with or directly **complementary** to a company's present activities. Sony, for example, started to compete in computer games, building on its presence in consumer electronics.

Vertical integration occurs when a company becomes its own:

(a) **Supplier** of raw materials, components or services (**backward vertical integration**). For example, backward integration would occur where a milk producer acquires its own dairy farms rather than buying raw milk from independent farmers.

(b) **Distributor** or sales agent (**forward vertical integration**), for example where a manufacturer of synthetic yarn begins to produce shirts from the yarn instead of selling it to other shirt manufacturers.

Table 3.2   Advantages and disadvantages of vertical integration

Advantages	Disadvantages
A **secure supply of components** or raw materials with more control. Supplier bargaining power is reduced.	**Overconcentration**. A company places 'more eggs in the same end-market basket' (Ansoff). Such a policy is fairly inflexible, more sensitive to instabilities and increases the firm's dependence on a particular aspect of economic demand.
Strengthen the relationships and contacts of the manufacturer with the 'final consumer' of the product.	The firm **fails to benefit from any economies of scale or technical advances** in the industry into which it has diversified. This is why, in the publishing industry, most printing is subcontracted to specialist printing firms, who can work machinery to capacity by doing work for many firms.
Win a share of the **higher profits**.	
Pursue a **differentiation strategy** more effectively.	
Raise **barriers to entry**.	

5.6 Unrelated diversification

Unrelated or conglomerate diversification 'is development beyond the present industry into products/markets which, at face value, may bear no close relation to the present product/market'.

Conglomerate diversification is now very unfashionable. However, it has been a key strategy for companies in Asia, particularly South Korea.

Table 3.3   Advantages and disadvantages of unrelated diversification

Advantages	Disadvantages
Risk-spreading. Entering new products into new markets offers protection against the failure of current products and markets.	The **dilution of shareholders' earnings** if diversification is into growth industries with high price : earnings ratios.
High profit opportunities. An improvement of the **overall profitability and flexibility** of the firm through acquisition in industries which have better economic characteristics than those of the acquiring firms.	**Lack of a common identity and purpose** in a conglomerate organisation. A conglomerate will only be successful if it has a high quality of management and financial ability at central headquarters, where the diverse operations are brought together.
Escape from the present business. For example, Reed International moved away from paper production and into publishing.	**Failure in one of the businesses will drag down the rest**, as it will eat up resources. British Aerospace was severely damaged by the effect of a downturn in the property market on its property subsidiary, Arlington Securities.
Better access to capital markets.	**Lack of management experience** in the business area. **Japanese steel companies** have diversified into areas completely unrelated to steel such as personal computers, with limited success.
No other way to grow. Expansion along existing lines might create a monopoly and lead to government investigations and control. Diversifications offer the chance of growth without creating a monopoly.	**No good for shareholders**. Shareholders can spread risk quite easily, simply by buying a diverse portfolio of shares. They do not need management to do it for them.
Use surplus cash.	
Exploit under-utilised resources.	

The Chartered Institute of Marketing

Advantages	Disadvantages	65
Obtain cash, or other financial advantages (such as accumulated tax losses).		
Use a company's image and reputation in one market to develop into another where corporate image and reputation could be vital ingredients for success.		

Arguably, vertical integration is the opposite of outsourcing some activities – do you buy them in or make your own? A problem with the integration model is that it is focused on a simple manufacturer rather than the service sector.

5.7 Withdrawal

It might be the right decision to cease producing a product and/or to pull out of a market completely. This is a hard decision for managers to take if they have invested time and money or if the decision involves redundancies.

Exit barriers make this difficult.

- **Cost barriers** include redundancy costs, the difficulty of selling assets.

- **Political barriers** include government attitudes. Defence is an example.

- **Marketing considerations** may delay withdrawal. A product might be a loss-leader for others, or might contribute to the company's reputation for its breadth of coverage.

- **Psychology**. Managers hate to admit failure. Furthermore, people might wrongly assume that carrying on is a low risk strategy, especially if they (wrongly) feel bound to carry on, as they have spent money already.

Reasons for exit may include:

- The **company's business** may be in buying firms, selling their assets and improving their performance, and then selling them at a profit.

- **Resource limitations** mean that less profitable businesses have to be abandoned. A business might be sold to a competitor, or occasionally to management (as a buy-out).

- A company may be forced to quit, because of **insolvency**.

- **Change of competitive strategy**. In the microprocessor industry, many American firms have left high-volume DRAM chips to Asian firms so as to concentrate on high value-added niche products.

- **Decline in attractiveness of the market**.

- **Funds can earn more elsewhere**.

6 Channel strategies

> ▶ **Key term**
>
> 'Managing the supply chain is by no means simple, and it is not always the role of the manufacturer to do so – many **supply chains** are managed by wholesalers, retailers or other members, using negotiation, coercion or reward to make the system operate more smoothly.'
> (Blythe, 2009)

Choosing distribution channels is important for any organisation, because once a set of channels has been established, subsequent changes are likely to be costly and slow to implement. Distribution channels fall into one of two categories: **direct** and **indirect** channels.

Direct distribution means the product going directly from producer to consumer without the use of a specific intermediary. These methods are often described as **active**, since they typically involve the supplier making the first approach to a potential customer.

Indirect distribution means systems of distribution, common among manufactured goods, which use an intermediary: a wholesaler or retailer for example. In contrast to direct distribution, these methods are **passive** in the sense that they rely on consumers to make the first approach by entering the relevant retail outlet.

Independently owned and operated distributors may well have their own objectives and these are likely to take precedence over those of the manufacturer or supplier with whom they are dealing. Suppliers may solve the problem by buying their own distribution route or by distributing direct to their customers. Direct distribution is common for many industrial and/or customised product suppliers. In some consumer markets direct distribution is also common, particularly with the advent of e-commerce via the internet.

6.1 General principles

A number of considerations will determine the choice of distribution strategy:

- The number of **intermediate stages to be used**. There could be zero, one, two or three intermediate stages of selling. In addition, it will be necessary to decide how many dealers at each stage should be used – ie how many agents should be used, how many wholesalers should be asked to sell the manufacturer's products, or what the size of the direct sales force should be.

- **The support that the manufacturer should give to the dealers**. It may be necessary to provide an efficient after-sales and repair service, or to agree to an immediate exchange of faulty products returned by a retailer's customers, or to make weekly, bi-weekly or monthly stock-checking visits to retailers' stores. To help selling, the manufacturer might need to consider advertising or sales promotion support, including merchandising.

- **The extent to which the manufacturer wishes to dominate a channel of distribution**. A market leader, for example, might wish to ensure that its market share of sales is maintained, so that it might, for example, wish to offer exclusive distribution contracts to major retailers.

- **The extent to which the manufacturer wishes to integrate its marketing effort up to the point of sale with the consumer**. Combined promotions with retailers, for example, would only be possible if the manufacturer dealt directly with the retailer (and did not sell to the retailer through a wholesaler).

6.2 Factors in channel decisions

In setting up a channel of distribution, the supplier has to take several factors into account:

- Customers
- Nature of the goods or services
- Distributor characteristics
- Competitors' channel choice
- The costs associated with available channels
- The supplier's own characteristics

6.2.1 Customers

The **number** of potential customers, their **buying habits** and their **geographical proximity** are key influences. The use of mail order and internet purchases for those with limited time or mobility (remote rural location, illness) is an example of the influence of customers on channel design.

Different distribution strategies may be adopted for **consumer** and **industrial** markets. Industrial channels tend to be more direct and shorter.

Industrial markets are generally characterised as having fewer, higher-value customers purchasing a complex total offering of products/services which fulfil detailed specifications. Industrial distribution channels therefore tend to be more direct and shorter, allowing partnership level relationships. There are specialist distributors in the industrial sector, which may be used as well as, or instead of, selling directly to industrial customers.

The Chartered Institute of Marketing

There have traditionally been fewer direct distribution channels from the manufacturer to the consumer in the consumer market. Even with the advent of e-commerce in some sectors, it is still more usual for companies in consumer markets to use wholesalers and retailers to move their products to the final consumer.

Understanding customers' buying behaviour is also a key part of deciding the appropriate channels: how do customers buy? Do they prefer traditional consumption channels or web-based channels? Further questions such as the time of delivery and the speed of delivery are also considerations, as well as whether organsations have the appropriate infrastructure in place to ensure that any channel can be appropriately managed.

6.2.2 Customer relationship management (CRM)

> ▶ **Key term**
>
> **Customer relationship management (CRM)** describes the methodologies and ICT systems that help an enterprise manage customer relationships.
>
> CRM consists of systems which:
>
> - Help an enterprise to identify and target their **most profitable customers** and generate quality leads
> - Assist the organisation to improve telesales and account and sales management by optimising **information sharing** and **streamlining** existing processes (for example, taking orders using mobile devices)
> - Provide employees with **information** to **integrate all communications** with customers: facilitating the 'recognition' of customers and consistent and up-to-date account/product/ delivery information.

Each time a customer contacts a company with an effective CRM system – whether by telephone, in a retail outlet or online – the customer should be recognised and should receive appropriate information and attention. CRM software provides advanced personalisation and customised solutions to customer demands, giving customer care staff a range of key information about each customer which can be applied to the transaction.

Basically, CRM involves a single **comprehensive database** that can be accessed from any of the points of contact with the customer. Traditional 'vertical' organisation structures have tended to create stand-alone systems developed for distinct functions or departments, which were responsible for the four main types of interaction with the customer: marketing, sales, fulfilment and after-sales. These systems need to be integrated into (or replaced by) a central customer database, with facilities for data to be **accessed from** and **fed into** the central system from other departments and applications (including the website), so that all customer information can be kept up-to-date and shared.

To ensure the organisation can develop a CRM strategy it is important to remember that it is more than just having a database and communicating with customers. It is ensuring that the organisation fully understands what its stakeholders expect and is able to manage the expectations of its customers. The vision also needs to be able to take account of the CRM focus; in doing so it needs to stand out from competitors and have a core proposition that is able to develop accordingly, often referred to as the customer value proposition (CVP). CRM cannot be regarded as just one activity of the organisation; for it to be fully effective it must be central to the organisation's activities and have management buy in.

These are the strategies for enhancing CRM.

Figure 3.4   Strategies for enhancing CRM

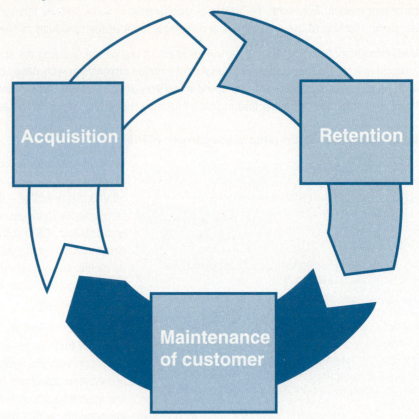

The acquisition of the customer is equally as important as retaining and enhancing the relationship with customer to ensure repeat business and long term advocacy as illustrated by Hilton Hotels.

THE REAL WORLD

CRM in action – Hilton Hotels

A key focus of Hilton Hotels is ensuring that the customer's needs are met and that individual choices can be catered for. As Jim VonDerheide stated in his interview for *Inside Scoop*: 'The customer promise from the family of brands really is hospitality. We consider ourselves to be synonymous, worldwide, with hospitality, and we try to bring hospitality to light in every one of our brands. So that is making your journey more of a pleasant experience.'

There are basic expectations that Hilton understand to be key to the success of any hotel: a clean room, security, a comfortable bed, alarm clock and a clean bathroom with hot water; however, their focus is to go over and above this: for example for a frequent guest they deliver a fruit basket or a complimentary plate of cheese. It is this investment that then brings customers back to the hotel, meeting their personal needs. This is based on four key points: identifying guests, knowing who they are, interacting with those guests and then differentiating.

A key enabler for this is technology. Hilton have an honours club, where frequent travellers and guests can join and so collect points and are rewarded. This gives Hilton valuable information to meet their individual needs and requirements; however, Hilton also recognise that some may not want to join the Honours club for whatever reason, so Hilton have tried to increase their touch points to gather customer data and then provide a service and product offerings that are unique to them. Technology has allowed Hilton to recognise and identify these customers accordingly and make their stay unique and memorable. Hilton management realise that the success of this depends on on going updates regarding the customers, understanding their needs without unduly bothering them and of course rewarding them for their loyalty.

The Chartered Institute of Marketing

6.2.3 Nature of the goods or service

Some product characteristics have an important effect on design of the channel of distribution.

Table 3.4 Product characteristics

Characteristic	Comment
Perishability	Fresh fruit and newspapers must be distributed very quickly or they become worthless. Speed of delivery is therefore a key factor in the design of the distribution system for such products. Fragile items need extra care and minimal handling.
Customisation	Customised products tend to be distributed directly. When a wide range of options is available, sales may be made using demonstration units, with customised delivery to follow.
After-sales service/technical advice	Extent and cost must be carefully considered, staff training given and quality control systems set up. Suppliers often provide training programmes for distributors. Exclusive area franchises giving guaranteed custom can be allocated to ensure distributor co-operation; the disadvantage of this is that a poor distributor may cost a supplier dearly in a particular area.
Franchising	Franchising has become an increasingly popular means of getting products to the customer. The supplier gains more outlets more quickly, and exerts more control than is usual in distribution.
Value	Highly valuable items might be better suited to direct delivery.

6.2.4 Distributor characteristics

The location, customer base, performance and reliability, promotion and pricing policies of different types of distributor, and specific distribution outlets, will have to be evaluated. Selling to supermarket chains in the UK, for example, is now very difficult as the concentration of grocery retailing into a few large chains has increased the power of the buyers. Some products (such as emergency medical supplies) will be dependent upon faultlessly reliable delivery systems.

6.2.5 Competitors' channel choice

For many consumer goods, a supplier's brand will sit alongside its competitors' products. For other products, distributors may stock one name brand only (for example, in car distribution) and in return be given an exclusive area. In this case new suppliers may face difficulties in breaking into a market because the distribution channel is in effect controlled by the competition.

6.2.6 Costs

There are considerable costs associated with distribution. In addition to the costs of importing goods from overseas suppliers, or exporting to overseas customers, products will often need to be stored (in warehouses for example) or held somewhere (such as on the shop floor, for the use of which rent will usually be payable) awaiting sale or collection. The cheapest method of transport (by road, as opposed to by air) will not always be the most effective.

6.2.7 Supplier characteristics

A strong financial base gives the supplier the option of buying and operating their own distribution channel; Boots is a good example in the UK. The market position of the supplier is also important; distributors are keen to be associated with the market leader, but other brands may experience distribution problems.

6.3 Making the channel decision

Producers have to decide the following:

- **What types of distributor** are to be used (wholesalers, retailers, agents)?

- **How many of each type will be used?** This depends on what degree of market exposure is required.

  - Intensive, blanket coverage
  - Exclusive, appointed agents for exclusive areas
  - Selective, some but not all in each area

- Who will carry out specific marketing tasks?

  - Credit provision
  - Delivery
  - After-sales service
  - Training
  - Display

- How will the **effectiveness** of distributors be evaluated?

  - In terms of cost
  - In terms of sales levels
  - According to the degree of control achieved
  - By the amount of conflict that arises

To develop an integrated system of distribution, the supplier must consider all the factors influencing distribution, combined with a knowledge of the merits of the different types of channel.

6.4 Direct distribution versus indirect distribution

Table 3.5 Direct distribution versus use of intermediaries

Factors favouring the use of direct distribution	Factors favouring the use of intermediaries
(a) The need for an expert sales force to demonstrate products, explain product characteristics and provide after-sales service. Publishers, for example, use sales reps to keep booksellers up-to-date with new titles or to arrange for the return of unsold books.	(a) Insufficient resources to finance a large sales force.
(b) Intermediaries may be unwilling or unable to sell the product.	(b) A policy decision to invest in increased productive capacity, rather than extra marketing effort.
(c) Existing channels may be linked to other producers.	(c) The supplier may have insufficient in-house marketing 'know-how' in selling to retail stores.
(d) The intermediaries willing to sell the product may be too costly, or they may not be maximising potential sales.	(d) The product line may be insufficiently wide or deep for a sales force to carry. A wholesaler can complement a limited range and make more efficient use of its sales force.
(e) Where potential buyers are geographically concentrated, the supplier's own sales force can easily reach them (typically an industrial market).	(e) Intermediaries can market small lots as part of a range of goods. The supplier would incur a heavy sales overhead if its own sales force took 'small' individual orders.
(f) Where e-commerce is well established, potential buyers can be reached online.	(f) Large numbers of potential buyers spread over a wide geographical area (typically consumer markets).

6.4.1 Multiple channels

A producer serving both industrial and consumer markets may decide to use:

- **Intermediaries** for the **consumer** division

- **Direct selling** for the **industrial** division

For example, a detergent manufacturer might employ a small sales team to sell to wholesalers and large retail groups in their consumer division. It would not be efficient for the sales force to approach small retailers directly.

The Chartered Institute of Marketing

6.5 Distribution strategy

There are three main strategies.

- Intensive distribution involves blanket coverage of distributors in one segment of the total market, such as a local area.

- Using selective distribution, the producer selects a group of retail outlets from amongst all retail outlets. The choice of selected outlets may be based on reflecting brand image (eg 'quality' outlets), or the retailers' capacity to provide after-sales service ('specialist' outlets).

- Exclusive distribution is where selected outlets are granted exclusive rights to stock and sell the product within a prescribed market segment or geographical area. Sometimes exclusive distribution or franchise rights are coupled with making special financial arrangements for land, buildings or equipment, such as petrol station agreements.

7 Growth strategies

Many firms are growing by **alliances** with other firms, short of a full scale merger or acquisition. These are supposed to offer synergies and mutual benefits.

Growth can involve:

- **Building up new businesses** from scratch and developing them (sometimes called organic growth)

- **Acquiring** already existing businesses from their current owners via the purchase of a controlling interest in another company

- A **merger** is the joining of two or more separate companies to form a single company

- Spreading the costs and risks (**joint ventures**, **alliances** or other forms of **co-operation**)

7.1 Acquisitions

7.1.1 The purpose of acquisitions

(a) **Marketing advantages**

   (i)   Buy-in a new product range
   (ii)   Buy a market presence (especially true if acquiring a company with overseas offices and contacts that can be utilised by the parent company)
   (iii) Unify sales departments or rationalise distribution and advertising
   (iv)   Eliminate competition or protect an existing market

(b) **Production advantages**

   (i)   Gain a higher utilisation of production facilities and reap economies of scale by larger machine runs
   (ii)   'Buy in' technology and skills
   (iii) Obtain greater production capacity
   (iv)   Safeguard future supplies of raw materials
   (v)   Improve purchasing by buying in bulk

(c) **Finance and management**

   (i)   Buy a high quality management team, which exists in the acquired company
   (ii)   Obtain cash resources where the acquired company is very liquid
   (iii) Gain undervalued assets or surplus assets that can be sold off ('asset stripping')
   (iv)   Obtain tax advantages (eg purchase of a tax loss company)

(d) **Risk-spreading**

(e)   **Independence**

A company threatened by a take-over might take-over another company, just to make itself bigger and so a more expensive 'target' for the predator company.

(f)   **Overcome barriers to entry**

7.2 Organic growth

Organic growth (sometimes referred to as internal development) is the primary method of growth for many organisations, for a number of reasons. Organic growth is achieved through the development of internal resources.

Table 3.6   Organic growth

Reasons for pursuing organic growth	Problems with organic growth
Learning. The process of developing a new product gives the firm the best understanding of the market and the product.	**Time** – sometimes it takes a long time to climb a **learning curve**.
Innovation. It might be the only sensible way to pursue genuine technological innovations and exploit them. (Compact disk technology was developed by Philips but Sony, which earn royalties from other manufacturers, is licensed to use it.)	**Barriers to entry** (eg distribution networks) are harder to overcome: for example a brand image may be built up from scratch.
There is **no suitable target for acquisition**.	The firm will have to **acquire the resources independently**.
Organic growth can be **planned more meticulously** and offers little disruption.	Organic growth may be **too slow for the dynamics of the market**.
Reasons for pursuing organic growth	Problems with organic growth
It is often **more convenience** for managers, as organic growth can be financed easily from the company's current cash flows, without having to raise extra money on the stock market (eg to fund an acquisition).	
The **same style of management and corporate culture** can be maintained.	
Hidden or unforeseen losses are less likely with organic growth than with acquisitions.	
Economies of scale can be achieved from more **efficient use of central head office functions** such as finance, purchasing, personnel, management services and so on.	

7.3 Alliances

Alliances are becoming more popular. An alliance is a business arrangement whereby firms share data, resources and activities to achieve mutually beneficial objectives. Alliances can take a number of forms:

- Agreements to co-operate on various issues
- Shared research and development
- Joint ventures, in which the partners create a separate business unit
- Supply chain rationalisation
- Licensing and franchising
- Purchase of minority stakes

7.3.1 Alliances and synergy

Synergy is achieved when combining resources results in a better rate of return than would be achieved by the same resources used independently in separate operations.

The Chartered Institute of Marketing

7.3.2 Obtaining synergy from alliances

(a) **Marketing synergy:** use of common marketing facilities such as distribution channels, sales staff and administration, and warehousing. Petrol stations can double as burger outlets.

(b) **Operating synergy** arises from the better use of operational facilities and personnel, bulk purchasing, a greater spread of fixed costs whereby the firm's competence can be transferred to making new products.

(c) **Investment synergy:** the joint use of plant, common raw material stocks, transfer of research and development from one product to another – ie from the wider use of a common investment in fixed assets, working capital or research.

(d) **Management synergy:** the advantage to be gained where management skills concerning current operations are easily transferred to new operations because of the similarity of problems in the two industries.

Hooley *et al* (2007) give an overview of some of the environmental factors that are stimulating the need for alliances:

- Scarce resources
- Increased competition
- Higher customer expectations
- Pressures from strong distributors
- Internationalisation of markets
- Changing markets and technologies
- Turbulent and unpredictable markets

7.4 Consortia

Organisations co-operate on specific business prospects. Airbus is an example: a consortium including British Aerospace, Dasa, Aerospatiale and Casa (of Spain). However, it does have an unusual financial structure, and it will soon turn into a normal company.

7.5 Joint ventures

Two firms (or more) join forces for manufacturing, financial and marketing purposes and each has a share in both the equity and the management of the business. A joint venture is a separate business unit set up for the reasons outlined below:

- **Share funding.** As the capital outlay is shared, joint ventures are especially attractive to smaller or risk-averse firms, or where very expensive new technologies are being researched and developed (such as the civil aerospace industry).

- **Cut risk.** A joint venture can reduce the risk of government intervention if a local firm is involved (eg Club Méditerranée pays much attention to this factor).

- Participating enterprises **benefit from all sources of profit**.

- **Close control** over marketing and other operations

- Overseas, a joint venture with an indigenous firm provides **local knowledge**, **quickly**.

- **Synergies**. One firm's production expertise can be supplemented by the other's marketing and distribution facility.

- **Learning** can also be a 'learning' exercise in which each partner tries to learn as much as possible from the other.

- **Technology**. New technology offers many uncertainties and many opportunities. Such alliances provide funds for expensive research projects, spreading risk.

The joint venture itself can generate innovations. The alliance can involve **'testing' the firm's core competence** in different conditions, which can suggest ways to improve it.

7.5.1 Disadvantages of joint ventures

Conflicts of interest can occur between the different parties. Disagreements may arise over profit shares, amounts invested, the management of the joint venture and the marketing strategy. One partner may wish to withdraw from the arrangement.

7.5.2 Licensing

A **licensing agreement** is a commercial contract whereby the licenser gives something of value to the licensee in exchange for certain performances and payments. The licenser may provide, in return for a royalty:

- Rights to produce a patented product or use a patented production process
- Manufacturing know-how (unpatented)
- Technical advice and assistance
- Marketing advice and assistance
- Rights to use a trademark, brand and so on

Subcontracting is also a type of alliance. Co-operative arrangements also feature in supply chain management, JIT and quality programmes.

7.6 Franchising

Franchising is a method of expanding the business on less capital than would otherwise be possible. For suitable businesses it is an **alternative business strategy to raising extra capital** for growth.

Franchisers include Budget, Dyno-Rod, Express Dairy, Holiday Inn, Kall-Kwik Printing, KFC, Prontaprint, Body Shop and even McDonald's.

The **franchiser** offers its:

- Name and any goodwill associated with it
- Systems and business methods
- Support services, such as advertising, training, help with site decoration etc

The **franchisee**:

- Provides capital, personal involvement and local market knowledge
- Pays the franchiser for being granted these rights and services
- Has responsibility for the running and profitability of its franchise

7.7 The virtual firm

An extreme example of an alliance is the so-called **virtual firm**. A virtual firm is created out of a **network of alliances** and subcontracting arrangements; it is as if most of the activities in a particular value chain are conducted by different firms, even though the process is loosely co-ordinated by one of them. It is outsourcing taken to its greatest extent.

For example, assume you manufacture small toys. You could in theory **outsource**:

- The design to a consultancy
- Manufacturing to a subcontractor in a low-cost country
- Delivery arrangements to a specialist logistics firm
- Debt collection to a bank (factoring)
- Filing, tax returns, bookkeeping to an accountancy firm

Virtual corporations effectively put market forces in all linkages of the value chain – this has the advantage of creating **incentives** for suppliers, perhaps to take risks to produce a better product, but can lead to a loss of control.

The Chartered Institute of Marketing

8 Hostile and declining markets

Markets decline because of **environmental factors**. Some can be revitalised. In others, a firm has to choose whether it wants to stay in the market or withdraw.

Many of the portfolio models assume that markets are growing. However, this is certainly not the case in many markets and firms within them still have to survive.

8.1 Declining markets

Why do markets decline?

- Obsolete technology
- Change in customer needs, leading to fall in demand
- Alternative satisfactions

Strategic alternatives include:

(a) Revitalising the market
(b) Becoming a profitable survivor
(c) Harvest and withdraw

8.2 Revitalising the market

- Identify new market segments or submarkets
- Introduce new products
- Introduce new applications of existing products
- Change the market

8.3 Becoming a profitable survivor

- Make a visible commitment to the market, as a signal to other competitors.
- Encourage competitors to leave by aggressive competition or by making it easier for them to quit.
- Purchase the competitor's capacity, close it down and carry on in a smaller niche.

8.4 Harvest and withdraw

Reduce investment and operating resources in order to make a graceful exit. Profits may still be made. However, employees and customers may fear the lack of commitment and go elsewhere. A milking or harvesting strategy can be reversed, as the firm still has a market presence.

8.5 Hostile environments

Aaker (1991) describes a six-phase cycle for hostile markets.

Table 3.7   Aaker's six-phase cycle for hostile markets

Phase 1: Margin pressure	Overcapacity leads to predatory pricing, benefiting large customers
Phase 2: Share shift	Each year, up to 5% of market share will shift under price pressure
Phase 3: Product proliferation	Firms create excess value by adding new lines
Phase 4: Self-defeating cost reduction	Firms cut costs but, in doing so, weaken themselves
Phase 5: Shakeout	Closures, mergers
Phase 6: Rescue	Some markets recover with fewer companies competing

8.6 Winning in hostile markets

- Focus on **large customers**, to benefit from economies of scale
- **Differentiate on intangible factors** such as reliability and relationships
- Offer a broad **array of products** at a variety of prices
- Turn price into a commodity by **removing price from the customer's buying criteria**
- **Control cost** structures

8.7 Wear-out and renewal

Strategic wear-out occurs when firms continue with old strategies that are no longer viable. Strategic and tactical **wear-out** is the problem that any organisation will face if it retains its current strategies and tactics without any review or consideration of changed circumstances.

The following factors give rise to wear-out:

(a) **Market changes**

- Customer requirements
- Distribution requirements

(b) **Competitor innovations**

(c) **Internal factors**

- Poor cost control
- Lack of consistent investment
- Ill-advised tinkering with successful strategies

Some organisations still continue to pursue marketing programmes long after their effectiveness has diminished. Many reasons can be put forward to explain this.

Table 3.8   Reason for pursuit of ineffective marketing programmes

Fear of change	Most people are afraid of change, preferring to stay in their own comfort zone. Change is becoming harder to forecast. Many organisations opt to stay with what is familiar.
'If it ain't broke, don't fix it!'	Market leaders, having developed a successful strategy, are understandably reluctant to change it.
Change too late	The need for change often only becomes apparent when the gap between what a company is doing and what it should be doing increases to a point at which performance suffers in an obvious way.
Failure to learn	Companies fail because managers' theory of the business no longer works. A theory of the business contains the assumptions (about markets, technology etc) that shape any organisation's behaviour.
The wrong customers	Keeping too close to existing customers, rather than thinking about future customers, can also result in strategic wear-out: 'an industry's leaders are rarely in the forefront of commercialising new technologies that do not initially meet the functional demands of mainstream customers'. New technologies are developed and take industry leaders unawares.
Failure to look	Some organisations do not have environmental monitoring and strategic review procedures embedded within their marketing planning systems.

Four interlinked avenues of action are required to overcome the danger of strategic wear-out:

(a)   Regular and detailed reviews of each of the significant elements of the external environment
(b)   Identification of the ways these elements are changing
(c)   Evaluation of the implications of these changes on the organisation
(d)   Internal audit to establish the appropriateness of actions both currently and for the future

The Chartered Institute of Marketing

In order to avoid strategic wear-out a multi-functional perspective is required. A combination of strategic, organisational and cultural change is required. Companies are likely to be unsuccessful in maintaining change unless five demanding criteria are met:

(a)   Coherence of direction, actions and timing
(b)   Environmental assessment of competitors, customers and regulatory climate
(c)   Leading change by creating the correct climate
(d)   Linking strategic with operational change (communication and reward systems)
(e)   Treating people as assets and investments rather than costs

---

▶ **Assessment tip**

It is important to ensure that before deciding on any type of strategy the overall vision and mission of the organisation is understood. Strategic development needs to be based on the analysis undertaken; for the organisation this can be through the strategic audit. Recent assessments ask candidates, to undertake a strategic audit and from the findings of the audit make recommendations for improvements to the organisation's value proposition as well as assess how the organisation's marketing strategy could be improved to bring about an increase in stakeholder value. This requires there to be an appropriate analysis of the strategic direction of the organisation. Before any recommendations can be made candidates need to understand the dynamics of the market, the organisation's current and future strategic objectives as well as the value proposition of the organisation.

Any strategy recommendations need to be supported with the appropriate evaluation and justification, linking it back to the organisation's core competences, strengths and long-term goals. Strategic goal decisions must take account of both internal and external factors of the organisation and so these factors need to clearly underpin the decisions made. It is important to remember that decisions may be difficult, especially when withdrawing from a market or undertaking an exit strategy; the rationale and the justification are as important as the decision.

CHAPTER ROUNDUP

- The key elements of the marketing strategy are understanding what the company's core businesses/areas of activity are and what they should be; this could mean developing a more marketing oriented approach and greater long-term sustainability amongst other strategies.

- Competitive strategies require actions to create a defendable position.

- Competitive advantage is anything which gives one organisation an edge over its rivals in the products it sells or the services it offers.

- A firm needs to consider how it should adopt a competitive strategy to secure a competitive advantage.

- There are three generic strategies for competitive advantage: cost leadership, differentiation and focus.

- There a number of competitive positions for an organisation to attack or defend its position.

- Different strategies are appropriate to challengers, followers, leaders and nichers (positioning strategies).

- Product-market strategy includes market penetration, market development, product development and diversification.

- Channel strategies concentrate on choosing distribution channels.

- A number of considerations will determine the choice of distribution strategy: intermediate stages to be used, the support that the manufacturer should give to the dealers, the extent to which the manufacturer wishes to dominate a channel of distribution and the extent to which the manufacturer wishes to integrate its marketing effort up to the point of sale.

- Growth in an organisation can happen in a number of ways: building up new businesses, acquiring, merger, joint ventures, alliances and co-operation.

- There can be a number of reasons why markets decline including internal and external factors (environmental factors).

FURTHER READING

De Wit, B. and Meyer, R. (2005) *Strategy synthesis: resolving strategy paradoxes to create competitive advantage, test and readings*. 2nd edition. London, Thomson.

Dibb, S. and Simkin, L. (2009) *Marketing essentials*. 1st edition. London, Cengage.

Doyle, P. and Stern, P. (2006) *Marketing management and strategy*. 4th edition. Harlow, Prentice Hall.

Hooley, G. *et al* (2007) *Marketing strategy and competitive positioning*. 4th edition. Harlow, Prentice Hall.

Mintzberg, H. (1994) *The rise and fall of strategic planning*. New York, The Free Press.

 The Chartered Institute of Marketing

REFERENCES

Aaker, D. (1991) *Managing brand equity*. New York, The Free Press.

Ansoff, H.I. (1965) *Corporate strategy: an analytic approach to business policy for growth and expansion.* New York, McGraw-Hill.

Bowman, C. and Faulkner, D. (1996) *Competitive and Corporate Strategy*. Chicago, Irwin.

Blythe, J. (2009) *Principles and practice of marketing*, 2nd edition. London, South-Western/Cengage Learning.

Doyle, P. and Stern, P. (2006) *Marketing management and strategy*. 4th edition. Harlow, FT Prentice Hall.

Gilligan, C. and Wilson, R. (2004) *Strategic marketing management*. 3rd edition. Oxford, Butterworth-Heinemann.

Hooley, G., Saunders, J., Piercy, N. and Nicouloud, B. (2007) *Marketing strategy and competitive positioning*. 4th edition. Harlow, FT Prentice Hall.

Johnson, G., Scholes, K. and Whittington, R. (2007) *Exploring corporate strategy*. 8th edition. Harlow, FT Prentice Hall.

Kotler, P. and Keller, K. (2006) *Marketing management*. 12th edition. Harlow, FT Prentice Hall.

Kotler, P.and Singh, P. (1981) Marketing Warfare in the 1980s. *McKinsey Quarterly 3*, pp62–81.

McDonald, M (2007) *Marketing Planning: Understanding Marketing Plans & Strategy*. London, Kogan Page.

Porter, M.E. (1998) *On Competition*. Boston, Harvard Business School.

Porter, M.E. (1980) *Competitive strategy: techniques for analysing industries and competitors*. New York, The Free Press.

QUICK QUIZ

1   What are the seven elements of a marketing plan?

2   How does Porter define competitive strategy?

3   Name Porter's three generic strategies.

4   Name four offensive competitive strategies.

5   Name five defensive competitive strategies.

6   Name the four different positions a firm can have in the market.

7   When might an organisation adopt a diversification strategy?

8   Why might an organisation decide to exit from a market?

Activity 3.1

This will depend on your own research. If you found it difficult to differentiate between the corporate and marketing strategies, try to discuss it with a colleague and see to what extent your opinions differ and why.

QUICK QUIZ ANSWERS

1 – Organisational mission, goals and corporate strategy
   – Organisational opportunities and capabilities
   – Strategic objectives
   – Target market strategy and brand positioning
   – Marketing objectives
   – Marketing programmes for implementation
   – Performance measurement and monitoring

2 Competitive strategy means 'taking offensive or defensive actions to create a defendable position in an industry, to cope successfully with...competitive forces and thereby yield a superior return on investment for the firm. Firms have discovered many different approaches to this end, and the best strategy for a given firm is ultimately a unique construction reflecting its particular circumstances.'

3 Cost leadership, differentiation and focus

4 Frontal attack, Flanking attack, Encirclement attack, Bypass attack

5 Position defence, Mobile defence, Pre-emptive defence, Flank position defence, Counter-offensive defence

6 Pioneers, Challengers, Followers, Nichers

7 Diversification occurs when a company decides to make new products for new markets. It should have a clear idea about what it expects to gain from diversification. There are two types of diversification: related and unrelated diversification.

8 – The company's business may be in buying firms, selling their assets and improving their performance, and then selling them at a profit.

   – Resource limitations mean that less profitable businesses have to be abandoned. A business might be sold to a competitor, or occasionally to management (as a buy-out).

   – A company may be forced to quit, because of insolvency.

   – Change of competitive strategy. In the microprocessor industry, many American firms have left high-volume DRAM chips to Asian firms so as to concentrate on high-value added niche products.

   – Decline in attractiveness of the market.

   – Funds can earn more elsewhere.

 The Chartered Institute of Marketing

CHAPTER 4

The concept of strategic marketing planning

Introduction

Within this chapter we look at the role of strategic marketing planning as a tool to deliver the value proposition. Although this chapter has several sections, it broadly covers two main themes. First, we introduce the wide subject of **corporate strategy**. An important aspect of this introduction is an explanation of the way that strategy and marketing relate to one another. Second, we cover the **strategic analysis** phase of the classic system of corporate strategy.

Topic list

The concept of strategy	1
Levels of strategy in an organisation	2
The strategic planning process	3
Is strategic planning necessary?	4
Corporate strategy and marketing strategy	5
The role of strategic marketing	6
Barriers to effective marketing planning	7
The concept of strategic marketing planning in charity and not-for-profit marketing	8

2.1.1	Critically evaluate the concept of strategic marketing planning as a tool to deliver an organisation's value proposition:
	■ Efficacy of formalised marketing planning
	■ The specification of sustainable competitive advantage and marketing planning and its contribution to commercial success and to delivering the organisation's value proposition
	■ Preparedness to meet change and implement market-focused orientation across the organisation
	■ Contextualisation of marketing planning in a corporate framework (McDonald, 2007)
2.1.2	Analyse the corporate objectives and translate into overarching marketing objectives to support giving direction to a marketing plan:
	■ The interactive process – balancing an organisation's ambitions with knowledge from individual business units
	■ Relevant marketing objectives to enhance the attainment of the firm's ability to satisfy customers and foster innovation
	■ From corporate objectives to setting a balanced array of marketing objectives that cover marketing and financial aspects
2.1.3	Assess the variables facing an organisation in order to assess the impact of the future corporate and marketing objectives against its current competences, resource capacity and financial positioning:
	■ Analyse key areas within an organisation:
	– Market share
	– Innovation
	– Resource
	– Productivity
	– Social aspects and profit
	– Alternative measures of success eg, for NFP
	■ Core competences:
	– Potential access
	– Significant contribution
	– Difficulty for competitors to copy
	■ Auditing resources:
	– Technical resources
	– Financial standing
	– Managerial skills
	– Information systems
	■ Ansoff matrix and Gap analysis
2.1.4	Make clear recommendations that determine either changes in the strategy or further resource requirements to support the delivery of the strategic marketing plan:
	■ Resource audit
	■ Core competences for the attainment of a successful marketing plan
	■ Marketing audit to underpin the marketing plan
2.1.5	Develop marketing plans utilising corporate planning frameworks to deliver an organisation's strategies and meet corporate objectives:
	■ Planning typologies
	■ Marketing design and implementation of planning systems
	■ Integration of the marketing planning process with organisation's overall strategy and objective (to include: corporate and strategic issues, competition, industry, SWOT, business environment [PEST], marketing objectives, strategy, monitoring evaluation)

2.1.6	Critically evaluate why marketing plans can fail:

- Design and implementation issues
- Gaining management support
- Separation of operational planning from strategic planning
- Integration of marketing planning into a total corporate planning system

1 The concept of strategy

1.1 What is strategy?

> **Key terms**
>
> **Strategy** is defined by Johnson, Scholes and Whittington (2007) in this way: 'the direction and scope of an organisation over the long term, which achieves advantage in a changing environment through its configuration of resources and competences with the aim of fulfilling stakeholder expectations'.
>
> **Strategic management** is the development, implementation and control of agreed strategies in order to achieve competitive advantage.
>
> **Strategy** exists on three levels: corporate, business and functional/operational. The marketing concept informs strategy: a defined course of action to achieve specific objectives.
>
> It is important to realise that a strategic decision can affect an entire organisation or at least key parts of the organisation. Often strategic decisions and the fulfilment of a strategy do not happen over time but are a more long term commitment. This commitment can be through resources, management support and potentially the longer term development of a particular internal culture.
>
> Raynor (2007) more recently defined strategy as 'how an organization creates and captures value in a specific product market'.

This section is about corporate strategy and how marketing relates to it. We have already discussed some ideas about this relationship and will return to it later. In this section we will look a little more deeply into the fundamental idea of strategy in business and what it involves.

Competitive advantage: a business achieves competitive advantage when it earns higher than average profits. Whatever overall objective is set for a firm – to survive, to create value, to make profit – the key to achieving it lies in the attainment of some form of **competitive advantage**. Business therefore revolves around the means by which competitive advantage may be attained and sustained. It can be challenging trying to create value over and above your competitors as they can develop a similar strategy potentially at a lower cost as has been discussed in Chapter 3.

Competitive advantage distinguishes the successful business from the average enabling it to earn an **above average level of profit**.

There are two main kinds of approach to achieving competitive advantage, each encompassing several strands of strategic thinking:

(a) **The positioning approach**. The positioning approach to strategy is closely related to the traditional concept of marketing orientation. It starts with an assessment of the commercial environment and positions the business so that it fits with environmental requirements.

(b) **The resource-based approach**. The resource-based approach starts with the idea that competitive advantage comes from the possession of distinctive and unique resources.

Strategic management can be analysed into four main groups of activities:

- Analysis
- Choice
- Implementation
- Control

2 Levels of strategy in an organisation

Any level of the organisation can have objectives and devise strategies to achieve them. The strategic management process is multi-layered.

Hofer and Schendel (1978) refer to three levels of strategy: corporate, business and functional/operational.

The distinction between corporate and business strategy arises because of the development of the **divisionalised** business organisation, which typically has a corporate centre and a number of strategic business units (SBUs).

Chandler (1962) described how four large US corporations found that the best way to divide strategic responsibility was to have the corporate HQ allocate resources and exercise overall financial control while the SBUs were each responsible for their own product-market strategies. Functional operational strategies are then developed for component parts of SBUs.

2.1 Corporate strategies

> ▶ **Key term**
>
> **Corporate strategy** is concerned with the overall purpose and scope of the organisation and how value will be added to the different parts (business units) of the organisation.
>
> Johnson, Scholes and Whittington (2007)

It is important to understand that while the wider concepts of marketing are closely allied to the concept of overall strategy, the **specific marketing activities** we are familiar with, such as product planning, advertising and channel management make up just **one function amongst many**.

We must be careful not to claim pre-eminence for this **functional** aspect of marketing.

2.1.1 Defining aspects of corporate strategy

Strategy and strategic management impact upon the whole organisation: all parts of the business operation should support and further the strategic plan.

- **Environment**. The organisation counters threats and exploits opportunities in the environment (customers, clients, competitors).

- **Resources**. Strategy involves choices about allocating or obtaining corporate resources now and in the future.

- **Values**. The value systems of people with power in the organisation influence its strategy.

- **Timescale**. Corporate strategy has a long-term impact.

- **Complexity**. Corporate strategy involves uncertainty about the future, integrating the operations of the organisation and change.

Corporate strategy needs to consider how there can be improvement in the competitive strategies of the operating units, whether they are at a domestic, international or global level. This is also the case when considering SMEs; the level of competitiveness still needs attention. Corporate strategy also needs to be considered as complementing the competitive strategy and helping to achieve it. There are two aspects to the strategy: an internal analysis of the different functions and how they can work with each other, as well as how the organisation can identify external opportunities and potentially manage uncertainty based on external influences.

2.2 Business strategy

Business strategy can involve decisions such as whether to segment the market and specialise in particularly profitable areas, or to compete by offering a wider range of product.

2.3 Operational strategies

Operational strategies are concerned with how the component parts of an organisation deliver effectively the corporate and business-level strategies in terms of resources, processes and people. (Johnson, Scholes and Whittington, 2007)

Individual operational strategies are often the concern of business functions, so they are also known as functional strategies. Every business unit develops functional strategies for each major department. Here are some examples of the considerations required:

- **Marketing**. Devising products and services, pricing, promoting and distributing them, in order to satisfy customer needs at a profit. Marketing and corporate strategies are interrelated.

- **Production**. Factory location, manufacturing techniques, outsourcing and so on.

- **Finance**. Ensuring that the firm has enough financial resources to fund its other strategies by identifying sources of finance and using them effectively.

- **Human resources management**. Secure personnel of the right skills in the right quantity at the right time, and ensure that they have the right skills and values to promote the firm's overall goals.

- **Information systems**. A firm's information systems are becoming increasingly important, as an item of expenditure, as administrative support and as a tool for competitive strength. Not all information technology applications are strategic, and the strategic value of IT will vary from case to case.

- **R&D**. New products and techniques.

3 The strategic planning process

3.1 Synergistic planning

Planning's function is to co-ordinate resources to increase the chances of achieving objectives. Planning involves making decisions about what has to be done, how and when it should be done and who should do it. An integral part of the planning process is **control**. If plans are to be successful then systems must be established for their modification in the light of outcomes.

3.2 The synergistic planning process

Any process of planning must start with a clear definition of what is to be achieved. This process of objective setting is frequently undertaken in a very superficial manner in the real world and sometimes hardly performed at all.

There may be an assumption that 'everybody knows what we are trying to achieve' or reference back to long-established objectives that have lost some or all of their relevance under current circumstances. Only when

objectives are clearly defined can possible courses of action be assessed and eventual success or failure be measured.

It is clear that any plan is only as good as the team or individual that is going to implement it. The effectiveness of a plan or decision is also impacted by the quality of the plan and also the level of acceptance from the team that is then going to implement it. The synergistic model looks at both the rational and human-centric models to develop effective plans and decisions that will be accepted by its implementors.

The **process of definition** is not complete until everyone concerned has agreed on a single clear statement of what is to be attained.

Vagueness and ambiguity of language are to be avoided, but appear all too often for political purposes, since they allow different interpretations to be used by parties pursuing different agendas. Vagueness and ambiguity hamper effective action.

Any plan must take into account circumstances that will affect attainment of the objective. The first step is to establish just where the individual or organisation stands to begin with. Current circumstances will include a vast array of factors, some of far more immediate importance than others. An important aspect of the current situation is the potential that exists for future developments that may affect possible future action.

You should be familiar with the idea of SWOT – strengths, weaknesses, opportunities and threats. Strengths and weaknesses exist now; opportunities and threats have potential for the future. SWOT is a very common model for analysing the existing situation and widely used in marketing.

Simple problems, when analysed, often suggest a single, fairly obvious route to a satisfactory solution. If you come home from a skiing holiday and find that a period of cold weather has left you with a burst pipe, you have little alternative to turning off the water at the mains and trying to find a plumber (unless you are a plumber yourself, of course).

The analysis of more complex problems will tend to suggest a **range of possible courses of action**. There is a requirement for both experience and imagination here. Experience will suggest routes that have proved satisfactory in similar circumstances in the past. Imagination suggests both modifications to such plans and the creation of completely new ones.

When a range of possible plans has been outlined, it then becomes necessary to go through a **process of selection**, normally by considering such matters as those below:

- Probability of success
- Resources required
- Acceptability of the proposed action and its implications
- Potential obstacles

In essence a plan must be simple, clearly written, needs to take account of the current situation and the organisation's future intent.

The process of planning is not complete when a course of action has been chosen. It is then necessary to prepare **detailed plans** for all the groups and individuals involved. These must be **integrated** in such a way that all action undertaken supports the attainment of the overall objective. **Performance measures** and **control mechanisms** must also be established so that effort is not wasted and obstacles can be overcome.

Corporate decisions relate to the scope of a firm's activities, the long-term direction of the organisation, and allocation of resources. The **'planning' model of strategy formation** suggests a logical sequence which involves **analysing** the current situation, **generating** choices (relating to competitors, products and markets) and **implementing** the chosen strategies.

It is important to recognise the **hierarchical** level of planning and control decisions, because decision-makers can only make plans or take control action within the sphere of the **authority** that has been **delegated** to them.

 The Chartered Institute of Marketing

3.3 A corporate strategic planning model

A marketing plan needs to take into account a number of factors, the strengths and weaknesses of the organisation, the market needs and wants, existing and potential competitors and the overall design to create value to gain competitive advantage.

Generally any planning model should help to the following:

- Identify sources of competitive advantage

- Force an organisational approach to develop specific strengths and core competences

- Develop communication to inform everyone in the organisation about the key priorities; this should then also be communicated to external stakeholders

- Obtain the resources required to implement the plan appropriately

- Engage with the organisation at all levels to ensure there is engagement at all levels and that the leadership team is also ensuring engagement

We identify three stages. These are described briefly in the paragraphs below.

(a)   **Strategic analysis**

Strategic analysis is concerned with understanding the strategic position of the organisation.

(i)   **Environmental analysis** (external appraisal) is the scanning of the business's environment for factors relevant to the organisation's current and future activities.

(ii)   **Position or situation audit**. The current state of the business in respect of resources, brands, markets etc.

The resource audit helps to identify the resources available to a business. Resources can vary from tangible resources to intangible resources (eg skill set, employees, plant, machinery)

(iii)   **Mission**

–   The firm's long-term approach to business
–   The organisation's value system

(iv)   **Goals** interpret the mission to the needs of different stakeholders (eg customers, employees, shareholders).

(v)   **Objectives** should embody mission and goals. Generally, they are **quantitative** measures, against which actual performance can be assessed.

(vi)   **Corporate appraisal**. A critical assessment of strengths, weaknesses, opportunities and threats (SWOT) existing in the internal and environmental factors affecting an organisation.

(vii)   **Gap analysis**. A projection of current activities into the future to identify if there is a difference between the firm's objectives and the results from the continuation of current activities.

Note that you might decide the mission after assessing the needs of the organisation and its environmental situation. You may have to suggest a new mission, sometimes for the organisation as a whole and sometimes for the marketing function and get people to engage with the new direction.

Another way of reaching understanding and ensuring the audit has been covered in the appropriate depth is to undertake a core competence analysis. Core competences are the capabilities that are critical to the organisation in achieving its competitive advantage (as discussed in Chapter 1). The understanding and the measurement of competences can help the organisation to fulfil its corporate and marketing objectives. The audit however needs to be critical in nature and underpin the decision making at a corporate level. An audit is a fundamental part of planning and should be used to underpin the direction and development of the marketing plan.

(b) **Strategic choice**

Strategic choice is based on strategic analysis.

(i) **Strategic options generation**. Here are some examples:

- Increase market share
- International growth
- Concentration on core competences (the identification of core competences or the changes of core competences can impact the strategic direction of the organisation)
- Growth through acquisition

(ii) **Strategic options evaluation**. Alternative strategies are developed and each is then examined on its merits:

- Acceptability to the organisation's stakeholders
- Suitability
- Feasibility

(iii) **Strategy selection**

- **Competitive strategy** is the generic strategy determining **how you compete**
- **Product-market strategy** determines **where you compete**
- Institutional strategies determine the **method of growth**

(c) **Implementation**

The implementation of the strategy has to be planned. This is the conversion of the strategy into detailed **plans or objectives for operating units**. Implementation also needs to be facilitated through the leadership team who need to have the appropriate skills, vision and motivation for implementation to be a success.

(i) Some plans go into detailed **specifications** as to how the activities should be carried out.

(ii) Others will specify **targets** which managers are expected to reach on their own initiative.

(iii) The planning of implementation has several aspects, namely:

- **Resource planning** (ie finance, human resources (HR)). This involves assessing the key tasks, and the resources to be allocated to them.

- **Systems**. Systems are necessary to provide the necessary strategic information, as well as essential operational procedures. Control systems are used to assess performance.

4 Is strategic planning necessary?

4.1 Advantages and criticisms of strategic planning

We looked at the advantages of a formal system of strategic planning and criticisms of the rational model in theory and in practice in Chapter 2. Refer to Chapter 2 if you need a reminder.

The problem is that the further ahead you look the more imprecise planning becomes.

Forecasting becomes more uncertain with each key variable, such as interest rates and employment levels, becoming more and more difficult to predict. Long-term plans therefore have to be broad brush pictures of the organisation's future.

Modification will be necessary as more information becomes available and managers need to be clear that long-term goals are most likely to be achieved by a series of short-term strategies which may not follow a direct path.

Long-term thinking, even beyond the **planning horizon** (the furthest time ahead for which plans can be usefully quantified) is still a useful activity as it provides managers with a picture of how the organisation should be developing a vision for the future.

Often SMEs question whether they need to develop such a plan as they are smaller and very aware of the developments in the organisation. The following are key points why planning is still important for the smaller organisation:

- Many industries are changing and developing at a pace that makes the environment within which an organisation operates complex. Planning can help to predict, foresee and react to market changes and so take advantage of opportunities and potentially identify areas that the organisation needs to develop in to gain the competitive advantage sought.

- Planning can also help to identify key competitors as well as their activities, as the smaller organisation may be competing with larger players.

- Planning can encourage financial planning which is very important for a smaller organisation to ensure it has the relevant resources as and when required.

- Planning can also help to engage employees at all levels so they too know what the vision is, especially when an individual or a family owns the smaller organisation.

- Planning also shows key stakeholders, whether funders or supporters of your organisation, that you are looking ahead and have a vision to take your business forward.

THE REAL WORLD

Aquastyle Waterbeds – the challenger

Aquastyle Waterbeds is a small company based on the South coast of England specialising in selling and maintaining waterbeds. As a market challenger it had a number of key competitors, some of whom were market leaders. Its competitors included already well-established regional providers as well as national waterbed companies benefitting from an array of distribution opportunities and economies of scale with suppliers. These distribution strategies included providing competitively priced products over the web allowing them to target a wider customer base. So how did a local company make a difference, how did Aquastyle maintain its market share, ensure it remained competitive in the market and develop a longer term marketing strategy that could compete with the key players? Read on…

- Aquastyle developed strong relationships with its suppliers, giving the company flexibility to order products and supply them on to its customers within 24 hours.

- Aquastyle worked with domestic customers as well as business to business customers, so widening their market and building its networks.

- Aquastyle provided a complete service to its target market, which the more dominant companies were not always able to do, from building bespoke beds, servicing beds, providing 24-hour service for any problems with the beds, to a waterbed helpline in case of any leakages. This changed the dynamics of the traditional waterbed market, this could not easily be mimicked.

- Aquastyle also made good use of technology, developing a marketing information system, to develop critical time points when customers needed to be reminded of servicing beds and providing conditioners for the bed as well as proactively seeking feedback from its customers to improve its service.

These are just some of the factors that allowed the company to keep the larger more dominant competitors away from its more local and regional market and to become a real competitor to the larger businesses in the marketplace.

Considering your own organisation, critically evaluate how marketing planning is undertaken.

How does your organisation benefit from a formal system of planning?

If there is an informal system of planning how could it benefit from a more formal system of planning?

5 Corporate strategy and marketing strategy

Marketing contributes significantly to **corporate planning** and formulating **corporate objectives**, as markets and customers are a key part of the corporate environment and are key to the firm's survival. Marketing therefore has a lead role in other business functions. Anticipated sales, for example, determine the **volume** produced by the production function. However, available **production capacity** can lead to constraints on what is produced, and **financial limitations** offer a limit to the resources available.

5.1 How marketing can contribute to the corporate plan

Marketing makes a particularly important input to the corporate planning decisions. Information inputs from marketing to the **corporate** planning decisions perform a double duty in that they also provide the bases for deciding marketing objectives and strategies. **Marketing research** is vital to **all stages** of the marketing plan hence the need for an effective marketing information system.

5.2 The environmental audit

This reviews the organisation's position in relation to changes in the external environment (social/cultural, legal, economic, political and technological) and provides information which directly affects the setting of corporate objectives. The marketplace is, by definition, part of the 'environment'.

- **Competitor analysis** provides competitor intelligence, competitor response models and so on which again influence corporate objectives, strategy and contingency planning.

- **The customer audit** assesses the existing and potential customer bases to provide information as to whether to develop new markets.

- **Product portfolio analysis** provides input for decisions as to whether to drop particular products and/or add new ones.

- **The sales forecast** provides the basis for all other functional activities as well as marketing. Students often find it difficult to relate marketing objectives clearly to corporate objectives and even more difficult to distinguish clearly marketing objectives from corporate objectives. There can be no corporate plan which does not involve products/services and customers.

The **marketing plan** is concerned with **products** and **markets**.

(a) These are typically stated in terms of market share, sales volume, levels of distribution and profitability.

(b) Decisions might be taken as to the type of products sold to particular customer groups. The marketing manager's plans are often frustrated by other people in the organisation. These 'blockers' can be people in the marketing department but are more likely to be people in other departments. The less an organisation is truly market-oriented, the more likely it is that marketing plans are ineffective.

Each functional area has its own particular concerns and constraints and, at strategic level, marketers have to take these into account if they want to achieve anything.

The Chartered
Institute of Marketing

6 The role of strategic marketing

The emphasis in this model is for marketing to contribute to the creation of value and competitive customer strategy. As such, it is practised in customer-focused and larger organisations. In a large or diversified organisation, it may also be responsible for the co-ordination of marketing departments or activities in separate business units. Strategic marketing decisions, when not made by professional marketers, are taken by business leaders.

Professional marketers are likely to be responsible for strategic marketing only in those organisations with a strong market (note, not necessarily marketing), or customer orientation or with separate marketing departments in business units that require co-ordination. In organisations with a weak customer orientation (typically those with a production, sales, product or technology orientation), the role of marketing is likely to be limited to one of sales support or marketing communications.

Corporate objectives are the overarching objectives of the organisation, the marketing objectives focus on marketing and may relate to the marketing mix. It is important that the marketing objectives link to the marketing strategy. The marketing objectives are a critical part of the marketing plan. Establishing clear objectives is as important as the development of the marketing strategy in ensuring the overall success of the marketing plan.

6.1 Strategic marketing activities

The full spectrum of strategic marketing activities is illustrated in the statements of marketing practice on which your syllabus is based.

Strategic marketing activities include those in the list below:

- Research and analysis
- Strategy making and planning
- Brand management
- Implementing marketing programmes
- Measuring effectiveness
- Managing marketing teams

6.2 Plans and planning processes

The planning processes used in organisations are typically geared to the annual operating and financial reporting cycle. In those organisations in which annual or longer-term plans are produced, these plans are usually at three levels: corporate, business and functional. Marketing contributes to corporate and business plans and develops its own functional plan at an operational level. In organisations with strong strategic management practices (often those with a strong customer orientation), plans are likely to contain the strategies of the organisation or business. In organisations where plans are effectively 'budgets', strategy is unlikely to be explicit. It is therefore important to recognise that:

- The terms 'strategy' and 'plan' may not be the same.
- Strategy making and planning may be different processes in organisations.
- Organisations approach strategy formulation in a range of formal and informal ways.

What is sometimes referred to as the 'strategic marketing plan' can take different forms in different organisations. For example:

- It may be the name given to the plans that co-ordinate the marketing activities of the different businesses or units throughout an organisation.

- It may be synonymous with the term 'business plan' or 'corporate plan' in an organisation with a strong customer focus or responsibility only for marketing products made elsewhere and bought in.

- It may simply be the name given to the marketing plan, which specifies the objectives or targets, activities, resources and budgets of the marketing function.

However, it should be recognised that the majority of organisations do not produce a strategic marketing plan. The major plans that specify and control the organisation's strategy are corporate or business plans, into which strategic marketing should have input.

The primary role of strategic marketing is to identify and create value for the business through **strongly differentiated positioning**. It achieves this by influencing the strategy and culture of the organisation in order to ensure that both have a strong customer focus.

In organisations where strategic marketing does not exist as a function, the process or decisions are still undertaken by senior managers or business leaders. Where it is an explicit function, the strategic marketing role will usually be performed by a marketing function in a business unit and by a corporate level marketing function, which may also have a responsibility for co-ordinating the activities of marketing departments in business units.

Strategic marketers should champion the customer experience and exert a strong influence on the organisation to adopt a customer orientation, contribute along with other directors and senior managers to its competitive strategy, align the organisation's activities to the customer, and manage the organisation's marketing activities.

During strategy formulation, strategic marketing is about **choices** that customer-focused organisations make on where and how to compete and with what assets.

It is also about developing a specific competitive position using tools from the marketing armoury including brands, innovation, customer relationships and service, alliance, channels and communications, and increasingly, price.

Strategic marketing does not own the business strategy but, like other departments and functions, should contribute to it and control the operational levers that make a strategy effective. However, marketing has an exceptional contribution to make in identifying opportunities and determining ways to create value for customers and shareholders.

During implementation, strategic marketing is the 'glue' that connects many aspects of the business. It will often manage one or a portfolio of brands. Increasingly, it works with HR to ensure that the culture and values in the organisation are consistent with the brand and to ensure that marketing competences are part of the overall framework for staff development across the business.

The recognition and development of a marketing strategy can help to develop continuous innovation concentration, also improve concentration on key areas of the organisation, including distribution, customer participation, sustainability and marketing performance, and potentially focus on the global market.

Strategic marketing also has responsibility for directing the implementation of marketing activities needed to execute the organisation's strategy. Other key tasks of strategic marketing in today's organisations are:

- Contributing to strategic initiatives being undertaken by the organisation, for example marketing input to a 'due diligence' evaluation of a prospective merger or acquisition. In some cases, strategic marketers will be managing multi-disciplinary teams.

- Co-ordinating and managing customer information across the organisation within the data protection and privacy legislation. This involves close relationships with the IT function.

- Advising on **competitive positioning:** that is, determining target market segments and how they will be approached. This will include developing and driving the business case for investment in brands, new products and services.

- Championing and developing innovation and entrepreneurship within the organisation.

- Ensuring that the marketing function is appropriately skilled and resourced.

- Providing input with finance on the valuation of brands for reporting and disclosure.

- This concept of strategic marketing draws heavily on the theory and practice of strategic management, not just of marketing. This is an important distinction since strategic marketing is as much a part of directing how the organisation competes as it is a part of marketing itself.

Professional marketers engage in relationships with most functions within the organisation and are 'business people' rather than 'technical marketers'. This is particularly so at the strategic level. It requires participants at this level to embrace a wider range of management theory and practice than has been the case in the past.

In addition to traditional marketing theory, strategic marketing also embraces:

- Business and corporate strategy
- Investment decisions
- Culture and change management
- Quality management
- Programme and project management

Marketers still have an essential role to play in contributing their specialist marketing skills to the formulation, implementation and control of strategy. While this syllabus does embrace the wider business skills also expected of the strategic marketer, it still places a high priority on these specialist marketing skills.

6.3 Sustainable competitive advantage

Competitive advantage has to be sustained. It can come from better products, customer perceptions, costs, competences, assets, economies of scale, attitudes and relationships, offensive and defensive. A key issue in competitive advantage is ensuring it is sustained.

Competitive advantage only really exists in the customer's mind. Competitive advantage can be easily lost as a result of market changes or new ways of doing business.

Competitive advantage will be lost, gradually or rapidly, if the organisation's chosen strategy loses its relevance, or if customers' needs are no longer met and market share declines. This is termed strategic wear-out.

6.3.1 Different types of advantage

- **Better product** in some way eg Renault – safest car in its class
- **Perceived advantage** or psychic benefit, exclusivity eg Harrods
- **Global skills** eg having global supply chains, competing on process
- **Low costs** via high productivity or focus eg discount retailers or supermarkets such as Lidl or Aldi
- **Better competences:** some firms are better at marketing or aligning technologies to markets than others eg Apple with the iphone
- **Superior assets** eg property, cash or brands
- **Economies of scale:** size can be a source of competitive advantage
- **Attitude:** this is partly related to culture and management abilities
- **Superior relationships:** companies can exploit business alliances and develop personal relationships

The most important competitive advantages depend on the market and existing competitors. Keegan and Davidson (2003) suggest the best advantages are the hardest to copy.

Key factors of sustainable competitive advantage

A key part of sustaining competitive advantage is ensuring that the organisation realises and maintains its distinctive competences. Competitive advantage is achieved by continuously developing existing and creating new resources and capabilities in response to rapidly changing market conditions.

Another key aspect of this is ensuring you have effective leadership, the relevant teams and the ongoing capabilities to sustain the competitive advantage. It is important that the leadership skills within the organisation can ensure employees are motivated to sustain the competitive positioning as well as motivate key internal stakeholders for ongoing innovation. The strength of the organisational culture is also a key facilitator in maintaining long-term sustainable competitive advantage. This means encouraging innovation, following the

mission and ensuring you are able to maintain the key factors that have made the organisation reach its current positioning.

6.4 Guidelines for effective marketing planning

Although innovation remains a major ingredient in commercial success, if companies wish to become and remain competitive, they must overcome a range of challenges.

Table 4.1   Market challenges

Nature of change	Marketing challenges
Pace of change ■ Compressed time horizons ■ Shorter product life cycles ■ Transient customer preferences	■ Ability to exploit markets more rapidly ■ More effective new product development ■ Flexibility in approach to markets ■ Accuracy in demand-forecasting ■ Ability to optimise price-setting
Process thinking ■ Move to flexible manufacturing and control systems ■ Materials substitution ■ Developments in microelectronics and robotisation ■ Quality focus	■ Dealing with micro-segmentation ■ Finding ways to shift from single transaction focus to the forging of long-term relationships ■ Creating greater customer commitment
Market maturity ■ Over capacity ■ Low margins ■ Lack of growth ■ Stronger competition ■ Trading down ■ Cost-cutting	■ Adding value leading to differentiation ■ New market creation and stimulation
Customer's expertise and power ■ More demanding ■ Higher expectations ■ More knowledgeable ■ Concentration of buying power ■ More sophisticated buyer behaviour	■ Finding ways of getting closer to the customer ■ Managing the complexities of multiple market channels
Internationalisation of business ■ More competitors ■ Stronger competition ■ Lower margins ■ More customer choice ■ Larger markets ■ More disparate customer needs	■ Restructuring of domestic operation to compete internationally ■ Becoming customer-focused in larger and more disparate markets

McDonald (2007) recommends the following guidelines to help the marketer focus on effective marketing strategies:

 The Chartered Institute of Marketing

(a) **Understand the sources of competitive advantage**

Be clear about your mission and build your competences around the needs of the market. Wherever possible organisations should seek to avoid competing with an undifferentiated product or service in too broad a market. Those organisations without something different (eg their USP) to offer will struggle.

(b) **Understand differentiation**

Companies should work relentlessly towards achieving differential advantage. The main sources of differentiation are:

(i)   Superior product quality
(ii)   Innovative product features
(iii)   Unique product or service
(iv)   Strong brand name
(v)   Superior service
(vi)   Wide distribution coverage

(c) **Understand the environment**

There is overwhelming evidence that failure to monitor the turbulent environmental changes is the biggest failure in both large and small organisations. This means devoting at least some of the key executives' time and resources to monitoring formally the changes taking place about them. PEST and competitive factors should be continually monitored in order to understand the opportunities and threats that are emerging.

(d) **Understand competitors**

Any organisation, large or small, that does not know much about its close competitors should not be surprised if it fails to stay ahead, or fails all together!

These include:

(i)   Direct competitors
(ii)   Potential competitors
(iii)   Substitute products
(iv)   Forward integration by suppliers
(v)   Backward integration by customers
(vi)   Competitors' profitability
(vii)   Competitors' strengths and weaknesses

(e) **Understand strengths and weaknesses**

There should be a written summary of all the conclusions which were obtained the above guidelines. If the sources of the company's competitive advantage cannot be summarised on a couple of sheets of paper then the chances are that the audit has not been done properly.

(f) **Understand market segmentation**

This is one of the key sources of commercial success. As a marketer, you know not every customer in a broadly-defined market has the same needs. The secret to success is to change the offer in accordance with changing needs and not to offer exactly the same product or service to everyone.

With the growth of digital marketing, understanding the market segment also requires the organisation to understand which consumer segments are engaging with digital marketing as this will impact how the organisation communicates with these consumers. This means that as part of the planning process the marketing environmental factors impacting the online marketing activity need to be considered, as well as investigating how the different marketing mix elements are evolving and changing in the digital environment.

(g) **Understand the dynamics of product/market evolution**

This applies to organisations of all types and sizes. Today's fad can be tomorrow's failure.

(h) **Understand a portfolio of products and markets**

You cannot be all things to all people. A deep understanding of portfolio analysis will enable you to set appropriate objectives and allocate resources effectively.

Figure 4.1   Portfolio analysis

	High	Low	
	Invest and build for growth	Selectively invest	High
Market attractiveness	Maintain and manage for sustained earnings	Managed for cash	Low

Competitive position

The matrix is divided into four boxes and each box is assessed by management as suggested. This gives at a glance a reasonably accurate picture of the business and will indicate whether or not it is a well balanced portfolio. Too much business in any one box should be regarded as dangerous.

ACTIVITY 4.2

Undertake a critical review of the portfolio of products and markets for your organisation and critically evaluate their position in the matrix. Based upon this analysis decide what course of action needs to be taken, including justifications.

(i) **Setting clear strategic priorities and sticking to them**

You need to commit to writing a strategic marketing plan. You and the rest of the organisation need to understand how you need to focus your best resources on the best opportunities for achieving continuous growth in sales and profits.

The Chartered
Institute of Marketing

This means having a three-year strategic plan which contains:

(i) The mission statement
(ii) Financial summary
(iii) Market overview
(iv) A SWOT on key segments
(v) Portfolio summary
(vi) Assumptions
(vii) Marketing objectives and strategies
(viii) A budget

The strategic plan can then be converted into a detailed one-year plan. To do this an agreed marketing planning process is necessary.

(j) **Understand customer orientation**

A key role of marketing is to ensure that every function understands their role in serving the needs of the customer and not just their own functional interests. This culture is essential in ensuring success and must be driven from the board of directors downwards.

(k) **Be professional**

Entrepreneurial skills combined with hard headed management skills will see many companies through the challenge of today's markets.

(l) **Give leadership**

As McDonald says:

(i) Do not let doom and gloom pervade your thinking

(ii) Lead your team strongly

(iii) Do not accept poor performance

Corporate objectives need to link clearly to marketing objectives, which will influence the development and the direction of the marketing plan.

6.5 Change management planning

The successful management of change involves a number of considerations from identifying the need for change, the justification of change to key stakeholders, the resource implications, gaining both internal and external buy in as well as planning change to ensure it fits in with the organisation's overall mission, vision and long-term strategic direction.

Change management also requires the organisation to undertake a resource audit, that clearly identifies the key resource implications of the change. Resource considerations need to go beyond financial resources but also the skillset within the organisation, the opportunity cost of change as well as the structural implications both in the short and long term. The need to identify the core competences is also a fundamental part of change; consideration needs to be made as to what the core competences are and why.

The implication of the change being recommended needs also to be considered from an organisational and leadership perspective, what skills currently exist and what are required, how will the structure of the organisation need to potentially be changed to account for the recommendations. Kotter (1996) identified eight steps to managing change successfully:

(a) **Increase urgency** – Inspire people to move, make objectives real and relevant.

(b) **Build the guiding team** – Get the right people in place with the right emotional commitment, and the right mix of skills and levels.

(c) **Get the vision right** – Get the team to establish a simple vision and strategy, focus on emotional and creative aspects necessary to drive service and efficiency.

(d) **Communicate for buy-in** – Involve as many people as possible, communicate the essentials, simply, and to appeal and respond to people's needs. De-clutter communications – make technology work for you rather than against.

(e) **Empower action** – Remove obstacles, enable constructive feedback and lots of support from leaders – reward and recognise progress and achievements.

(f) **Create short-term wins** – Set aims that are easy to achieve – in bite-size chunks. Manageable numbers of initiatives. Finish current stages before starting new ones.

(g) **Don't let up** – Foster and encourage determination and persistence – ongoing change – encourage ongoing progress reporting – highlight achieved and future milestones.

(h) **Make change stick** – Reinforce the value of successful change via recruitment, promotion, new change leaders. Weave change into culture.

7 Barriers to effective marketing planning

Table 4.2   Why marketing plans can fail

Issue	Comment
Weak support from chief executive and top management	Without support from senior management for the marketing planning process it is unlikely to work. Where marketing is seen as an unworthy activity this is a major barrier to marketing planning.
Lack of a plan for planning	Failure or partial failure is often the result of developing a timetable for implementation. A sense of purpose and dedication is required tempered by patience and a willingness to appreciate and deal with the issues associated with implementation of a new system.
Lack of line management support	Hostility, lack of skills, lack of data and information, lack of resources and an inadequate organisational structure add up to a failure to obtain the willing participation of operational managers.
Confusion over planning terms	An over use of jargon will cause resentment and hostility towards the planning system. Planning systems that are successful use terminology familiar in operational management and are clearly defined.
Numbers in lieu of written objectives and strategies	Most managers are used to completing sales forecasts and the financial implications without considering the underlying factors or opportunities. Successful systems only ask for essential data and place greater emphasis on narrative to explain the underlying thinking behind the objectives and strategies.
Too much detail, too far ahead	Systems that generate a large amount of paper and bureaucracy are generally de-motivating for all concerned. Companies try to do too many things at once in too many directions, and key strategic issues do not get the attention they deserve.
Once-a-year ritual	Managers treat the writing of a once-a-year plan as an unpleasant duty. Resulting plans are not used or are relegated to a position of secondary importance. Successful companies spread the planning activity over the entire 12-month period with a clear timetable of activity. This ensures a better chance of the plan being converted into action.
Separation of operational planning from strategic planning	This is a major cause of missed opportunities and an inability of management to consider any alternatives. This also discourages operational managers from thinking strategically with the result that detailed operational plans are completed in isolation. Strategic plans are seen as an ivory tower exercise.

Issue	Comment
Failure to integrate marketing planning into a total corporate planning system	This results in a lack of participation of key functions such as production, engineering, finance and HR. Where their involvement is a key determinant of success this makes the marketing planning system virtually ineffective.
Delegation of planning to a planner	Without the co-operation of operational management a planner becomes little more than an HQ administrative assistant and is virtually powerless.

There are a number of reasons why plans can fail.

Communications

Poor communications or a lack of communication can impact the development and execution of a plan. If the mission and vision are not appropriately communicated to internal and external stakeholders it can impact the development and fulfilment of the strategy, as these individuals or groups of individuals may not have the appropriate information. Also a lack of information can mean that team members do not know when and potentially how to make certain decisions. This can then impact the organisational culture.

Leadership

The leadership team is fundamental in ensuring the success of a strategy. If the leadership underestimates the requirements of the plan, the plan will fail. Also weak leadership can be a key factor in a plan failing as the appropriate resource allocation may not take place. It is therefore imperative that the leadership skill requirements are constantly audited and evaluated. The management team must ensure it has the relevant skilled leaders to help implement the plan.

Planning the plan

For a plan to be successful it needs to be appropriately written and developed. Plans are often incomplete, based on little evidence or experience or can be very tactical rather than strategic in nature. The plan needs to be at a strategic level but also have an action plan. However the action plan cannot be central to the plan but rather a breakdown of how to execute the plan.

Inactive management

Another reason why plans can fail is because of passive management. Plans can start off with management providing impetus and momentum but this needs to be continuous. Management needs to make sure the plan does get implemented and the tactical plan is also followed; however, leadership needs to ensure the plan is still engaging with the mission and vision.

ACTIVITY 4.3

Critically analyse, using examples, why you think plans can fail. What factors can be used to avoid failure?

8 The concept of strategic marketing planning in charity and not-for-profit marketing

Marketing is as valuable in **NFP** organisations as in those properly driven by shareholder value. Measures of efficiency and effectiveness replace profit-based measures and several kinds of audience or stakeholder exist.

Although most people would 'know one if they saw it', there is a surprising problem in clearly delimiting what counts as a **not-for-profit (NFP) organisation**. Local authority services, for example, would not be marketing in order to arrive at a profit for shareholders, but nowadays they are being increasingly required to apply the same disciplines and processes as companies which are oriented towards straightforward profit goals.

Oxfam has almost 15,000 shops all over the world. It opened its first charity shop in 1948. The proceeds from these usually get paid to different charities, or are used to further Oxfam's relief efforts around the globe. The stock originally came from public donations, but is increasingly based on products from developing countries in Africa, Asia and South America, including handcrafts, books, music CDs and instruments, clothing, toys and food.

In 2008, Oxfam GB worked with over 20,000 volunteers in shops across the UK, raising £17.1 million for Oxfam's programme. Of the 750 Oxfam charity shops around the UK, around 100 are specialist bookshops or book and music shops. Oxfam is the largest retailer of second-hand books in Europe, selling around 12 million per year.

NFP enterprises need to be **'non-loss' operations** in order to cover their costs, and profits are only made as a means to an end (eg providing a service, or accomplishing some socially or morally worthy objective).

A **not-for-profit organisation** be defined as: '...an organisation whose attainment of its prime goal is not assessed by economic measures. However, in pursuit of that goal it may undertake profit-making activities'.

This may involve a number of different kinds of organisation with, for example, differing legal status – charities, statutory bodies offering public transport or the provision of services such as leisure, health or public utilities such as water or road maintenance.

Marketing management is now recognised as equally valuable to profit-oriented and NFP organisations. The tasks of marketing auditing, setting objectives, developing strategies and marketing mixes and controls for their implementation can all help in improving the performance of charities and NFP organisations.

While the basic principles are appropriate for this sector, differences in how they can be applied should not be forgotten. Dibb *et al* (2000) suggest that four key differences exist related to **objectives**, **target markets** (and hence buyer behaviour), **marketing mixes** and **controlling marketing activities**.

8.1 Objectives

Objectives will not be based on profit achievement but rather on achieving a **particular response** from various target markets. This has implications for reporting of results. The organisation will need to be open and honest in showing how it has managed its budget and allocated funds raised. **Efficiency and effectiveness** are particularly important in the use of donated funds.

The concept of target marketing is different in the not-for-profit sector. There are no buyers but rather a number of different **audiences or stakeholder groups**. A target public is a group of individuals who have an interest or concern about the charity. Those benefiting from the organisation's activities are known as the **client public**. Relationships are also vital with **donors and volunteers** from the general public. In addition, there may also be a need to lobby local and national government and businesses for support.

Charities and NFP organisations often deal more with **services and ideas** than products. In this sense the extended marketing mix of people, process and physical evidence is important.

- **Appearance** needs to be business-like rather than appearing extravagant.

- **Process** is increasingly important, for example, the use of direct debit to pay for council tax reduces administration costs leaving more budget for community services.

- **People** need to offer good service and be caring in their dealings with their clients.

- **Distribution channels** are often shorter with fewer intermediaries than in the profit-making sector. Wholesalers and distributors available to a business organisation do not exist in most non-business contexts.

- **Promotion is usually dominated by personal selling**. Advertising is often limited to public service announcements due to limited budgets. Direct marketing is growing due to the ease of developing databases. Sponsorship, competitions and special events are also widely used.

- **Pricing** is probably the most different element in this sector. Financial price is often not a relevant concept. Rather, opportunity cost, where an individual is persuaded of the value of donating time or funds, is more relevant.

It is important to note that a marketing plan needs to feed into the marketing objectives and the corporate objectives, these are all linked.

▶ **Assessment tip**

Task 3 of the December 2009/March 2010 assignment involved developing an outline marketing plan, and utilising an appropriate framework to allow the successful delivery of the recommended strategy. Key considerations/elements of a marketing plan need to be considered this context.

▶ **Assessment tip**

When undertaking strategic decisions or recommending the development of a strategy it is important to think of the following:

Scope and scale – what is the actual scope and scale of your decisions? How are they going to impact your organisation, its activities and potentially the value chain and the resource requirements? What will be the implications of these resource requirements? While an exact figure may not be required it is important to have an understanding of the amount as key stakeholders will be interested in this decision and its potential implications.

Is the strategy being recommended something completely new or a development of what currently exists within the organisation? Will it impact the organisation as a whole? Consideration also needs to be given to the investment required if the level of innovation is high especially when trying to gain competitive advantage.

There also needs to be an analysis of the risk involved in the strategy being recommended, in terms of development in areas where the organisation has little experience. It can be that a recommendation is made that the organisation carries on doing what it is currently doing with little or no change; however, there needs to be clear justifications as to why this is the case and how it will fit in with the organisation's overall strategic direction, as well as the vision and mission.

CHAPTER ROUNDUP

- Strategy exists on three levels: corporate, business and functional/operational.

- Strategic management is the development, implementation and control of agreed strategies in order to achieve competitive advantage.

- There are a number of aspects of corporate strategy: environment, resources, values, timescales and complexity.

- There are a number of parts to the strategic planning model; there are three stages:
  - Strategic analysis
  - Strategic choice
  - Strategy selection

- The above parts include a number of subsections/parts that need to be considered to ensure the planning is appropriately written and underpinned.

- Marketing planning can fail due to a number of reasons.

- The third sector (charity and not-for-profit marketing) also needs to consider strategic marketing planning to ensure stakeholders' needs are met and internal targets are understood by all involved in the organisation.

FURTHER READING

Ahmed, P.K., Rafiq, M. and Saad, N.M. (2003) Internal marketing and the mediating role of organisational competencies, *European Journal of Marketing*, Vol37(9), pp1221-1241. (article available via library photocopying service)

Anon (2008) Building a timeline for marketing success. *Folio: The Magazine for Magazine Management.* Sept, Supplt, pp10-13. Ebsco link

Beaman, L. (2008) Planners must embrace strategic change. *Money Management*, Vol22(35), p8.

Gordon, D. and Allen, R. (2008) Plan for your marketing 2009. *Electrical Wholesaling,* Oct, Vol89(10), pp62-63. Ebsco link

Hafeez, K. and Essmail A.E. (2007) Evaluating organisation core competences and associated personal competencies using analytical hierarchy process. *Management Research News*, Vol30(8), pp530-547.

Hill, J., McGowan, P. and Maclaran, P. (1998) Developing marketing planning skills: combining theory and practice. *Journal of Marketing Practice: Applied Marketing Science,* Vol4(3), pp69-84. (article available via library photocopying service)

Pearson, G. and Proctor, T. (1994) The modern framework for marketing planning. *Marketing Intelligence & Planning*, Vol12, 4, pp22-26. (article available via library photocopying service)

Piercy, N.F. and Morgan, N. (1994) The marketing planning process: behavioural problems compared to analytical techniques in explaining marketing plan credibility. *Journal of Business Research*, Vol29(3), pp167-178.

Simpson, D. (1994) How to identify and enhance core competencies. *Strategy and Leadership,* Vol22(6), pp24-26.

The Chartered Institute of Marketing

REFERENCES

Baker, M. and Hart, S. (2008) *The marketing book.* 6th edition. Oxford, Butterworth Heinemann.

Bell, B., Grosholz E. and Stewart, J. (1997) *WEB Du Bois on race and culture: critiques and extrapolations.* London, Routledge.

Chandler, A.L. (1962) *Strategy and structure: chapters in the history of the American industrial enterprise.* Cambridge, MA, MIT Press.

Dibb, S. *et al* (2000) *Marketing concepts and strategies.* London, Houghton Mifflin.

Gilligan, C. and Wilson, R. (2004) *Strategic marketing management.* 3rd edition. Oxford, Butterworth Heinemann.

Hofer, C. and Schendel, D. (1978) *Strategy formulation: analytical concepts.* West Pub. Co (St Paul).

Johnson, G., Scholes K. and Whittington, R. (2007) *Exploring corporate strategy.* 8th edition. London, FT Prentice Hall.

Keegan, W.J. and Davidson, H. (2003) Offensive Marketing, Gaining Competitive Advantage. Boston, Butterworth Heineman.

Kotter, J.P. (1996) *Leading Change.* Harvard Business School Press.

McDonald, M. (2007) Marketing plans – how to prepare them how to use them. 6th edition. Oxford, Butterworth Heinemann.

Palmer, J., Cockton, J. and Cooper, G. (2007) *Managing marketing.* 1st edition. Oxford, Butterworth-Heinemann.

Raynor, M.E. (2007) What is corporate strategy really? *Ivey Business Journal*, December (71)8.

QUICK QUIZ

1   What are the two main kinds of approach to achieving competitive advantage?

2   Hofer and Schendel refer to three levels of strategy – what are they?

3   How do Johnson, Scholes and Whittington define operational strategies?

4   How does marketing contribute to the corporate plan?

5   What is the role of strategic marketing?

6   Identify potential sources of competitive advantage.

7   What guidelines does McDonald recommend to help the marketer focus on effective marketing strategies?

8   Provide five reasons why marketing planning fails.

Activity 4.1

The problem is that the further ahead you look the more imprecise planning becomes. Long-term plans therefore have to be broad brush pictures of the organisation's future. Modification will be necessary as more information becomes available and managers need to be clear that long-term goals are most likely to be achieved by a series of short-term strategies which may not follow a direct path. Long-term thinking, even beyond the planning horizon (the furthest time ahead for which plans can be usefully quantified) is still a useful activity as it provides managers with a picture of how the organisation should be developing a vision for the future. So while formalisation has its benefits there are clear weaknesses too, particularly in turbulent and uncertain economic times.

Activity 4.2

A business with a range of products has a portfolio of products. However, owning a product portfolio poses a problem for a business. It must decide how to allocate investment (eg in product development, promotion) across the portfolio.

Another way of analysing a portfolio of products can be using the Boston Group Consulting Matrix. This categorises the products into one of four different areas, based on:

- Market share – does the product being sold have a low or high market share?

- Market growth – are the numbers of potential customers in the market growing or not?

The four categories can be described as follows:

- Stars are high-growth products competing in markets where they are strong compared with the competition. Often Stars need heavy investment to sustain growth. Eventually growth will slow and, assuming they keep their market share, Stars will become Cash Cows.

- Cash Cows are low-growth products with a high market share. These are mature, successful products with relatively little need for investment. They need to be managed for continued profit so that they continue to generate the strong cash flows that the company needs for its Stars.

- Question Marks are products with low market share operating in high-growth markets. This suggests that they have potential, but may need substantial investment to grow market share at the expense of larger competitors. Management has to think hard about Question Marks – which ones should they invest in? Which ones should they allow to fail or shrink?

- Unsurprisingly, the term Dogs refers to products that have a low market share in unattractive, low-growth markets. Dogs may generate enough cash to break-even, but they are rarely, if ever, worth investing in. Dogs are usually sold or closed.

Ideally, a business would prefer products in all categories (apart from Dogs!) to give it a balanced portfolio of products.

Activity 4.3

There are a multitude of reasons why marketing plans fail. Was the plan discussed, but never written? Is the plan too vague? Is the plan too detailed? Have internal roles been clearly defined? Have all essential elements of the plan been considered? Do leaders disagree with elements and execution of the plan?

To avoid these and other marketing mistakes, stick to the following process. You'll spend your resources wisely and realise measurable, positive returns.

- Get to know your customers, their needs and purchasing influences.

- Set goals according to validated customer needs and your business's resources.

- Develop action items that address these needs as individually as possible.

The Chartered
Institute of Marketing

- Share your plan with others in your company.

- Carefully choose delivery methods that have proven exposure, credibility and response rates amongst your audiences.

QUICK QUIZ ANSWERS

1
– The positioning approach. The positioning approach to strategy is closely related to the traditional concept of marketing orientation. It starts with an assessment of the commercial environment and positions the business so that it fits with environmental requirements.

– The resource-based approach The resource-based approach starts with the idea that competitive advantage comes from the possession of distinctive and unique resources.

2 Corporate, business and functional/operational.

3 Operational strategies are concerned with how the component parts of an organisation deliver effectively the corporate and business-level strategies in terms of resources, processes and people.

4 Marketing makes a particularly important input to the corporate planning decisions. Information inputs from marketing to the corporate planning decisions perform a double duty in that they also provide the bases for deciding marketing objectives and strategies. Marketing research is vital to all stages of the marketing plan hence the need for an effective marketing information system.

5 The emphasis in this model is for marketing to contribute to the creation of value and competitive customer strategy. As such, it is practised in customer-focused and larger organisations. In a large or diversified organisation, it may also be responsible for the co-ordination of marketing departments or activities in separate business units.

6
– Better product in some way
– Perceived advantage or psychic benefit
– Global skills
– Low costs via high productivity or focus
– Better competences
– Superior assets
– Economies of scale
– Attitude
– Superior relationships

7
– Understand the sources of competitive advantage
– Understand differentiation
– Understand the environment
– Understand competitors
– Understand strengths and weaknesses
– Understand market segmentation
– Understand the dynamics of product/market evolution
– Understand a portfolio of products and markets
– Set clear strategic priorities and stick to them
– Understand customer orientation
– Be professional

8
– Weak support from chief executive and top management
– Lack of a plan for planning
– Lack of line management support
– Confusion over planning terms
– Too much detail, too far ahead

CHAPTER 5

Assessing resource requirements

Introduction

This chapter explores the internal focus required to ensure the successful implementation of the marketing strategy. We explore the importance of organisational structure and culture and their impact on the resultant performance of the organisation in the marketplace. We explore the systems and processes required to ensure a strategy can be evaluated, monitored and communicated and the budgetary framework required to ensure the required funds are in place to deliver the marketing strategy effectively.

Topic list

Organisational structures	1
Teams in organisations	2
Virtual and self-managed teams	3
Organisational life phases	4
The importance of corporate culture on marketing strategy	5
The importance of communications in the implementation of marketing strategy	6
Improving marketing management	7
Budgets	8
Effective marketing feedback and control systems	9
Features of basic strategic control systems	10

2.2.1	Assess an organisation's structure and critically evaluate its appropriateness to align and deliver its strategy and fulfil its vision:
	■ Centralisation versus decentralisation ■ Lines of authority and communications ■ Committees, teams, taskforces required ■ Organisational life phases
2.2.2	Critically evaluate existing systems and processes and identify future needs in line with an organisation's strategy requirements:
	■ Budget setting ■ Planning systems ■ Accounting systems ■ Information management and flows
2.2.3	Assess the competency of an organisation's workforce in order to establish future capability and capacity requirements:
	■ Skills, knowledge and expertise ■ Quality and fit ■ Employee expectations ■ Attitudes
2.2.4	Ascertain where the new marketing strategy will impact and how it will fit into the broader organisation:
	■ Impact on other organisational strategies ■ Fit with systems and culture ■ Required organisational changes ■ Communication strategies
2.2.5	Establish a clear funding framework in order to deliver the marketing strategy effectively and ensure sufficient and realistic financial resource is available:
	■ Bid for funding at board level ■ Sufficient funds for implementation and delivery of the strategy ■ Full measuring, control and evaluation frameworks in place

1 Organisational structures

All organisations have some form of structure that refers to the clustering of tasks and people into smaller groups. This encompasses several aspects (Mintzberg, 1990):

(a) **Departmentalisation**

The principles by which an organisation is organised: by functions, markets or product.

(b) **Specialisation**

The extent to which tasks are defined and allocated to a specific person. There are two types of specialisation:

(i) Vertical specialisation – the number of hierarchical levels
(ii) Horizontal specialisation – the number of different functions that have been identified

(c) **Standardisation**

The number of procedures that explain how tasks should be accomplished.

(d) **Co-ordination**

According to Mintzberg this can be achieved through:

(i) Mutual adjustment on a one-to-one basis
(ii) Direct supervision that applies hierarchical authority
(iii) Standardisation of procedures, results, qualifications or norms

(e) **Formalisation**

The use of written documents in communication and information processes.

(f) **Decentralisation/centralisation**

Relates to the levels at which decisions are taken. The lower the decision level is, the more decentralised the organisation.

(g) **Control**

This refers to the evaluative process by which tasks are judged. Results, or the implementation of control, can be evaluated.

(h) **Differentiation and integration**

These can and may overlap. Differentiation reflects the degree to which each department develops its own way of functioning, behaving and accomplishing tasks. In order to develop coherent strategies an organisation needs mechanisms for integration. These involve: mutual adjustment, hierarchy, standardisation of procedures, committees, task groups, co-ordinating agents, project managers, product managers, common objectives, common norms and values and training and so on.

All organisations need at least some division of labour in order to function efficiently and effectively, requiring them to structure into smaller parts.

Structure can be considered in two main forms: hierarchical and matrix.

1.1 Hierarchical structures

Hierarchical structures can be divided into three types:

Table 5.1 Hierarchical structures

Type	Features
Functional	<ul><li>Typical of smaller businesses</li><li>Sensible balance between managers and operational staff</li><li>Subdivisions of specialisations as appropriate</li><li>Tend to lack flexibility due to one size fits all approach</li></ul>
Product/market	<ul><li>More appropriate to focus resources more specifically where company diversifies into different markets with same or different products</li><li>This may occur as an organisation grows in size and scope</li><li>Discussions will need to take place as to the degree of centralisation versus decentralisation that is required and with which of its activities</li></ul>
Divisional	<ul><li>Product/market operations may become stand-alone profit centres or strategic business units with agreed divisions of responsibility between the 'centre' and the 'division'</li><li>Division by product, market or geography is commonly seen</li></ul>

There are a number of advantages and disadvantages to the hierarchical structure:

- Authority and responsibility is well defined and so teams know exactly what needs to done; this can also impact the promotional path that is followed.

- Specialist managers can be employed where required and so gaps in skills can be highlighted.

- Often there are clear departments which mean the structure is clearly defined throughout the organisation.

- There can often be a lot of bureaucracy internally which means that the organisation is slow to change or respond to the changing environment.

- Hierarchy can often mean that there is poor communication.

- Departments can often make decisions that will benefit them rather than the organisation as a whole and so impact the greater good of the organisation.

1.2 Matrix structures

A matrix organisation operates several types of structures in tandem with the objective of integrating specialist knowledge areas around common objectives in a grid-like structure.

Those who operate in such a structure may find they have two bosses which can often create ambiguities for all concerned. Therefore, the culture and attitude of those concerned is an important factor. In practice, it has proved problematic.

Sy and D'Annunzio (2005) have proposed five factors that compromise the operation of a matrix structure:

(a) **Misaligned goals**

With at least two bosses there is possibility of competition or conflict of objectives as well as problems of co-ordination and communication.

(b) **Unclear roles and responsibilities**

Often seen as confusion regarding what is required, by and to whom, resulting in tension and ambiguity.

(c) **Ambiguous authority**

Lack of managerial and staff experience in working in a matrix leads to lack of clarity in decision making.

The Chartered Institute of Marketing

(d) **Matrix guardian**

Difficult to measure individual performance; therefore, reward system may conflict with the way a matrix operates.

(e) **Functional focused employees**

There is potential for tension if employees are attitudinally focused to their functional area of expertise which can result in a lack of trust, communication and reluctance to commit resources.

The matrix structure also brings with it a number of advantages and disadvantages:

A matrix structure organisation contains teams of people created from various sections of the business. Often there is a project manager for each of the teams. The advantages of a matrix structure can include the following:

- Staff can be chosen according to the needs of the project.
- Different specialists are a part of the team working together in a new environment.
- There can be specific deadlines and budgets within which the team operates.

The disadvantages of the matrix structure can include the following.

- Internal conflicts between actual line managers and project managers over resource allocation.

- Teams may not follow the central strategy of the organisation; their independence may be difficult to monitor.

- There can be high costs associated with the matrix structure due to project teams.

THE REAL WORLD

AREVA T&D Corporation

AREVA T&D Corporation (formerly Alstom Esca) is a global supplier of energy management systems for the generation, transmission, and distribution of electricity. For many years AREVA T&D was organised along independent lines of business, each responsible for a specific customer market segment. To reduce costs, and to leverage common products and services across all market segments, AREVA T&D decided to shift to a matrix organisation with centralised functional groups supporting each line of business. Although the matrix organisation changed, AREVA T&D realised many of their procedures did not, causing a high degree of business friction within the organisation. An assessment revealed the primary cause of business friction was an inconsistent view of management roles under the new matrix structure. AREVA T&D's CEO accepted a recommendation to perform an organisational structure design that included performance measurements and enabled a series of senior leader events to move beyond the organisation chart and lay the foundation for putting the organisation back to work. As a result management tension surrounding the matrix structure dissolved.

THE REAL WORLD

Coca-Cola

Coca-Cola has key strategic priorities; they are broken down into six key points:

- Accelerate carbonated soft drinks growth, led by Coca-Cola

- Broaden the family of products wherever appropriate eg bottled water, tea, coffee, juices, energy drinks

- Grow system profitability and capability together with the bottlers

- Creatively serve customers (eg retailers) to build their businesses

- Invest intelligently in market growth

■ Drive efficiency and cost effectiveness by using technology and large-scale production to control costs enabling our people to achieve extraordinary results every day

There are a number of different organisational structures; however, organisations need to understand that the structure has to help with communication, flexibility and decision making. Coca-Cola has developed flexible structures that encourage teamwork, based on employees' skills bases and employees are brought together based on their specialism.

Coca-Cola also has a head office that is responsible for the overall direction of the organisation. This central office can provide direction, support and resources to the regional structure and so can work to the organisation's benefit.

However, due to the global nature of the organisation it operates in a number of regions and so it is managed regionally. Regionally each of the SBUs are subdivided into divisions; for example there are Africa, North America, European, Latin America, South East Asia and North Asia regional divides. These geographical structures are then able to develop markets based on regional tastes, lifestyles and cultures. This also allows Coca-Cola to understand the consumer behaviour of these individuals appropriately and so develop its product range accordingly. It is also important to note that different markets are at differing stages of development; this type of structure allows organisations to develop them accordingly.

In summary, Coca-Cola needs to manage a global brand and have the appropriate organisational structures in place to ensure that all parts of the organisation are managed to get the best out of the team.

http://www.businesscasestudies.co.uk

ACTIVITY 5.1

Compare both case studies above. Critically evaluate the organisational structure for both and make recommendations as to how you think changes can be made, if any. If you are not recommending any changes, give justifications.

1.3 International and multinational firms

As organisations and industries grow and develop, issues of structure and organisation become more complex. As they develop a global presence a number of factors assume higher priority (Palmer *et al*, 2007):

(a) **World-wide value chains**

For instance time frames become important in delivering certain products along the supply chain.

(b) **International firms, local markets**

There is potential for conflict when international firms enter into local markets where different standards, business practices, legislation and cultures apply.

(c) **Greater influence of NGOs**

NGOs, pressure groups and other influences are capable of scrutinising every element of a firm's operation as it grows in size.

(d) **Government intervention**

Governments may act unilaterally in what they perceive to be their best interest. This may have an impact on the international firm at a country specific level.

Such organisations face the challenge of managing diverse products and services in local markets, and perhaps with limited knowledge. In such circumstances there are four main options summarised in the table below.

The Chartered Institute of Marketing

Table 5.2   Organisational management

Option	Features
International divisions	■ Enables the core business of the firm to develop strategy appropriate to the markets in which it operates ■ Good vertical co-ordination between divisions
International subsidiaries	■ Internationally co-ordinated by means of financial and top level planning ■ Managers enjoy a high level of autonomy for operational matters and implementation
Global product companies	■ One size fits all approach ■ High degree of central co-ordination ■ Planning is often undertaken on a global basis
Traditional corporations	■ Comprise many different business units as part of a network of interdependent operations ■ Providing local response and presence ■ Such organisations tend to be powerful economic and political forces, exercising significance influence

1.4 Centralisation versus decentralisation

A centralised organisation tends to hold authority and power of the organisation centrally, this traditionally is held by a few people in the organisation. This can mean that planning, decision-making and the delegation of authority is undertaken centrally. This means that the control is in the hands of these individuals/groups. Contrastingly decentralisation can mean that the power is distributed at different levels across the organisation, this can also be in different parts of the country or the world. Decision making is not concentrated necessarily at just the top of the organisation but can be distributed across the organisation. There are advantages and disadvantages to both, from speed of decision-making, levels of control to the speed of implementation. The macro and micro environment of the organisation, as well as its growth strategy and overall mission and vision need to be analysed before any change is recommended or implemented.

2 Teams in organisations

There are two basic approaches to the organisation of cross-functional team working: **multi-disciplinary** teams and **multi-skilled** teams.

2.1 Multi-disciplinary teams

Multi-disciplinary teams bring together individuals from different functional specialisms, so that their competences can be **pooled or exchanged**. They are appropriate when a significant degree of technical expertise in divergent disciplines is required, as in most large technical projects.

Multi-disciplinary teams are useful in:

■ Increasing team members' **awareness of the big picture** of their tasks and decisions, by highlighting the dovetailing of functional objectives.

■ Helping to generate **solutions to problems**, and suggestions for performance or process improvements, by integrating more pieces of the puzzle.

■ Aiding **co-ordination across functional boundaries**, by increasing the flow of communication, informal relationships and co-operation.

On the other hand, the members of multi-functional teams have different reporting lines and responsibilities within their line departments, creating the **ambiguity of dual responsibility**.

They may have a range of different backgrounds, work cultures, specialist skills and terminology. This creates a particular challenge for the team leader: to build a sense of team identity, role clarity and co-operative working.

2.2 Multi-skilled teams

Multi-skilled teams bring together a number of functionally versatile individuals, each of whom can perform any of the group's tasks: work can thus be **allocated flexibly**, according to who is best placed to do a given job when required. The advantages of multi-skilling may be as follows:

- Performing a **whole**, **meaningful job** is more satisfying to people than performing only one or two of its component operations (as in scientific job design).

- Allowing team members to see the big picture enables and encourages them to **contribute information and ideas** for improvements.

- Empowering team members to take initiative **enhances organisational responsiveness** to customer demands and environmental changes (particularly in 'front-line' customer service units).

- A focus on overall task objectives **reduces the need for tight managerial control** and supervision.

- Labour resources can be allocated more **flexibly and efficiently**, without potentially disruptive demarcation disputes.

- Multi-skilled teams are particularly appropriate when a high degree of flexibility is required.

However, because of human limitations, there are likely to be large areas of competence outside their capabilities. They are therefore suited to broad but still limited areas of activity, whereas a multi-disciplinary team can be assembled to cover any desired range of functions.

2.3 Project teams

Project teams may be set up to handle specific **strategic developments** (such as the introduction of a Just-in-Time approach), tasks relating to **particular processes** (such as the computerisation of the payroll system), tasks relating to particular **cases or accounts** (such as co-ordination of work for a client or client group) or special **audits or investigations** of procedures or **improvement opportunities** (such as a review of recruitment and selection methods).

Short-term projects pose particular time constraints on building and managing a successful team. The challenge for project managers and co-ordinators is to accelerate the process of team development, while at the same time keeping pace with the immediate targets set out in the project plan.

3 Virtual and self-managed teams

It is no longer essential that teams have all their members in a single location, or even have a single formal leader. Virtual teams function via electronic links; self-managed teams collaborate to discharge most routine management functions themselves.

3.1 Virtual teams

The development of information and communications technology has enabled communication and collaboration among people at a diverse and far-flung range of locations, via teleconferencing and video-conferencing, locally networked PCs and the internet.

The Chartered Institute of Marketing

This has created the concept of the **virtual team:** an interconnected group of people who may never be present in the same office – and may even be on different sides of the world – but who share information and tasks, make joint decisions and fulfil the collaborative functions of a physical team.

Solomon (2001) describes the virtual team as follows:

> 'Virtual teams may be composed of full-time or part-time employees. They might have a global reach, or involve combinations of local telecommuting members and more traditional in-house workers. A senior executive might be on one planning committee for a product release, for example, another for identifying minority vendors, another to study relocating a plant, and another to evaluate software tracking. He may deal with key players who not only are out of the country but also are working for another company, or perhaps as suppliers who are on the virtual team to add information and technical support.'

Localised virtual teams have been used for some time in the form of **teleworking:** the process of working from home, or from a satellite office close to home, with the aid of computers, facsimile machines, modems or other forms of telecommunication equipment. The main benefits cited for such work include savings on office overheads and the elimination of the costs and stresses of commuting for employees.

More recently, however, the globalisation of business, the need for fast responses to marketplace demands and the increasing sophistication of available technologies has brought about an explosion in global virtual team working.

More and more organisations are attempting to conduct business 24 hours a day, seven days a week, with people on different continents and in different time zones. Electronic collaboration allows organisations to do the following:

(a) Recruit and collaborate with the best available people without the constraints of **location** or **relocation**. A team can co-opt a specialist when required, from a global pool of skills.

(b) Offer more **scheduling flexibility** for people who prefer non-traditional working hours (including the handicapped and working parents, for example).

(c) Maintain close contact with customers **throughout the world**.

(d) Operate **24-hour working days** (for example, for global customer support) – without having to have staff on night shifts.

3.2 Self-managed teams

Self-managed teams are the most highly-developed form of team working. They are permanent structures in which team members collaboratively decide all the major issues affecting their work: work processes and schedules, task allocation, the selection and development of team members, the distribution of rewards and the management of group processes (problem-solving, conflict management, internal discipline and so on).

The team leader is a member of the team, acting in the role of coach and facilitator: leadership roles may be shared or rotated as appropriate.

Self-managed teams generally have the following features:

- They contract with management to assume various degrees of **managerial responsibility** for planning, organising, directing and monitoring (which may increase as the team develops).

- Team members learn and share the jobs usually performed by a manager: no 'visible' immediate manager is present. They often report to 'absentee' managers with broad responsibilities for several functions, whose role is to act as integrators/facilitators.

- They perform **day-to-day planning and control functions:** scheduling and co-ordinating the daily and occasional tasks of the team and individuals; setting performance goals and standards; formulating and adopting budgets; collecting performance data and reviewing results.

- They perform **internal people management functions:** screening and interviewing candidates to join the team, and contributing to selection/hiring decisions; providing orientation for new members; coaching and providing feedback on member performance; designing and conducting cross-training on all tasks.

- Team members cross-train in all the tasks necessary for a particular process, and members rotate flexibly from job to job.

- Weekly team meetings are used to identify, analyse and solve task and relationship problems within the team: reviewing team working and progress; getting team members to research and present team issues and so on.

Self-managed team working is said to have advantages in:

- Saving in managerial costs
- Gains in quality and productivity, by harnessing the commitment of those who perform work

4 Organisational life phases

Organisations are required to adapt, reflect and reason to change. Greiner's organisational growth model (1972) provides a framework against which managers can derive a framework within which they can understand their circumstances as a basis for decision making.

Greiner's (1972) model indentifies five stages of growth, summarised with the table below.

Table 5.3   Greiner's five stages of growth

Stage	Features
1 **Creativity**	■ An entrepreneurial organisation finds a niche in the market ■ Those involved in the business are product or technology-focused ■ Solutions to managerial problems tends to be viewed in terms of better technology and more new products rather than strategic direction and management ■ SMEs can get stuck at this level as the owner/manager fails to put in place the management resource necessary to grow the business
2 **Direction**	■ Appropriate management structures, financial controls and planning procedures are put in place to enable next phase of growth and development ■ Speed and pace of change means decisions need to be taken closer to where the action occurs
3 **Delegation**	■ Decision making becomes decentralised ■ Senior management sets performance criteria and operational management runs the business ■ Greater freedom given to managers which can lead to conflicting action to the overall mission of the organisation
4 **Coordination**	■ A better solution than increased control and regulation is to look for more effective ways of co-ordinating activities
5 **Collaboration**	■ As the organisation grows co-ordination becomes more difficult to manage ■ Further evolution of the organisation is achieved through such techniques as team building, matrix structures and process orientation

While this framework does not provide a description of solutions it helps managers understand the influences upon the organisation and possible routes to a solution.

Figure 5.1   Greiner's growth model (1972)

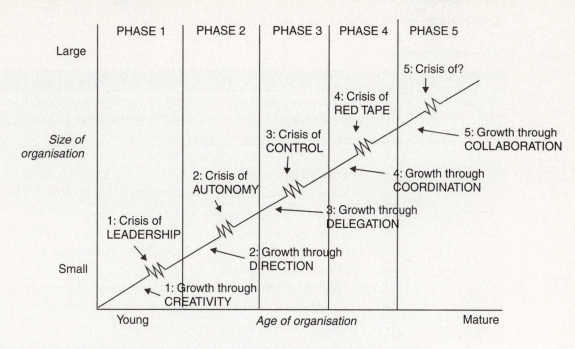

5 The importance of corporate culture on marketing strategy

> **▶ Key term**
>
> **Culture:** '…a pattern of basic assumptions that a given group has invented, discovered, or developed in learning to cope with its problems of external adaptation and internal integration, a pattern of assumptions that has worked well enough to be considered valid, and therefore, to be taught to new members as the correct way to perceive, think and feel in relation to those problems'.
>
> Schein (1993)

Culture represents a problematic but extremely powerful integrating mechanism for organisations. Organisations function coherently as a result of the 'glue' provided by culture (Ouchi, 1980). Cultures develop over time and become stable entities that can be relied upon to respond in specific ways to given stimuli.

Schein (1993) distinguishes three layers that comprise organisational culture:

(a) **Basic assumptions**

Fundamental beliefs that are shared within the organisation.

(b) **Values**

Principles that guide social interaction, constituting a goal in themselves because of their intrinsic value.

(c) **Artefacts**

Historical artefacts are the most tangible or visible manifestation of the way the organisation has previously worked and include rituals and practices.

5.1 Types of culture

Charles Handy (1976) identifies four types of culture:

Table 5.4   Four types of culture

Cultural type	Features
Role culture	<ul><li>Typical of hierarchies in which the job and pace within an organisation is well defined</li><li>Personal power is derived from the job and its position within the hierarch.</li><li>Encourages introversion and bureaucracy</li><li>Can develop a 'silo mentality' where cross functional communication is poor</li><li>Inflexible and slow to change</li><li>Typical of larger organisations and those in which routine processing is the norm</li></ul>
Power culture	<ul><li>This culture is best described as a 'web'.</li><li>A few people in the organisation have power and their connections radiate out in a 'web-like' way.</li><li>Flexible and quick to change as a few but highly significant people have power</li><li>Encourages congruent thinking</li><li>Can become 'political' as members associate themselves with the powerbrokers</li><li>Typical of family businesses and organisations with charismatic leaders</li></ul>
Task culture	<ul><li>Focused on task completion and problem-solving with success judged on outcomes</li><li>Structure is flexible and dynamic, drawing on the task in hand</li><li>Draws on skills and capabilities of individuals in the organisation who are respected regardless of their place in the hierarchy</li><li>An organisation supporting this culture is typically a matrix. Typical of many consulting organisations</li></ul>
Person culture	<ul><li>Not very typical of many organisations</li><li>Individuals become stars in the organisation and have substantial power due to their knowledge and expertise.</li><li>While these experts are brought together by the common interest of the organisation they exert a high level of individual discretion.</li><li>Typical amongst professional partnerships such as legal firms, advertising agencies and so on</li></ul>

Giddens (1984) discusses structure as the society we inhabit. In effect the organisation that we work for has a set of rules and procedures in place, and resources available to it. Resources tend to be constrained and this sets limits or boundaries on what we are able to do.

This suggests that in order to bring about change and ensure the successful implementation of our marketing strategy, simply changing the organisation will not have the desired effect.

Giddens identifies the central role of rules and resources. When you first join an organisation you learn the 'way things are done around here'. All of these norms are part of the social structure. These processes and procedures are prescribed.

As Handy (1976) suggests, the organisational structure overlays the social structure and this sets boundaries on the degree of discretion and the opportunity for participation that is available.

To bring about change we need to question some of these activities. We also know that there are ways around the rules and procedures and things we can do to get the job done, despite the rules, rather than because of them.

So in bringing about change we need to think about the intangible as well as the tangible things, typically based around the way that people think, act and behave.

The McKinsey 7s Model is a useful tool for helping us understand this.

The Chartered Institute of Marketing

Figure 5.2 The McKinsey 7s model

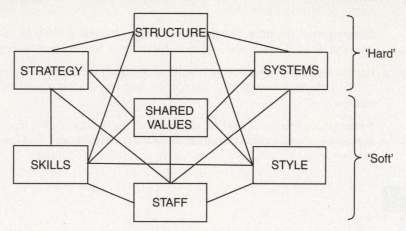

Three of the elements were considered 'hard' originally, but in today's context they are becoming more flexible.

(a) **Structure**. The organisation structure determines division of tasks in the organisation and the hierarchy of authority from the most senior to junior. As discussed above, today's company is likely to be made up of flat, empowered networks.

(b) **Strategy**. Strategy is the way in which the organisation plans to outperform its competitors; it will be market-led.

(c) **Systems**. Systems include the technical systems of accounting, personnel, management information and so on, with particular emphasis on how market-related information is distributed and used.

The McKinsey model suggests that the 'soft' elements are equally important.

(d) **Shared values** lie at the heart of the organisation and are the guiding principles for the people in it. They are vital for developing the motivation to drive the organisation to achieve.

(e) **Staff** are the people in the organisation. They have their own complex concerns and priorities. The successful organisation will recruit the right staff and develop their motivation to pursue the right goals.

(f) **Style** is another aspect of the corporate culture, and includes the shared assumptions, ways of working and attitudes of senior management.

(g) **Skills** are the core competences that enable the company to create value in a particular way. The importance of the 'soft' elements for success was emphasised by Peters and Waterman (1982) in their study of 'excellent' companies.

The cultural web

Corporate culture involves a learned set of behaviours that is common knowledge to all the stakeholders within the organisation. This should help to promote a shared set of meanings which guide the employees and other key stakeholders within the organisation.

Culture should help individuals and groups share particular patterns of behaviour; culture can evolve and change overtime, and often with new leadership and management the culture changes accordingly. The cultural paradigm, which includes the following, has often been referred to as the key components of culture (the cultural web) within an organisation (www.mindtools.com).

- **Stories:** the past events and people talked about inside and outside the company. Who and what the company chooses to immortalise says a great deal about what it values, and perceives as great behaviour.

- **Rituals and routines:** the daily behaviour and actions of people that signal acceptable behaviour. This determines what is expected to happen in given situations, and what is valued by management.

- **Symbols:** the visual representations of the company including logos, how plush the offices are, and the formal or informal dress codes.

- **Organisational structure:** this includes both the structure defined by the organisation chart and the unwritten lines of power and influence that indicate whose contributions are most valued.

- **Control systems:** the ways in which the organisation is controlled. These include financial systems, quality systems, and rewards (including the way they are measured and distributed within the organisation).

- **Power structures:** the pockets of real power in the company. This may involve one or two key senior executives, a whole group of executives, or even a department. The key is that these people have the greatest amount of influence on decisions, operations and strategic direction.

ACTIVITY 5.2

Critically evaluate your own organisational and apply the McKinsey 7s model to your organisation. Make recommendations of the changes required to your organisation.

6 The importance of communications in the implementation of marketing strategy

6.1 Communications and vision, mission and strategy

The role of strategic communications is to clarify what the mission and vision mean to people internally and what markets can expect from the organisation.

The purpose is then reinforced through planned communication activities. Marketing communications signal future intentions and aspirations in the market.

Fundamental to the believability of the messages is credibility. Developing credibility underlies the messages of the organisation's purpose and vision and therefore its capabilities and competences are given prominence. Since capabilities and competences are delivered through people, credibility depends to a large extent on their performance.

Competitive positioning and growth strategies depend on effective marketing communications to achieve the overall goal. Organisations must ensure than any messages about what customers can expect can and will be matched by their experiences.

Marketers have a duty to ensure that communications do not raise expectations or make claims that will not or cannot be met.

6.2 Communications, culture and management style

Trust and respect can be passed on to customers through employee attitudes to service. Customers will either have an impersonal experience where they do not feel valued or a personal experience where expectations are met or exceeded.

6.3 Communications strategy

Fill (2009) has identified three important dimensions to communications:

(a) **Pull strategies**

    (i)   Targeted at customers, consumers and end-users

The Chartered Institute of Marketing

(ii)   Designed to pull customers into 'outlets'

(iii)   Key to this strategy are generating awareness, forming attitudes and motivating behaviour that ultimately result in demand availability of the brand.

(b)   **Push strategies**

(i)   Targeted at channels or networks that provide the brand

(ii)   Key to this strategy is encouraging suppliers to hold stocks and allocate resources to actively sell the brand.

(c)   **Profile strategies**

(i)   Strategic and targeted at all stakeholders of the organisation, both internal and external

(ii)   Key to this strategy are the creating, building and maintaining of the desired image of the organisation, what it stands for and its reputation.

6.4 Communication and change management

The need to communicate change is as important as the change itself. The communication needs to be clear and understood. The content and the actual delivery of the communication is important, the key content of the message regarding change may need to be communicated over a period of time rather than just being a one off occurance. This also means providing enough information as is available. The delivery of the message also needs to be reiterated by management to ensure all those at different levels of the organisation are engaged and can 'buy into' the change. The communication also needs to be two way to ensure that anything that has not been covered can be in the future. A change management communication plan that engages stakeholders both internally and externally may need to be implemented.

6.5 The role of internal marketing

Marketing knowledge should be part of an internal marketing system and internal marketing can be one of the most powerful activities management can engage in.

- It communicates management intentions and expectations.
- It informs, educates and persuades employees regarding intended courses of action.
- It motivates.
- It clarifies responsibilities.

Internal marketing is an activity that unites the workforce behind the organisation's mission and strategy.

By communicating management intentions of an intended strategy it minimises any potential conflict that may arise. It provides a better understanding of why an organisation is following a particular direction.

For it to be successful, senior management must be committed to the concept of internal marketing and be prepared to commit resources to it. Open communication, honesty and trust should be a cultural norm and attention to developing communication skills part of everyone's development.

In developing an internal marketing strategy you should consider the following:

(a)   **Objectives**

These might include:

(i)   Uniting the workforce behind organisational goals

(ii)   Promoting organisational change

(iii)   Encouraging sharing and living the organisation's values

(iv)   Encouraging commitment to customer service

The purpose of the internal marketing programme determines the style and tone. During times of change education and information are important.

During times of difficulty, reassurance and transparency take priority.

(a) **Stakeholders**

Identify internal stakeholders and their perceptions and expectations, what their needs, motives and concerns are, and design messages accordingly.

(b) **Communications**

You need to consider what messages need to be communicated, through what mechanisms and how. The more difficult the situation the more personal the communication should become.

(c) **Alliances**

Alliances involve personnel exchanges across different departments. These can promote better relationships and will encourage cross-functional networking, break down barriers and improve idea and information sharing.

Such alliances can take the form of secondments, shadowing, presentations or briefings.

(d) **Training and development**

Ensure people are equipped with the necessary knowledge and skills to facilitate internal marketing such as improved networking skills, communication skills and so on.

(e) **Appraisals and feedback**

As part of the internal marketing programme they should reflect components of the objectives of the programme.

(f) **Control**

An internal marketing communications plan requires a budget, schedule and performance measurement, so ensure you apply as much effort to this as to the wider communications strategy.

Since marketing is often the driver of change it should therefore take responsibility, in collaboration with others, for internal marketing, aligning people behind organisational goals and strategy, and encouraging a behavioural norm that leads to excellent customer service. Developing an internal marketing strategy is a relatively new challenge for marketers and is not helped by structures that separate marketing activities.

The fundamental thinking of internal marketing is based on the principle that satisfied and highly motivated employees will be better aware of customer needs. Based on the latter, internal marketing focuses on the principle that if internal employees are satisfied it will benefit the organisation. Kotler (2000) stated that internal marketing should precede external marketing. In addition to this, Ahmed and Rafiq (2004) stated that there are five key elements to internal marketing:

(1) Employee motivation and satisfaction;
(2) Customer orientation and customer satisfaction;
(3) Inter-function co-ordination and integration;
(4) Marketing-like approach to the above;
(5) Implementation of specific corporate and functional strategies.

Key authors have suggested that organisations need to apply the external concept of external marketing to the organisation internally, in as much as an internal marketing mix should be developed for the organisation.

A clear internal marketing plan and strategy should also help to identify any skill gaps within the organisation. It should also help to assess employee expectations from the management and leadership team. This will further develop and identify the required organisational changes and the necessary communication strategies

The Chartered Institute of Marketing

that are required or need to be implemented to ensure the overall aim and goals of the organisation are achieved.

ACTIVITY 5.3

Choosing an industry of your choice critically evaluate how the implementation of internal marketing across organisations from one sector could help organisations to better respond to changing external needs.

7 Improving marketing management

▶ **Assessment tip**

An important aspect of the process of assessing resources is ensuring that you have the right people with the right skills doing the right things. Task 4 on the December 2009/March 2010 assignment concerned the analysis of leadership skills and the approach required in order to successfully implement a marketing plan.

The June 2011 assignment also focused on critically analysing the changes required to realign the proposed marketing strategy to the new value proposition as well as critically evaluating the different approaches to leadership that would be appropriate to bring about the necessary changes identified.

Developing and improving the marketing skills and capabilities of the organisation starts with an assessment of the overall learning and development needs.

7.1 Skills assessment

Skills assessment should aim to establish current competence, required competence, and any gap that may exist between the two. You will need to assess strengths and weaknesses, and prioritise these in terms of essential strengths and undesirable weaknesses.

Skills assessment can be achieved by or through:

- Performance appraisals with managers, where skills will be identified
- Diagnostic tests, from (for example) simple questionnaires to sophisticated psychometric tests
- Feedback from colleagues and peers

Skills assessment should be undertaken at all levels of the organisation from the front-line staff, to middle management and even at leadership and management level. It is important to identify the key gaps in the skills as this will then determine whether a particular marketing strategy can be achieved or not. Assessing the skills gap can also help to identify personal development plans for individuals, training required as well as the resource requirements to ensure the organisation can develop appropriately.

7.2 Learning and development objectives

Once it is understood where an organisation wants to improve the next step is to set clear objectives.

7.3 Skills development

The next step is to identify opportunities for development and improvement. This can be achieved through a combination of on-the-job and blended learning techniques.

ACTIVITY 5.4

Critically evaluate your own personal development needs against the current marketing strategy. Assessing your own role within the organisation. Outline the key skills you need to develop and what training you need to fulfil your role within the organisation.

8 Budgets

The **principal budget factor** should be identified at the beginning of the budgetary process. It is often sales volume and so the sales budget has to be produced before all the others.

A **budget** is a consolidated statement of the resources required to achieve objectives or to implement planned activities. It is a planning and control tool relevant to all aspects of management activities.

8.1 Purposes of a budget

- **Co-ordinates** the activities of all the different departments of an organisation; in addition, through participation by employees in preparing a budget, it may be possible to motivate them to raise their targets and standards and to achieve better results.

- **Communicates** the policies and targets to every manager in the organisation responsible for carrying out a part of that plan.

- **Control** by having a plan against which actual results can be progressively compared.

8.2 Preparing budgets

Procedures for preparing the budget are contained in the **budget manual**, which indicates:

- People responsible for preparing budgets
- The order in which they must be prepared
- Deadlines for preparation
- Standard forms

The preparation and administration of budgets is usually the responsibility of a **budget committee**. Every part of the organisation should be represented on the committee.

The preparation of a budget may take weeks or months, and the budget committee may meet several times before the master budget is finally agreed. Functional budgets and cost centre budgets prepared in draft may need to be amended many times over as a consequence of discussions between departments, changes in market conditions, reversals of decisions by management and so on during the course of budget preparation.

8.3 The budget period

A budget does not necessarily have to be restricted to a one-year planning horizon. The factors which should influence the **budget period** are as follows:

- **Times**. A plan decided upon now might need a **considerable time** to be put into operation. Many companies expect growth in market share to take a number of years.

- **In the short-term some resources are fixed**. The fixed nature of these resources, and the length of time which must elapse before they become variable, might therefore determine the planning horizon for budgeting.

- All budgets involve some element of **forecasting and even guesswork**, since future events cannot be quantified with accuracy.

- Since **unforeseen events** cannot be planned for; it would be a waste of time to plan in detail too far ahead.

- Most budgets are prepared over a one-year period to enable managers to plan and control **financial results for the purposes of the annual accounts**.

8.4 The principal budget factor

The first task in budgeting is to identify the principal (key, limiting) budget factor. This is the factor which puts constraints on growth. The principal budget factor could be:

- Normally, sales demand: ie a company is restricted from making and selling more of its products because there would be no sales demand for the increased output at a price which would be acceptable/profitable to the company

- Resources: machine capacity, distribution and selling resources, the availability of key raw materials or the availability of cash

Once this factor is defined then the rest of the budget can be prepared.

8.5 Methods of setting the marketing budget

Table 5.5   Methods of setting the marketing budget

Method	Comment
Competitive parity	Fixing promotional expenditure in relation to the expenditure incurred by competitors. (This is unsatisfactory because it presupposes that the competitor's decision must be a good one.)
The task method (or objective and task method)	The marketing task for the organisation is set and a promotional budget is prepared which will help to ensure that this objective is achieved. A problem occurs if the objective is achieved only by paying out more on promotion than the extra profits obtained would justify.
Communication stage models	These are based on the idea that the link between promotion and sales cannot be measured directly, but can be measured by means of intermediate stages (for example, increase in awareness, comprehension, and then intention to buy).

Method	Comment
All you can afford	Crude and unscientific, but commonly used. The firm simply takes a view on what it thinks it can afford to spend on promotion given that it would like to spend as much as it can.
Investment	The advertising and promotions budget can be designed around the amount felt necessary to maintain a certain brand value.
Rule-of-thumb, non-scientific methods	These include the percentage of sales, profits and so on.

8.6 Budgetary control

One of the purposes for which budgets are used is to provide an input into the corporate control system. Their use for control purposes is enhanced by detailed analysis of **variances** and **ratios**.

8.7 Variance analysis

It is fine to have a set of budgets and standards, but how do you apply them in practice? The use of budgets as a control device is often achieved through **variance analysis**. Quite complex variance analysis systems are applied to production costs: these need not concern us here, but a brief description of the technique might help, as it is relevant to marketing costs.

Other applications of sales variances include the **sales mix variance**. A firm might sell more of one product in a range and less of another than you anticipated, or there might have been some difference in prices. Variances can also be used in analysing other marketing costs, such as distribution expenditure.

8.8 Tolerance limits for variances at planning level

No corporate plan has the detail or accuracy that a budget has. Consequently, the tolerance limits giving early warning of deviations from the plan should be wider. For example, if tolerance limits in budgetary control are variance ± 5% from standard, then corporate planning tolerance limits might be set at ± 10% or more from targets.

Whatever the tolerance limits are, the reporting of results which go outside (either favourably or adversely) the limits must be prompt. If sales have dropped well below target, the reasons must be established quickly and possible solutions thought about. For example, if a company's products unexpectedly gain second highest market share, the questions that should be asked are:

- How did it happen?
- Has profit suffered?
- Can second place be made secure, and if so, how?
- Can the market leader be toppled? (And if so, is this profitable?)

8.9 Ratio analysis

Ratio analysis is a very important aspect of performance measurement. However, it is important to remember that the computation of ratios is in itself an almost worthless exercise: like most numerical information, ratios are only of value if they are **assessed for their significance**.

Generally speaking, the value of ratios lies in the making of comparisons year-on-year and, sometimes, between comparable functions, projects or operations.

The Chartered Institute of Marketing

8.10 Corporate ratios

The main corporate ratios are return on capital employed and, in the case of a quoted company, the price/earnings ratio. Marketing strategies **contribute** towards these, but they are at **too high a level of control** to be useful as control measures over marketing activities in particular.

- **Profitability**. Marketing personnel have little direct control over the cost structure of the company, and so while they do contribute to profitability, they cannot control it.

- **Return on Capital Employed (ROCE)**, as conventionally measured, is a control measure for the company as a whole.

Marketing relevant ratios are a **mix of financial ratios and non-financial ratios**.

For example:

(a) **Financial ratio only**

(i) Sales revenue or marketing expenditure can be compared: **over time**, against **budget** or against **competition**.

	20X7	20X8
Revenue	£10m	£15m

20X7/20X8 gives an increase of 1.5:1.

(ii) There may be relationships between different variables. For example

	20X7	20X8
Revenue	£10m	£15m
Bad debts	0.5m	1.2m
Bad debts/revenue	1:20 or 5%	2:25 or 8%

Comparing these over time suggests that while **income has increased**, the **quality of sales** (in terms of **creditworthiness**) has fallen, as bad debts are 8% of revenue rather than 5%. Perhaps the sales force has been too generous.

(b) **A mixture of financial ratios and non-financial data**

	20X7	20X8
Revenue	£10m	£15m
Sales personnel	50	60

Revenue has increased by 50% whereas the sales force has increased by 20%.

	20X7	20X8
Revenue per sales employee	£0.2m	£0.25m

The sales force is more productive in 20X8 than in 20X7.

(c) **Non-financial data only**

This can refer to almost any aspect of a company's operations. We are concerned with marketing.

	20X7	20X8
Sales orders	250	300
Sales leads	1,000	1,025
Sales personnel	50	60

9 Effective marketing feedback and control systems

Special problems occur in marketing feedback and control systems because markets are made up of people and therefore are not very predictable.

Marketing feedback and control systems need to recognise the volatile nature of human beings. After all, markets are people or rather people's wants and needs, modified by affordability and availability.

Problems of unsatisfactory feedback and control can occur.

(a)   People change.
(b)   Reasons for change are not always apparent or identifiable.
(c)   The same product can be bought by the same person for different purposes.
(d)   Delays occur in the system due to suppliers being remote from consumers.
(e)   Competitor actions can seriously affect the systems.
(f)   Rarely is complete information affordable so that inadequacies occur in feedback.
(g)   Distortions inevitably occur in the data transfer between people. The more often the data is transcribed the more distortion will occur.

There is a need for **information feedback at each stage of the marketing process**.

(a)   Only if marketing managers are kept informed of what is happening and what is likely to happen, can they make sensible decisions. For example, **contingency planning depends upon 'what if' scenarios**. Only when managers receive information indicating a particular scenario is taking place can the right contingency plan be invoked. The information in this case acts as an identifier, a selector and a trigger.

(b)   The dimensions of marketing feedback and control systems are in fact wide-ranging and flexible. One of the most important marketing planning philosophies is to avoid a *laissez faire*, complacent attitude to good news. We need to remember that **good sales figures represent the past situation**, so we need to worry about the future longer-term survival and growth.

Some items have greater immediacy than others. Failure to act on a serious complaint could lead to the loss of an important customer, adversely affecting future sales and profitability.

9.1 Basic control concepts

Basic control systems depend upon comparing results with plans: single loop feedback produces control action to modify performance; double loop feedback is used to modify the plan itself.

A good starting point in thinking about basic control concepts is to take the example of driving a car. In doing this we receive various **feedbacks** such as visual feedback to tell us if we are driving in the right direction, in the correct position on the road, at the right speed and so on. Instruments such as the speedometer and our senses – eyes, touch (vibration) provide the basic data.

We measure this data against **standards** such as the speed limit, the Highway Code and laws and so on and, where necessary, take **corrective action** using control devices like the steering wheel and the accelerator.

The marketing planning and implementation process follows similar precepts. We cannot implement a plan in the first place until we know where we are going. In planning where we are going we need to know where we are now. It also helps if we know where we have come from.

Figure 5.3 Generic control system

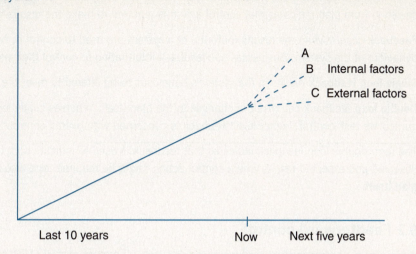

A
B   Internal factors
C   External factors

Last 10 years   Now   Next five years

The past determines not only where we are now relative to it but also our **future direction** (extrapolation of past trend assuming no change = position B).

Control is, however, only partial in marketing.

(a)   We can change internal factors (ie the 7 Ps) positively so as to aim for position A.

However, external factors (political, economic, sociological, technological and competition) might act positively or negatively, in the latter case dragging us down to position C.

(b)   Nevertheless, the more information we have about the so-called uncontrollable external factors, the more we can anticipate, ride or avoid the blows.

Here is a diagram of a **generic control system**.

Figure 5.4 Control system

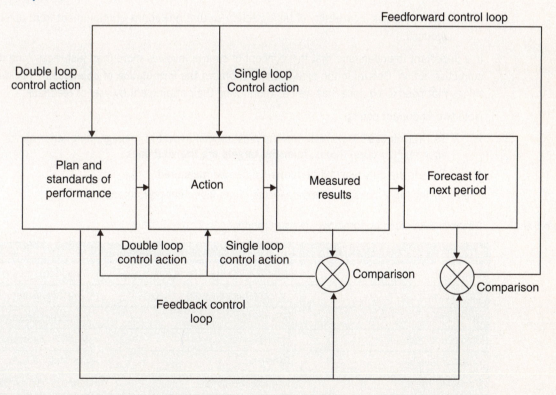

The essence of control is the measurement of results and comparison of them with the original plan. Any deviation from plan indicates that control action is required to make the results conform more closely with plan.

Feedback occurs when the results (outputs) of a system are used to control it, by adjusting the input or behaviour of the system. Businesses use feedback information to control their performance.

Single loop feedback results in the system's behaviour being altered to meet the plan.

Double loop feedback can result in changes to the plan itself. Whereas single loop feedback is concerned with immediate task control, higher level feedback is concerned with overall control.

The term double loop feedback indicates that feedback is used to indicate both divergence between the observed and expected results where control action might be required, and also the need for **adjustments to the plan itself**.

9.2 Feedforward control

▶ **Key term**

Feedforward control uses anticipated or forecast results, and compares them with the plan. Corrective action is thus taken in advance, before it is too late to do anything effective. Control is exercised before the results, rather than after the event.

Emmanuel *et al* (1990) describe four necessary conditions that must be satisfied before any process can be said to be controlled. These will help us to put control into a wider context still.

(a) Objectives for the process being controlled must exist, for without an aim or purpose control has no meaning.

(b) The output of the process must be measurable in terms of the dimensions defined by the objectives.

(c) A predictive model of the process being controlled is required so that causes for the non-attainment of objectives can be determined and proposed corrective actions evaluated.

(d) There must be a capability of taking action so that deviations of attainment from objectives can be reduced.

It is important to understand that this concept of control involves more than just measuring results and taking corrective action. Control in the broad sense embraces **the formulation of objectives** – deciding what are the things that need to be done – as well as monitoring their attainment by way of feedback.

Note two important points:

■ As Drucker (1999) pointed out, the most crucial aspect of management performance in business is economic success: that is, **financial targets are the vital ones**.

■ Targets are only useful if performance can be **measured**.

The following table looks at different aspects of management performance.

Table 5.6 Different aspects of performance measurements

Feedback	Standards	Control actions
Sales figures	Against budget plus or minus	Stimulate/dampen down demand
Complaints	Number, frequency, seriousness	Corrective action
Competitors	Relative to us	Attack/defence strategies
Market size changes	Market share	Marketing mix manipulation
Costs/profitability	Ratios	Cost cutting exercises
Corporate image	Attribute measures	Internal/external communications
Environmental factors	Variances from norm	Invoke strategic alternatives

10 Features of basic strategic control systems

Control must influence the behaviour of individuals and groups towards the implementation of the corporate strategy and towards progressive change.

(a) **Distinguish between control at different levels** in the management hierarchy (strategic, tactical, operational). Is the control measure intended to have an immediate impact (for example, 'firefighting', at an operational control or budgetary level) or will it take time for the measure to have a tangible effect?

    (i) Define **strategic objectives** (ie the organisation's eventual objectives in terms of competitive strategy).

    (ii) Identify **strategic milestones** on the way to achieving strategic objectives. These could be the specific tasks by which strategic objectives are achieved. These are short-term steps along the way to long-term goals.

    (iii) The **key assumptions** on which the strategy is based must also be monitored. A strategy drawn up from a position of limited competition (eg a protected national market) would have to be changed if the market was opened to foreign companies.

(b) **Individual managers** should be identified as having the responsibility for certain matters, and authority to take control measures.

(c) The **key factors for control** should be identified. Managers responsible for taking control action must be informed about what the key factors are, and why they are critical.

(d) **Control reporting should be timed sensibly**. Depending on the level of control, control reports should vary from occasional to regular and frequent.

(e) Apply targets and standards.

    ■ Targets for market share, in absolute and relative terms, compared with competitors'
    ■ Targets for relative product quality
    ■ Timetables for strategic action programmes
    ■ Targets for costs relative to the competitors' costs

(f) Control reports should only contain **relevant information** for the manager receiving the report.

(g) **Selective reporting**. Selective reporting means identifying **key points for control**.

    (i) The **position of each product** in the product-market matrix or in its life cycle will suggest how much close watching the product needs.

    (ii) A product which performs **inconsistently** might need close watching and control.

    (iii) **Information and control reporting costs money**.

    (iv) The **key item might be qualitative**. For example, within the marketing function it might be considered vitally important that there should be a rapid and significant improvement in employee commitment and enthusiasm. Control reporting at the corporate planning level should therefore emphasise these points, and shift back to other matters when appropriate.

10.1 The trade-off between short-term and long-term for control action

It is often the case that in order to rectify short-term results, control action will be at the expense of long-term targets.

Similarly, controls over longer-term achievements might call for short-term sacrifices.

Examples of the reasons for short-term/long-term trade-offs are as follows:

(a) **Short-term losses**

A company has a target of building up its market share for a new product to 30% within four years. It has decided to do this with a low price market penetration strategy. As a short-term target, it wants the product to earn a small profit (£100,000) in the current year. Actual results after three months of the year indicate that the market share has already built up to 18%, but that the product will make a £50,000 loss in the year. The short-term/long-term (S/L) trade-off involves a decision about what to do about short-term profitability (raise prices? cut back on advertising? reduce the sales force?) without sacrificing altogether the long-term market share target.

(b) **Capital expenditure**

There is a trade off with short-term costs against long-term benefits. It can mean that there is a reduction in short-term profits.

(c) **Research and development**

This is another area where short-term profitability is boosted, by cutting back on R&D expenditure at the expense of the longer-term need to continue to develop new products.

(d) **Behaviour**

Very often managers are under pressure to produce good short-term results (for example, immediate profitability) in order to get their next promotion.

10.2 Ensuring that the short-term/long-term trade-off is properly judged and well balanced

- Managers should **recognise** whether or not S/L trade-offs in control action could be a serious problem.

- **Managers should be aware** that S/L trade-offs take place in practice.

- Controls should exist to prevent or minimise the possibility that short-term controls can be taken which damage long-term targets.

- Senior management must be given **adequate control information** for long-term as well as short-term consequences.

- The planning and review system should **motivate** managers to keep long-term goals in view.

- **Short-term goals should be realistic**. Very often, the pressure on managers to sacrifice long-term interests for short-term results is caused by the imposition of stringent and unrealistic short-term targets on those managers in the first place.

- **Performance measures should reflect both long-term and short-term targets**. There might be, say, quarterly performance reviews on the achievement of strategic goals.

The Chartered Institute of Marketing

> **Assessment tip**

The marketing leadership and planning assignments in one context or another require candidates to assess the competency of the organisation's workforce; this can include assessing the resources required and critically evaluating the culture of the organisation to identifying leadership skill gaps. This then impacts the personal development needs of individuals within the organisation. It is important that candidates have a sound understanding of the resource implications at a broad level rather than focusing merely on the budget.

Resource analysis needs to include a critical evaluation of the structure and its alignment with the organisation's vision and mission. A clear understanding is required of the organisation's systems and processes in place and how they help or potentially hinder the strategic goals of the organisation. Levels of competency within the organisation also need to be assessed so appropriate changes can be recommended at a corporate level. Fundamental to these recommendations is ensuring a clear funding framework is identified to ensure that marketing strategy can be developed effectively and that the candidate has a realistic understanding of the financial resources available.

CHAPTER ROUNDUP

- There are a number of different organisational structures: hierarchical, functional, product/market, divisional and matrix.

- Teams in organisations can be multi-disciplinary, multi-skilled, or project teams.

- Virtual and self-managed teams can involve the team having to use their own initiative as well as following the core philosophy of the business.

- Different organisational life phases can influence management decision making; the following are the life stages: creativity, direction, delegation, co-ordination and collaboration.

- There are many different types of culture: role culture, power culture, task culture and person culture.

- Communications is the means with which to understand the vision, mission and strategy.

- Internal marketing is often regarded as the part of marketing that needs further consideration and development as most businesses tend to focus on external marketing activities.

- Leadership requires leaders to reflect and understand the skills they possess or need to develop in order to implement the marketing strategies.

- Evaluation, feedback and control are a central part of the planning process.

FURTHER READING

De Wit, B. and Meyer, R. (2005) *Strategy synthesis: resolving strategy paradoxes to create competitive advantage, test and readings.* 2nd edition. London, Thomson.

Doyle, P. and Stern, P. (2006) *Marketing management and strategy.* 4th edition. Harlow, Prentice Hall.

Hooley, G. *et al* (2007) *Marketing strategy and competitive positioning.* 4th edition. Harlow, Prentice Hall.

McDonald, M. (2007) *Marketing plans: how to prepare them, how to use them.* 6th edition. Oxford, Butterworth-Heinemann.

REFERENCES

Ahmed, P.K. and Rafiq, M. (2004) *Internal marketing: tool and concepts for customer focused management.* Oxford, Butterworth-Heinemann.

Baker, M. and Hart, S. (2008) *The marketing book* (6th edition). Oxford, Butterworth-Heinemann.

De Wit, B. and Meyer, R. (2005) *strategy synthesis: resolving strategy paradoxes to create competitive advantage.* 2nd edition. London, Cengage.

Drucker, P. (1999) *Management challenges for the 21st century.* New York, Harper Business.

Emmanuel, C.R., Otley, D.T. and Merchant, K. (1990) *Accounting for management control.* Thomson Learning, London.

Fill C (2009) *Marketing Communications, Interactively, Communities and Content*, 5th edition. FT Prentice Hall, Harlow, UK.

The Chartered Institute of Marketing

Giddens, A. (1984) *The constitution of society. Outline of the theory of structuration.* Cambridge, Cambridge University Press.

Greiner, L.E. (1972) Evolution and revolution as organizations grow. *Harvard Business Review*, July/August, pp55-60, 62-6, 68, Vol.76, Issue 3.

Handy, C. (1976) *Understanding organizations*, 3rd edition. Harmondsworth, Penguin Books.

Kotler, P. (2000) *Marketing management analysis, planning: implementation and control.* 10th edition, Englewood Cliffs, NJ, Prentice Hall.

Mintzberg, H. (1990) Strategy formation: schools of thought. *In:* Fredrickson, J. (ed) *Perspectives on strategic management*. Boston, MA, Ballinger pp105-235.

Ouchi, W.G. (1990) *Administrative Science Quarterly*, 25, pp129-141.

Peters T. & Waterman R. (1982) *In Search of Excellence: lessons from America's Best-Run Companies*. New York, Harper-Row Publishers.

Palmer, J., Cockton J., and Cooper, G., (2007) *Managing marketing*. 1st edition. Oxford, Butterworth-Heinemann.

Ranchhod, A. and Gurau, C. (2007) *Marketing strategies: a twenty-first century approach*. 2nd edition, London, FT Prentice Hall.

Schein, E. (1993) Organizational culture and leadership. *In:* Shafritz, J. and Ott, J. S. (eds) (2001) *Classics of Organization Theory*. Fort Worth, Harcourt College Publishers.

Sekhon, Y. and Robson, J. (2008) ESRC Sponsored Event. How can financial services companies get the best from their marketing? http://business.bournemouth.ac.uk/events/events/marketing_in_a_recession.html

Solomon, C.M. (2001) Managing virtual teams. *Workforce*, Accessed 31-05-2012. Vol. 80, No. 6 pp 60-65.

Sy, T. and D'Annunzio, L. (2005) Challenges and strategies of matrix organizations: top-level and mid-level managers' perspectives. *Human Resource Planning Journal*, 28, pp39-48.

www.mindtools.com/pages/article/news_STR_go.htm. [Accessed on 31 May 2012].

QUICK QUIZ

1   According to Mintzberg an organisation encompasses several aspects. What are they?

2   Sy and D'Annunzio (2005) have proposed five factors that compromise the operation of a matrix structure. What are these five factors?

3   What are the advantages and potential drawbacks of multi-disciplinary teams?

4   What are the five phases of growth in Greiner's organisational growth model?

5   How did Schein describe culture?

6   In 1985 Charles Handy identified four types of culture. What are they?

7   What are the 7Ss of the McKinsey 7s Model?

8   What are typical sources of 'organisational rigidity'?

9   Fill (2010) has identified three important dimensions of communications. What are they?

10   What are the principal purposes of a budget?

11   Name six ways in which a budget can be set.

12   What are the main reasons why unsatisfactory feedback and control can occur?

13   How can managers ensure that the short-term and long-term trade-offs are properly judged and well balanced?

ACTIVITY DEBRIEFS

Activity 5.2

The 7s model is based on the theory that, for an organisation to perform well, these seven elements need to be aligned and mutually reinforced. So, the model can be used to help identify what needs to be realigned to improve performance, or to maintain alignment (and performance) during other types of change. You can use the 7s model to help analyse the current situation (Point A) and a proposed future situation (Point B) and to identify gaps and inconsistencies between them. It's then a question of adjusting and tuning the elements of the 7s model to ensure that your organisation works effectively and well once you reach the desired endpoint.

Here are some of the questions to consider to help you understand your situation in terms of the 7s framework.

Structure:

- How is the company/team divided?
- What is the hierarchy?
- How do the various departments co-ordinate activities?
- How do the team members organise and align themselves?
- Is decision making and controlling centralised or decentralised? Is this as it should be, given what we're doing?
- Where are the lines of communication? Explicit and implicit?

Strategy:

- What is our strategy?
- How do we intend to achieve our objectives?
- How do we deal with competitive pressure?
- How are changes in customer demands dealt with?
- How is strategy adjusted for environmental issues?

Systems:

- What are the main systems that run the organisation? Consider financial and HR systems as well as communications and document storage.
- Where are the controls and how are they monitored and evaluated?
- What internal rules and processes does the team use to keep on track?

Shared values:

- What are the core values?
- What is the corporate/team culture?
- How strong are the values?
- What are the fundamental values that the company/team was built on?

Staff:

- What positions or specialisations are represented within the team?
- What positions need to be filled?
- Are there gaps in required competences?

Style:

- How participative is the management/leadership style?
- How effective is that leadership?
- Do employees/team members tend to be competitive or co-operative?
- Are there real teams functioning within the organisation or are they just nominal groups?

Skills:

- What are the strongest skills represented within the company/team?
- Are there any skills gaps?
- What is the company/team known for doing well?
- Do the current employees/team members have the ability to do the job?
- How are skills monitored and assessed?

Using the information you have gathered, now examine where there are strengths and weaknesses between the elements.

Activity 5.4

In thinking about your own development ask yourself the following questions:

- How you benefited overall from studying for this qualification?
- What impact have you had on other members of your team while studying for this unit?
- What impact have you had on the organisation itself while studying for this qualification?
- What skills have you developed in the course of studying for this qualification which will be valuable in the development of your career?

These questions can help in the formulation of an Individual Development Plan (IDP). An IDP is an action plan that develops employee skills and competences. It is separate from the normal performance review and goal-setting process because it is focused solely on an employee's individual development and required training. It is a commitment by an employee and his or her supervisor to personal and professional growth. The IDP focuses on career-development goals, both short-term and long-term, as they relate directly to the business.

The IDP process is intended to:

- Establish a process for individual reflection on work progress by the employee and any feedback from his or her manager
- Create a system of professional development
- Provide an organised approach for career planning and learning mapping so that desired learning is clearly communicated to the employee

IDP planning is a dynamic process and plans are often revised over time. Reasons for revisions include assuming additional responsibilities or changing strategic direction as a company responds to **new challenges and opportunities**. Realistic plans often require financial resources that must be managed. Therefore, the employee and his or her manager should sign off on the IDP before these resources can be approved.

1   –   Departmentalisation   –   Formalisation
       –   Specialisation   –   Decentralisation/Centralisation
       –   Standardisation   –   Control
       –   Co-ordination   –   Differentiation and integration

2   –   **Misaligned goals**

With at least two bosses there is the possibility of competition or conflict of objectives as well as problems of co-ordination and communication

–   **Unclear roles and responsibilities**

Often seen as confusion regarding what is required, by and to whom, resulting in tension and ambiguity

–   **Ambiguous authority**

Lack of managerial and staff experience in working in a matrix leads to lack of clarity in decision making

–   **Matrix guardian**

Difficult to measure individual performance, therefore reward system may conflict with the way a matrix operates

–   **Functional focused employees**

Potential for tension if employees are attitudinally focused to their functional area of expertise which can result in a lack of trust, communication and reluctance to commit resources

3   **Multi-disciplinary teams are useful in**:

–   Increasing team members' awareness of the big picture of their tasks and decisions by highlighting the dovetailing of functional objectives.

–   Helping to generate solutions to problems, and suggestions for performance or process improvements by integrating more pieces of the puzzle.

–   Aiding co-ordination across functional boundaries by increasing the flow of communication, informal relationships and co-operation.

On the other hand, the members of multi-functional teams have different reporting lines and responsibilities within their line departments, creating the ambiguity of dual responsibility.

They may have a range of different backgrounds, work cultures, specialist skills and terminology. This creates a particular challenge for the team leader: to build a sense of team identity, role clarity and co-operative working.

4   **Greiner's model identifies five stages of growth**:

–   Creativity
–   Direction
–   Delegation
–   Co-ordination
–   Collaboration

 The Chartered Institute of Marketing

5   Schein describes culture as '…a pattern of basic assumptions that a given group has invented, discovered, or developed in learning to cope with its problems of external adaptation and internal integration, a pattern of assumptions that has worked well enough to be considered valid, and therefore, to be taught to new members as the correct way to perceive, think and feel in relation to those problems.'

6   –   Role
    –   Power
    –   Task
    –   Person

7   –   **Structure**

    The organisation structure determines division of tasks in the organisation and the hierarchy of authority from the most senior to junior. As discussed above, today's company is likely to be made up of flat, empowered networks.

    –   **Strategy**

    Strategy is the way in which the organisation plans to outperform its competitors; it will be market-led.

    –   **Systems**

    Systems include the technical systems of accounting, personnel, management information and so on, with particular emphasis on how market-related information is distributed and used.

    –   **Shared values**

    Lie at the heart of the organisation and are the guiding principles for the people in it. They are vital for developing the motivation to drive the organisation to achieve.

    –   **Staff**

    The people in the organisation. They have their own complex concerns and priorities. The successful organisation will recruit the right staff and develop their motivation to pursue the right goals.

    –   **Style**

    Style is another aspect of the corporate culture, and includes the shared assumptions, ways of working and attitudes of senior management.

    –   **Skills**

    Skills are the core competences that enable the company to create value in a particular way.

8   –   Psychological resistance to change
    –   Cultural resistance to change
    –   Political resistance to change
    –   Investment lock-in
    –   Competence lock-in
    –   System lock-in
    –   Stakeholder lock-in

9   **Pull strategies**

    –   Targeted at customers, consumers and end-users

    –   Designed to pull customers into 'outlets'

– Key to this strategy is generating awareness, forming attitudes and motivating behaviour that ultimately results in demand availability of the brand

Push strategies

– Targeted at channels or networks that provide the brand

– Key to this strategy is encouraging suppliers to hold stocks and allocate resources to actively sell the brand

Profile strategies

– Strategic and targeted at all stakeholders of the organisation, both internal and external

– Key to this strategy is the creating, building and maintaining of the desired image of the organisation, what it stands for and its reputation

10 **The purposes of a budget are that it:**

– Co-ordinates the activities of all the different departments of an organisation; in addition, through participation by employees in preparing a budget, it may be possible to motivate them to raise their targets and standards and to achieve better results.

– Communicates the policies and targets to every manager in the organisation responsible for carrying out a part of that plan.

– Gives control by having a plan against which actual results can be progressively compared.

11 – Competitive parity
– The task method (or objective and task method)
– Communication stage models
– All you can afford
– Investment
– Rule-of-thumb, non-scientific methods

12 **Problems of unsatisfactory feedback and control can occur because of the following reasons:**

– People change.

– Reasons for change are not always apparent or identifiable.

– The same product can be bought by the same person for different purposes.

– Delays occur in the system due to suppliers being remote from consumers.

– Competitor actions can seriously affect the systems.

– Rarely is complete information affordable so that inadequacies occur in feedback.

– Distortions inevitably occur in the data transfer between people. The more often the data is transcribed the more distortion will occur.

13 – Managers should recognise whether or not S/L trade-offs in control action could be a serious problem.

– Managers should be aware that S/L trade-offs take place in practice.

– Controls should exist to prevent or minimise the possibility that short-term controls can be taken which damage long-term targets.

– Senior management must be given adequate control information for long-term as well as short-term consequences.

– The planning and review system should motivate managers to keep long-term goals in view.

The Chartered Institute of Marketing

–   Short-term goals should be realistic. Very often, the pressure on managers to sacrifice long-term interests for short-term results is caused by the imposition of stringent and unrealistic short-term targets on those managers in the first place.

–   Performance measures should reflect both long-term and short-term targets. There might be, say, quarterly performance reviews on the achievement of strategic goals.

CHAPTER 6

Measuring and evaluating marketing strategies

Introduction

It is often said that 'what isn't measured isn't done'! The techniques and measures used for monitoring and measuring marketing effectiveness are considered in this chapter. The role of different stakeholders in measuring success is also considered as one stakeholder may evaluate a strategy differently to another.

This chapter also explores the increasing importance of ethical considerations in developing strategy and the importance of environmental marketing. There does now seem to be widespread acceptance that commercial organisations should devote some of their resources to the promotion of wider environmental aims given the growing global nature of business.

Topic list

The importance of marketing metrics	(1)
Developing appropriate marketing measures	(2)
Shareholder value analysis	(3)
Value-based management	(4)
Benchmarking analysis	(5)
Monitoring competitor performance	(6)
Setting targets	(7)
The balanced scorecard	(8)
Ethics and strategy	(9)
Understanding environmental marketing	(10)
Marketing and due diligence	(11)

1.2.4	Determine a series of measures that enable an estimation of desired results for an organisation: ■ Marketing metrics ■ Relative perceived quality ■ Loyalty retention ■ Customer satisfaction ■ Relative price (market share/volume) ■ Market share (volume/value) ■ Perceived quality/esteem
2.3.1	Critically evaluate the concepts of adaptability, efficiency and effectiveness as means of measuring the success or otherwise of marketing strategies for a range of organisational sectors: ■ Efficiency/effectiveness matrix in measuring longevity of marketing strategies (McDonald, 2007) ■ Tactical versus strategic orientation
2.3.2	Critically evaluate and use quantitative techniques for evaluating business and marketing performance and delivery of the marketing strategy, including: • Brand equity and brand value ■ Shareholder value analysis ■ Benchmarking analysis ■ Comparative assessments with previous strategies and budgetary control techniques
2.3.3	Measure financial returns achieved as a result of specific investment decisions and compare them to the original investment appraisal or business case: ■ Historic decisions informing current decision-making ■ Short-term versus long-term ■ Linkages between strategic and financial appraisal from manager's own perspective (in a strategic management context – Grundy and Johnson, 1993 BJM)
2.3.4	Propose and critically evaluate the development of sustainable marketing strategies and ethics, and analyse the value generated by these strategies to the organisation's overall strategy: ■ Investment in sustainable marketing strategies ■ Developing appropriate messages to stakeholders and shareholders ■ Sustainable product development strategies and communication methods to influence consumer behaviour in a long-term sustainable context
2.3.5	Assess the value that the marketing proposition has generated and how it can contribute to shareholder value: ■ Value-based planning models ■ Creation of additional value ■ Role of marketing due diligence

1 The importance of marketing metrics

> ▶ **Assessment tip**
>
> In today's challenging environment marketing expenditure is under more scrutiny than ever before. You can be pretty sure that the question of funding of marketing plans to ensure delivery will feature regularly in assignment briefs.

Where organisations only use accountancy measures for measuring marketing performance there are a number of drawbacks:

- Accounts can be difficult to interpret, even if financial data are reported
- Accounting measures can vary from organisation to organisation, making it difficult to compare performance
- While financial performance measures are clearly very important they tend to only show the economic dimensions of performance and perhaps neglect the organisation's other important goals (Venkatramen and Ramanujam, 1987).
- An organisation's performance measures indicate whether and how well an organisation is delivering on its intended mission.
- They indicate whether an organisation's strategy and its implementation and execution are contributing to bottom-line improvements.
- Performance measures provide managers with better insights into planning, control and improving organisational performance.

Marketing at all levels has a responsibility to account for any investments it makes and the budget that is utilised. It is important to realise the difference between a marketing analytic and marketing metric. Marketing analytics are the actual tools used to produce the marketing metrics. There can be a resistance to using marketing metrics for a number of reasons: individuals find them difficult to use; they do not see the benefits of using the metrics; they are not sure of which metric to use and why; and they do not have the resources, either financial or time-related.

To ensure that there is a greater use of marketing metrics there are a number of factors that need to be considered:

- Organisations should use marketing metrics that are appropriate to specific business operations.
- Organisations need to identify their key business and marketing challenges and have an understanding of key areas for improvement.
- Where there are a number of marketing metrics to choose from it is recommended to begin with marketing profitability metrics and then move on to others.

There are three major marketing attributes that performance measures should include:

(a) **The adaptability or innovativeness of an organisation**

Measuring adaptability reflects an organisation's understanding of the changing environment and its ability to create and market new products and innovations.

Key performance measures

(i) New product success rate
(ii) New products and services
(iii) Patents
(iv) Registered trademarks

(b) **The effectiveness of particular marketing strategies**

This analysis helps to foster a clearer understanding of the competitive stances adapted by the organisation.

(i) Key performance measures
(ii) Unit sales
(iii) Market shares by unit and volume
(iv) Market share by segment
(v) Number of customers
(vi) Customer loyalty
(vii) Customer complaints
(viii) Relative quality
(ix) Relative value

(c)   **Efficiency in the execution of particular strategies**

The efficiency with which an organisation executes particular strategies needs to be understood and measured. Such measures reflect whether an organisation is utilising its asset base to the best of its ability.

(i)   Key performance measures

(ii)   Capacity utilisation

(iii)   R&D productivity

(iv)   Percentage employee turnover

(v)   Turnover per employee

(vi)   Distribution levels and efficiency

(vii)   Inventory levels

(viii) Speed of service delivery

(ix)   IT efficiency

(x)   Productivity per employee

(xi)   ROI

(xii)   Product availability in different geographic locations

It is important that any organisation, whether a large one or a SME is able to make the right choices and do the right thing; this will then lead to greater efficiency and effectiveness. The efficiency/effectiveness matrix can be used to analyse the organisation and the potential consequences of being part of one category over another:

(a)   The effectiveness/efficiency matrix outlines that if organisations fail to get the right combination it can have long-term consequences on the organisation.

(b)   Organisations that are effective and efficient in what they do are more likely to 'thrive' as they are pursuing a strategy that fits in with the organisation's overall goals and vision; this can also help with their long-term sustainability. However, those that are effective but inefficient are more likely to survive rather than thrive; lack of efficiency can be a result of poor management and inefficient processes in place internally. While survival may be accepted, it can impact the long-term sustainability of an organisation if efficiency does not improve. If an organisation is both ineffective and inefficient it will 'die slowly'. These types of organisations do not have the necessary focus and vision to take them into the future; it also a clear sign of poor management and unfocused leadership. Those organisations that are ineffective and efficient tend to be labelled as 'die quickly' as often resources are being invested in completely the wrong area, and the internal vision and mission have not taken account of the external environment and what is happening in the marketplace.

Kumar and Gulati (2009) analysed both effectiveness and efficiency amongst public sector banks in India and found that high efficiency does not always mean high effectiveness in this sector and that overall performance needs to be analysed from an effectiveness perspective to help with income generation.

Aldi

Aldi is an example of an organisation being able to gain competitive advantage through is efficient processes. Aldi operates in a very competitive market. Supermarkets nationally and internationally need to meet customers' ever changing needs and ensure they are able to provide products that cater for a price sensitive market, where customers are wanting good value for money and promotions that offer quality products at affordable prices.

Aldi wants to be a supermarket that caters for the price sensitive customer but does not compromise on quality. In 1913 Aldi opened its first store and since then has become a key player in the international market, having stores in Germany, the United Kingdom, Australia and the US. Aldi has over 7,000 stores and its key focus is to provide quality products at a low cost. How is it able to do this? This is done through efficiency. This is achieved through lean thinking and its business is run using this approach. Aldi's core purpose states that it is to 'provide value and quality to our customers by being fair and efficient in all we do'. This level of efficiency and low cost means Aldi can reinvest in the organisation and so meet its targets and objectives. The investment in lean production is a long-term commitment by Aldi.

The aim of lean production is to ensure that minimal resources are used to provide the goods and services to the customer base; in doing so the organisation will then become more efficient. This efficiency can be gained from reducing waste, whether time or materials, and potentially needing less labour. However, fundamental to this is ensuring that the savings are passed on to the customer. Aldi is able to do this by providing better value for money and lower priced products to the customer. Key components of lean production are as follows:

- Continuous improvement – a culture whereby all employees are constantly involved in making improvements to quality

- Just-in-time production – materials are received just as they are needed, eliminating the need to maintain large stock levels

- Time based management – an approach that aims to reduce the time wasted in business operations. This usually requires a multi-skilled and flexible workforce

- Total quality management (TQM) – a quality assurance ideal where all workers have a responsibility for getting it 'right first time'

- Aldi applies lean production principles in its supply chain; for example, when sourcing fruit and vegetables over 50% of them are sourced locally where possible, so delivery times are reduced and less storage space is required, so reducing inventory costs.

- There is strong investment in training Aldi employees so that they know what to do, how to do it and have the knowledge to respond to customers, so reducing waste and having a more efficient and effective workforce

- With regards to stock, Aldi sells a narrower range of products in each category, for example one size rather than many, limited brands and packaging, in return it is able to benefit from economies of scale and be more cost-effective.

The three core values of Aldi are simplicity, consistency and responsibility. These values lend themselves neatly to lean production:

- Simplicity – product ranges, offerings, store layout and design

- Consistency – in training, product offerings and the overall goals of the organisation

- Responsibility – empowering employees so they can be responsible in fulfilling their duties

These values enable Aldi to constantly improve efficiency, so having a positive benefit on their overall effectiveness as an organisation.

Critically analyse your organisation and evaluate how it could be more efficient with its processes and practices. Link this back to the vision and mission, and make recommendations for change, including justifications.

1.1 Brand equity

In addition to these measures, it is also important to understand the concept of brand equity and branding equity measures such as:

- Customer preferences
- Purchase intent
- Brand value
- Brand strength
- Level of trust in the brand
- Brand image

> ▶ **Key term**
>
> **Brand equity** is the 'added value endowed by the brand to the product'.

The success of a particular brand provides an organisation with profits and the potential to gain future profits, thereby creating an asset that has a value. The level of success can be determined by understanding the level of brand equity achieved, taking into consideration the effect of advertising (Ambler, 1997).

Boulding *et al* (1993) consider that the level of trust associated with a brand is also important and may be regarded as:

- Part of the brand-consumer relationship and therefore brand equity
- Dynamic and non-linear, slow to build and fast to destroy
- Both an antecedent and a consequence of success
- A habit

Effective promotion and consistently meeting or exceeding customer thoughts creates positive brand equity. There needs to be consistency with regards to the brand and people's expectations of it. To ensure these there needs to be appropriate leadership in place to give direction and management to ensure that it can be appropriately managed and delivered. The stronger the company's brand equity the more successful its marketing strategy, as key stakeholders have an understanding of what the organisation represents and what to can expect from the organisation, and this can help when launching a new product, diversifying or entering new markets. This means these decisions are less risky, less costly and give the organisation greater control.

2 Developing appropriate marketing measures

In choosing appropriate performance measures it is useful to divide them into the following categories:

2.1 Strategic

These are used to measure the overall performance of an organisation, such as market share or return on investment. They could include market share in geographic regions and the overall effectiveness of branding strategies.

It is increasingly important that environmental measures such as eco-efficiency are considered as the environmental responsibility of a company is becoming increasingly important.

2.2 Tactical

These can include short-term measures to improve customer satisfaction, loyalty rates and promotional effects.

When selecting and developing measures it is useful to adopt a screening procedure to assess the acceptability, suitability and feasibility of the proposed measures (Johnson and Scholes, 2002).

2.2.1 Acceptability

The issues to consider are:

- Are these measures acceptable to the various stakeholders?
- Do they make sense?
- Do they measure the right areas of business activity and the right issues?

If unacceptable measures are adopted by those responsible for delivering against them then the outcome will be unreliable since the results may well be 'fudged'. Measures adopted must demonstrate something tangible, meaningful and of value to the various stakeholders.

2.2.2 Suitability

An assessment of the most suitable performance measures that could be adopted is likely to be based on the following:

- The industry sector in which the organisation operates
- The service or product orientation of the organisation
- Whether the organisation is a commercial, not-for-profit or public sector organisation
- The level of technology used for automatic measurement
- The vision of the organisation
- Whether the measure is likely to be of value in the long-term
- Whether the measure chosen can be used to benchmark the organisation against its competitors

2.2.3 Feasibility

The test of whether it is practical and useful to adopt certain measures. For example, an organisation wanting to measure the visits to its website during a certain campaign will need to ensure that it has the necessary analytical tools to measure the impact.

3 Shareholder value analysis

> **▶ Key term**
>
> **Shareholder value analysis** (SVA) is a method of approaching the problem of business control by focusing on the creation of value for shareholders.

Independent financial analysts measure the value offered by a company's shares by considering the market value of all the shares in existence (the market capitalisation), in the light of the company's prospects for generating both cash and capital growth in the future. If the current market capitalisation is less than the estimate of actual value, then the shares are undervalued.

Investment is necessary to produce either assets that grow in value or actual cash surpluses, so the process of shareholder value analysis is essentially one of estimating the likely effectiveness of the company's current investment decisions. It is both a system for judging the worth of current investment proposals and for judging the performance of the managers who are responsible for the company's performance.

In the past, marketing managers have tended to pursue purely marketing objectives, such as sales growth, market share, customer satisfaction and brand recognition. None of these marketing objectives necessarily translates into increased shareholder value, and as a result, marketing has suffered from a lack of perceived relevance to true business value. An emphasis on profitability as a measure of success has led to a certain

amount of short-termism in strategic management, with an emphasis on containing and reducing current costs in order to boost current profits.

Unfortunately, this approach tends to underestimate the longer-term effect of such action and can lead to corporate decline. Investment in intangible assets such as brands can make a positive contribution to long-term shareholder value.

3.1 Computing value

Shareholder value created by past performance is measured by **economic profit**. The **cash flow** approaches are more appropriate for assessing plans for the future.

According to Doyle (2002), the extent of a company's success may be measured in two ways. The first is by using the concept of economic profit (trademarked by Stern Stewart and Company as Economic Value Added®, (1991). The expression 'economic profit' is used to distinguish the measure from accounting profit, which is computed according to the strict rules of accountancy.

> **▶ Key term**
>
> Economic profit is created when the return on a company's capital employed exceeds the cost of that capital.
>
> **Economic profit = NOPAT – (capital employed × cost of capital)**
>
> where **NOPAT** is net operating profit after tax

These feature, in particular, the principle of prudence. This makes it impossible for accounting profit to recognise spending on pure research, for instance, as an investment in an asset, since there is no guarantee that it will ever produce anything worth having; the same would be true of much marketing spend on building long-term effectiveness.

Cost of capital is, effectively, **the return that has to be made to providers of capital** in the form of interest on loans and dividends on shares. It may be calculated as a **weighted average**, which takes account of both the expectations of shareholders and lenders who have provided loans.

Economic profit is related to capital employed by **return on capital employed** (ROCE). This is a percentage and may thus be compared directly with cost of capital. When ROCE exceeds the cost of capital (r), economic value is created: under these circumstances (ROCE > r), the company is offering a greater return on capital than is available elsewhere.

Economic profit is useful for examining the company's **current and past performance**, but is less useful for assessing **future prospects**. For that purpose it is more appropriate to use the **cash flow approach**.

Be aware that both the economic profit method and the cash flow method should produce the same result when applied to a particular company.

The **cash flow approach** may be used to estimate the degree of economic value a company may be expected to create in the future. It is based on an estimation of likely future **cash flows**, both positive and negative, as indicated in the corporate plans. (A cash flow is simply a sum of money paid or received by the company.) This is easier to do than to compute future NOPAT, because it is far less complex and depends on far fewer variables.

4 Value-based management

Purely marketing objectives are no longer acceptable; value-based management aims always to maximise shareholder value by developing competitive advantage. Creating value is not about applying a systematic set of tools or processes but about creating competitive advantage in the marketplace. Strategy is central to achieve this success: 'Managing for value begins with strategy and ends with financial results' (Knight, 1998).
A fundamental part of value-based management is ensuring there is strategic planning, so that value can be managed; there is a focus that structures the decisions made. Greater time needs to be devoted to the

company's long-term value. To help achieve this the organisation needs good quality information to make both strategic and operational decisions. Some of this information is readily available; however, some might require auditing of the organisation both internally and in the marketplace within which it operates.

Doyle (2002) tells us that business success should be measured by shareholder value analysis (SVA) because of the property rights of shareholders and the 'pressures to oust management that does not deliver competitive returns'. Purely marketing objectives are no longer acceptable to investors or the analysts whose reports they rely on.

What Doyle (2002) calls **value-based management** is based on three elements:

(a)   A **belief** that maximising shareholder returns is the objective of the firm.

(b)   The **principles**, or strategic foundations of value, are first to target those market segments where profits can be made, and second to develop competitive advantage 'that enables both the customer and the firm to create value'.

(c)   The **processes** 'concern how strategies should be developed, resources allocated and performance measured'.

SVA is particularly appropriate for judging strategic investment decisions and applies the same principles that have been used for appraising investment in such tangible assets as premises and plant for many years. It is necessary to consider both the **cash costs** of the strategic investment to be made, and the **positive cash flows** that are expected to be produced by it.

These may then be discounted to a net present value (NPV) using an appropriate cost of capital, and a judgement made on the basis of the NPV. Any specifically marketing proposal, such as an enhanced advertising spend or a new discount structure may be assessed in this way, though it will almost certainly be necessary to take advice from the finance function on the process.

4.1 Value-based management

Value-based management means that purely marketing investment proposals will be judged as described above. It will be necessary for marketing managers to justify their spending requests in such terms, on the basis that such spending is not a cost burden to be minimised but an investment in intangible assets such as the four that Doyle suggests:

- Marketing knowledge
- Brands
- Customer loyalty
- Strategic relationships with channel partners

The obstacle that lies in the path of this approach to marketing use of SVA is the common perception that marketing spending is merely a cost to be controlled and minimised. The onus is on marketing managers to demonstrate that their budgets do in fact create assets that provide competitive advantage for the business and that the benefits exceed the costs.

4.2 Value drivers

The creation of value depends on three categories of value driver: **financial**, **marketing** and **organisational**.

Doyle (2002) suggests that it is possible to identify the factors that are critical to the creation of shareholder value. These he calls value drivers; he divides them into three categories:

- Financial
- Marketing
- Organisational

BPP LEARNING MEDIA

It is important to remember that **the financial drivers should not be targeted directly**: they are objectives, not the components of strategy. The company influences them by the proper management of the **marketing** and **organisational** drivers.

Value drivers can include the following:

- A stable, motivated management team
- Operating systems that improve sustainability of cash flows
- A solid, diversified customer base
- Facility appearance consistent with asking price
- A realistic growth strategy
- Effective financial controls
- Good and improving cash flow

Value drivers are characteristics of a business that help to reduce the risk of being part of the business and can help the business to grow and have longer-term sustainability.

4.3 Financial value drivers

There are four drivers of financial value:

(a) Cash flow volume
(b) Cash flow timing
(c) Cash flow risk
(d) Cash flow sustainability

4.3.1 Cash flow volume

Clearly, the higher that positive cash flows are and the lower negative cash flows are, the greater the potential for creating value:

4.3.2 Profitability

In the most simple terms, profit margin is measured by net operating profit after tax (NOPAT). NOPAT can be increased in three ways:

(a) **Higher prices.** Marketing strategies such as building strong brands can enable the charging of premium prices. A particularly powerful route to higher prices is **innovation**, since desirable new products will normally justify increased prices.

(b) **Reduced costs.** Cost reduction depends on increased efficiency in all aspects of the business operations.

(c) **Volume increases.** Other things being equal, volume growth increases the absolute profit margin and may increase the profit rate as well.

4.3.3 Sales growth

If increases in sales volume can be achieved without disproportionate increases in costs or, in particular, excessive discounting, positive cash flows will naturally increase. Increased sales can also bring increased **economies of scale**, which will take the form of reduced costs of all types. Overheads are spread over greater volumes and purchasing discounts reduce the cost of sales.

4.3.4 Investment

Investment provides the resources necessary to do business. These include premises, equipment, stocks, transport and well-trained, experienced staff. However, ill-advised investment can destroy value faster than profitable investment can create it, so any proposal for investment must be judged on its potential for generating acceptable returns.

The **net present value** (NPV) approach is the investment appraisal method best suited to the shareholder value principle, in that any project that has a NPV greater than zero provides a return greater than the cost of capital used in the discounting arithmetic.

4.4 Cash flow timing

The further into the future a cash flow occurs, the lower its present value. If positive cash flows can be achieved in the near future and negative ones put off until later, the company benefits. This is why companies and individuals put off paying their bills for as long as possible. Buying on credit and selling for cash is another approach.

Doyle (2002) gives five examples of ways that marketing managers can accelerate cash flows:

(a) **Faster new product development** processes, including the use of cross-functional teams and conducting projects concurrently rather than consecutively.

(b) **Accelerated market penetration** through pre-marketing campaigns, early trial promotions and word-of-mouth campaigns using early adopters.

(c) **Network effects**: that is, achieving market status as the industry standard. This is a self-reinforcing, feedback effect in which success leads to even greater success. It was seen, for instance, in the videotape market in the 1980s when VHS displaced the technically superior Betamax. Aggressive marketing measures to build the installed base are required.

(d) **Strategic alliances** speed market penetration, normally by providing extra distribution effort.

(e) **Exploiting brand assets**: new products launched under a suitable, established brand are likely to be more successful than others.

4.5 Cash flow risk

The higher the degree of **risk** associated with future cash flows, the greater the proportion of them that will not actually come to pass.

High risk can produce low returns as easily as high ones. Apart from this overall averaging effect, there is the disadvantage associated with **infrequent large cash flows**: failure of such a cash flow to occur can have catastrophic consequences.

Risk is also associated with timing: the further into the future that a cash flow is expected to occur, the greater the risk associated with it, since there is a greater likelihood of **changed conditions** affecting its eventual value and even whether or not it actually occurs.

Doyle (2008) suggests that the most effective marketing route to reduced cash flow risk is 'to increase customer satisfaction, loyalty and retention' by deploying such techniques as loyalty programmes and measures to increase satisfaction. Building **good channel relationships** also helps, both by building an element of loyalty based on good service and by sharing information on demand patterns to smooth stock fluctuations.

4.6 Cash flow sustainability

A single positive cash flow is useful. A positive cash flow that is repeated at regular intervals is much more useful. Quite apart from the extra cash involved, sustainable cash flows make it easier to plan for the future. Positive cash flows derive from the creation of competitive advantage and a sustainable advantage will lead to sustainable cash flows.

There are many **threats to sustainable profits**, including aggressive competition from copies and substitutes and, particularly in B2B markets, the bargaining power of customers. Part of the role of marketing management is to counter such threats using techniques such as those outlined above in connection with reducing risk.

Sustainable advantage also offers a benefit in the form of **enhanced options** for future development. Just as financial options to buy and sell securities and currency have their own value, so a strategy that creates **real options** for future activity has a value over and above any immediate competitive advantage it may offer.

A simple example is the development of a completely new product for a given market that can also be made viable in other markets at low incremental cost. Richard Branson's ability to use his brand Virgin with almost any consumer product is another example. There are network effects here too, in that as more and more dissimilar Virgin products become available, the brand's suitability for use with even more types of product grows.

4.7 Marketing value drivers

Doyle (2008) analyses four marketing value drivers. The first, choice of markets, is only applicable to the large, diversified organisation, but the remaining three apply to all companies.

4.7.1 Choice of markets

A large organisation operating a number of strategic business units (SBUs) must apply a continuing **portfolio analysis** to them. You will be familiar with such portfolio analysis tools as the BCG matrix and the GE business screen from your earlier studies, but you may only have considered their use at **the product level**. Nevertheless, it is both feasible and appropriate to apply the concept at **the SBU level** in order to determine priorities for investment and policies for exploitation. Doyle suggests a very simple, one dimensional classification of SBUs:

(a)   **Today's businesses** generate the bulk of current profits and cash, but probably have only modest growth potential. If successful, they attract modest investment for incremental developments; if performing badly they are put right rapidly or sold off.

(b)   **Tomorrow's businesses** have high potential and require major investment.

(c)   **Options for growth** are the seeds of more distant businesses such as research projects, market trials and stakes in new, small businesses that are a long way from success. Recognising the worth of such ventures is a difficult task; in the world of venture capital it is recognised that many good ideas will come to nothing in the end.

A large company needs a suitable mix of the three types of SBU each with its own appropriate strategic objectives, though there may be opportunities for **synergy**, such as the use of common brand names. SBUs that do not fit into one of the categories should be divested.

Srivastava, Shervani and Fahey (1999) looked at developing a framework for understanding how marketing can be integrated into business processes and shareholder value. In particular, they focused on product development management, supply chain management and customer relationship management and how these can be integrated to create shareholder value. However, these need to be embedded into the organisation rather than just being viewed as parts of the organisation with little integration and focus.

ACTIVITY 6.2

Identify the key stakeholders for your organisation and identify the key drivers in creating shareholder value.

The Chartered Institute of Marketing

5 Benchmarking analysis

Benchmarks can be set on a variety of key performance indicators as an objective form of control. Marketing research and competitor intelligence would be needed to establish benchmarks and to monitor progress.

The practice of benchmarking is becoming increasingly popular. There are two principal approaches:

(a)   **Process benchmarking**, where data is exchanged between companies with similar administrative and manufacturing processes. For example, one of the factors affecting aircraft turnaround away from home is the availability of spare parts required for routine maintenance. This process is very similar to the provision of field maintenance for office systems such as photocopiers and computers.

(b)   **Competitor benchmarking** focuses on the performance and relative strengths of direct competitors using information from customer and supplier interviews and published data from any source available. A firm tries to be as good as its competitors.

6 Monitoring competitor performance

When an organisation operates in a competitive environment, it should try to obtain information about the financial performance of competitors to make a comparison with the organisation's own results. It might not be possible to obtain reliable competitor information, but if the competitor is a public company it will publish an annual report and accounts.

6.1 Financial information that might be obtainable about a competitor

- Total profits, sales and capital employed
- ROCE, profit/sales ratio, cost/sales ratios and asset turnover ratios
- The increase in profits and sales over the course of the past twelve months (and prospects for the future, which will probably be mentioned in the chairman's statement in the report and accounts)
- Sales and profits in each major business segment that the competitor operates in
- Dividend per share and earnings per share
- Gearing and interest rates on debt
- Share price, and Price/earnings (P/E) ratio (stock exchange information)

6.2 Advantages of benchmarking

- The comparisons are carried out by the managers who have to live with any changes implemented as a result of the exercise.
- Benchmarking focuses on improvement in key areas and sets targets which are challenging but achievable. What is really achievable can be discovered by examining what others have achieved: managers are therefore able to accept that they are not being asked to perform miracles.

6.3 Disadvantages of benchmarking

- Benchmarking is reactive; rather than imitating a competitor, another competitive strategy may be more focused.

- It is not focused on the customer. The firm should set itself targets that customers value.

6.4 Market share performance

When a market manager is given responsibility for a product or a market segment, the product or market segment will be a profit centre, and measures of performance for the centre will include profits and cost variances and so on. However, another useful measure of performance would be the **market share** obtained by the organisation's product in the market. A market share performance report should draw attention to the following:

- The link between **cost and profit** and market performance in both the short-term and the long-term
- The performance of the **product or market segment** in the context of the product life cycle
- Whether or not the product is gaining or losing ground as its market share goes up or down

Changes in market share have to be considered against the change in the **market as a whole**, since the product might be increasing its share simply when the market is declining, but the competition is losing sales even more quickly. (The reverse may also be true. The market could be expanding, and a declining market share might not represent a decline in absolute sales volume, but a failure to grab more of the growing market.)

6.5 Monitoring customers

In some industrial markets or reseller markets, a producer might sell to a small number of key customers. The performance of these customers would therefore be of some importance to the producer: if the customer prospers, he will probably buy more and if he does badly, he will probably buy less. It may also be worthwhile monitoring the level of profitability of selling to the customer.

6.6 Key customer analysis calls for seven main areas of investigation:

(a) **Key customer identity**

- Name of each key customer
- Location
- Status in market
- Products they make and sell
- Size of firm (capital employed, turnover, number of employees)

(b) **Customer history**

- First purchase date
- Who makes the buying decision in the customer's organisation?
- What is the average order size, by product?
- What is the regularity/periodicity of the order, by product?
- What is the trend in size of orders?
- What is the motive in purchasing?
- What does the customer know about the firm's and competitors' products?
- On what basis does the customer reorder?
- Were there any lost or cancelled orders? For what reason?

(c) **Relationship of customer to product**

- Are the products purchased to be resold? If not, why are they bought?
- Do the products form part of the customer's service/product?

The Chartered Institute of Marketing

(d) **Relationship of customer to potential market**

- – What is the size of the customer in relation to the total end-market?
- – Is the customer likely to expand, or not? Diversify? Integrate?

(e) **Customer attitudes and behaviour**

- – What interpersonal factors exist which could affect selling processes?
- – Does the customer also buy competitors' products?
- – To what extent may purchases be postponed?
- – What emotional factors exist in buying decisions?

(e) **The financial performance of the customer**

- – How successful is the customer in its own markets?
- – Similar analysis can be carried out as with competitors.

(f) **The profitability of selling to the customer**

7 Setting targets

The organisation's objectives provide the basis for setting targets and standards. Each manager's targets will be directed towards achieving the company objectives. Targets or standards do two things:

(a) They tell managers what they are **required to accomplish**, given the authority to make appropriate decisions.

(b) They indicate to managers **how well their actual results** measure up against their targets, so that control action can be taken where it is needed. It follows that in setting standards for performance, **it is important to distinguish between controllable or manageable variables and uncontrollable ones**. Any matters which cannot be controlled by an individual manager should be excluded from their standards for performance.

8 The balanced scorecard

▶ **Key term**

The **balanced scorecard** is 'a set of measures that gives top managers a fast but comprehensive view of the business. The balanced scorecard includes financial measures that tell the results of actions already taken. And it complements the financial measures with **operational** measures on customer satisfaction, internal processes, and the organisation's innovation and improvement activities – operational measures that are the drivers of future financial performance.'

(Robert Kaplan, January–February 1992, *Harvard Business Review*)

At the strategic level it is necessary to form an overview of the business's progress towards its goals. To do this it is not enough to look at the performance of marketing alone, or even at summary financial results. A more rounded picture is needed. This is provided by the four **perspectives** of the **balanced scorecard**.

The reason for using such a system is that 'traditional financial accounting measures such as return on investment and earnings per share can give misleading signals for continuous improvement and innovation'. The balanced scorecard allows managers to look at the business from four important perspectives:

- ■ Customer
- ■ Internal business
- ■ Innovation and learning
- ■ Financial

8.1 Customer perspective

'How do customers see us?' Given that many company mission statements identify customer satisfaction as a key corporate goal, the balanced scorecard translates this into specific measures. Customer concerns fall into four categories:

- **Time**. Lead time is the time it takes a firm to meet customer needs from receiving an order to delivering the product.

- **Quality**. Quality measures not only include defect levels – although these should be minimised by TQM – but also accuracy in forecasting.

- **Performance** of the product. (How often does the photocopier break down?)

- **Service**. How long will it take a problem to be rectified? (If the photocopier breaks down, how long will it take the maintenance engineer to arrive?)

In order to view the firm's performance through customers' eyes, firms hire market researchers to assess how the firm performs. Higher service and quality may cost more at the outset, but savings can be made in the long-term.

8.1.1 Complaints

All businesses need systems for handling complaints since complaints are a most important aspect of the way their customers view them. Complaints indicate **dissatisfaction:** the degree of dissatisfaction a firm is willing to tolerate is an important strategic decision that should be informed by **analysis of the rate**, **severity and topic** of complaints.

It is important to remember that complaints are not an accurate index of dissatisfaction since many of those dissatisfied will not bother to complain; they will vote with their purses and go elsewhere. In fact, willingness to complain may be encouraged by proper handling of complaints, while an absence of complaints may simply indicate customers' belief that complaining will be a waste of effort.

8.2 Internal business perspective

The **internal business perspective** identifies the **business processes that have the greatest impact on customer satisfaction**, such as quality and employee skills.

Companies should also attempt to identify and measure their **distinctive competences** and the critical technologies they need to ensure continued leadership. Which processes should they excel at?

To achieve these goals, **performance measures must relate to employee behaviour**, to tie in the strategic direction with employee action.

An information system is necessary to enable executives to measure performance. An **executive information system** enables managers to drill down into lower level information.

8.3 Innovation and learning perspective

The question is **'Can we continue to improve and create value?'** While the customer and internal process perspectives identify the current parameters for competitive success, the company needs to learn and to innovate to **satisfy future needs**.

- How long does it take to develop new products?
- How quickly does the firm climb the experience curve to make new products?
- What percentage of revenue comes from new products?
- How many suggestions are made by staff and are acted upon?
- What are staff attitudes?
- The company can identify measures for training and long-term investment.

8.3.1 Financial perspective

'How do we appear to shareholders?' Financial performance indicators indicate 'whether the company's strategies, implementation and execution are contributing to bottom-line management'.

Table 6.1   Financial Performance Indicators

Measures	For	Against
Profitability	Easy to calculate and understand	Ignores the size of the investment
Return on investment (profit/capital)	▪ Accounting measure: easy to calculate and understand ▪ Takes size of investment into account ▪ Widely used	▪ Ignores risk ▪ Easy to manipulate (eg managers may postpone necessary capital investment to improve ratio) ▪ What are 'assets'? (eg do brands count?) ▪ Only really suited to products in the maturity phase of the life cycle, rather than others which are growing fast
Residual income	Head office levies an interest charge for the use of asset	Not related to the size of investment except indirectly
Earnings per share	Relates the firm's performance to needs of its shareholders	Shareholders are more concerned about future expectations; ignores capital growth as a measure of shareholders' wealth
DCF measures	Relates performance to investment appraisal used to take the decision; cash flows rather than accounting profits are better predictors of shareholder wealth	Practical difficulties in predicting future cash flows of a whole company

8.4 Linkages

Disappointing results might result from a failure to view all the measures as a whole. For example, increasing productivity means that fewer employees are needed for a given level of output.

Excess capacity can be created by quality improvements. However, these improvements have to be exploited (eg by increasing sales).

The financial element of the balanced scorecard 'reminds executives that improved quality, response time, productivity or new products, benefit the company only when they are translated into improved financial results', or if they enable the firm to obtain a sustainable competitive advantage.

The balanced scorecard only measures performance. It does not indicate that the strategy is the right one. 'A failure to convert improved operational performance into improved financial performance should send executives back to their drawing boards to rethink the company's strategy or its implementation plans.'

When applying the balanced scorecard, it is important to remember that it is a management tool rather than a measurement tool. For the balanced scorecard to be used appropriately it needs to be linked to the organisation's vision and strategies, which are clearly linked to the teams within the organisation. This analysis looks at financial as well as non-financial operating measures.

The balanced scorecard needs to be applied down the organisation's hierarchy to ensure that complementary scorecards are then applied. This allows management at corporate level to align individual efforts at all levels with the overall focus being on the vision and longer-term strategy.

Figure 6.1   A balanced scorecard

Balanced Scorecard

Financial Perspective	
GOALS	**MEASURES**
Survive	Cash flow, net margin
Succeed	Monthly sales growth and operating income by division
Prosper	Increase market share and ROI

Customer Perspective	
GOALS	**MEASURES**
New products	Percentage of sales from new products
Responsive supply	On-time delivery (defined by customer)
Preferred supplier	Share of key accounts' purchases
Customer partnership	Ranking by key accounts
	Number of co-operative engineering efforts
Value for money	Customer survey

Internal Business Perspective	
GOALS	**MEASURES**
Technology capability	Manufacturing configuration vs competition
Manufacturing excellence	Cycle time
	Unit cost
	Yield
Design productivity	Safety record
New product introduction	Engineering efficiency
	Actual introduction schedule vs plan

Innovation and Learning Perspective	
GOALS	**MEASURES**
Technology leadership	Time to develop next generation of product
Manufacturing learning	Process time to maturity
Product focus	Percentage of products that equal 80% sales
Time to market	New product introduction vs competition
Staff empowerment	Staff survey

ACTIVITY 6.3

For a project you are working on now, consider developing a set of performance measures according to the balanced scorecard model. What questions do you think you need to ask in determining the right set of measures?

Apply the balanced scorecard to your organisation and critically evaluate its findings to the organisation's overall vision and mission.

Many firms use profit or investment centre organisation to control the performance of different divisions.

A profit centre is where managers are responsible for revenues and costs; an investment centre is a profit centre in which managers have some say in investment decisions. Always keep in mind the following:

(a)   Different divisions may offer different risk/return profiles.
(b)   Managers will take dysfunctional decisions if these put their performance in a better light.
(c)   An economically efficient, fair transfer pricing system must be devised.
(d)   There are problems in assessing how shared fixed assets or head office costs should be charged out.

The Chartered Institute of Marketing

9 Ethics and strategy

In this Study Text we have emphasised that what the organisation wishes to achieve – its **mission** – is fundamental to any focused control of its activities.

It is important to understand that if ethics is applicable to corporate behaviour at all it must therefore be a fundamental aspect of **mission**, since everything the organisation does flows from that. Managers responsible for strategic decision making cannot avoid responsibility for their organisation's ethical standing.

They should consciously apply ethical rules to all of their decisions in order to filter out potentially undesirable developments.

THE REAL WORLD

BP

'I want my life back'. These words from Tony Hayward, CEO of BP, in the wake of the Deepwater Horizon oil spill in the Gulf of Mexico, coupled with his statement that he expected the environmental impact of the spill to be quite small, provoked an angry response from President Obama.

9.1 The stakeholder view

As Anita Roddick (founder of the Body Shop) stated: 'being good is good business'; ethical behaviour can impact the organisation, its performance, the stakeholders and its reputation both in the short- and long-term.

The stakeholder view is that many groups have a stake in what the organisation does. This is particularly important in the business context, where shareholders own the business but employees, customers and government also have particularly strong claims to having their interests considered.

This is fundamentally an argument derived from natural law theory and is based on the notion of individual and collective rights.

It is suggested that modern corporations are so powerful, socially, economically and politically, that unrestrained use of their power will inevitably damage other people's rights. For example, they may blight an entire community by closing a major facility, therefore forcing long-term unemployment on a large proportion of the local workforce.

Similarly, they may damage people's quality of life by polluting the environment. They may use their purchasing power or market share to impose unequal contracts on suppliers and customers. And they may exercise undesirable influence over government through their investment decisions. Under this approach, the exercise of corporate social responsibility constrains the corporation to act at all times as a good citizen.

Another argument points out that corporations exist within society and are dependent upon it for the resources they use. Some of these resources are obtained by direct contracts with suppliers but others are not, being provided by government expenditure. Examples are such things as transport infrastructure, technical research and education for the workforce.

Clearly, corporations contribute to the taxes that pay for these things, but the relationship is rather tenuous and the tax burden can be minimised by careful management. The implication is that corporations should recognise and pay for the facilities that society provides by means of socially responsible policies and actions.

9.2 The ethical stance

An organisation's **ethical stance** is the extent to which it will exceed its minimum obligations to stakeholders. There are four typical stances:

- Short-term shareholder interest
- Long-term shareholder interest
- Multiple stakeholder obligations
- Shaper of society

9.2.1 Short-term shareholder interest

An organisation might limit its ethical stance to taking responsibility for **short-term shareholder interest** on the grounds that it is for **government** alone to impose wider constraints on corporate governance.

This minimalist approach would accept a duty of obedience to the demands of the law, but would not undertake to comply with any less substantial rules of conduct. This stance can be justified on the grounds that going beyond it can **challenge government authority**; this is an important consideration for organisations operating in developing countries.

9.2.2 Long-term shareholder interest

There are two reasons why an organisation might take a wider view of ethical responsibilities when considering the **longer-term interest of shareholders**:

(a)   The organisation's **corporate image** may be enhanced by an assumption of wider responsibilities. The cost of undertaking such responsibilities may be justified as essentially promotional expenditure.

(b)   The responsible exercise of corporate power may prevent a build-up of social and political **pressure for legal regulation**. Freedom of action may be preserved and the burden of regulation lightened by acceptance of ethical responsibilities.

9.2.3 Multiple stakeholder obligations

An organisation might accept the legitimacy of the expectations of stakeholders other than shareholders and build those expectations into its stated purposes. This would be because without appropriate relationships with groups such as suppliers, employers and customers, the organisation would not be able to function.

A distinction can be drawn between rights and expectations. The *Concise Oxford Dictionary* defines a right as 'a legal or moral entitlement'. One is on fairly safe interpretative ground with legal rights, since their basis is usually clearly established, though subject to development and adjustment.

The concept of moral entitlement is much less well defined and subject to partisan argument, as discussed above in the context of natural law. There is, for instance, an understandable tendency for those who feel themselves aggrieved to declare that their rights have been infringed. Whether or not this is the case is often a matter of opinion.

For example, in the UK, there is often talk of a 'right to work' when redundancies occur. No such right exists in UK law, nor is it widely accepted that there is a moral basis for such a right. However, there is a widespread acceptance that governments should make the prevention of large-scale unemployment a high priority.

Clearly, organisations have a duty to respect the legal rights of stakeholders other than shareholders. These are extensive in the UK, including wide-ranging employment law and consumer protection law, as well as the more basic legislation relating to such matters as contract and property.

Where moral entitlements are concerned, organisations need to be practical: they should take care to establish just what expectations they are prepared to treat as obligations, bearing in mind their general ethical stance and degree of concern about bad publicity.

The Chartered Institute of Marketing

Acceptance of obligations to stakeholders implies that measurement of the organisation's performance must give due weight to these extra imperatives.

9.2.4 Shaper of society

It is difficult enough for a commercial organisation to accept wide responsibility to stakeholders. The role of **shaper of society** is even more demanding and largely the province of public sector organisations and charities, though some well-funded private organisations might act in this way.

The legitimacy of this approach depends on the framework of corporate governance and accountability. Where organisations are clearly set up for such a role, either by government or by private sponsors, they may pursue it. However, they must also satisfy whatever requirements for financial viability are established for them.

9.3 Two approaches to managing ethics

A compliance-based approach highlights conformity with law and regulation. An integrity-based approach suggests a wider remit, incorporating ethics in the organisation's values and culture.

Lynne Paine (*Harvard Business Review*, March–April 1994) suggests that ethical decisions are becoming more important as penalties, in the US at least, for companies which break the law become tougher. (This might be contrasted with the UK, where a fraudster whose deception ran into millions received a sentence of community service.) Paine suggests that there are two approaches to the management of ethics in organisations:

- Compliance-based
- Integrity-based

9.3.1 Compliance-based approach

A compliance-based approach is primarily designed to ensure that the company **acts within the letter of the law**, and that violations are prevented, detected and punished. Some organisations, faced with the legal consequences of unethical behaviour, take legal precautions such as those below:

- Compliance procedures to detect misconduct
- Audits of contracts
- Systems for employees to report criminal misconduct without fear of retribution
- Disciplinary procedures to deal with transgressions

Corporate compliance is limited in that it relates only to the law, but legal compliance is 'not an adequate means for addressing the full range of ethical issues that arise every day'. This is especially the case in the UK, where **voluntary** codes of conduct and self-regulation are perhaps more prevalent than in the US.

An example of the difference between the **legality** and **ethicality** of a practice is the sale in some countries of defective products without appropriate warnings. 'Companies engaged in international business often discover that conduct that infringes on recognised standards of human rights and decency is legally permissible in some jurisdictions'.

The compliance approach also overemphasises the threat of detection and punishment in order to channel appropriate behaviour. Arguably, some employers view compliance programmes as an insurance policy for senior management, who can cover the tracks of their arbitrary management practices. After all, some performance targets are impossible to achieve without cutting corners: managers can escape responsibility by blaming the employee for not following the compliance programme, when to do so would have meant a failure to reach a target.

Furthermore, mere compliance with the law is no guide to **exemplary** behaviour.

9.3.2 Integrity-based approach

'An integrity-based approach combines a concern for the law with an **emphasis on managerial responsibility** for ethical behaviour. Integrity strategies strive to define companies guiding values, aspirations and patterns of thought and conduct.

When integrated into the day-to-day operations of an organisation, such strategies can help prevent damaging ethical lapses, while tapping into powerful human impulses for moral thought and action'.

From this it should be clear to you that an integrity-based approach treats ethics as an issue of organisational culture.

Ethics management has several tasks:

- To define and give life to an organisation's defining values
- To create an environment that supports ethically sound behaviour
- To instil a sense of shared accountability amongst employees

It is commonly accepted there are two approaches to managing ethics, as detailed above. However, organisations can also fit into the following categories:

- **Amoral firm:** this wants to achieve its goal/aim at any cost to society or the environment and from its perspective anything is acceptable.

- **Legalistic firm:** this type of organisation is happy to stay on the right side of the law but is not willing to give resources or time to do any more.

- **Responsive firm:** this understands that to be ethical it can have its advantages and pay offs, and so is interested in ethical behaviour however it is not its main priority.

- **Ethically engaged firm:** this has the intention to follow a code of ethics; ethics are important to the organisation; however, ethics are not fully integrated into culture.

- **Ethical firm:** ethics are a part of the core values of the organisation and an inherent part of the culture.

ACTIVITY 6.4

Analyse the culture and ethos of your organisation; which category do you think it fits in? Recommend a strategy that is ethically focused; critically evaluate how you think it will improve the organisation's positioning.

THE REAL WORLD

Ethical decisions

There are organisations that have been labelled as 'ethical firms' but then have sold out to organisations that do not necessarily have a similar ethical culture, for example:

Body Shop – in 2006 the Body Shop was taken over by L'Oréal; Anita Roddick claimed that L'Oréal could continue and would have the same ethical values as the Body Shop.

Pret A Manger – sold a third of its business to McDonald's stating that these resources would help it expand further. More recently a private equity firm Bridgepoint bought Pret for £345m.

Green & Black's – was taken over by Cadbury Schweppes; this shocked many supporters of fair trade chocolates as it conflicted with the key values and ethos of Green & Black's.

The Chartered Institute of Marketing

10 Understanding environmental marketing

As production, marketing and consumption behaviour become increasingly global, marketers have to deal with a complex set of interconnecting strands that affect the production and perception of a single product and brand.

Social and ecological issues are inextricably linked and a truly green organisation has to address both areas simultaneously in order to create sustainable businesses and environments.

Ethics are part of understanding sustainable marketing strategies.

10.1 Life cycle analysis (LCA)

According SPOLD (Society for the Promotion of Life Cycle Analysis Development) life cycle thinking reflects the acceptance that key company stakeholders cannot limit their responsibilities to those phases of the life cycle of the process or activity with which they are involved.

The implication is therefore that all organisations upstream and downstream in the life cycle share responsibility, so the individual share of responsibility for each of them will be greatest in parts of the life cycle under their direct control.

There are a number of different concepts related to developing ecologically sound products. We discuss these briefly.

10.1.1 Design for the environment

In designing for the environment technologists are concerned with reducing energy consumption (both in the production of an item and when it is in use) and generally conserving resources. The main trends are:

- The incorporation of information from LCA into design

- The definition of environmental objectives

- A focus on the relationship between the product and the consumer and how the design can encourage environmentally responsible behaviour in the consumer

10.1.2 Clean technology

Providing a human benefit which overall uses fewer resources and causes less environmental damage than alternative means with which it is economically competitive

Organisations that implement some of these concepts can have a significant impact on the environment and have to be proactive in producing ecologically friendly products. Bennet and James (1999) suggest that companies have become much more sensitive to the demands of customers such that:

- The growing economy value of a good corporate reputation can be put at risk by adverse criticism of environmental and social performance.

- The growing number of customers who are becoming more 'green aware' impacts the organisation and its activities.

- A highly educated and more informed and literate workforce and market means the organisation cannot ignore these stakeholders.

10.1.3 Green marketing strategies

In order to gain competitive advantage organisations have to exhibit the following characteristics:

- Offering products that address ethical, moral and sustainability issues

- Using some of the profits for environmental and social improvement at the source of production

- Segmenting markets effectively so that the complexity of the niche markets and the 'new' consumer are targeted and understood

- Communicating honest and credible messages to the customers – transparent and understood by all stakeholders

- Developing transportation and logistics systems that meet the organisation's environmental objectives

- Developing a life cycle approach to products

- Understanding the needs of customers and stakeholders today and tomorrow

11 Marketing and due diligence

11.1 Marketing due diligence

The a number of areas to consider when focusing on due diligence:

Financial due diligence

This focuses on the analysis of the organisation's assets, revenues, financial situation and budgeting, in other words the organisation's earning power and financial stability.

Legal due diligence

The focus here is on the organisation's legal situation, for example the current contracts in place, the deeds and any special circumstances that should be highlighted.

Environmental due diligence

The quantification and evaluation of environmental risks with regards to production or the buildings that the organisation may use or own.

Market due diligence

Information that exists focusing on market-relevant data (pricing, market share, market share opportunities, organisation buying and marketing activities, level and quality of communication, product portfolios, supplier/distributor activities, customer behaviour, needs, activities, competitors).

The Chartered Institute of Marketing

A fundamental part of the Marketing Leadership and Planning unit is ensuring that any recommendations made are appropriately justified, evaluated and critically analysed. A common theme of the unit is to critically analyse the marketing strategies of an organisation; in doing so it is important that candidates are able to evaluate the current marketing strategy from a number of different contexts: competitiveness, long-term sustainability, and ethically, as well as through the application of the appropriate marketing measures.

A recent assessment asked candidates to assess how the organisation's marketing strategy could be improved to bring about an increase in stakeholder value and a more competitive, innovative and customer-focused value proposition. This would require candidates to measure and evaluate the current marketing strategy, as well as assessing it against the desired results of the organisation. This required candidates to understand the core competences of the organisation, its ethos, value, mission, how to identify key stakeholders (and other analysis) and then critically analyse the organisation in the wider, corporate level context.

CHAPTER ROUNDUP

- Marketing metrics need to be utilised to measure the efficiency and effectiveness of organisations as well as measure performance at different levels.

- Marketing measures can be both at a strategic and tactical level.

- Shareholder value analysis (SVA) is a method of approaching the problem of business control by focusing on the creation of value for shareholders.

- Value based management is based on three key elements: belief, principles and processes.

- Benchmarking is widely used by businesses, focusing on its performance against other external businesses.

- The use of the balanced scorecard includes both financial and operational measures, bringing together the internal and external perspective.

- Ethics are a key part of strategy development, but the extent of the ethical stance varies considerably.

FURTHER READING

Anderson, B.B. (2000) The move toward sustainable marketing. *Agri Marketing*, Vol38(2), pp38.

Bridges, C.M. and Wilhelm, W.B. (2008) Going beyond green: the 'why and how' of integrating sustainability into the marketing curriculum. *Journal of Marketing Education*, Apr, Vol30(1), pp33-46.

De Wit, B. and Meyer, R. (2005) *Strategy synthesis: resolving strategy paradoxes to create competitive advantage, test and readings.* 2ⁿᵈ edition. London, Thomson.

Doyle, P. and Stern, P. (2006) *Marketing management and strategy.* 4ᵗʰ edition. Harlow, Prentice Hall.

Hooley, G. *et al* (2007) *Marketing strategy and competitive positioning.* 4ᵗʰ edition. Harlow, Prentice Hall.

Kucharsky, D. (2006) Sustainable marketing. *Marketing Magazine*, 27 Feb, Vol111(8), p4 Ebsco abstract.

Peattie, K. (2001) Towards sustainability: the third age of green marketing. *Marketing Review*, Vol2(2), pp129-146.

REFERENCES

Ambler, T. (1997) How much of brand equity is explained by trust? *Management Decision*, 35(3-4), pp283-92.

Bennet, M. and James, P. (1999) *Sustainable measures: evaluating and reporting of environmental and social performance*. Sheffield, UK, Greenleaf Publishing.

Boulding, W. A., Kalra, R., Staelin, and Zeithaml, A. (1993) A dynamic process model of service quality: from expectations to behavioural intentions. *Journal of Marketing Research*, 30 (February), pp7-27.

Clark (N) (2008) 'From ethical consumerism to political consumption'. *Geography Compass* 2 (6) pp1870-84.

De Wit, B. and Meyer, R. (2005) *Strategy synthesis: resolving strategy paradoxes to create competitive advantage.* 2ⁿᵈ edition. London, Cengage.

Dibb, S. and Simkin, L. (2009) *Marketing essentials*. 1ˢᵗ edition. London, Cengage.

Doyle, P. (2002) *Marketing management and strategy*. 3rd edition. Harlow, Prentice Hall International.

Doyle, P. and Stern, P. (2006) *Marketing management and strategy*. 4th edition. Harlow, FT Prentice Hall.

Doyle, P. (2008) *Value-based marketing: marketing strategies for corporate growth and shareholder value*. Chichester, John Wiley & Sons Inc.

Gilligan, C. and Wilson R. (2004) *Strategic marketing management*. 3rd edition. Oxford, Butterworth-Heinemann.

Johnson G. and Scholes K. (2002) *Exploring Corporate Strategy*. Harlow, Essex. Pearson Education Limited.

Johnson, G., Scholes K. and Whittington R. (2007). *Exploring corporate strategy*. 8th edition. Harlow, FT Prentice Hall.

Kaplan, R.S. and Norton D.P. (1992) The balanced scorecard: measures that drive performance. *Harvard Business Review*. Jan–Feb, pp71-80.

Knight, J.A. (1998) *Value based management – developing a systematic approach to creating shareholder value*. New York, McGraw-Hill.

Kumar, S. and Gulati, R. (2009) *Measuring efficiency, effectiveness and performance of Indian public sector banks. International Journal of Productivity and Performance Management*, Vol59 Issue 1, pp51-74.

Paine, L.S. (1994) Managing for organizational integrity. *Harvard Business Review* 72, No 2 (March-April), pp106-117.

Palmer, J. Cockton, J. and Cooper, G. (2007) *Managing marketing*. 1st edition. Oxford, Butterworth-Heinemann.

Ranchhod, A. and Gurau, C. (2007) *Marketing strategies: a twenty-first century approach*. 2nd edition. London, FT Prentice Hall.

Rajendra, K., Srivastava, Tasadduq, A., Shervani and Fahey, L. (1999) *The Journal of Marketing.* Vol63 Fundamental issues and directions for marketing. pp168-179. American Marketing Association, www.jstor.org/stable/1252110

Srivastava, R, Shervani, T and Fahey, L (1999) Fundamental Issues and Directions for Marketing, pp168-179, Vol.63.

Venkatramen (N) and Ramanujan (V) 1987, "Measurement of business economic performance: An examination of method convergence". *Journal of Management* 13 (1): 109-122 "Directory of Life Cycle Inventory Data Sources" Society for Promotion of LCA Development (SPOLD) (Brussels), Nov 1995.

Wasik, J.E. (1996) *Green marketing and management: a global perspective*. Cambridge, MA., Blackwell.

QUICK QUIZ

1   What are the drawbacks of organisations that only use accountancy measures for measuring marketing performance?

2   What are the three major marketing attributes that performance measures should include?

3   What is shareholder value analysis (SVA)?

4   According to Doyle the extent of a company's success may be measured in two ways. What are they?

5   What are the four drivers of financial value?

6   There are two principal approaches to benchmarking. What are they?

7   Name two advantages and two disadvantages of benchmarking.

8   What roles do setting standards and targets play in marketing management?

9   How does Robert Kaplan describe the balanced scorecard?

10   There are two reasons why an organisation might take a wider view of ethical responsibilities when considering the longer-term interest of shareholders. What are they?

11   According to SPOLD (1995) what does life cycle analysis thinking reflect?

ACTIVITY DEBRIEFS

Activity 6.3

To verify the design of the initial balanced scorecard, here is a list of possible questions to ask of every strategic initiative:

Alignment questions

- What is the strategic goal that is being addressed by this activity?
- What organisational mission does it relate to?
- Do we have a hypothesis as to how this initiative will eventually improve results (ie a strategy map)?

Baseline questions

- What is the existing level of performance? Do we know?
- Are we collecting this data and storing it somewhere?
- What are the statistical parameters of this data, eg how much random variation does it contain?

Cost and risk questions

- What is the existing cost of operation?
- How much will that increase when we do the initiative?
- What is the risk that this cost will be exceeded?
- Is the money being spent on this initiative the best use of the funds, or is there a better use?
- What is the risk that the initiative will fail? Has this assessment been included in the planning?

Customer and stakeholder questions

- Have you listed all the communities of interest that have a stake in this initiative?
- Who are the kinds of customers/stakeholders who will benefit directly from this initiative?
- Who will benefit indirectly?
- Is the specified initiative the best way to increase satisfaction for all kinds of customers, or is there a better way?
- How will we know that the initiative benefits these customers?

Metrics questions

- What metrics will be used to define the benefit?
- Are these the best metrics? How do we know that?
- How many metrics need to be tracked? If this is a large number (it usually is), what kind of system are you planning to use to track them?
- Are the metrics standardised so they can be benchmarked against performance in other organisations?

Measurement methodology questions

- How will the metrics be measured? What methods will be used, and how frequently will data be collected?
- Is this the best way to do the measurements? How do we know that?

Results questions

- How can we demonstrate that this strategic initiative, and not something else, contributed to a change in results?
- How much of the change was probably random?

Activity 6.4

The very act of creating a written code of ethics demands that you really think about what ethics drive your decision making and the direction you want to go in. Consider obtaining employee input when creating your company code of ethics.

Try to tailor your company code of ethics to your particular business and industry. Throughout your code of ethics you may want to cite a few examples or common scenarios employees may face. Your code of ethics may include but, not be limited to the following:

- Your company's values and commitment to ethical behaviour
- Ethical and unethical behaviour, and guidance on making good decisions
- Conflicts of interest
- Acceptance of gifts
- Confidentiality of company information
- Reporting code of ethics violations (including method of confidential reporting)
- Written pledge
- Consequences and remedies of breaches of the code

Reduced turnover and improved employee morale and satisfaction are just a few added bonuses of being a business employees can be proud of.

QUICK QUIZ ANSWERS

1.   –   Accounts can be difficult to interpret, even if financial data are reported

    –   Accounting measures can vary from organisation to organisation, making it difficult to compare performance

2.   –   The adaptability or innovativeness of an organisation

    –   The effectiveness of particular marketing strategies

    –   Efficiency in the execution of particular strategies

3.   Shareholder value analysis (SVA) is a method of approaching the problem of business control by focusing on the creation of value for shareholders.

4.   According to Doyle (2002), the extent of a company's success may be measured in two ways:

The first is by using the concept of economic profit (trademarked by Stern Stewart and Company as Economic Value Added®). The expression 'economic profit' is used to distinguish the measure from accounting profit, which is computed according to the strict rules of accountancy.

The cash flow approach may be used to estimate the degree of economic value a company may be expected to create in the future. It is based on an estimation of likely future cash flows, both positive and negative, as indicated in the corporate plans.

5.   –   Cash flow volume

    –   Cash flow risk

    –   Cash flow timing

    –   Cash flow sustainability

6   Process benchmarking, where data is exchanged between companies with similar administrative and manufacturing processes. This process is very similar to the provision of field maintenance for office systems such as photocopiers and computers.

Competitor benchmarking focuses on the performance and relative strengths of direct competitors using information from customer and supplier interviews and published data from any source available. A firm tries to be as good as its competitors.

7   **Advantages of benchmarking**

–   The comparisons are carried out by the managers who have to live with any changes implemented as a result of the exercise.

–   Benchmarking focuses on improvement in key areas and sets targets which are challenging but achievable. What is really achievable can be discovered by examining what others have achieved: managers are therefore able to accept that they are not being asked to perform miracles.

Disadvantages of benchmarking

–   Benchmarking is reactive; rather than imitating a competitor, another competitive strategy may be more focused.

–   It is not focused on the customer. The firm should set itself targets that customers value.

8   The organisation's objectives provide the basis for setting targets and standards. Each manager's targets will be directed towards achieving the company objectives. Targets or standards do two things:

–   They tell managers what they are required to accomplish, given the authority to make appropriate decisions.

–   They indicate to managers how well their actual results measure up against their targets, so that control action can be taken where it is needed. It follows that in setting standards for performance, it is important to distinguish between controllable or manageable variables and uncontrollable ones. Any matters which cannot be controlled by an individual manager should be excluded from their standards for performance.

9   The balanced scorecard is a set of measures that gives senior managers a fast but comprehensive view of the business. The balanced scorecard includes financial measures that tell the results of actions already taken. It complements the financial measures with operational measures on customer satisfaction, internal processes, and the organisation's innovation and improvement activities – operational measures that are the drivers of future financial performance.

10   There are two reasons why an organisation might take a wider view of ethical responsibilities when considering the longer-term interest of shareholders:

–   The organisation's corporate image may be enhanced by an assumption of wider responsibilities. The cost of undertaking such responsibilities may be justified as essentially promotional expenditure.

–   The responsible exercise of corporate power may prevent a build-up of social and political pressure for legal regulation. Freedom of action may be preserved and the burden of regulation lightened by acceptance of ethical responsibilities.

11   According to SPOLD (1995) life cycle thinking reflects the acceptance that key company stakeholders cannot limit their responsibilities to those phases of the life cycle process or activity with which they are involved.

CHAPTER 7

Leadership theories and strategies

Introduction

Leadership theories and thinking have developed and changed rapidly in recent years as leaders, authors and academics try to interpret what is practised and what is needed in our increasingly dynamic business environment. It would be easy to assume that new ideas have emerged with new solutions to leading in the next few decades. A review of research studies, texts and articles and many of these ideas and themes reveal that much of this new thinking on leadership is based on established theories.

However, there are some new ideas, often built on a foundation of established leadership theories, and there are changes, some subtle, on the thinking of what makes a good leader today. We can learn from all of these ideas and thinking and they provide useful guidance to how people might develop their personal growth as leaders and equip themselves for our rapidly changing environment and demanding stakeholder needs.

Topic list

3.1.1	Critically evaluate and identify the methods for measuring successful and effective leadership strategies in determining and defining an organisation's strategic focus and intent

	▪ Different leadership theories in achieving strategic focus:
	  – Trait approach/Behaviour approach
	  – Power/influence approach
	  – Situational approach
	  – Integrative approach

3.1.2	Critically evaluate a range of approaches to successful leadership of the organisation and of the marketing function:
	  ▪ Characteristics of a successful leader
	  ▪ Characteristics of followers
	  ▪ Characteristics of the situation
	  ▪ Relating and integrating the primary types of leadership approaches in order to ensure successful and effective leadership strategies
	  ▪ Ethics of leaders

3.1.3	Critically evaluate and analyse the dominant leadership paradigms
	  ▪ Classical/Visionary/Transactional/Organic
	  ▪ Organisational considerations according to different leadership paradigms

3.1.4	Critically evaluate the concept of power and influence in promoting a coherent philosophy regarding sources of power and how it can be exercised in the organisation
	  ▪ Influence processes (Kelman proposed three different types of influence processes – instrumental compliance, internalisation and personal identification)
	  ▪ Different types of power according to their source (French and Raven, 1959)
	  ▪ Control over information power
	  ▪ Dichotomy between position power and personal power (Bass 1960, Etzioni 1961)

1 Leadership and management

1.1 Difference between leadership and management?

▶ **Key terms**

Leadership outlines what needs to be done by creating and identifying new ideas and trends and establishing a vision and clear direction.

Management works out how to achieve the vision and gets things done through organising, planning, motivating, co-ordinating and controlling resources.

There are differences in the roles of leaders and managers and it is worth noting what these differences are. Both leaders and managers can and do share skills and both need to sometimes lead and sometimes manage. However, leaders and managers also have distinct roles that complement each other and one without the other will eventually lead to failure, very broadly, it is important to note that leaders and managers need to work with each other and complement each other's activities; if they do not have a clear understanding as to what each other is doing this can lead to a breakdown of communication in other parts of the organisation as well as objectives not being achieved.

If leaders spend their time submerged in the detail of how to achieve a vision they are unlikely to have the time, or develop the skills, to conceptualise the future and the organisation's role in that future.

If managers are preoccupied with the future and developing a vision for it they will overlook or ignore designing and implementing strategies and plans to achieve the vision.

The Chartered Institute of Marketing

This is not to say leaders and managers do not work together on both vision and its implementation. As with the best of teams, ideas are explored, practicalities investigated and the process of exchanging ideas and thoughts between leaders, managers **and staff** is essential. This collaboration and each person understanding the essential role they play is what leads to successful organisation performance.

Understanding the difference is important for knowing where the majority of your time should be spent and what skills should be improved and developed and where you leave or delegate responsibility for aspects of organisation success to someone else.

Many of us will have experienced organisations where the leaders are focused on day-to-day tactical activities at the cost of any sort of strategic direction and where managers dabble in visionary ideas neglecting or relinquishing responsibility for the design and management of implementation. The result can often be chaos, even in very small organisations. The exception in very small organisations is that the leader and manager may be the same person and here the challenge is often either having the right skills or knowing when and what role to play. The following are key points that need to be considered when analysing the leadership and management team of an organisation:

- Leadership and management must go hand in hand.

- Workers need their managers not just to assign tasks but to define purpose and link it back to the organisation's vision and mission as well as the long-term marketing strategy; this will help to ensure the marketing strategy is fulfilled and key objectives met.

- Managers must organise workers, not just to maximise efficiency, but to nurture skills, develop talent and inspire results, especially if the organisation is trying to improve its level of efficiency and effectiveness (see Chapter 6 for more in depth discussion on efficiency and effectiveness).

THE REAL WORLD

What makes a good leader?

Richard Branson discusses the key elements of being a good leader: 'Having a personality of caring about people is important. You can't be a good leader unless you generally like people. That is how you bring out the best in them.'

Branson does things somewhat differently to other leaders; he is known for not holding regular board meetings and has a fairly informal approach to leadership. However, central to his leadership skills is ensuring others are treated with respect. Leadership for him involves trouble shooting, having time to concentrate on new projects and ensuring the company continually promotes and markets his businesses. A key element of Branson's leadership strategy is ensuring there is conviction in the decisions he makes, stating that you have to believe in a project 100% for it to have any chance of success.

Another key element of Branson's leadership strategy is ensuring that he hires are people that can engage with his brand, believe in the business and are bright. In return he is happy to give them a stake in the business, which in turn will make them more motivated, committed and interested in working well for the organisation.

Branson also states: 'As much as you need a strong personality to build a business from scratch, you also must understand the art of delegation. I have to be good at helping people run the individual businesses, and I have to be willing to step back. The company must be set up so it can continue without me.'

A key factor for good leadership, as far as Branson is concerned, is being able to relate to other people: 'If you're good with people…and you really care, genuinely care about people then I'm sure we could find a job for you at Virgin. The companies that look after their people are the companies that do really well. I'm sure we'd like a few other attributes, but that would be the most important one.' Hence, treating employees as the most important part of the organisation for Branson is the key to success.

http://richardbranson.evancarmichael.com (accessed March 2012)

1.2 Ethics and leadership

The importance of ethical behavior is fundamental to leading and managing. Leaders should be able to show their ethics through their leadership style and actions. The visibility of ethics and values is a key consideration for leadership teams. This can help to build trust, gain brand credibility as well fulfill key stakeholder expectations. The judgement of ethics can be subjective however it has a key role to play in the leading, development and long-term sustainability of an organisation as well as its leader. Stakeholders at all levels expect ethical considerations as central to the organisation's success.

2 Strategic leadership theories

There are still some prevailing myths of leadership it is worth dispelling:

(a) **Leaders are born not made:** there is no doubt that some people have certain characteristics that predispose them to being effective leaders. However, we can all learn and do all the time from the examples of leadership we experience early on of what makes good and bad leaders. If we have a personal interest in being a good leader we automatically adopt good practices and try to avoid bad leadership.

(b) **Leaders must have charisma:** if this were true we would be seriously short of leaders. More importantly it supposes that charisma automatically leads to good leadership, which is not true. There are charismatic people that are poor at leadership; they may be able to inspire but lack the skills to do anything positive or productive with inspired people. This is not to say that charisma, in a good leader, is not an advantage; it certainly is and, used appropriately, can be very powerful. However, there are good leaders that do not have charisma and are successful.

(c) **Leaders can only lead in one particular way:** there are some people who are inflexible and cannot adapt to different situations and usually these people will not make good leaders. We also cannot change our personality to be someone different. However, any effective leader can be flexible and modify their leadership style to reflect the requirements of the situation.

(d) **Leaders need status to lead:** often used inappropriately as a crutch for employee compliance, status (job title, formal position higher up the hierarchy) is seen as all that is needed to lead people. If this were true we would never experience those occasions when some people take control of a difficult situation or crisis regardless of their status and lead people to a successful outcome, often seen during a natural disaster. In the workplace there are examples of a leader's assistant or deputy being seen as the force behind the leader and employees see them as the real leader.

(e) **Leaders have power and authority:** this is often true as it comes with the territory, so a job title or formal position higher up the hierarchy bestows a certain amount of power and authority. However, if a leader is not trusted or respected this power and authority can quickly diminish, even disappear. Real power and authority comes from the trust and respect of others, employees and other stakeholders. This trust and respect is only conferred on leaders who are seen to be effective leaders.

Leaders may all lead in their own very distinct and different ways but effective and successful leaders often share some common characteristics.

2.1 Leadership characteristics

You do not have to be in the workplace for very long before you can identify what characterises good and bad leaders. You will also have observed the impact certain leadership styles have on you and others. It can be positive and inspiring, negative and destructive or somewhere in between. The **traits** typically found in successful leaders include:

The Chartered Institute of Marketing

- Self-confidence and energy
- Tolerance of stress and willingness to assume responsibility
- Persistence and determination
- Decisive, assertive and fair
- Adaptable and co-operative
- Humility

These traits are complemented with the most typical **skills** of successful leaders:

- Fluent and articulate
- Socially skilled
- Organisation and co-ordination
- Conceptually skilled and creative
- Diplomatic, tactful and persuasive

Many people may start with some innate traits and skills but most leaders develop skills throughout their careers and usually because they want to be successful leaders, and success does not necessarily mean being financially successful. The trait theory of leadership proved to have shortcomings when it came to defining leadership, not least showing that leaders are not necessarily born but can be made. Focusing on ideal leadership traits exposed that people with these traits did not always make good leaders and not having all of these traits early on did not always stop people from becoming successful leaders.

In particular, it was recognised that successful leaders are not just intelligent and technically skilled. Increasingly emotional intelligence is seen as essential to good leadership. There are also key principles to a good leader which can be summarised as follows:

- **Know yourself and seek self-improvement:** leaders must know how to self reflect and look at what gaps there are in their skill base; as a strategy changes and developing different skill sets may be required.

- **Be technically proficient:** as a leader, you must know your job as well as understanding what others are doing.

- **Seek responsibility and take responsibility for your actions:** it is important that different challenges are identified and understood.

- **Make sound and timely decisions:** use good problem solving, decision making and planning tools; the time of the decision making is just as important as the decision itself.

- **Set the example:** a leader must be a good role model and lead by example; this helps others to aspire to the leader and can help with motivating individuals and teams: 'We must become the change we want to see', Mahatma Gandhi (quotationsbook.com).

- **Know your people and look out for their well-being:** if employees feel that leaders care and are concerned this can help to create loyalty and increase motivation.

- **Keep your workers informed:** knowing how to communicate with key stakeholders is an imperative part of good leadership.

- **Develop a sense of responsibility in your workers:** help to develop good character traits which help them to develop in their role.

- **Ensure that tasks are understood, supervised, and accomplished:** it is important that people know what they are doing and why, so that they can take ownership of their actions.

- **Train as a team:** leaders should be a part of the training and personal development process themselves, they also need to be aware of where they need to train and develop further to ensure that they can develop strategies appropriately.

2.2 Emotional intelligence

Emotional intelligence emerged in the 1980s, from psychological works from the 1930s, when John Mayer and Peter Salovey (1990) looked at the different factors of emotional intelligence.

Salovey and Mayer (1990) described four key factors:

- **Identify emotions:** the ability to perceive emotions in oneself, others, and in objects, art and events

- **Use emotions**: the ability to generate, use and feel emotions to communicate feelings, or employ them in thinking or creating

- **Understand emotions:** the ability to understand emotional information, how emotions combine and progress, and to reason about such emotional meanings

- **Manage emotions:** the ability to regulate emotions in oneself and others to promote personal understanding and growth

It was the 1990s before the concept became popular in leadership writing, on the publication of Daniel Goleman's book (1995) *Emotional intelligence: why it can matter more than IQ*. Goleman originally identified numerous factors under two headings but these have evolved into the following:

- **Self-awareness:** emotional self-awareness, accurate self-assessment, self-confidence

- **Self-management:** emotional self-control, transparency, adaptability, achievement orientation, initiative, optimism, conscientiousness

- **Social awareness:** empathy, organisational awareness, service orientation

- **Relationship management:** inspire, influence, develop others, change catalyst, conflict management, building bonds, teamwork, collaboration, communication

Goleman (1995) believes that emotional intelligence competences are not innate skills but rather they are abilities that can be learned. He also suggests that you cannot teach emotional competences using traditional methods designed for cognitive learning. Emotional learning involves thinking and acting in ways that are fundamental to a person's identity: their personality. This will inevitably bring some people into conflict with their deep-rooted beliefs and attitudes and the need to change their behaviour. This can be difficult; it requires new ways of thinking and acting.

We will discuss this in more detail in Chapter 9.

Higgs and Dulewicz (2002) *Making sense of emotional intelligence* identified seven elements of emotional intelligence and broke down the elements into three areas:

- **Drivers:** motivation and decisiveness, traits that energise people and drive them towards achieving goals

- **Constrainers:** conscientiousness, integrity, emotional resilience, factors that control, traits that curb the excesses of the drivers

- **Enablers:** sensitivity, influence and self-awareness, traits that facilitate performance and help individuals to succeed

Higgs and Dulewicz (2002) argue that their components of emotional intelligence divide into two categories for learning:

(a) People can learn through established methods, such as personal development strategies eg sensitivity, influence and self-awareness.

(b) More enduring elements of an individual's personality that are more difficult to learn, such as motivation, emotional resilience and conscientiousness, can be learnt through training strategies that exploit each

The Chartered Institute of Marketing

individual's characteristics to the full and through developing 'coping strategies' that minimise the impact of potential limitations.

Appraising emotional intelligence is best undertaken through a combination of methods including self-assessment, peer assessment, manager assessment and subordinate assessment. This should produce a well-rounded perspective and help identify areas for improvement.

> ▶ **Assessment tip**
>
> A fundamental part of the leadership and planning assessment is understanding what leadership skills are required to develop recommendations and ensure they can be implemented. This may involve reflecting on one's own leadership style and identifying gaps that need developing.

2.3 Leadership styles

> ▶ **Key term**
>
> **Leadership style** is the outward expression of the beliefs, values and assumptions held by an individual that lead to typical attitudes and behaviour towards others and influence approaches to leading and managing people.

The trait theory of leadership was followed by other theories. During this time the idea of leadership evolved from being directive and controlling to being more participative, visionary and collaborative. Much has been written on leadership styles over the last six decades and many schools of thought have emerged.

Figure 7.1   The journey and evolution of leadership styles

Leadership and management styles vary considerably and the following covers some examples of better known and more enduring theories. Many styles have their value as well as their disadvantages. Leadership styles come in and go out of fashion (and come back into fashion). The leadership styles described emerged in different eras but are still relevant today as they are still practised.

2.3.1 Behavioural leadership

Behavioural leadership theory focused on what people did rather than what traits they had. Different ideas emerged but essentially focused on four main themes:

(a)   **People-oriented** leadership: focuses on people to achieve the objectives.

(b)   **Task-oriented** leadership: focuses on tasks to achieve the objectives.

(c)   **Directive** leadership: authority and decisions are retained by the leader.

(d)   **Participative** leadership: authority and decisions are shared with employees.

Tannenbaum and Schmidt (1973) developed their continuum of possible leadership styles illustrating the degree of control exercised by leaders and the extent of freedom for subordinates to participate. Tannenbaum and Schmidt believed that the leadership style adopted depended on three forces:

(a)   **Forces in the manager:** eg values, attitudes, personality, behaviour

(b)   **Forces in subordinates:** eg personality, need for independence, willingness to take responsibility

(c)   **Forces in the situation:** eg environmental factors such as internal (organisational, the problem, time) and external (challenges)

Figure 7.2   Leadership style continuum

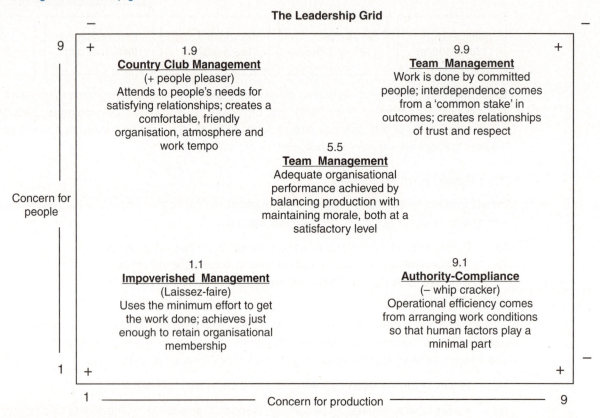

Dictatorial	Autocratic			Democratic			Laissez faire
Manager makes decision and enforces it	Manager makes decision and announces it	Manager sells decision	Manager presents ideas and invites questions	Manager presents tentative decisions subject to change	Manager presents problem, gets suggestions, makes decision	Manager defines limits, asks group to make decision	Manager permits subordinates to function within limits defined by superior

High degree of control exercised by leader
Low employee involvement

Low degree of control exercised by leader
High employee involvement

Adapted from Tannenbaum and Schmidt (1973) continuum

The assumptions of behavioural leadership that leaders either focus on **people (goal accomplishment)** to achieve goals or focus on **tasks (goal attainment)** suggests, for example, an autocratic style of leadership would tend to focus on task and assume people need to be directed and controlled if the task is to be achieved. A more democratic style of leadership would assume that people can be trusted to complete the task and therefore it is more important to focus on people and their needs. Behavioural leadership can, and expects to, adapt and change depending on circumstances.

Blake and Mouton (1985) developed their managerial/leadership grid: a two dimensional grid using 'concern with people' and 'concern with production' as the axes. They later added another axis: 'motivation'.

Figure 7.3   Managerial/leadership grid

The Leadership Grid

	9.9
1.9	**Team Management**
Country Club Management	Work is done by committed
(+ people pleaser)	people; interdependence comes
Attends to people's needs for	from a 'common stake' in
satisfying relationships; creates a	outcomes; creates relationships
comfortable, friendly	of trust and respect
organisation, atmosphere and	
work tempo	

9

Concern for people

5.5
Team Management
Adequate organisational
performance achieved by
balancing production with
maintaining morale, both at a
satisfactory level

1.1
Impoverished Management
(Laissez-faire)
Uses the minimum effort to get
the work done; achieves just
enough to retain organisational
membership

9.1
Authority-Compliance
(– whip cracker)
Operational efficiency comes
from arranging work conditions
so that human factors play a
minimal part

1

1 ———————— Concern for production ———————— 9

The concern refers to the leader's attitudes, assumptions and style of leadership and the grid reflects how the leader expresses concern for people or production. The research of Blake and Mouton revealed that leaders

The Chartered Institute of Marketing

may change from one style to another or use a combination of different styles for different situations but that leaders typically have one dominant style that usually asserts itself. However, leaders are known to have a 'secondary' style that they use if the dominant style is not getting the desired results.

Styles that leaders can adopt are affected by those they are working with and the environment they are working in. The problem with behaviour approaches to leadership is that they don't look properly at the context or setting in which the style is used.

2.3.2 Situational (contingency) theory of leadership

Situational leadership believes that a leader will adopt a leadership style that is appropriate to the needs of the situation. It is based on the assumption that the person most qualified and experienced to do the job will emerge as leader.

There are four types of behaviour:

(a) **Directive leadership** – letting people know exactly what is expected and giving specific directions. People expected to follow rules

(b) **Supportive** – friendly, approachable, concerned for needs and the welfare of employees

(c) **Participative** – consulting and evaluating opinions and suggestions from employees and stakeholders

(d) **Achievement-oriented** – setting challenging goals, seeking improvement in performance and confident that subordinates who have ability will perform well

There are two main situational factors:

(a) **Personal characteristics of subordinates** – determines how they will react to the manager's behaviour and the extent to which they see behaviour as an immediate or a potential source of need satisfaction

(b) **Nature of task** – extent to which it is routine and structured or non-routine and unstructured

Hersey and Blanchard (1993) based situational leadership on 'readiness' (the followers' ability and willingness to accomplish task) and the level of people the leader is attempting to influence. The leadership style reflects the amount of direction and support that the leader provides to their followers. They describe leadership styles as four types of behaviour named S1 to S4:

Figure 7.4   Situational leadership model

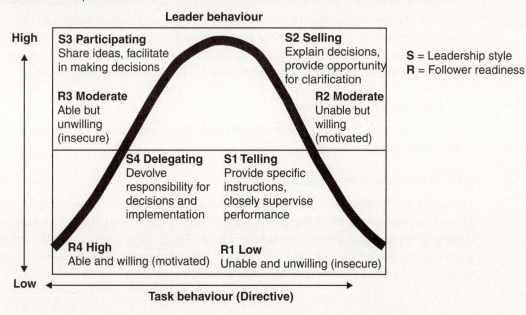

The different styles require a different focus, either on the task or on the relationship between the leader and follower, depending on the situation. For example when the follower is unable and unwilling to do the job, and reasons may include lack of training or confidence, the style is more directive. When followers are able, willing and motivated the leader can allow followers to lead and the style devolves responsibility to followers.

No one style is considered the best or even necessary for all leaders. Because of personality leaders will lean towards a particular style and the challenge for effective leaders is to be flexible in their style and able to adapt to the situation and assume a leadership style more appropriate to the situation.

2.3.3 Transformational leadership theory

Transformational leadership is based on transforming organisation performance and such leaders are willing to make changes where necessary to improve and achieve the organisation's goals. The focus of the transformational leader is to create a vision that appeals to the values of followers and in so doing create a feeling of justice, loyalty and trust. Transformational leadership can be democratic but the leader expects to shape and change events rather than adapt to changing events which can result in a more autocratic style. They are focused on strategic issues and believe charisma, intellectual stimulation, inspiration and using motivation will get things done.

Transformational leaders challenge and assume people can be inspired to achieve high standards of performance. Learning and development is therefore a driving force. They can be inflexible, single minded, obstinate, stubborn.

Table 7.1   Transactional/Situational/Transformational Leadership

Critical difference	
Transactional/situational	**Transformational**
'Do what is required'	'Go the extra mile'
Leader adapts to various situations	Organisation adapts, focus on consistency
Focus in on day-to-day activities	Strategic emphasis, vision
Development of task and people behaviours	Symbolic influence
Situational analysis decides emphasis	Focus is on the organisation
Management by exception (Active: seek deviation, correct. Passive: correct if exposed)	Inspire individuals to transcend self-interest, activate higher level needs
Exchange rewards for effective performance	Growth and development of individuals

As has already been stated the next two leadership styles are actually centuries old but have become increasingly relevant to a broader range of organisations driven by social, environmental and ethical goals and by the urgent need for organisations to nurture creativity and exploit innovation. Attention has therefore refocused on these styles and research and studies resulted in new emerging themes.

2.3.4 Entrepreneurial leadership

Entrepreneurial leadership is recognised as desirable in both small and large organisations and yet, particularly in large organisations, often seems elusive.

2.3.5 What is entrepreneurial leadership?

The fundamental difference between transformational leadership and entrepreneurial leadership is focus. Transformational leaders try to change the existing order; entrepreneurs create a new order. Entrepreneurial leadership has also been around for a very long time. The problem is that in recent decades, particularly as the leadership trends we have discussed emerged and influenced leadership styles, entrepreneurial leadership was sidelined and seen as the domain of start-ups and small businesses.

Creativity and innovation feature high on the list of entrepreneurial characteristics. The ability and willingness to challenge current thinking and ways of doing things and come up with new ideas is part of the entrepreneur's make-up.

The entrepreneurial instinct is not seen as a threat or the domain of only the leader. It is seen as desirable in many people in the organisation and actively encouraged. The leader should not see themselves as the only person who can be the entrepreneur but be prepared to lead and facilitate entrepreneurship. This of course means giving up control and being willing for others to take risks and make mistakes.

Developing strategy and building operational efficiency is essential to organisation success and to realising entrepreneurial output and there is no good reason why efficiency should stifle the entrepreneur. As long as organisation design remains flexible and bureaucracy does not take over, entrepreneurship can flourish.

It is important to clarify entrepreneurial behaviour. Entrepreneurs challenge and change things. They do not rigidly follow rules but they also do not break them for the sake of it. They break rules for good reasons, for example if they are constraining organisation success, but they follow tried and trusted principles that work to ensure effectiveness and efficiency. Entrepreneurs also do not instigate change for no valid reason; there is always a well thought through purpose.

Neal Thornberry's book *Lead like an entrepreneur* explores and describes some of the factors and behaviour of entrepreneurial leadership. He distinguishes between transformational and entrepreneurial leadership entrepreneurial leadership is similar to the factors outlined in Table 7.1.

Key characteristics of the entrepreneur include:

- **Internal locus of control:** most entrepreneurs have strong internal locus of control to determine their own fate
- **Tolerance for ambiguity:** chaos, uncertainty and disorder comes with the territory
- **Willingness to hire smarter people:** accept personal limitations and seek to balance
- **Consistent drive to create, build or change:** driven by challenge rather than money
- **Passion:** enthusiastic even obsessive
- **Optimism:** glass half full
- **Sense of urgency:** impatience, don't waste time or miss the boat
- **Perseverance:** not sidetracked or derailed
- **Resilience:** accept mistakes, learn, bounce back
- **Sense of humour about oneself:** being prepared to accept flaws

Thornberry (2006) describes two dimensions to entrepreneurial orientation:

- **Activist orientation:** adopt a direct driver/owner orientation towards value creation. They push others in new directions. They are serial changers, spotlight flaws and factors that will hold the organisation back.
- **Catalyst orientation:** tend not to be direct drivers of opportunity. They help to set up or induce conditions to allow innovation and entrepreneurial opportunities to be consistently and persistently pursued. They are often cultural value setters, believe in innovation, taking risks, allow mistakes and encourage continual learning. They build a structure and climate where others can create value.

Figure 7.5   Entrepreneurial leadership – focus and roles

	Internal	External
Activist	Miners (Operational value chain)	Explorers (Market)
Catalyst	Accelerators (Unit)	Integrators (Enterprises)

Entrepreneurial role (label positioned between Activist and Catalyst on left)

Thornberry goes on to describe commitment to entrepreneurship and attitudes to control and how this influences the way an entrepreneur might behave. The horizontal axis refers to how much organisational commitment the entrepreneur must pursue. The less control they have the more they must negotiate, sell, or persuade others to achieve their objectives.

- **Accelerator:** internally-focused leadership but indirect entrepreneurs, instead focusing on how to get people to be more creative, innovative, stimulate different thinking and behaviour

- **Miner:** operationally-focused leadership, creating, designing operations to deliver new value propositions

- **Explorer:** market-focused leadership, developing new markets or products or both

- **Integrator:** organisation-level focus developing an organisation-wide entrepreneurial strategy. They are focused on the external environment and on creating an internal environment for opportunism.

Figure 7.6   Different types/different requirements

- **Accelerator:** typically need little permission as they run their own unit and have more control

- **Miner:** usually need permission and have less personal control because they embark on internal opportunities that cross organisational lines

- **Explorer:** have to assemble resources and need to enlist the help of senior management. They often have to act like start-up entrepreneurs if they want their goals achieved.

- **Integrator:** embed entrepreneurship as part of their strategy and build the support, through structure, systems etc necessary to keep the momentum going

Entrepreneurial leaders often lose interest when they have achieved their goal and unless they are in an environment where they can activate their vision for the next goal they will move on to new challenges elsewhere. For the entrepreneur it is about new beginnings, risk and change.

Entrepreneurs often utilise a servant leadership style to achieve their goals, recognising that success depends on committed people.

Steve Jobs from Apple was regarded as an entrepreneurial leader; he recommended 12 tips to be a successful leader:

1   Do what you love to
2   Be different
3   Do your best

The Chartered Institute of Marketing

4   Undertake a SWOT analysis
5   Be entrepreneurial
6   Start small, think big
7   Strive to become a market leader
8   Focus on the outcome
9   Ask for feedback
10   Innovate
11   Learn from failures
12   Learn continually

(http://www.1000ventures.com [accessed March 2012])

2.3.6 Servant/stewardship leadership

Servant leadership goes back thousands of years, with the idea of the leader of a kingdom serving his/her people and it can also be found in the teaching of various religions. The idea of servant leadership in the modern organisation first emerged in 1970 following an essay by Robert Greenleaf on the subject of 'The servant as leader' where he explained that servant leadership requires a belief that as a leader your role is to serve others first, prioritising the needs of others before focusing on personal needs. Evidence of this servant leadership is found in the personal growth of others. At the centre of servant leadership is collaboration and the ethical use of power. Stewardship requires sharing power and decision making.

Greenleaf identified eleven characteristics of the servant leader:

(a)   **Calling** to serve in the interests of others and put that interest before self interest

(b)   **Listening** with commitment to others and to oneself. Hearing and valuing what people say and acting on it when appropriate

(c)   **Empathy** to understand others in order to better understand their individual concerns and needs

(d)   **Healing** oneself and others in times of change or crisis, being prepared to understand and allow for reactions of various sorts and work towards solutions

(e)   **Awareness** of self and others

(f)   **Persuasion** rather than authority or coercion

(g)   **Conceptualisation** to cultivate dreams and rise above day-to-day tasks

(h)   **Foresight** based on learning from the past, comprehend the present and visualise the future

(i)   **Stewardship** looking after something with the intention of passing it on to others

(j)   **Growth** of people through formal and informal encouragement of learning and development

(k)   **Building community** within the organisation and harmonising relationships

The advantages of servant leadership include nurturing a collaborative and supportive culture that encourages personal and organisation growth that facilitates transformation. Its main disadvantage is that such a culture requires time and the commitment of everyone and can lead to a lack of decision.

Stewardship is very similar with more of an emphasis on passing something on that is as good or in better condition than when the leader took over; therefore, it has a much longer-term perspective and it protects continuity. A leader is the guardian of the organisation during their leadership and has a duty to at least maintain, but ideally improve, the strength and performance of the organisation during their stewardship. Stewardship goes beyond fiscal performance and requires attention to broader economic impact, community responsibilities and social inclusion and governance. These issues are currently being addressed by some organisations pursuing the goal of corporate responsibility. Pivotal to stewardship is accountability, and stakeholders of many organisations would benefit from leaders being more accountable beyond share price or financial performance.

We might be forgiven for thinking too many leaders have a narrow transient approach to corporate responsibility and are too preoccupied with self-interest. It is interesting that many CEOs argue that it is more difficult to adopt a stewardship style of leadership in a public company. This argument is weakened with shareholders increasingly demanding a more long-term, responsible approach to business and one of the biggest investment growth areas is in ethical investors. Many leaders would benefit from at least some of the stewardship principles to leading an organisation and increasingly good leaders are doing just that.

Servant and stewardship leadership has been more easily embraced, as a concept at least, by public sector organisations, charities, institutions and religious organisations. However, the re-emergence of corporate responsibility, as a corporate goal influencing organisation design and leadership behaviour, has seen a renaissance of servant leadership and stewardship thinking.

For many small- to medium-sized organisations, particularly family run businesses, servant stewardship leadership can be automatic with a desire to see their business thrive and continue, whether passed on to the next generation of family or to managers.

All these leadership styles will include a particular way of relating to and motivating people. For example, an autocratic style of leadership assumes people need to be directed and controlled. If the national cultural characteristics support this assumption it may well be true. However, if people are motivated by taking responsibility and having some autonomy they will be demotivated by such a style.

ACTIVITY 7.1

Now you have read examples of different leadership style theories.

(a)   Critique these theories for their application in the workplace.
(b)   In the context of your own organisation, how relevant and useful do you think they are?

2.4 Leadership and employee engagement (motivation)

▶ Key terms

Motives are needs and desires existing within us which act as driving forces to search for satisfaction, contentment, a sense of well being and happiness, internal drivers that energise behaviour to satisfy a need.

Incentives are the external 'carrots', objects, goals, satisfactions or circumstances outside the individual which he or she feels will satisfy a need and are inducements to respond. Incentives can be financial or material, for example a holiday or some gift or competition, that are seen as of value as a reward, including the admiration of others or fear of disapproval.

Disincentives are the external circumstances or behaviours that cause individuals to lose interest, for example lack of recognition of good work, long unpaid overtime working hours or poor working conditions, and this may result in a person possibly rebelling quietly or openly.

Leadership characteristics and style lead to assumptions about how to manage people and accordingly leadership behaviour towards people. This belief and behaviour will either motivate people or not.

2.4.1 What is motivation?

You could argue it does not exist; it is an abstract idea. Behavioural scientists and psychologists have undertaken numerous studies to try to understand why people behave in a particular way and in doing so understand the drivers. Simply put, there is some broad agreement on motivation.

Money is often cited as a motivator and while it can have a short-term effect it is an external incentive. Problems arise if incentives are confused with people's motives for behaviour. For example, if we rely on money to motivate it can only do so for a very short

time and then people come to expect that money. The only way to motivate again is more money which may not be available. It also assumes that people only work for money. Money is a necessity but many of us work for a variety of other reasons as well. Many, of course, work willingly for no money at all.

To understand motivation and typical assumptions a useful starting point is McGregor's theory X and theory Y.

2.4.2 McGregor's theory X and theory Y

McGregor's (1957) **theory X and theory Y** go to the heart of people's assumptions about each other that can still be seen in the workplace today. McGregor argued managers' attitudes to, and assumptions about, employees lead them to manage in a particular way and offered two opposing views on these assumptions.

Theory X assumptions:

(a)   The average human being has an inherent dislike of work and will avoid it if they can.

(b)   People work mostly for money, status and rewards.

(c)   Because of the characteristic dislike for work most people must be coerced, controlled, directed and/or threatened to get them to put adequate effort into achieving organisation goals.

(d)   The average human being prefers to be directed, wishes to avoid responsibility, has relatively little ambition and wants security above all else.

Such assumptions are likely to lead to a more directive and autocratic, even bullying, style of leadership and a 'carrot and stick' approach to rewarding good or bad behaviour. The assumption is that people will not take initiative and the best that can be achieved is to push people hard and often only provide money as a reward. This neglects significant drivers for performance.

Theory Y assumptions:

(a)   The expenditure of physical and mental effort in work is as natural as play or rest.

(b)   External control and the threat of reprisals are not the only means of encouraging commitment to organisation objectives. People exercise self-direction and control in the service of objectives and commitment to objectives is a function of the rewards associated with their achievement.

(c)   The average human learns under proper conditions to accept and also to seek responsibility.

(d)   The capacity to exercise a high degree of imagination, ingenuity and creativity in the solution of organisational problems is widely, not narrowly, distributed in the population.

(e)   Intellectual potential of the average person is only partially utilised in the conditions of modern life.

Theory Y assumptions lead to a more democratic style of leadership and tapping into people's desire for work and for achievement is the route to success. If the right conditions are created people will take initiative, are prepared to solve problems and can be motivated by a range of factors other than money.

2.4.3 Maslow's hierarchy of needs theory

Maslow's **hierarchy of needs theory** (1943) was developed to understand motivation purporting that individual needs are hierarchical with the stronger, more basic needs at the bottom and weaker more complex needs higher up.

Needs

(i)   **Self-actualisation/self-fulfilment** needs are about personal development and achieving one's own potential to the full in ways far broader than just work being part of life.

(ii)   **Self-esteem** needs are about how one is regarded internally to self and externally to others including respect from others, recognition and status, self-confidence, independence and achievement.

(iii)   **Love/belonging/security** needs concern relationships with others, how a person interacts with others, whether or not they belong and or are part of a group.

(iv)   **Safety** needs are concerned with danger, deprivation, the ability to work and provide security for dependants.

(v)   **Physiological** needs are the basics: food, drink, sleep and shelter from the elements.

Figure 7.7   Maslow's hierarchy of needs

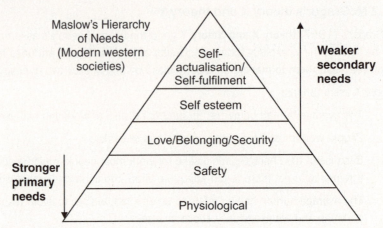

The primary needs must first be met before a person can move up to satisfying secondary needs. Moving up to higher order needs does not mean a person will not, at some time, find they again need to satisfy lower order needs. In the workplace, if a job is threatened or change proposed this can often lead people to abandoning weaker needs and refocusing on primary needs.

Managers need to be aware that once a need is satisfied it no longer motivates. A need satisfied results in other needs emerging and now these needs are the source of motivation. The challenge for the leader is recognising when needs are met, when other needs emerge and how to redesign work to motivate.

It is important to note that Maslow's motivation model has been subject to criticism; these criticisms need to be taken into account when applying this model.

Limitations:

- Individual behaviour cannot be neatly categorised and can fit into a number of categories, depending on context, situation and external factors.

- The categorisation of needs may result in different behaviour in different individuals and there may be a number of other factors to consider before any conclusion can be made.

- How does one decide when a level has been satisfied? This can be very subjective and so not consistent across all individuals.

- The model is not able to take account of factors that are not objective, for example individuals who tolerate low pay for the promise of future benefits.

- There is limited empirical evidence to support the model. Some critics suggest that Maslow's model is only really relevant to understanding the behaviour of middle-class workers in the UK and the US, as this was the basis of his empirical research, and its relevance in today's society is questioned.

2.4.4 Herzberg's two factor theory

Frederick Herzberg's **two factor theory** (1966) undertook more comprehensive research in organisations to discover why people enjoyed some aspects of work and found others dissatisfying. Of the factors that emerged as influencing motivation, Herzberg identified what he called motivators (or satisfiers) and hygiene (or maintenance) factors.

(a)   **Hygiene factors** were lower order needs, the relationship to the environment and factors that could cause dissatisfaction if they were missing or found wanting. Improving hygiene factors reduces

dissatisfaction or possibly provides a short lived sense of satisfaction. They include salary, status, working conditions, supervision and job security.

(b) **Motivators** were intrinsic higher order needs that had the potential to provide sustainable satisfaction to individuals. They include achievement, recognition, responsibility and job interest.

If hygiene factors are causing dissatisfaction, for example salary or poor social conditions, motivators such as recognition or responsibility will have limited, if any, success.

2.4.5 McClelland's achievement, affiliation and power needs theory

McClelland's (1961) **achievement, affiliation and power needs theory** believed that strong needs are not inherited but are learnt and identified three kinds of needs:

- **Need for achievement:** to be able to affect desirable outcomes
- **Need for power:** to be able to influence and control events
- **Need for affiliation:** to connect and associate with others that leads to belonging and relationships

Entrepreneurs are often people with a high **achievement** need characterised by a preference for more difficult tasks, personal responsibility for performance, clear and unambiguous feedback and they are more innovative. They may enjoy teamwork or may be happy to work in isolation depending on the individual.

Power motivates those who have a strong desire to have an impact and be influential which tends to be more important than getting things done. They do not necessarily have to be highly visible or seek the limelight; they are not interested in personal power. What is important is their need for impact and influence and each will interpret this differently. The very nature of how these people are motivated means interaction with others is important but usually as a means to a group or organisation goal. Their need to belong will depend on the individual but it will not be a primary need.

People who prioritise relationships and belonging have a high **affiliation** need and will be motivated by teamwork. Working on tasks that are designed for individuals with little interaction with others will quickly see them feeling isolated and demotivated. Satisfaction comes from working with others to achieve task goals and in sharing success.

Victor Vroom's (1960s) **expectancy theory** is based on three variables:

- **Valence:** reward value, a person's feeling about specific outcomes, the value placed on it, a preference for or the attractiveness of a particular outcome to the individual

- **Expectancy:** that if effort is made it will result in performance (eg quality, quantity)

- **Instrumentality:** is that performance will result in reward (eg praise, promotion, bonus)

Expectancy theory proposes that people are motivated by different needs depending on the value they attribute to different outcomes and rewards and different people have different expectations. People will only put effort into doing a task if the expected outcome or reward is seen as achievable and desirable. The value placed on needs will be influenced by whether they are internal higher order needs, such as self-esteem or self-fulfilment which are decided by the individual, and/or external lower order needs given by others such as recognition or promotion.

Figure 7.8   Expectancy theory

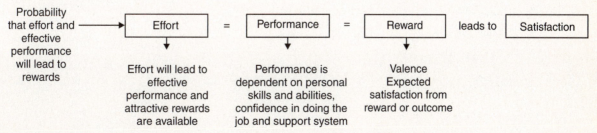

This requires leaders to relate what people are doing to achieving an outcome and reward they value. The following is an example of how marketing tasks can be linked to motivation and reward resulting in satisfaction or dissatisfaction.

Table 7.2   Motivation and reward

Motivation	Effort	=	Performance	=	Reward	Leads to
Chris is motivated by achievement	Design and implementation of new segmentation process	=	Successfully implemented simple, effective process leading to improved results	=	Recognition from leader and congratulations from peers	Satisfaction
					Process ignored or unjustly criticised	Dissatisfaction
Nic is motivated by money	Increase customer base and/or repeat purchases	=	Won new valuable customers from competition and increased value of key existing customers	=	Bonus	Satisfaction
					Congratulated but no financial reward	Dissatisfaction
Sam is motivated by power	Design and implementation of a marketing orientation	=	Successfully influenced changes in design that lead to greater efficiency	=	Impact of changes lead to promotion	Satisfaction
					Contribution raised but no opening available for promotion	Dissatisfaction

Each of these people have different perspectives on rewards, outcomes and their value so the way they each go about tackling and prioritising projects and tasks will be different.

Motivation theories have also evolved over time as one study after another brings a new perspective.

Leadership comes with authority, power and influence and different leadership styles result in power and influence being used differently.

> **▶ Assessment tip**
>
> Another potential pitfall of assignments is being too tactical. Management might be tempted to 'get a job done' rather than provide the right level of assignment. This is a test of your management and leadership potential. You therefore need to identify a project that benefits the business strategically.

The Chartered Institute of Marketing

3 Authority, power and influence

Organisation culture and leadership style strongly influence the nature, sources and use of authority, power and influence in an organisation. If the organisation is hierarchical, the culture subservient and leadership style autocratic the sources of power may be from formal status or seniority and positions held. Power will typically be used to dictate and control.

In some organisations, particularly where a high level of expertise is required power may reside, for example with technicians or scientists, by virtue of their expertise.

Employees have become more powerful partly as a result of changing attitudes and employment law but also because in many industries where high levels of skill and/or knowledge are required employees have power by virtue of that skill or knowledge.

3.1 Sources of power

It might be assumed that a leadership position automatically leads to a position of power. However, power does not inevitably come with leadership. As we acknowledged earlier power comes with the territory but it is worth considering the sources of this power.

Different types of power were identified by French and Raven (1959):

Legitimate power comes with authority as it is based on holding a formal position. People who accept this legitimate power will comply and actively seek direction and guidance from such a source of power.

Reward power is based on giving something of value to someone in exchange for particular behaviour. These rewards may be financial, for example a bonus, or non-financial, for example an award for achievement.

Coercive power stems from the threat of punishment, the most obvious being no salary increase or bonus, no promotion or dismissal. Less obvious, and potentially more damaging, are bullying and social exclusion. In the real world we know there are some people who just do not want to work or work well for a variety of reasons. However coercive power, while suggested by some as an acceptable form of power, is a last resort. With current legislation, quite apart from the potential to pitch the organisation into an unpleasant, expensive and time consuming tribunal, the use of coercive power can suggest a failure in leadership and people management. This does not mean we should tolerate poor performance or paralyse ourselves with political correctness. If a person is not responding to every opportunity to improve, disciplinary action or dismissal are necessary.

Expert power comes from knowledge and experience and being seen as talented, gifted and the best in the business. It is usually narrow in its ability to exert power, constrained by the nature of the expertise.

Referent power comes from people with, for example, special qualities, poise, great personality, ability to inspire, interpersonal skills and charisma. People acquiesce to this power because they admire, respect or identify with the qualities this person has.

A leader can possess and utilise a number or all of these sources of power. A leader can hire and fire, dictate terms and decide on rewards, particularly if they own the company. A leader can impress and reassure people with their advice and mesmerise. This power may only achieve obedience, compliance and even loyalty. But today's leaders have to achieve so much more.

One of the greatest influences on leadership style evolution today is the recognition that amongst other goals leadership style needs to inspire and empower people, build employee commitment and loyalty and nurture an

ethical culture of creativity for innovation to improve organisation performance through excellent people and performance. These goals require a leader to build credibility, respect and trust. And this is where real power comes from. It is useful to understand sources of power and to utilise them.

3.2 Politics and power

We all recognise politics is a reality in most organisations and it is suggested by many authors that organisation politics is always desirable. This is interesting in light of the DDI research, referred to later, where leaders saw politics as their fourth most challenging problem with many admitting they had failed to deal with the negative impact.

The reason politics tends to have such a bad reputation is because it is usually discussed when it has had a negative, often destructive impact.

Politics is part of human nature and leaders need to use and cultivate the more positive and productive forms of politicking and be very clear that negative politicking is unacceptable. The many forms it takes include:

- **Networking and coalitions:** positive eg building contacts and nurturing relationships across the organisation and externally to advance group and organisation goals. Negative eg to identify potential competitors (individuals) and allies to recruit in order to destroy those seen as being in competition

- **Ingratiation:** negative eg using compliments, flattery, agreeing with someone considered important regardless of the right or wrong or truth; are all designed to create a favourable impression and win approval and support

- **Personal promotion:** positive eg establishing credibility to sway and influence decisions in order to secure desired outcomes for the organisation or group. Negative eg egotistical promoting of often exaggerated achievements no matter how small or relevant for reasons such as self-importance

- **Information:** positive eg used to convince, persuade and provide evidence for a particular argument or justify a particular point of view. Negative eg 'information is power' syndrome and information can be used for the other forms of politics mentioned

- **Upstaging:** negative eg publicly criticising a subordinate, peer or manager, bragging about 'what you have done' or 'how you would have done it', taking credit for the ideas and achievements of others

Usually the tactics employed, while having some self-interest, have the interest of a task or project or department etc as the goal. In these circumstances, people are finding ways to get what they think are the right things done. They may be competing for resources or a project that is not necessarily a priority for others, particularly those in control.

Politics becomes negative when all or some of these tactics are used purely for self-interest and often in conflict with the goals of others and the organisation. When political tactics cause others to be seen in a poor light or it damages performance it can be a destructive force in the organisation.

How often have you wondered or heard others say they do not know how a decision got made as it seems irrational or did not appear to go through the formal decision-making process or channel etc. Politics will often be the reason behind what appear to be irrational decisions and leaders should never underestimate the power of politics in the informal decision process. This process includes many more people than a formal decision process and they are not always easy to identify.

One of the reasons people engage in politics is because people have different perspectives, agendas and interpret needs and decisions differently. This can bring people into conflict and result in negative politicking.

The Chartered Institute of Marketing

3.3 Influence

Leaders with authority and power still need to be able to influence, particularly today in organisations where employees are technically skilled or are knowledge workers or in organisations where equality is emphasised or workers are volunteers. Influence often results in people conforming to particular decisions and behaviour.

Herbert Kelman (1974) identifies three major types of social influence:

- **Compliance:** people will agree with each other to ensure they receive a positive response and avoid unfavourable reactions. Influence is exercised because of people's apprehension about the social consequences of agreeing or not agreeing with others who have the power to reward or punish.

- **Identification:** people will agree with others who they perceive as having qualities they value in order to establish or maintain a fulfilling relationship that re-enforces their self image. Influence is exercised because of a desire to promote goals associated with forming and maintaining a relationship which is in harmony with their social identity.

- **Internalisation:** people will agree with others who they perceive as having attitudes that are credible and believable. Influence is exercised because the issues fit broadly with their own values and goals.

Two main **types of influence** used in organisations are:

- **Informational influence:** people can be manipulated by providing both accurate and inaccurate information to achieve a desired outcome. People look for information when what they have is ambiguous, when they want expert advice or when a problem or crisis occurs. If people giving the information believe the information may have a significant impact they are more likely to want to be accurate. The less important the outcome, the more likely people are to conform to the group rather than worry about the accuracy of the information.

- **Normative influence:** is about being liked; therefore, people will conform to the behaviour and decisions of the rest of the group. They may not necessarily agree with what others are doing or saying but will conform. The more people in the group, the less influence one person has.

3.4 Use of power and influence

Much of what has been discussed under leadership styles provides clues to how leaders use power and influence, and the organisation culture will determine how much people feel they must conform or have the freedom to disagree or be different. Leaders and employees in organisations are often trying to influence each other in different ways and for a variety of reasons. Typically we are:

- **Convincing** others through logical argument
- **Persuading** others by presenting a compelling case
- **Negotiating** with others to gain agreement

and usually with the best of intentions and the interests of the group or organisation.

ACTIVITY 7.2

Identify and critically analyse the power and influence in your organisation, and observe how it is used. Identify whether you think it is used in a positive or negative way and the impact of it on the overall organisation.

4 Approaches to leadership

4.1 Leadership realities

It is one thing to know and understand good marketing leadership practices, concepts and principles but another to implement them. Leaders might know what they should be doing but the organisation and environmental contexts present challenges to implementing improvements and change. If, for example, you have an autocratic leader who has been entrepreneurial and successful as a result but is now losing touch with the marketplace and is not interested in whether or not employees are motivated, it is very difficult to convince such a leader to change. If an employee appears to be impossible to motivate it may be because they are in the wrong job and/or organisation and no amount of effort or doing the right thing is going to change that.

Working in these conditions can be challenging in a good way, particularly when you can realise a change and have a positive effect on the organisation. The sense of achievement can be very rewarding. It can also be demoralising and frustrating when you cannot effect change. But this is the leadership reality. Even at the top of organisations there are constraints and factors out of the control of the leader; influences and factors that have to be negotiated and navigated, and compromise is part of the way we achieve some of what we want and live with what we cannot achieve.

Being promoted to a leadership role is often the ultimate goal and reward for many executives and they usually work hard to achieve that goal. Having achieved it many find themselves with expected challenges in terms of their tasks and objectives and unexpected challenges in terms of making the transition to leadership.

THE REAL WORLD

The Chartered Institute of Personnel and Development (CIPD) research by Development Dimensions International (DDI), on leadership transitions revealed some of the dilemmas leaders face as they move to more responsible roles. All leaders rated the ability to get work done through others as being in their top three most difficult challenges. More than 92% of senior leaders said understanding that the new role would require different ways of thinking would have helped them be successful. One in three said their company provided little or very poor support to them in making the mental shift for the transition. Interestingly, all leaders complained that politics is one of their main challenges as they move to a more senior role, rating it as the fourth most difficult challenge.

4.2 Leadership paradigms

As we have discussed, leadership styles have come into fashion, evolved, gone out of fashion and become relevant again as the external environment changes. Leadership style can be dominated by thinking and behaviour of the era; for example when greed becomes acceptable some leaders see no relevance in stewardship and can be driven by narrow goals and self-interest. New agendas emerge and thinking on what is acceptable leadership changes; for example, corporate responsibility is having an effect on what is seen as desirable leadership.

So what leadership style? There is no one right leadership style; many factors influence what is possible (personal traits and skills), what is right (the situation and circumstances) and what is appropriate (ethical and social goals). As we have discussed, leadership styles need to be able to adapt.

Across the hundreds of thousands of different organisations it would be difficult to declare there are dominant leadership styles; all the styles described are, and will continue to be, practised in varying degrees. An entrepreneurial leader can adopt at one moment a democratic style and at another an autocratic style depending on their characteristics and the situation.

Modern leadership is showing signs of being more fluid and increasingly reflects a combination of the best of the styles. There is a thread of servant leadership and stewardship across some leadership styles and as the demand for leaders to become more accountable increases, such styles would be more relevant today.

Taking the best principles from the theory and reflecting on our changing social and business environment can help frame a leadership style that meets a variety of needs and allows for a range of adaptations as appropriate.

4.3 Leadership strategies

Leaders set the goals for the organisation, the strategic direction and desired competitive position. Strategy is influenced by the leader's personality and their personal goals. As we saw, an entrepreneurial leadership style is likely to result in being first to market with new products and services and first to exploit new market opportunities. They are likely to design innovative business models to exploit those opportunities. It will be difficult to keep up with them and they might be exciting to work with but they may be demanding and difficult. With entrepreneurs, change is continuous and a way of life.

An organisation leader with a follower mentality is unlikely to build an organisation that is a market leader (assuming the organisation has the necessary competences). They may be particularly good at utilising the resources they have very efficiently and effectively and be strong at maintaining follower strategies and a follower position. However, if the organisation has the ability to be a market leader in such circumstances this leader's follower mentality will hold the organisation back.

A leader who believes in stewardship is likely to take a more considered approach to all they do. Their strategy is influenced by the desire to build a strong company for future generations rather than just share price factors, and the culture of this organisation will be built on ethical values. Strategy will not compromise short-term goals for longer-term objectives. The down side is in dynamic markets or periods of unprecedented change a lack of speed to respond to events can be damaging.

All leadership styles influence the culture of organisations and the culture of organisations, influences leadership style, which is the subject of Chapter 10.

ACTIVITY 7.3

Evaluate the different leadership styles in your organisation. Is there a common style or different styles, and what is the impact on motivation, positive and negative?

Critically evaluate where your leadership style fits in with leadership theories outlined in this chapter. Do you have the necessary skills to perform your role accordingly? What are your personal development needs as a result of your analysis?

▶ **Assessment tip**

Leadership features strongly in the marketing leadership and planning assessment. A key part of the leadership tasks is for candidates to demonstrate they have fully understood the key leadership theories and in, addition to understanding them, are able to apply them to their own context, situation and organisation. Often candidates are expected to critically evaluate their own leadership skills as well as identify gaps and make recommendations for their own personal development. This involves candidates having a good understanding of the overall strategic goals of the organisation: what is its focus? What is it trying to achieve and why? This understanding then needs to be applied to leadership, and consideration needs to be given as to how leadership can help to achieve this: what might be the skill gaps and why?

Another key consideration is not to provide a 'mind dump' of all the leadership theories, but rather apply them according to the task; if a critical analysis of the leadership theories is requested candidates need to ensure they are able to critically analyse them rather than just describing them. Also, when outlining personal development needs these need to be linked back to the critical thinking and there need to be clear reasons why these have been identified, rather than just listing general strengths and weaknesses.

CHAPTER ROUNDUP

- There is a difference between the role of leaders and managers.

- Leadership theories and styles can impact the organisation as a whole, how decisions are made, by who, when and how and also the achievement of the organisation's vision and mission.

- Understanding motivation can help leaders to understand the needs and wants of their teams further and more accurately.

- Levels of authority, power and influence are embedded in leadership decisions and can impact the facilitation of strategic marketing decisions.

- Approaches to leadership, leadership realities, paradigms and strategies will impact how decisions are made.

FURTHER READING

Bowerman, J.K. (2003) Leadership development through action learning: an executive monograph. *Leadership in Health Services*. Vol16(4), Case study. Emerald abstract.

Doyle, P. and Stern, P. (2006) *Marketing management and strategy.*4th edition. Harlow, Prentice Hall.

Harris, L.C. and Ogbanna, E. (2001) Leadership style and market orientation: an empirical study. *European Journal of Marketing*, Vol35(5/6), pp744–764 (article available via library photocopying service).

Kasper, H. (2002) Culture and leadership in market–oriented service organisations. *European Journal of Marketing*, Vol36(9/10), pp1047–1057 (article available via library photocopying service).

Lee, Y. –I. (2004) Customer service and organizational learning in the context of strategic marketing. *Marketing Intelligence and Planning;* Vol22(6), pp652–662 (article available via library photocopying service).

Quotationsbook.com (accessed 31 May 2012)

Salovey, P. & Mayer J. (1990) Emotional Intelligence. *Imagination, Cognition, and Personality*, 9 (3), pp185-211.

Sharma, B. (2004) Marketing strategy, contextual factors and performance: an investigation of their relationship. *Marketing Intelligence and Planning*, Vol22(2), pp128–143 (article available via library photocopying service).

Terrill, C. and Middlebrooks, A. Marketing leadership strategies for service companies: creating growth, profits, and customer loyalty. Book review in*: Marketing Health Services*, Winter 99/Spring 2000, Vol19(4), p50.

Vecchio, R.P. (2007) *Leadership, understanding the dynamics of power and influence in organisations.* 2nd revised edition. University of Notre Dame.

The Chartered Institute of Marketing

REFERENCES

Blake, R.R. and Mouton, J.S. (1985) *The managerial grid III*. Doha, Gulf Publishing Company.

CIPD (2007) *Leadership Transactions*, research conducted by Development Dimensions International (DDI), Chartered Institute of Personal and Development (CIPD).

French, J.R.P. and Raven, B. (1959) The bases of social power: In Cartwright, D. (ed) *Studies in social power*. Ann Arbour, MI: Michigan, University of Michigan Press, pp130-167.

Goleman, D. (1996) *Emotional intelligence: why it can matter more than IQ*. London, Bloomsbury.

Greenleaf, R.K. (1970) *Servant leadership: a journey into the nature of legitimate power and greatness*. London, Spears.

Hersey, P. and Blanchard, K.H. (1993) *Management of organisational behaviour: utilising human sources*. London, Prentice Hall.

Herzberg, F. (1966) *The Motivation to Work*. London, Wiley.

Higgs, M.J. and Dulewicz, V. (2002) *Making sense of emotional intelligence*. 2nd edition. Windsor, NFER Nelson.

Kelman, H.C. (1974) *Social influences and linkages between the individual and the social system: further thoughts on the processes of compliance, identification and internalisation*: In Tedeschi, J. (ed). *Perspectives on social power*, pp125-171. Aldine, Chicago.

Maslow, A.H. (1943) *Motivation and personality*. London, Harper & Row.

Mayer, J. and Salovey, P. (1990) Emotional intelligence: imagination, cognition and personality. *Journal of Personality Assessment*. 54, pp772-781.

McClelland, D. (1961) *The achieving society*. London, Van Nostrand Reinhold.

McGregor, D. (1957) *The human side of enterprise*. Oxford, McGraw Hill.

Tannenbaum, R. and Schmidt, W.H. (1973) How to choose a leadership pattern. *Harvard Business Review*, May–June, p162.

Thornberry, N. (2006) *Lead like an entrepreneur*. Oxford, McGraw Hill.

Vecchio, R.P. (2007) *Power, politics and influence*. Paris, University of Notre Dame Press.

Vroom, V. (1960) *Work and motivation*. London, Wiley.

1   How might leadership style affect teams?

2   What are typical symptoms of poor motivation?

3   What is Maslow's hierarchy of needs?

4   What are Herzberg's hygiene factors and motivators?

5   What are McClelland's three motivation needs?

6   What is Vroom's theory of motivation?

7   What are McGregor's theory X and theory Y?

8   What are the causes of poor motivation?

ACTIVITY DEBRIEFS

Activity 7.1

Your organisation context will influence your critique of leadership theories but the sort of issues that might emerge are that some styles described are irrelevant; for example, if you are in a very creative environment autocratic leadership is unlikely to exist. If you work in a very hierarchical and bureaucratic organisation that operates in a simple and stable environment entrepreneurship may be impossible or seem irrelevant. If you work in a highly competitive, fast moving environment you may think servant leadership or stewardship is appropriate. However, if you tackle this task with an open mind see what you can take from the different styles that may inform your own personal development.

Activity 7.2

Sources of power will be affected by the organisation structure and culture, the type of industry and, for example, the level of expertise required by your industry. Sources may be obvious, such as position in the organisation or the esteem and respect with which someone is held, or less obvious, for example, someone with strong influential skills. Identifying when it is used positively might include achievement of organisational goals or resources allocated to an essential project, and when it used negatively might include goals that have more to do with personal ambitions than the good of the organisation and others, or slowing down activities through the introduction of unnecessary steps in a process.

Activity 7.3

If you identify a common leadership style it may be the result of a deliberate strategy, supported by organisation culture and designed to support the maintenance of a particular orientation. This might include recruiting people of a certain 'type' who fit the profile or only recruiting from within. If styles differ, to what extent is this appropriate and does it support a positive organisation environment, and to what extent does it hamper presenting a united organisation identity? How does leadership influence motivation – are people empowered, challenged, supported, trusted or are they demoralised, over supervised and have adopted a 'work to rule' mentality?

1   –   An autocratic manager would be happiest when 'leading' the team. Individual and team responsibility for tasks and development would be discouraged.

       –   A more democratic style would actively encourage people in the team to take responsibility for their team activities and development. This would be supported with plans for training and development to improve the effectiveness of individuals and the team.

       –   A laissez faire style could result in two outcomes: (a) the leader has assessed and determined they are capable and is there to facilitate and guide; the team make their own decisions and take responsibility for outcomes, and (b) a leader who abdicates without assessing team capabilities can result in poor performance, low morale with little emphasis on formal support for the team.

2   –   Absenteeism, possibly symptoms of stress

       –   Reduction in productivity and a refusal or reluctance to do anything except the minimum that has to be done

       –   Behaviour reflecting non co-operation, withdrawal, aggression or defensiveness

       –   Increasing complaints about work loads, routines and conditions and opposition to any new ideas, changes etc

       –   Poor time keeping and a general sense of 'it can wait'

       –   Increasing staff turnover

3   A description of human needs that should be satisfied if people are to be happy and work productively. These needs are arranged in order of importance with the most basic needs – physiological, security and safety – being the most important, and social, esteem and self-fulfilment needs being less important until basic needs are met. The 'hierarchy' indicates that basic needs must be satisfied before other needs higher up in the hierarchy become important and can be satisfied. If circumstances change and basic needs are under threat eg with changes in the workplace or redundancy, the higher needs become less important again and lower needs become important and are defended.

4   –   Hygiene factors are lower order needs which do not motivate but can cause dissatisfaction if they are missing or wrong eg salary, status, working conditions, working relationships, supervision, job security

       –   Motivators are higher order needs that do motivate but cannot do so (or it is difficult for them to do so) if lower order needs are missing eg achievement, recognition, job interest, responsibility, advancement

5   –   Need for achievement – being able to take responsibility for design and development that results in successful outcomes

       –   Need for power – to have control and influence over events and people

       –   Need for affiliation – to have relationships and belong

6   Expectancy theory – people are motivated by what they value and different people value different things. The reward must be easily understood and perceived to be of value to the person receiving the reward; so for example one person might be motivated by promotion, another by recognition for achievement. People will interpret the route to achieving the reward differently and therefore will put in the effort and performance they believe appropriate to achieving the reward.

7 – Theory X assumptions – people are lazy, untrustworthy and dislike work or responsibilities. They therefore require high levels of supervision and control and will be uninterested in the organisation or its activities.

– Theory Y assumptions – people are willing to work and are interested in work and personal development and growth. They are prepared to take responsibility, are self-disciplined and creative. They require minimal levels of supervision and control and should be encouraged to use their creativity in improving the organisation's performance.

8 – Poor management – eg criticism, threats, lack of interest in employees

– Poor working conditions

– Poor pay – inequality in pay structures or bonuses

– Poor communications – lack of information, one way

– Poor training and development – people poorly equipped to carry out their tasks and responsibilities

– Unreasonable targets and lack of explanation of expected standards

CHAPTER 8

Leadership and the organisation

Introduction

Leaders have the potential to have the most powerful influence on the organisation and its structure, operations, culture, people, competence and performance. Of course, they do not do this alone; management, employees and in many organisations other stakeholders all influence the shape and form of the organisation.

A strong leader can have the most direct influence in shaping, for example, a creative environment, a learning organisation, strategy formulation, collaboration and alliances and stakeholder relationships. The larger the organisation gets the more challenging it is for leaders, working together, to create the sort of organisation they want. Knowing what they should do is a small part of achieving their goals. However, knowing what to do is a good starting point and if the right objectives and measures are put in place leaders can monitor their progress and take corrective action where and when necessary.

Topic list

Innovation and learning	1
Thought leadership	2
Knowledge management and learning	3
Risk management	4
Competition and collaboration	5
Stakeholder relationship management	6
Your leadership style	7

3.1.5	Critically evaluate the concept of bi-cultural leadership in developing capabilities effectively within new sub-cultures and across boundaries:
	■ Examine how leaders create an organisational climate that encourages a healthy balance between collaboration and competition
	■ Which encourages risk-taking and risk assessment and which is boundary-less
3.1.6	Explore ways of developing thought leadership within the organisation to assist in the development of a culture of innovation and learning, including:
	■ Keeping stakeholders connected
	■ Engaging and expediting learning
	■ Developing a learning organisation
	■ Investing in knowledge capital through knowledge management
	■ Maintaining knowledge of innovation and passing it on
3.1.7	Utilise the management team, internal resources and networks to develop tools to access key stakeholders, including:
	■ Setting up steering committees
	■ Establishing formal links with strategic planners and leaders
	■ Establishing communities and networks with business leaders
	■ Continuously seeking internal and external customer information
3.1.8	Assess your own leadership style and recommend how it can be improved and maximised to aid business thinking, working with colleagues, inspiring people and achieving goals:
	■ Leadership styles (Transitional, Transformational, Traditional)
	■ Group dynamics/team motivation
	■ Reflective thinking and feedback
	■ Different methods of measuring leadership effectiveness
	■ Difficulties of measuring effectiveness of a leader

1 Innovation and learning

> ▶ **Key terms**
>
> **Creativity** is the ability to think differently, to generate new ideas and requires freedom, inspiration, originality, ingenuity.
>
> **Innovation** is the first attempt to put invention (the idea, novelty, something unique) into practice and requires a process.

Few people question the value of creativity and innovation, particularly in our rapidly changing world today. Organisation success and survival are dependent on innovation. Leaders and managers do not deliberately try to inhibit creative and innovative behaviour but for a variety of reasons this is what often happens, even when the opposite is a clearly stated objective.

Reasons include:

■ **Risk averse:** past failures, costs, fear of getting it wrong

■ **Organisation culture:** responses to past failure eg a 'name and blame' culture

■ **Leadership style and practice:** discourage creativity by emphasising and rewarding uniformity, task completion and unwilling to allocate appropriate resources

Often there is a common misconception as to what innovation actually is. Many regard innovation as developing new products, dramatically entering new markets or making decisions that will give them the competitive edge. While elements of this are true, it involves having a culture of innovation and learning. Leaders need to have the appropriate skills to ensure innovation is encouraged but also managed, as well as organisational culture that can deal with innovative ideas and practices. Innovation does not have to be dramatic but can in fact be more cognitive and promote a culture of learning and development.

Procter and Gamble

Procter and Gamble is an example of an organisation that has used innovation and its leadership skills to develop in a number of markets as well as remain responsive to customer needs. The central ethos of P&G is 'Touching lives, improving life'; it has just under 150,000 employees and a world-wide customer base. Due to the heavy demand for its products it has had to develop marketing strategies that take into account the global environment, which is very diverse.

P&G claims its success is based on its innovative practices and strategies. So what are these innovative strategies? An important focus of P&G is the speed of commercialisation of new products. As strong players in the health and personal care industry it wanted to be and has been the first to get products into the market. Another equally aggressive strategy was the acquisition of domestic and foreign competitors; however, central to this was also acquiring the manufacturing processes of companies, such as Norwich Eaton Pharmaceuticals, Richardson-Vicks and Noxell amongst others.

Leadership practices within P&G are also another focus with regards to innovation; they encourage a participatory and empowering leadership style. This means that the organisation is able to train employees to understand the central ethos and values of P&G but still have the autonomy to make decisions, be flexible and central to the overall decision making process. It has a decentralised management structure which means that key decision-makers are not having to endure a bureaucratic process but are able to make decisions as and when required with P&G vision and mission in their minds. Davila *et al*, 2006 p74) states that leadership is pivotal in the success of P&G. Commenting on the CEO: 'He restored focus on leading brands and reminded everyone in P&G that the measure of success was not innovation per se, but the customer.' Leadership clearly focuses on the customer against the backdrop of the global environment. P&G, in summary, is an organisation that continues to be innovative in its practices but also realises that innovation alone cannot achieve success; it needs to be supported by the organisation's core values, the management team, the leadership and the facilitation of decision making at all levels and across all countries.

Often the necessary effort put into maximising efficiency of operations results in standardising everything the organisation does using rigid processes and procedures to protect the organisation from deviation and this has the effect of inhibiting creativity. Establishing an environment for innovation benefits from an understanding of what drives innovation and what is required.

Not everyone can be creative but many never have the opportunity to realise their full creative potential. Organisations need creativity that leads to innovation on new ways of doing things and new things to do. Innovation requires a rigorous process to ensure what emerges from creativity is commercially viable. This is how businesses grow and prosper.

1.1 Environmental scanning and different contexts

Ideas come from a network of sources and are often driven by external environmental change. Monitoring the external environment is part of the innovation process and interpreting analysis findings, in the right organisation climate, stimulates creativity. Creativity responds to changing market dynamics whether it is macro, for example legislation and economic conditions, or micro, for example a change in customer or competitor behaviour.

Figure 8.1   Drivers of the need for innovation

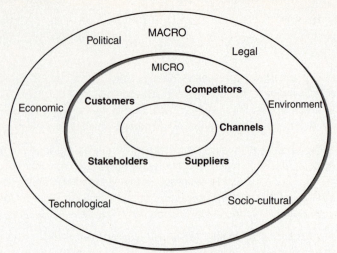

In a creative climate, ideas are also created internally, sometimes without outside influence. This is a natural process and should be encouraged. The innovation process will check the viability of internally generated ideas for their suitability and feasibility to the organisation and externally.

No organisation is exempt from the need to innovate. Private companies, public sector organisations, charities, organisations in stable and simple environments, those in dynamic, complex environments and small, medium and large organisations all at some time or another need to innovate what they do and/or how they do it. What differs is the speed of response and the nature and extent of innovation required.

Our environment continually changes but organisations need to assess the nature of change to decide whether it is appropriate or necessary to respond. Many managers are frustrated by a culture of continuous change that is not always necessary or beneficial. This leads to following every fad and fashion regardless of its relevance or value. The skill of leadership is to recognise what to change and when.

1.2 Who is responsible for innovation?

Leadership is responsible for creating the vision for the organisation and the right climate for creativity that leads to innovation that will help achieve the vision. Only when the right climate has been created can everyone else take responsibility for creativity and innovation.

Many leaders genuinely believe they encourage creativity and innovation. However, there are a number of obstacles unintentionally created by leaders and actively maintained by management including a lack of resources, a 'get it right first time' mentality, and time.

1.3 What innovation and where?

Innovation is not confined to new products and services and is required at various times in other areas including:

- **Operations:** technology and systems that produce products or services

- **Processes:** for managing and delivering value to customers

- **Value:** products and services produced for customers and stakeholders

- **Marketing:** research can require creativity when information is difficult to get and communications require adopting different approaches to rise above the 'noise' and reach the desired targets

Leaders need to enthuse managers and employees with the task of finding both short-term innovation, often the marketing mix, and longer-term innovation, for example operations.

The Chartered Institute of Marketing

1.4 Type of innovation

Incremental innovation is less risky, less costly and more likely to succeed and the business learns as it evolves. Incremental innovation supports consistency and continuity and usually builds on something customers understand so they can appreciate the 'new' benefits.

Revolutionary innovation involves 'megaprojects' or 'do everything' and requires heavy investment. The 'unknowns' are greater, including market response, and learning curves are far steeper. It is only usually an option if a matter of survival or the innovation is known to meet a significant identified need and has guaranteed commercial viability. Revolutionary innovation may not be consistent and a concerted effort, usually by marketing, is required to establish or maintain a clear competitive position, and not lose or confuse customers and stakeholders.

All innovation should lead to competitive advantage and opportunities for differentiation. How long-term or sustainable this competitive advantage is depends on the nature of innovation.

Teresa M. Amabile (1998) suggests there are three components to creativity: 'Within every individual, creativity is a function of three components: expertise, creative-thinking skills, and motivation. Can managers influence these components? The answer is an emphatic yes – for better or for worse – through workplace practices and conditions.'

Figure 8.2   Three components to creativity

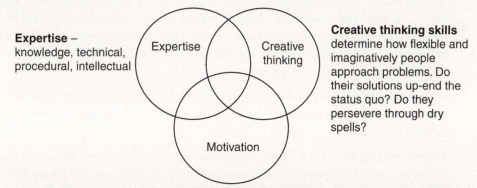

Expertise – knowledge, technical, procedural, intellectual

Creative thinking skills determine how flexible and imaginatively people approach problems. Do their solutions up-end the status quo? Do they persevere through dry spells?

Not all **motivation** is created equal. An inner passion to solve the problem at hand leads to solutions far more creative than do external rewards, such as money. This component called intrinsic motivation is the one that can be most immediately influenced by the work environment.

The point about motivation is important. Those people motivated by money to solve a problem will not necessarily be motivated to solve it in a creative or innovative way. It does not automatically follow that it will encourage exploration, experimentation and so on. If money is the reward then solving a problem as quickly as possible, rather than finding the best solution, is likely to be the goal.

Many innovations are improvements on existing ideas or re-designed for new and different purposes and in different contexts. As many trends, preferences and tastes usually change gradually many innovations respond gradually, with modifications and adjustments. During periods of significant change innovation requires a leap into the unknown and leadership that succeeds in creating and maintaining a creative climate will have built an organisation in a better position to take that leap.

No matter how successful, or if the organisation is a market leader, leaders can never be complacent. A leader should never lose sight of the need to nurture creativity. This is most successfully achieved through people.

2 Thought leadership

It is worth noting there are some different views on what thought leadership is and how it works. Some believe it is about leading an organisation and others believe that anyone in the organisation can be a thought leader and it is about thinking differently, creating leading edge knowledge and influencing others to think differently and how new ideas are generated and assimilated.

Thought leadership (Kurtzman, 2010) encourages the development of new ideas and practices. These do not need to be all encompassing or at a higher corporate level; they can also be small changes rather than organisation wide. It is important that thought leaders are aware of the organisation's overall goals and strategies so that ideas link in with the organisation's goals and objectives.

Thought leadership is shared by all who can think creatively or differently, and at any point in a meeting, casual discussion, solving a problem or heated debate different individuals may be demonstrating thought leadership. It is immediate and does not have to have a vision or journey. It is argued that thought leaders are more like artists and therefore do not need to worry about their interpersonal skills or ability to get on with people. Thought leaders include the mavericks and rebels in the organisation who cannot and will not conform: the plant (in Belbin's team role terms). Thought leaders are also willing to accept rejection of ideas within the team; however, this does not imply that they will give up, but potentially present an idea or a concept from another perspective. A key aspect of thought leadership is that it is not conventional top down, but may be bottom up leadership, organic leadership or sideways.

We need people who can think differently. When it comes to thinking differently one of the most popular and enduring writers on the subject is Edward De Bono (1970). He recognised there are broadly two approaches to thinking as follows.

Vertical thinking tends not to come up with new ideas or different perspectives, it follows trusted paths so comes up with similar ideas and solutions. De Bono contrasted this with lateral thinking which requires different ways of looking at things. **Lateral thinking** should:

- Generate **alternatives:** never accept one or two solutions, and the more unlikely the alternative the more promising the potential solutions for being different.

- Adopt a **random** approach avoiding following a logical order; instead join up a number of apparently disconnected themes and see what emerges.

- **Deviate:** avoid the obvious path and follow a different one, preferably several different ones.

De Bono (1970) believed both vertical and lateral thinking were important, both needed for different purposes and situations.

ACTIVITY 8.1

Critically analyse the level of innovation in your organisation, analysing to what extent leadership helps or potentially hinders an innovative culture.

Robin Ryde (2007) picks up this theme in his book *Thought Leadership*. He shares experiences from running programmes for leaders and potential leaders and for problem-solving workshops. He describes two dominant patterns in the way people explore issues when they come together:

(a) **Deficiencies:** a tendency to look for the faults and deficiencies in any information they have acquired and in ideas, discussion or possible solutions. Deficient thinking can put a lot of time and energy into proving there are deficiencies. These are the people who see the 'problem, difficulty or impossibility' of anything different or new.

(b) **Commonsense:** thinking applies a broad and general set of principles to a situation to advance the thinking on the subject. As you would expect it is sensible. A problem arises when commonsense can be sensible but not necessarily appropriate. Sometimes a variety of factors, not all obvious, need also to be considered that might result in a different outcome.

We know people come to various situations such as solving problems or generating ideas in two ways:

(a) With a **closed mind:** they already have the solution or think there is no need for a solution and are less likely to listen to different views except to criticise or find fault.

(b) With an **open mind** and willing to listen to different points of view, ideas and explore these ideas. They will build on the ideas of others, contribute and challenge constructively.

2.1 Standard thinking repertoire

Ryde (2007) describes six standard thinking repertoires that can stifle creativity because they take the most direct route or a path already taken by others.

(a) **Deficit** thinking focuses on faults, shortcomings and weaknesses of the topic.

(b) **Rational** thinking: logical, sequential approach to problems or ideas, fails to deal with feelings and emotions, typical of business interactions

(c) **Commonsense** thinking applies general and inexpert knowledge to find a solution not always fit for purpose.

(d) **Equity** thinking uses fairness as its overriding principle; people make comparisons to look for inconsistencies that support the view it is 'unfair' and seek to even things up.

(e) **Binary** thinking assumes solutions are one thing or another, opposing ends of a spectrum, black or white. There are no possibilities in variations or of combinations.

(f) **Sticky** thinking forms associations from one person's contribution to the next; conversations wander through association from one subject to another, often avoiding the topic.

Ryde (2007) also acknowledges that some of the above standard thinking repertoires have their place. For example, challenging and pointing out shortcomings can be important where there are shortcomings. The problem for thinking is when the above becomes a habit, particularly just one way of thinking.

Therefore, the first step is to recognise and understand your thinking habit: do you just have one way of thinking? How rigid is it and what productive outcomes result? Why has this thinking habit emerged? What is the trigger? What factors influence your way of thinking?

The next step is to develop broader thinking skills. This requires discipline and determination, particularly in everyday interactions and with the pressure of work. In a meeting or conversation when you recognise you are slipping into your thinking habit try a different approach; deliberately think and say something different. If you have a tendency to see shortcomings try instead to develop the discussion to possible 'what ifs'.

Ryde recommends developing a broader repertoire by adopting what he calls the 'shadow side' of the dominant standard ways of thinking.

Table 8.1   Ryde's dominant and shadow thinking functions

Dominant function	Shadow function
Deficit thinking	Strengthen-based thinking
Rational thinking	Feeling thinking
Commonsense thinking	Insight thinking
Equity thinking	360 degree thinking
Binary thinking	Re-integrated thinking
Sticky thinking	Exit thinking

Shadow function:

(a) **Strengthen-based** thinking: searches for the positive in a situation and supported by evidence, 'can do' mentality.

(b) **Feeling** thinking: allows for emotions and feelings in a conversation and is not threatened or embarrassed by them, it is accepted as part of what we are. It does not mean events are overtaken by emotions but rather that we acknowledge likely reactions and emotions and we use good interpersonal skills to manage feelings.

(c) **Insight** thinking: draws on experience and expertise and uses this to inform ideas and possible solutions.

(d) **360 degree** thinking requires adopting multiple rather than single perspectives on any given problem, sees ideas and problems from many perspectives and tries to understand how these different perspectives change as a result.

(e) **Re-integrated** thinking avoids 'either/or' and looks to integrate, combine, adjust where it is appropriate to do so. It requires exploring, investigating and being prepared to work on ideas or solutions with a broader perspective.

(f) **Exit** thinking: avoids slipping into meandering conversations that go off topic and is prepared to refocus, also prepared to bring discussions to an end when they cease to add value or contribute something useful.

Changing unproductive thinking habits and developing effective thinking encourage and enable us to think differently, creatively and come up with new ideas and approaches to solving problems.

Thought leadership works on knowledge and is also about learning. Learning is essential for creativity and innovation and thought leaders value learning and actively encourage the creation of a learning climate where creativity can flourish and innovation emerges.

3 Knowledge management and learning

Knowledge is a source of competitive advantage or for non-profit organisations, an advantage. In an era of information technology you might expect that we must be better than we have ever been at management knowledge. Unfortunately, many studies have shown the contrary is true.

A focus on technology has led to a tendency to focus on gathering data and because it is so easy, vast quantities of it can be gathered. A lack of selectivity in data collection can add to the problem but the main problem is that too often it remains as data never making the transition, through analysis and interpretation to knowledge.

The Chartered Institute of Marketing

Knowledge is vital for innovation whether we formally gather, analyse and disseminate knowledge or whether it is the informal process that goes on in our heads all the time. We use knowledge from a variety of sources to generate and build on ideas.

Hargadon and Sutton (2000) describe a 'knowledge brokering cycle' that allowed organisations to innovate time and time again, which might look something like this.

Figure 8.3   Knowledge brokering cycle

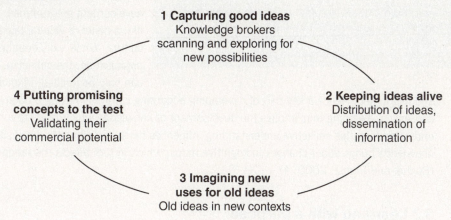

3.1 Knowledge ownership and creating the right climate

A good starting point is to establish the ownership of knowledge in an organisation, particularly in knowledge organisations. There is no question that knowledge acquired and developed in the pursuit of organisation strategies and goals belongs to the organisation. However, the concept of shared ownership is more likely to create a culture of sharing and exchanging knowledge which is more likely to lead to innovation. Policy and contractual arrangements will be needed to protect intellectual property but there should also be acknowledgement and recognition of those contributing to the knowledge pool. If this is neglected a 'knowledge is power' mentality can quickly emerge with people being protective of the knowledge they have and very selective about what they share with others. This is not conducive to innovation.

Creating the right climate requires:

- **A culture** of freedom, constructive challenge and confrontation, as well as other factors already mentioned is essential for knowledge sharing and innovation. The culture will also see people as central to knowledge and innovation and technology and process as support activities.

- **Honest and open communications** will encourage the sharing and exchanging of knowledge. If employees are kept informed of decisions and events they are more likely to reciprocate with information.

- **People:** it is not just about acquiring knowledge. People develop and use knowledge and this is where the real value exists. It is not simply a collection of disparate pieces of data but interpreted and stored as intelligence – connections are made and assumptions and conclusions are drawn. The knowledge they hold is the sum total of this activity and the experience that goes with it. People are the experts in knowledge management. Staff should be motivated and rewarded for sharing and using knowledge.

- **Recognition and reward** help encourage the sharing and exchanging of knowledge and acknowledging the contribution employees make to the overall wealth of organisational knowledge. Performance measurement should take account of the value of knowledge and its contribution.

- **Processes** provide the method for gathering, analysing, interpreting, disseminating and using knowledge. Good processes are kept simple and minimal if they are going to be effective. Processes should evolve to support knowledge management.

- **Technology** is the tool to support knowledge management. The connectivity of technology across the organisation and extending it to external stakeholders is essential. The brief to technological requirements is not driven by finance and IT; it is a collaboration across the organisation resulting in a specification that meets marketing needs, collaboration with stakeholders and knowledge management and innovation needs.

3.2 A learning culture

Organisational learning goes beyond sending people off on training courses or internal management or other development programmes. Learning should be a way of life, a belief, a value integral to the organisation's culture. While individual beliefs are important in an organisation, the collective belief of the organisation can only be fulfilled if individual beliefs are discussed and negotiated. Hence a key part of developing a learning culture is having a balance between diversity and consensus. 'Learning thus implies the development of knowledge which leads to a new collective understanding, this collective understanding influences behaviour since the acquisition and interpretation of knowledge brings about changes in cognitive maps; which in turn affects the range of potential behaviours.' (Buchel and Probst, 2000: 4)

3.3 Learning with a purpose

External training courses, learning and development programmes are all relevant. What sets apart good learning and development from poor is how connected it is to the organisation's goals and strategy and how well numerous learning events have objectives that have emerged from learning needs and whether these events are co-ordinated, integrated and evaluated for their outcomes.

Where learning and development are unintentionally designed in isolation of the workplace and no attention is paid to the transfer of learning, positive outcomes and benefits of the learning are either not realised or short lived. This can be de-motivating for employees keen to make a positive difference and implement learning.

Figure 8.4   Systematic learning and transfer cycle

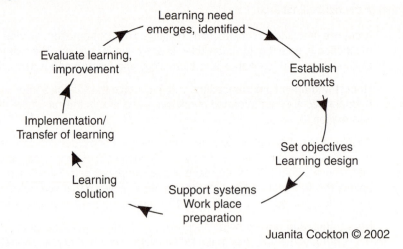

Juanita Cockton © 2002

Attention to the transfer of learning is required, whether it is informal or formal learning, external courses or internal on the job learning. Line managers should establish support systems, however simple, and with the learner and colleagues give thought to how the learning can be implemented into new work practices or as a change in behaviour. Work as usual is unlikely to result in the acceptance of learning.

 The Chartered Institute of Marketing

Leaders can create a learning organisation starting with its culture. Leaders provide examples of learning behaviour and signal its importance through their commitment to objectives set and resources allocated. A learning culture requires acceptance of mistakes and encouragement of exploration and investigation. Therefore cultures that are risk averse and strong on maintaining the status quo will struggle to develop a learning culture.

Learning comes from reviewing and evaluation of tasks and activities; for example on completion of a project a meeting to review and evaluate what can be learned from the experience can result in identifying improvements for the next project.

Properly managed delegation is powerful for supporting learning. Delegation that provides the right level of challenge with a balance of appropriate support can develop new skills and improve existing skills. The role of coach or mentor is not restricted to the domain of leadership and management. Skills for coaching and mentoring for most employees are developed by providing opportunities, no matter how small, to coach and mentor another.

Actions, behaviour, success and failures are all assessed for what can be learnt, not as an opportunity to apportion blame but to explore for improvements. The activity of avoiding mistakes and problems is a different one: that of risk management.

ACTIVITY 8.2

Critically identify the barriers and drivers of creativity and innovation in your organisation. Review the impact on your organisation of the internal barriers.

4 Risk management

▶ **Key term**

Risk is defined as the probability of an event and its consequences. Risk management is the practice of using processes, methods and tools for managing these risks.

Risk management is about avoiding or reducing a negative or damaging impact or a potential crisis by anticipating in advance likely events or threats. Because risks can be difficult to identify, particularly their impact, and difficult to interpret risk management is about managing uncertainty. The intention broadly is about identifying, avoiding or managing, monitoring and limiting risks. Not all risks can be avoided but some can and those risks that cannot be avoided are monitored and action taken to reduce risk where possible.

Bauer identifies key steps in risk management (www.martinbauer.com, accessed 14 June 2012):

- Risk assessment
- Risk reduction/minimisation/containment
- Risk monitoring
- Risk reporting
- Risk evaluation

With increasing legislation and corporate responsibility pressures, an organisation's risk management becomes a priority. Leaders and managers have a legal obligation to identify risks and hazards and proactively take action to eliminate, reduce and manage risks.

BPP
LEARNING MEDIA

For risk management to be truly successful it should be integrated into the culture of the organisation. This in itself can do much to reduce risk if people are alert to the nature of risks and their possible consequences.

There are four stages to risk management:

(a) **Identification**

- Nature of risks and hazards
- Sources of risk
- Approaches to identifying risk

(b) **Analysis and assessment**

- Categories of risk
- Assessing risk
- Evaluation criteria

(c) **Risk management and mitigation plan**

- Types of techniques to manage risk
- Mitigation plan

(d) **Risk reporting and policy**

- Strategic, operational and tactical reporting
- Risk management policy

▶ **Assessment tip**

A risk with assignments is not completing within the stated deadlines. You do not want to put work into a project and then find you miss the submission deadline because you could not meet an interim deadline eg allowing enough time for review and feedback. A schedule of learning as well as assignment activities should be built into weekly work routines.

4.1 Risk identification

The task is to identify risks and hazards which are sometimes the same but sometimes not. Risks typically have impact and the nature of damage tends to be to the organisation and its strategies, resources and plans. Hazards typically do harm, for example physical damage in the workplace (layout, ease of access and exit), activity (using machinery, repetitive actions) and environmental (dust, pollution).

Nature of risks and hazards to an organisation takes many forms including:

- **Legal and professional risk** (compliance): lack of compliance with laws and industry and professional codes of conduct

- **Financial risk:** investment in capital, strategies, resources, cash flow, funding, debtors, interest rates, foreign exchange, debtors

- **Health and safety risk:** to employees, customers and other stakeholders. This could be included in legal but it is such an important and ongoing issue for leaders it is worth separating out

- **Hostile action risk:** military forces or guerrilla groups, employee sabotage or pressure groups

- **Third party risk:** for example, a stakeholder or member of the extended value chain of the organisation that has indirect influence or impact on products and services offered and customers

- **Environmental risk:** natural hazards such as earthquakes, extreme weather, pollution

During the audit stage of business and marketing planning the external audit and environmental monitoring will alert leaders and managers to their exposure to possible risks and threats that will or may damage the achievement of organisation goals and performance.

Sources of risks can be identified as internal or external and are shown in the table below.

The Chartered Institute of Marketing

Table 8.2   Sources of risk

Internal sources of risk	External sources of risk
Leadership competence	Political/legal
Management competence	Economic
Employee competence	Social
Operational (systems, processes, technology)	Technological
Financial	Environmental
Customer	Competitive

This gives us clues as to the degree of control we may have over the risk. Internal risks should be within the control of the organisation. External risks are unlikely to be controllable.

It is also worth considering risk in terms of its scope, the extent of impact on the organisation and where the impact will occur. The scope of risk broadly covers:

(a)   **Strategic** (corporate/organisation, leadership): this type of risk is likely to impact on the entire organisation and have serious consequences, possibly beyond the organisation, for example the extended value chain, intellectual capital and other stakeholders. Mergers and acquisitions, changes in customers or demand, changes in competition, changes in the industry.

(b)   **Operational** (systems, processes, technology, management): this type of risk impacts on one or all of the organisation's operations or aspects of operations. It may extend to specific areas of the value chain. Technology advances, materials and inventory management, transportation and fuel, sources of supply, security (including IT), privacy and data protection.

(c)   **Tactical** (tasks, teams, individuals): this type of risk is more likely to be a hazard and is typically confined to immediate workspace, individual behaviour and task execution, for example untidy office, ventilation, sufficient breaks. However, individuals can behave in a way or take action that can have more serious consequences such as sabotaging an IT system.

4.1.1 Approaches to identifying risk

There are risk consultants and management companies that an organisation can use and they have the advantage of expertise. However, because of increasing legislation a more effective approach, in some organisations, is to manage risk internally. Everyone should be responsible and accountable for reducing risks and hazards; this cannot be delegated externally. Even risk experts criticise the culture of 'protecting backs'. Risk management that has emerged from external risk management organisations (and some internal) wanting to make sure everything is covered can result in cumbersome, over engineered risk management processes.

Setting out to identify risk can be daunting and, if not done properly, time wasting and expensive. Having a framework for identifying risk is useful and brings some focus to the activity. Amongst approaches to identifying risk are the four discussed below.

(a)   **Objectives-based risk identification** focuses on the objectives of the team, section or organisation and identifies anything that may jeopardise the achievement of those objectives. This approach has the potential to miss risks not directly linked to objectives but that may be high risk.

(b)   **Resources-based risk identification** focuses on the resources needed for particular plans and projects and identifies issues and factors that may limit or prevent those plans or projects from succeeding. This has the same shortcoming as above.

(c)   **Functional audit-based risk identification:** as audits are now increasingly a common practice in organisations and part of the audit process is to identify threats to the business, the process can be extended to identify specific functional risks. This provides the scope of risk identification to help focus the process. The approach has the potential to miss risks associated with strategies and plans.

(d)   **Scenario planning** focuses on identifying the 'what ifs': those events, patterns and behaviours that might happen beyond the expected and planned for. It requires looking into the future and imagining alternative future states to the ones predicted.

These approaches all have their value and depending on the circumstances it may be useful to adapt and use the above approaches to design an approach appropriate to your organisation. Market scanning and quality marketing research are essential to the successful identification of risk.

4.2 Risk analysis and assessment

Assessing risk can be difficult because often information is missing and variables are unknown. Risk assessment can be quantitative or qualitative in terms of probability and possible consequences. Many small- to medium-sized businesses effectively assess risk using high, medium or low rating without the need for more complex methods. However, some organisations require sophisticated programmes to measure risk, for example financial organisations and major construction companies.

Categories of risk determine the extent of impact and whether or not the risk is within the control of the organisation or not.

Figure 8.5   Categories of risk

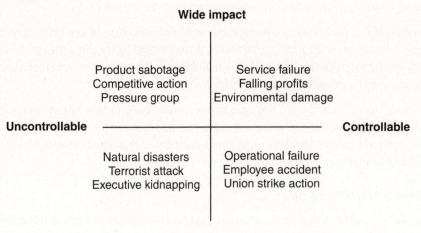

Wide impact

Product sabotage	Service failure
Competitive action	Falling profits
Pressure group	Environmental damage

Uncontrollable ———————————————— **Controllable**

Natural disasters	Operational failure
Terrorist attack	Employee accident
Executive kidnapping	Union strike action

Local impact

There are three aspects of assessing risk:

(a)   The probability of it occurring
(b)   The seriousness of the consequences, against attractiveness, should the risk occur
(c)   The attractiveness of the activity or strategy

Figure 8.6   Risk matrix

Probability of occurrence

<table>
<tr><th rowspan="2">Severity of consequences</th><th></th><th>High</th><th>Medium</th><th>Low</th></tr>
<tr><td>High</td><td>Damage limitation</td><td>Contingency</td><td>Monitor</td></tr>
<tr><td></td><td>Medium</td><td>Contingency</td><td>Contingency</td><td>Monitor</td></tr>
<tr><td></td><td>Low</td><td>Monitor</td><td>Monitor</td><td>Ignore</td></tr>
</table>

Another matrix, with different criteria, can be used to evaluate the attractiveness, for example the GE matrix which includes competitive position or business strength.

This exercise can be subjective as evidence for **probability** cannot always be precise. However, evidence can be provided by indicators, for example number of times a risk has occurred and the consequences, therefore number of times it might reasonably be expected to occur in future depending on conditions.

Severity of **consequences** might be reasonably easy to identify, for example damage to property, a lost major customer or a product recall. The severity of some risks is more difficult to identify particularly where all the variables are not known, for example environmental where the risk of pollution in the atmosphere cannot accurately predict climate or weather variables.

It is important to include **vulnerable groups** where appropriate; for example disabled people or trainees must also be considered in risk assessment.

Approaches to assessing risk can be simple and typically in smaller businesses do not involve sophisticated computer programmes. Assessing risk includes prioritising and ranking consequences and probability and mapping risk. **Mapping risks** provides a means of both assessing and communicating to others the degree of risk.

Figure 8.7   Spider gram/positioning web of risk

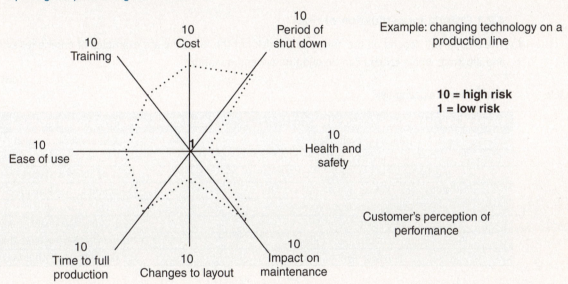

Alternatively risks can be plotted on a **risk radar**. The nearer the middle the greater the **probability** of the risk happening. The concentric circles can represent timescales, for example months or years. The severity of consequences can be represented by the size of filled in circles.

Figure 8.8 Risk radar

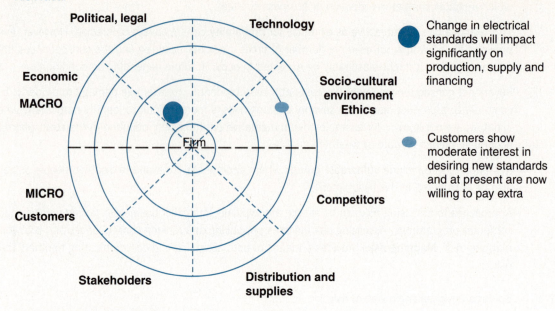

Figure 8.8 Risk radar

4.2.1 Criteria for evaluation of risk

The criteria will depend on the nature of the risk but the following are examples of criteria for evaluating risk and illustrate where criteria can be quantitative and qualitative.

Table 8.3 Criteria for evaluating risk

Financial risk: launch new product range	Ethical risk: outsourcing manufacturing abroad
Criteria for evaluation	Criteria for evaluation
Market demand and size	Health and safety of employees
Marketing growth of not less than X%	Working terms and conditions
Potential market share of not less than X%	Recruitment of employees
Profitability of not less than X%	Training
Differentiation of range	Ease of managing relationship
Speed of market penetration	Cost of outsourcing not more than X%
Payback period	Contractual constraints

4.3 Managing risk and mitigation

When risks have been assessed the next stage is to decide the most appropriate courses of action to deal with risk. These include:

- Avoid the risk
- Accept risk
- Reduce the risk
- Transfer risk

The most obvious way of **avoiding a risk** is to decide not to undertake the strategy or activity that carries the risk. This has to be balanced against the potential loss, financial or otherwise, of deciding not to act.

Reducing risk includes taking additional steps such as health and safety precautions (hard hats, protective clothing) and innovating incrementally.

Accepting risk is viable when, for example, an insurance premium might be too high and the probability of the risk occurring is medium to low or the risk cannot be insured against such as war, and often, natural disasters.

The Chartered Institute of Marketing

Marketers take risks all the time. Every time a produce or service and marketing communications campaign are launched there is the opportunity for things to go wrong and result in an expensive disaster. To reduce these risks:

- **Marketing intelligence** is used extensively during product and campaign development to reduce the risk of external threats and internal weaknesses.

- **Informing and communicating** with those involved with potential risks and consequences alerts people to possible problems and allows them to prepare for managing, typically a crisis, should it arise.

- **Training** of people equips them with the necessary skills and reduces the risk of incompetence leading to problems.

- **Guidelines and procedures** can provide a point of reference for dealing with different or difficult situations and reduces the risk of neglecting or not dealing with problems.

- **Transferring risk** to another party in exchange for an agreed benefit takes the form of, for example, insurance cover and hedging. Outsourcing is another form of transferring risk.

For marketers the use of technology in data collection and storage can expose them to the risk of inadequate data protection or it being leaked or sabotaged. Inadequate protection can lead to expensive litigation and damage to reputation.

4.3.1 Mitigation

As with any plan resources are limited and not everything can be prioritised. The same is true of risk. Our assessment of risk in terms of understanding the scope and impact allows us to **prioritise**. This prioritisation needs to take account of organisation goals and strategies but importantly ensures that the necessary resources are allocated to priority risks so if the worse does happen corrective action is immediate.

Methods for mitigating risk include:

- **Contingency planning:** brainstorming, scenario planning to identify possible 'what ifs' and develop outline plans to deal with situations if they arise.

- **Keeping a record** allows the tracking of problems and risk to be taken into account in future planning.

- **Measures and monitoring**: a quality management system will set quality standards against which compliance, performance and risk can be measured, for example measuring errors and their consequences.

- **Auditing and inspection**: including guidelines, procedures, manuals, instructions etc for their value in preventing risks occurring.

4.4 Risk reporting

Risk reporting should be designed for appropriate levels:

Strategic/board: senior management should be informed of the most significant risks facing the organisation and the possible impact on key stakeholders. They should be kept aware of risk issues and how they are being managed and alerted if problems arise. It is then their responsibility to report on risk internally and externally if necessary and as appropriate.

Senior management also report on the effectiveness of the organisation's risk management policy and any changes that may be required. Their report should include the risk management process – how risks are assessed, monitored and managed.

Operational/unit/function: managers should be aware of risks that fall within their area of responsibility and the possible impact and consequences including where these might affect other areas of the organisation. KPIs are established to monitor and assess risk and then to report to senior management and individuals where appropriate.

Tactical/team/individuals: employees should be aware of risks within their jobs and working space and take responsibility for risk assessment and avoidance. If problems arise they report to their line manager.

4.5 Risk management policy

In some organisations because of the nature of the industry, eg chemicals, there will be a risk management function. For many organisations it will be enough to have a robust risk management policy. This policy will establish:

- **Role of leaders:** responsible and accountable for creating an organisation environment and structure that eliminates or reduces risks and hazards for employees and other stakeholders. They provide resources for risk management.

- **Role of unit/function managers:** responsible and accountable for managing the organisation environment and operations within their unit or function to eliminate or reduce risks and hazards for employees and other stakeholders. They allocate resources for risk management.

- **Role of team leaders/individuals:** responsible and accountable for executing tasks and engaging in daily interactions within their area of work in a way that eliminates or reduces risks and hazards for themselves and each other.

All of these roles and responsibilities are guided by the risk management process we have covered.

THE REAL WORLD

Land Securities

Land Securities is an example of a business that is willing to take risks to gain rewards and is keen to enter new markets and offer a varied product range; having a balanced portfolio means that risk is minimised. Land Securities has six steps as part of its risk management strategy:

1. Identify the business goals and objectives
2. Identify the risks
3. Measure the level of risk
4. Develop action plans to manage the risks
5. Assess the risks again after they have been managed
6. Report at each stage

These steps help to reduce risks as there are key steps that have to be followed. While there is a very linear approach to the management of risk, the company encourages innovation in particular with its product/service offerings, which range from property outsourcing to landflex. Land Securities is keen to develop a varied portfolio; however, it keeps a close watch on its current portfolio to ensure it is engaging with changes in the sector and is meeting ever evolving customer needs.

Land Securities has taken on a number of high profile projects; however, a key factor that is important is ensuring it takes care of the environment: for example it has been involved in a number of recycling projects, such as Terminal 5 Heathrow that was built using recycling aggregate. It also chooses to work with subcontractors that are energy efficient. A key focus of Land Securities is working closely with its employees and ensuring constant communication. The communication include:

- An employee intranet

- Regular presentations and updates of business activities

- Management training days

- E-mail updates

- Different forms of communication, in paper and online

The Chartered Institute of Marketing

This encourages staff to suggest ideas that will help them and the organisation and encourages innovative practice. Also, employees are rewarded accordingly. Land Securities is very much focused on its labour force and ensuring it keeps its labour force happy, as well as meeting all regulatory requirements. Overall Land Securities focuses on meeting shareholder needs, having a balanced portfolio, ensuring it invests in appropriate projects and remaining an enterprising organisation with minimal risk.

ACTIVITY 8.3

Identify your organisation's risk strategy. What are the key factors that need to be considered?

5 Competition and collaboration

As we have established a leader's own ambitions can determine whether or not they desire to be leaders in their field or have less ambitious goals and are content to follow, entrepreneurs are typically pioneers. Far more challenging for leadership than formulating competitive strategies today is building an organisation that has a strong, consistent and sustainable competitive advantage. It is no longer enough to engage in competitive tactics such as price cutting, heavy promotions or even rapid product launches.

Competition and competitive strategies have been covered comprehensively in previous chapters so this section is intended as a brief reminder of some of the issues around competition and the increasing developments in collaboration.

5.1 Competition

Managers may be responsible for influencing, designing and implementing competitive strategy, but leaders are responsible for deciding a clear, distinct position for profit-making organisations, a competitive position. Even the public sector or not-for-profit organisations increasingly find themselves being compared with others, for example a private hospital or school, or another charity competing for similar funds. Even government departments are compared with similar organisations or other governments overseas for the public to decide whether or not they are competent. In these cases they also need a competitive position. A clear and distinct position requires that the whole organisation is designed for a particular purpose and does things in a particular way that reinforces their desired position.

Competition by its nature is trying to do something better than others and beating others to win customers. There are some well known strategies for competitive positioning.

5.2 Positioning

▶ **Key term**

Positioning is the deliberate effort by an organisation to positively influence stakeholder perceptions of what it is and what it does.

Trout and Ries (1991) were the first to clarify what the purpose of positioning was for organisations and their focus was on what the customer actually received. The three bases of positioning are:

(a)   **Functional** (solves problems, provides benefits)
(b)   **Symbolic** (self-image enhancing, ego identification, belonging/socially meaningful, affective fulfilment)
(c)   **Experiential** (provides sensory stimulation, provides cognitive stimulation)

BPP
LEARNING MEDIA

They proposed that positioning can be based on:

- Product benefits, needs solutions
- Use categories
- Usage occasions
- Placing and comparing relative to another offer
- Dissociation of the product class

Positioning became more strategic with the works of Michael Porter (1980) and Treacy and Wiersema (1993).

Porter (1980) argues that to build an effective, sustainable competitive position an organisation must focus on developing a specific source of competitive advantage. If they do not design the organisation to build a specific source of advantage they end up 'stuck in the middle' through inefficiencies and little opportunity to compete.

Figure 8.9   Michael Porter's generic competitive strategies

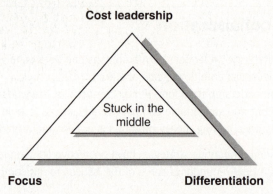

Organisation goals, strategies and operations are designed to build advantage and require one of the following:

Table 8.4   Porter's generic competitive strategies

Cost leadership	Differentiation	Focus
Cost and efficient objectives	Investment in:	Either differentiation in cost leadership in a niche market
Tight cost and overhead control	- Design or brand image	
Pursuit of high value customers only	- Technology and features	
Cost minimisation in all areas	- Customer service	
Achieving critical mass	- Dealer network	
Achieving economies of scale	or combination of these to differentiate	

Treacy and Wiersema (1993) recommended developing **value disciplines** for competitive positioning and provided four rules for success.

5.2.1 Four rules for developing value (Treacy and Wiersema,1993)

(a)   Excel in one specific dimension of value – develop a compelling, unmatched value proposition
(b)   Maintain threshold standards on other dimensions of value – to support core value
(c)   Continuous improvement in core value to remain dominant
(d)   Dedicated operating model built to deliver unmatched value

A company must choose one value discipline and consistently act upon it as indicated by the four rules above.

5.2.2 Three generic value disciplines (Porter, 1980)

- **Operational excellence:** focus on efficiency and volume, reasonable quality/no frills, very low price, task-oriented towards people, streamlined operations, supply chain management, limit range

- **Product leadership:** strong innovation and brand marketing, focus on development, innovation, design, time to market, high margins, short timeframe, flexible company cultures

- **Customer intimacy:** excel in customer attention and service, tailor products/services, large variety, CRM, deliver above expectation, lifetime value concepts, reliability, authority to employees close to customers

All of these approaches are designed to differentiate and compare better against the competition. In all examples the intention is that the entire organisation, from structure to operations, systems and processes, the sort of people recruited, trained and developed and the way leaders lead and managers manage, is designed to build and sustain a distinct and different competitive position.

From this distinct competitive position the organisation can design strategies to aggressively or offensively attack other competitors and defend its position whether its goal is market leader, follower, challenger or pioneer.

So what happens when players in the market either find it desirable to, or have no choice but to, work with their competitors? This is a trend that has been growing for some time and it requires a different approach.

5.3 Collaboration

Collaboration between competitors and with other stakeholders has been growing rapidly over the last decade. Various forms of collaboration exist, driven by different organisation goals.

Burton (1995) emphasises the co-operative rather than competitive arrangements between industry participants and describes collaborative advantage as a foundation of superior business performance. The five sources of collaborative advantage are:

- **Horizontal collaborations** with other enterprises operating at same stage of product, process, producing the same group of closely related products

- **Vertical collaborations** with suppliers of components or services

- **Selective partnering:** arrangements with specific channels or customers

- **Related diversification:** alliances with producers of both complementary and substitutes

- **Diversification alliances** with firms based in previously unrelated sectors but between which a blurring of industry borders is potentially occurring

Figure 8.10   Burton's (1995) five sources framework

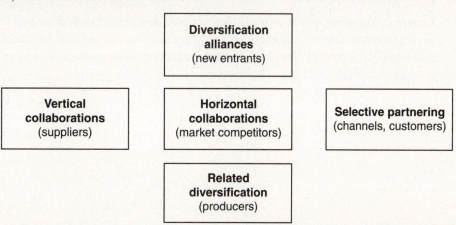

Each of the five approaches will have its own particular requirements, but broadly bringing together a strategy that is both competitive and collaborative requires:

- Trust, openness and willingness to share ideas, innovation and information

- Identification and exploitation of collaborative advantage
- Joint strategic planning teams and good communication skills and processes
- Compromise and showing consideration in areas of differences
- Integrity and professionalism

In our internet world these five sources of collaboration have evolved into strategic e-mediary networks.

Characteristics of e-mediary networks are high connectivity and transaction focus. To achieve advantage requires synergistic strategic value. Partnerships must reciprocally add value to enable network advantage over competing networks. Being able to transfer organisational know-how and learning is important. This 'knowledge resource' from the network is the 'core competency'. These factors can lead to sources of competitive advantage that are difficult to copy and 'lock' e-mediaries together making switching difficult. Working together the network can increase chances of profitability and increase power in the industry, leading to being able to set the 'rules of the game', even build barriers to entry. Crispin Dale (2002) described the role and purpose of competitive networks of tourism e-mediaries as:

- Channel
- Collaborative
- Communicate
- Complementary
- Converse

Channel: global distribution systems (GDSs) primarily drive this relationship. **Value:** Channel relationships enable one e-mediary to access the channels of another and provide breadth of distribution and multi-channel objectives. There is an exchange of strategic resources and capabilities, combining resources, concurrently.

Collaborative: alliances to strengthen competitive offer through 'co-opetition' where there is synergy in the products/services of two or more providers and they are valued more together. **Value:** for example, access to new geographic markets, off-line alternative channels (eg call centres, agencies). Issues include managing different business operations, culture and so on.

Communicate: 'infomediary' channels and portals. **Value:** disseminate information through specific (relevant) channels for specific (relevant) purposes eg comparison websites. Also disseminate ancillary information eg destination information.

Complementary: cross-sell or distribute complementary products or services. **Value:** connecting related services eg travel with a sports event. Opportunities for maximising sales ratio of e-mediaries and yield of distressed inventory for suppliers. Can re-enforce brand credibility through association with respected brands.

Converse: where one e-mediary distributes the unrelated product or another and vice versa. **Value:** allows access to distribution channel expertise and to tap into new markets that have possibly not previously been interested in the product or service or have not accessed those products or services through the primary e-mediary channel.

Figure 8.11   Example of a strategic networks in tourism 'e-mediary'

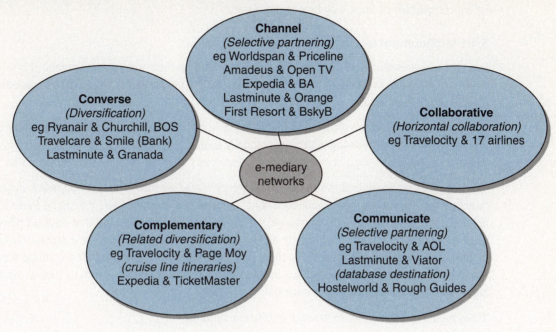

5.4 Organisation design in collaboration

These themes in organisation development require leaders to design organisations to be able to exploit opportunities for creative, innovative and competitive partnerships. These partnerships are very different in nature so a 'one size fits all' approach will not work. We discussed the fluid nature of leadership style and this is also true for organisation design.

As collaborations have increased and market conditions changed so organisations have responded with new business models emerging. Interestingly, as organisations have become flatter (or claim to be) they have become broader through alliances and collaboration which can be rather more difficult to manage than a hierarchical structure. As well as creating a learning organisation, leaders need to resource connectivity through technology to be able to work with collaborative networks and virtual self-managed teams.

Developing strategic networks and collaboration needs clear objectives, strategy, stakeholder relationship management and control. Of course, the nature of collaboration means control might be rather challenging. However, some level of control is essential as there are obviously risks associated with collaboration including:

- Sharing sensitive information or intellectual property and the risk of it ending up in the hands of the competition, or in the marketplace before it should, with damaging consequences

- Losing innovative ideas to others

- Exposing sources of sustainable competitive advantage that are then leaked to competitors

Collaborations should therefore be assessed for potential risks.

We should not forget where we started: how might collaboration impact on competitive position? Some collaborations should not, for example those where the purpose of a collaborative network is innovation, unless something radically new emerges. Collaborative networks may well be competing with other collaborative networks so leaders have to work with each other across networks on consistency and collaborative advantage that establishes a distinct position – difficult enough when it is just the organisation you are trying to position competitively.

Collaborations between competitors can change competitive positions either deliberately or unintentionally. Where deliberate, the decisions are about what competitive position and how operations and marketing change as a result. The real challenge here is how much each organisation wants to change or can change.

Consistency and continuity are important factors in deciding to form a collaborative partnership, particularly where competitive position may be compromised.

5.4.1 Multicultural leadership

Even if an organisation does not consider itself international there are very few organisations that are not influenced by or in contact with international markets. This is particularly true in an organisation that has collaborative networks.

Collaborative networks are global with potentially anyone contributing to some process and increasingly that process is innovation. Working with teams globally even if they are virtual still means leaders need to be culturally aware and skilled at managing the differences if positive outcomes are to be realised.

There is much evidence that the culture convergence feared by many has not happened and most cultures remain intact. However, the interconnectivity of cultures has increased and managing those aspects that influence the organisation is the challenge. Managing any form of operation that involves different cultures requires leaders to manage the diversity and ensure the best emerges from the cultural differences. For organisations with overseas operations there may be more control and need for a consistent corporate identity but, even if what is being managed is a collaborative network of people or enterprises not part of the organisation, cultural sensitivity is essential.

There are three approaches to managing different cultures:

(a)   **Ignore** the differences and carry on as usual. This risks the best from the cultures being lost and ignoring can result in cultural insensitivity leading to focusing negatively on the differences.

(b)   **Eliminate** the differences and drive conformity. First, it is usually impossible to eliminate the differences and any attempts to do so will antagonise, demoralise and result in active or passive resistance or withdrawal. Second, while it might be desirable for good reasons to have a 'one way of doing things around here' it should focus on operations and harmonising what is commonly shared rather than stifle the diversity that can bring positive contributions.

(c)   **Accept** the differences and work on commonalities. If groups are going to be working together for some time it is worth identifying commonalities early on, as it can avoid focusing on differences that might be perceived as threats, with a greater focus on the positives.

Processes and systems for doing things can be standardised but even here a consultation process and negotiations and compromise should result in something everyone finds acceptable.

The emphasis for leaders is to encourage cultural co-operation by providing examples through their own behaviour. Their challenge is to manage diversity in a way that makes the most of all that is best. For leaders to succeed cultural awareness is not enough. They need a deeper understanding of cultural differences and diversity and that means going beyond what is reasonably familiar to the edges of their organisation's world and towards what is unfamiliar, being open and willing to engage with the unfamiliar sends a positive signal.

Multi-cultural leadership involves understanding different cultures but also subcultures it is not enough just to understand the national culture, but having a clear understanding of the subcultures can also help to identify differences and commonalities amongst the workforce. Looking at Hofstede's value orientations can also help leaders understand country differences, as teams may come from a number of different countries.

Hofstede's value orientations (1984) are:

■   **Power/distance (PD)**

This focuses on the level of inequality that exists, for those with or without power; high PD indicates that this society is happy to accept an unequal distribution of power and people understand their place in the system.

- **Individualism (IDV)**

  This refers to the strength of ties that people have with the community and their family and the extent to which this influences their decision making. Those with high IDV scores generally are more individualistic and make decisions that will benefit them first and the community second; however, those communities/groups with low IDV scores have stronger group cohesion and are very concerned with meeting others' needs as well as their own.

- **Masculinity/femininity (MAS)**

  This focuses on how much a society follows the traditional gender (male and female) roles. High MAS scores indicate countries where men are expected to be the main breadwinner, assertive and strong, while low MAS scores are societies where roles are not so gender defined.

- **Uncertainty/avoidance index (UAI)**

  This relates to the degree of anxiety a society or individual feels when things are not planned out or there are uncertain and unknown situations. Those societies that have high UAI scores tend to avoid ambiguity, whereas those with lower scores are happy with the uncertainty and almost thrive on it. In fact, there are less stringent rules and people are encouraged to explore and develop freely.

- **Long term orientation (LTO)**

  This looks at the extent to which society values long-standing versus short-term. For those that had high LTO scores they were very much focused on social obligations and saving face within the community.

Often these value orientations have been categorised according to eastern and western societies, as eastern societies are more collectivistic and western societies more individualistic. However, there is an argument that these categorisations may need updating as there is a global flow of people who have a hybrid of cultural values that are constantly evolving.

---

6 Stakeholder relationship management

> ▶ **Key term**
>
> A **steering committee** is an advisory committee, usually a group of high level stakeholders, that is responsible for providing guidance on overall strategic direction. They can provide guidance on key issues such as company policy and objectives, budgetary control, marketing strategy, resource allocation and expenditure decisions.

Keeping track of who the organisation is or should be collaborating with is not simple. Typically and most obviously an organisation is involved with:

- Customers
- Shareholders
- Financial institutions and other investors
- Distribution channels
- Suppliers

and in some cases:

- Trade association and industry institutions
- Regulatory and licensing bodies
- Analysts
- Non-government organisations (NGOs)

It is easier with competitor collaborations to identify who you might want to collaborate with and why. The challenge then is making it happen and making it work.

Identifying other collaborators in innovation may be more difficult. With the web the possibilities are endless and then the challenge is one of being open enough to collaborate but balancing this with protecting intellectual property and creativity.

Stakeholders, other than employees, who collaborate in the innovation process include:

- Customers
- Suppliers and intermediaries
- Shareholders/members
- Media and industry analysts
- Industry associations, regulatory bodies
- Universities, business schools

Mapping collaborative networks can be very useful for understanding who is involved.

Figure 8.12   Collaborative innovation network or innovation communities

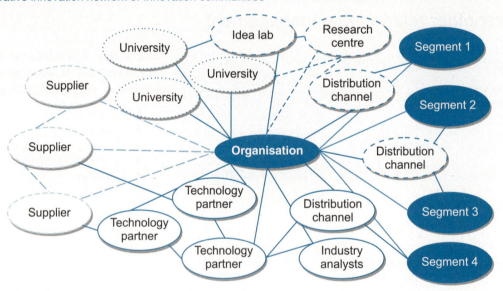

When all stakeholders of any collaboration have been identified the next step is to establish their power and impact.

6.1 Stakeholder influence and involvement

Stakeholders other than customers need to be understood and their impact on the organisation can be just as important. Some stakeholders' involvement with the organisation will be far greater than others as will their

The Chartered
Institute of Marketing

impact on value. It will also vary from organisation or organisation. It can be useful to identify a stakeholder's level of involvement with the organisation and their influence on you.

Figure 8.13   Stakeholder influence and involvement

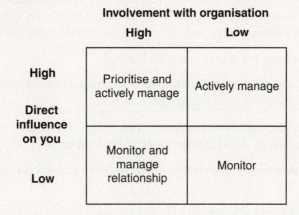

Factors that contribute to and define influence and impact include:

- Investment in organisation: for example finance, knowledge or expertise
- Authority over organisation: for example government or regulatory body
- Power of stakeholder: for example pressure group or key distribution outlet

---

▶ **Assessment tip**

You may want to think about stakeholder relationships to gain workplace support – you will require the support and co-operation of your managers and colleagues during assignments. Explain your needs and what is to be undertaken and any resources that may be required.

It may mean returning the favour at some point!

6.2 What is involved in building and managing relationships?

Working relationships often fail because of a lack of strategy and management. They can fail or not work effectively due to misunderstandings, misinterpretations, conflicts and antagonism that can arise from poor communications and no effort to manage. To work effectively there needs to be a formalised process for building and managing a working partnership. Therefore a plan and guidelines are needed on managing the partnership.

6.3 Compatibility

To what extent do people share values, beliefs and practices? If there are differences these will either need to be acknowledged and allowances made for them or changes managed. If allowances or changes are not made conflicts can emerge quickly distracting people from the purpose of the relationship.

6.4 Partnership

The leader signals the emphasis is on co-operation and managers work on:

- Building the relationship
- Commitment to quality improvement
- Regular face-to-face meetings
- Collaborative effort – understanding each others' responsibilities and commitments
- Exchanging information (ideas etc)
- Sharing mutual goals and some risks
- Flexible arrangements

6.5 Boundaries and learning curve

As people begin to work together there will be a period of learning about the relationship itself. Allow time for the network to learn about each other. Setting clear boundaries establishes the role of the network in achieving strategic goals and defining expectations and commitment. This avoids misunderstandings. It is rather like an induction for new employees and can shorten and speed up the learning curve and build loyalty to the network.

(a) **Objectives:** the desired outcomes clarified

(b) **Role and defining responsibilities:** who is responsible for what, eg providing funds, changing systems, supporting and encouraging practices

(c) **Reporting and communication:** formal written reports and their purpose, eg to inform, update, meetings and briefings, informal reporting lines and structure

(d) **Agreeing review procedures:** timing, methods and monitoring

6.6 Communications

Implicit in the partnership is the need for good communications both formal and informal. As well as communicating expectations, feedback and exchanging information, the following established at the start will provide a foundation:

- Communications: used to inform, educate, promote and persuade. For example, informing people of the standards expected, promoting best practice

- Establishing the standards: how they are identified, how they are validated

- Knowledge and information: sharing and exchanging, using the best, selectivity and processes

- Leading by example: being advocates of best practice and demonstrating through everyday practice

6.7 Control and evaluation

Feedback should be part of the communications process. To what extent can existing internal controls be used? Do new controls need to be established? You would need:

- Evaluation: commitment to meeting standards by measuring the effectiveness of performance and establishing whether or not it has met the standard

- Standard of reporting (ease of understanding, does it enlighten, address issues, are recommendations actionable?)

- Impact on relationships (steady and consistent or surprises and crisis)

- Partnership development (knowledge of each others' activities etc)

- Added value (what benefits have been derived from the partnership?)

This provides us with a framework for forming and managing partnerships that clarifies what people are expected to do. Without this formalisation stakeholders might be disinclined to take responsibility for outcomes. Our approach to managing partnerships must be flexible and will form and re-form over time as different needs and change are implemented.

We should also ensure we have mechanisms in place for learning from the partnership, what worked well, what was problematic etc. An end of project review of the actual partnership would provide an opportunity to honestly and openly discuss how effective partnerships were with a view to improving next time.

How effectively partnerships work, particularly collaboration, will depend on the culture of the organisation. Some cultures will act as inhibitors to the effectiveness of the partnership. A driver of effective partnerships will be a learning culture.

Identify key stakeholders you collaborate with either informally or formally. How could you improve this collaboration and what would the benefits be?

7 Your leadership style

Now you have had time to think about and evaluate different leadership styles, motivation and other organisation factors that affect leadership you can start to work on your own career progression. Self-reflection when analysing leadership is important; whether you are in a position to lead or potentially want a leadership role, understanding your own strengths and weaknesses is a key part of development. Identifying gaps is an important part of development as well as understanding how to respond to these gaps and move forward; this can mean knowing where training is needed and the benefits that it will bring to one's own development.

Identify your leadership style. You may already have done this or completed a diagnostic test to establish your leadership style. If not, having read Chapters 7 and 8 you will no doubt have been reflecting on your leadership style, wherever you are in the hierarchy, and in the context of your organisation. From this analysis, identify key gaps and strengths in your style and decide what recommendations you would make to fill these gaps.

7.1 Developing your leadership style

Following the identification of your leadership style you can then set personal objectives and goals. In developing your leadership style there are a number of factors you need to take into account including:

- Of the leadership styles described, what style/s would you like to develop? What sort of leader do you want to be?

- What is appropriate and possible in your organisation?

- What are the barriers to developing your preferred leadership style, internal and personal to you and within your organisation?

- What are the opportunities to develop leadership skills, for example leading projects, learning and development programmes?

Leadership style is strongly influenced by organisation culture and the next chapter explores this issue.

Goleman (2002) describes six different styles of leadership, suggesting leaders can move among these styles depending on the context and what is required.

- **Visionary**

  The style is recommended when an organisation requires direction or a change of direction. The role of the visionary leader is direct people towards the new vision and direction, allowing people to innovate, take risks and experiment as required.

- **Coaching**

  This style focuses on developing the individuals encouraging people to improve their performance by achieving their own goals and the goals of the organisation. Coaching works better with certain individuals over others, ie those that show initiative and want further training and professional development.

- **Affiliative**

  This style focuses on team work, encouraging individuals to work with each other. This style can work well when the leadership team would like greater harmony and the development of stronger teams. However, the risk of using this in isolation can mean that group praise can mean that individual poor performance is not spotted or corrected.

- **Democratic**

  This leadership style ideally works better where the overall direction of the organisation is not certain and is subject to change, the leader needs to work with the team and use their collective knowledge to make decisions. However, the risk of this is that decision making can be slower and urgency maybe required for certain decision making.

- **Pacesetting**

  In this style the leader or leadership team set high standards for performance, things need to be done better, more efficiently and faster and this is expected from everyone. However, this style may need to be used in conjunction with other styles to avoid a loss of morale and confidence.

- **Commanding**

  This style has been likened to a 'military' style of leadership, generally lacking praise and focusing more on criticism, this can have a direct impact on morale and job satisfaction. Goleman believes this is better applied in times of crisis when things need to be turned around fast, its usefulness is however questioned.

7.2 Personal development plans

An effective personal development plan needs to be self reflective, taking account of the individual's developmental needs. This will involve identifying key areas of strength and weaknesses, along with a rationale and justification as to why these have been identified, and potential development requirements over and above just training courses. Also, there will be a requirement to self reflect and understand one's role within the organisation and at leadership level. If an individual is aspiring to reach a certain level what self development is required and why? Skills that may need developing may range from communication, decision making, leadership, analysing, planning , motivating , supporting others among others. A PDP needs to be critical rather than just descriptive, a well thought through PDP will help an individual develop with the organisation and at leadership level. A PDP can also be linked back to any changes and developments within the organisation and how an individual's development will help them to deal with any changes both now and in the future.

ACTIVITY 8.6

Develop a personal development plan (PDP) to improve an aspect of leadership and discuss how this improvement will be beneficial to yourself and your organisation.

You do not have to be in a senior management role to do this activity. This is about improving leadership skills whether you are in such a role or in preparing for a leadership role.

The Chartered Institute of Marketing

CHAPTER ROUNDUP

- Understanding innovation and learning is a fundamental part of ensuring the long-term sustainability and success of an organisation.

- Thought leadership looks at leadership from a different perspective to traditional leadership styles.

- Knowledge management and learning can help a business gain competitive advantage.

- The need to identify and understand risk is a key part of management in today's business environment. Levels and types of risk vary across organisations and industries.

- Managing risk is a fundamental part of doing business in today's world.

- Collaboration between competitors and stakeholders is growing rapidly and is something that is becoming increasingly popular.

- Managing stakeholders at all levels within the organisation is a fundamental activity for leaders and managers.

FURTHER READING

Barksdale, H.R. and Darden, B. (1971) Marketer's attitudes toward the marketing concept. *Journal of Marketing*, Vol35(4), pp29–36.

Bruning, E.R. and Lockshin, L.S. (1994) Marketing's role in generating organizational competitiveness. *Journal of Strategic Marketing*, Vol2(3), pp163–87.

Cadogan, J.W. and Diamantopoulos, A. (1995) Narver and Slater, Kohli and Jaworski and the market orientation construct: integration and internationalization. *Journal of Strategic Marketing*, Vol3(1), pp41-60.

Day, G.S. (1994) The capabilities of market-driven organizations. *Journal of Marketing*, Vol58(4), pp37–52.

Doyle, P. and Stern, P. (2006) *Marketing management and strategy.* 4th edition. Harlow, Prentice Hall.

Newcombe, K. (2007) Smart marketing and leadership for survival. *Debt Cubed*, Sep/Oct, Vol22(5), pp20–21.

Vecchio, R.P. (2007) *Leadership, understanding the dynamics of power and influence in organizations.* 2nd revised edition. University of Notre Dame.

REFERENCES

Amabile, T.M. (1998) How to kill creativity. *Harvard Business Review,* September–October.

Bauer, Martin. www.martinbauer.com (accessed June 2012).

Buchel, B. and Probst, G.J.B. (2000) *From organisational learning to knowledge management*

Burton, J. (1995) Composite strategy: the combination of collaboration and competition. *Journal of General Management*, Vol21, No 1, Autumn.

Cockton, J. (2002) *Systematic learning and transfer cycle.* London, CIPD.

Dale, C. (2002) Competitive networks of tourism e-mediaries. *Vacation Marketing*, Vol9, No 2, pp109-118.

Davila, T., Epstein, M.J. and Shelton, R. (2006) *Making innovation work*. Upper Saddle River, NJ, Wharton School Publishing.

De Bono, E. (1970) *Lateral thinking*. London, Penguin.

Goleman D., Boyatzis R., McKee A. (2002) Primal leadership realising the power of emotional intelligence Harvard Business School Press., USA002E.

Hargadon, A. and Sutton, R. I. (2000) Building an innovation factory. *Harvard Business Review*, May–June, pp157-166.

Hofstde, G. (1984) *Culture's consequences: international differences in work-related values*. 2nd edition. Beverly Hill, CA, SAGE Publications.

Kurtzman, J. (2010) *Common purpose. How greater leaders get organisations to achieve the extraordinary* ISBN 978-0-470-49009-9.

Porter, M. (1980) *Competitive strategy*. New York, The Free Press.

Ryde, R. (2007) *Thought leadership*, London, Palgrave.

Treacy, M. and Wiersema F. (1993) Customer intimacy and other value disciplines. *Harvard Business Review*, January–February.

Trout, J. and Ries, A. (1991) *Positioning: the battle for your mind*. London, McGraw Hill.

QUICK QUIZ

1 Who is responsible for innovation?

2 What sort of thinking is unlikely to result in new and different creative ideas?

3 What types of risk are organisations exposed to?

4 Briefly, what categories of risk are there?

5 What are the four main ways of dealing with risks?

6 What is risk reporting and policy?

7 What types of collaboration are possible for organisations?

8 What is relationship marketing?

ACTIVITY DEBRIEFS

Activity 8.2

You may identify a mix of the external and internal barriers we discussed in this chapter. You may also identify triggers of change that seem to have come from nowhere, do not seem to have been in response to an obvious external or internal trigger. If this is the case what was the trigger? Was it the result of a leadership whim or an internally created problem? If you identify internal barriers, what is the nature of these barriers? Do these barriers keep recurring? Is it possible to eliminate or reduce these barriers and to what extent have efforts been made to do this? Finally, what was the impact? Did it force people to look for creative ways of managing or dealing with the barrier? Was it ignored? Did it actually prevent change or damage its success?

Activity 8.3

Some organisations will have a very informal risk management process, particularly where the organisation is small or where risks are typically minimal, and there is nothing wrong with this approach. The test is: are risks proactively identified and, when they are, what actions are taken to evaluate the nature and extent of risks and either reduce or eliminate risks? Improvements might include the auditing process and activity, developing checklists of typical risks, developing effective criteria for evaluating risk, improving risk reporting or a risk management policy. There are plenty of general guidelines that are useful, but essential to success is tailoring risk management to your particular industry and organisation.

Activity 8.4

For many organisations collaboration might be informal and this might be appropriate. Where it is not appropriate is where the organisation's core competence or competitive advantage is dependent on the collaboration. The task is to identify the objectives of the collaboration, the desired outcomes and then establish measures to ensure those outcomes are realised. Building good relationships with those with whom the organisation collaborates is essential and communications in various forms is the best way of achieving this. Benefits will very much depend on your own particular situation but may include, for example, increased customer added value, improved core competence or innovation, and reduced risk and costs.

Activity 8.5

Evaluating your leadership style can be achieved in a number of ways and, as well as ideas discussed in these chapters, diagnostic techniques that can help include:

- Multifactor Emotional Intelligence Scale (Mayer, Caruso and Salovey, 1998)
- Emotional Competence Inventory (ECI) (Goleman, 1998) – a 360° instrument
- Myers-Briggs Type Indicator (MBTI) – personality questionnaire

There are many more and many can be accessed on the web.

Activity 8.6

In developing your PDP you might include improving conceptual skills, for example, and working on creatively interpreting the future and a vision for your organisation for that future. Your improvements could work on improving your ability to motivate your staff or even work with peers to improve overall motivation.

QUICK QUIZ ANSWERS

1   –   Leaders signal a new vision and are responsible for scoping ideas around that vision. They are also responsible for creating an environment for creativity and providing the necessary resources.

      –   Managers are responsible for managing the environment to nurture creativity.

      –   In the right environment employees are responsible for thinking up new ideas and contributing to the creative process.

2   –   Vertical thinking – typically analytical, considered, sequential, predictable

      –   Standard thinking repertoires – eg deficit (can't do mentality), rational (vertical thinking), sticky (aimless and meandering)

The Chartered Institute of Marketing

3   You may have come up with a long list but some examples include:

–   Political and legal – changes in policy and law

–   Financial – funding, cash flow, actions of shareholders

–   Environment – pollution, natural disasters

–   Operations – investment in technology, serious breakdowns

4   –   Wide impact and uncontrollable eg sudden decline of or crisis in an industry (your customers)

–   Wide impact and controllable eg product failure

–   Local impact and uncontrollable eg major flood

–   Local impact and controllable eg breakdown in machinery

5   –   Avoid risk by not undertaking or accepting the task or strategy

–   Reduce risk eg by taking precautions such as water sprinkler systems to reduce the risk of fire

–   Accept risk eg if the cost is not too high or the return is seen as worth the risk

–   Transfer risk eg if it can be covered by insurance or transferred to another

6   –   Risk reporting requires alerting appropriate target audiences and making them aware of the risks the organisation, department or people might be exposed to and the consequences of not managing these risks

–   Risk policy is the document that sets out responsibilities and accountability for risk

7   –   Diversification alliances eg with new entrants to market

–   Vertical collaborations eg with suppliers

–   Horizontal collaborations eg with competitors

–   Selective partnering eg with outlets or channels

–   Related diversification eg with other producers

–   Innovation collaborations eg with universities

8   Relationship marketing is a concept that encourages commitment to customers over the long-term. This is achieved through actively building long-term relationships with customers by delivering quality products/services and good customer service co-ordinated through strategic marketing planning. It requires understanding customers and their needs and designing business activities to meet these needs. There is an emphasis on continuous improvements to meet the continually changing and evolving needs of customers throughout the long-term relationship.

Relationship marketing extends to other stakeholders eg distribution channels, supplier and innovators. Managing these relationships effectively can be the difference between success and failure.

CHAPTER 9

Developing a marketing-oriented culture

Introduction

We live and work in cultures most of the time not thinking much about what the cultures are or their influences on us. Leaders do need to think about this perhaps more often as they can have the greatest influence on organisation culture and need to maintain a healthy culture.

The task of developing and maintaining a desirable culture in a long established and large organisation is always going to be more difficult than in a small organisation. In a small, young organisation the challenge will be establishing cultural norms, particularly if there are a number of founders with strong and different personalities.

This chapter explores some of the research and work on organisation cultures and then reviews what a marketing orientation looks like and how to establish one.

Topic list

Culture or climate	1
Organisational culture types	2
Functional orientations and cultural drivers	3
Creating a marketing-oriented culture	4
Shared values	5
Measuring marketing orientation	6

3.2.1	Critically evaluate the concept of a market-oriented culture and consider the implications for an organisation in achieving it, including: ■ Customer orientation ■ Cross and inter-functional orientation ■ Competitor orientation ■ Profit orientation
3.2.2	Assess the different characteristics of culture in a broad context and evaluate the need for change to achieve true market orientation, including: ■ Values, beliefs and assumptions ■ Symbols ■ Heroes ■ Rituals ■ Culture and strategic implications ■ Organisational climate
3.2.3	Explore ways in which the organisation can go about creating and shaping a market-oriented culture: ■ Working towards common goals ■ Collective identity ■ Embracing differences and diversity ■ Common goals ■ Fostering support ■ Focus on innovation ■ Focus on performance ■ Focus on learning and development
3.2.4	Critically evaluate the concept of shared values and show how they can be effectively communicated in a market-oriented organisation: ■ Organisational values, eg CSR, sustainability ■ Cultural values ■ Ethical values ■ Economic values
3.2.5	Determine measures for success in transforming an organisation's culture to one of true market orientation: ■ Externally focused organisation ■ Market orientation matrix (Heiens 2000) ■ Customer/Competitor focused – toward an integrated approach (Slater and Narver 1994) ■ Market orientation and business performance

1 Culture or climate

> ▶ **Key terms**
>
> **Culture:** is the underlying, internal values, beliefs and attitudes that shape behaviour and the structure of perceptions. Culture goes deep and is stable. It is often difficult to assess and change culture.
>
> **Climate:** is the atmosphere, recurring patterns of behaviour, interactions and feelings. It is fluid and often easier to assess and change.

Culture and climate are often used interchangeably but do have slightly different meanings.

1.1 Characteristics of culture

Culture is often described as 'how we do things around here' (Deal and Kennedy, 1982) and the description certainly reflects the outward manifestation of culture. Understanding culture is essential for leaders as they not only can have the greatest influence on culture, they can also be influenced by culture and not always positively. The destiny of the organisation is in the hands of leadership and one of the most enduring ways they can affect desirable behaviour and performance is through culture.

The make-up of organisation culture is:

(a)   **Artefacts and behaviours:** the most visible and superficial expressions of culture, for example organisation practices, structures, systems, rituals, routines, stories, myths, jokes, heroes, symbols and atmosphere. Organisation climate is one of these artefacts. Artefacts are easy to observe but difficult to decipher.

(b)   **Beliefs, values and attitudes:** go deeper and are part of the foundation organisational culture. Beliefs are what people think is true or not true, or what is important or not important. Values are what people hold to be right or wrong, good or bad, their ethical code of conduct for example integrity, transparency and fairness. It can be difficult to recognise the difference between beliefs and values because beliefs about how to do something are often driven by values. For example, if people believe the only way to conduct business is by being honest, open and accountable is this based on their values or beliefs? Attitudes make the link between beliefs and values with feelings.

(c)   **Underlying assumptions:** are at the deepest level and the most difficult to reach. Assumptions are mainly formed unconsciously by values over time as we interpret and make sense of our experiences and the world around us. This unconscious interpretation emerges as deeply embedded assumptions that guide perceptions, feelings and emotions that people share.

Figure 9.1   Organisation culture

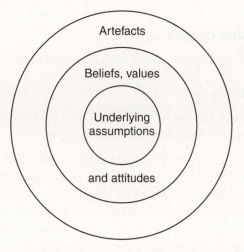

Schein (1985) suggests that when all these three levels are aligned a homogeneous culture exists and that organisations with a homogeneous culture are more likely to be successful than those that are culturally out of alignment.

There has been much research on organisations, particularly since the 1980s, and some useful and enduring typologies have emerged that help us describe and understand what sort of organisational culture exists and therefore what works for and against us in achieving organisation goals.

Previous units cover national culture and we should never underestimate the strong influence national culture has over organisation culture.

Fairchild (1970) links culture primarily to behaviour; behaviour that is collective to particular grouping or society. This is also supported by Wallendorf and Reilly: 'Culture is reflected in behaviour patterns which are expressions of collective values and beliefs'. (1983,p292). Behaviour is regarded as a central part of culture.

There are a number of views on culture; it is learned and something that is shared with other people. The impact of culture is far-reaching and it influences an individual's behaviour and one's expectations of others' behaviour. This behaviour is not just restricted to society but also within an organisation and the culture that is an inherent part of culture.

Three important aspects of culture come out of the varying definitions:

(1)   That culture is shared by the members of a given society and influences behaviour
(2)   That culture is, by its very nature, dynamic and transmissible
(3)   Visible manifestations

Culture influences behaviour and the way people work and make decisions as well as interact with one another.

> ▶ **Assessment tip**
>
> While planning your assignment it can be tempting to 'sort the problem' and forget to incorporate the learning and/or try and shoehorn a loosely related work project into a CIM assignment. The task must match the objectives of the CIM assignment and to incorporate learning use marketing management concepts applied to demonstrate understanding and skills.
>
> Answers need to clearly demonstrate how decisions are made, and the rationale, justification and evaluation that have been undertaken.

---

2 Organisational culture types

2.1 Typologies of culture

Four typologies of organisation culture were developed by Charles Handy (1978).

2.1.1 Power culture

Power culture or web has few rules and regulations but there are strong policy decrees. Behaviour exhibited in such a culture includes aggressive, flexible and responsive.

A power culture is typically only as strong as the central figure who exercises control through a small circle of executives who usually retain financial control. Politics are a feature of this culture and decisions are often based on political themes rather than for logical or operational reasons. Lack of formality means management development is difficult. Personal development is achieved through a system of apprenticeship to the central power and this special place is dependent on the quality of the relationship. People are promoted because of who they know/get on with not what they do/have achieved.

Figure 9.2   Power culture

Perceptions of infallibility can lead to risk-taking and competition between employees is encouraged. A lack of rules, quick responses and competitive behaviour lead to a higher chance of surviving a crisis.

Examples: Robert Maxwell kept tight control of all aspects of a large business; few executives had a complete picture of what was happening or a role in strategic decisions. Anita Roddick, founder of Body Shop, developed questionnaires for prospective franchisees to ensure like-minded people were appointed.

2.1.2 Person culture

Person culture is a cluster of individuals. The focus in this culture is on the individual and the organisation is not hierarchical; it only exists to support an individual or small number of individuals. There is little structure imposed in this culture or control exercised. People have usually come together to share administrative resources. Its lack of structure and formality is challenged as the business grows, and if it is to survive the culture it will eventually need to change to allow for growth.

Figure 9.3   Person culture

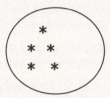

Examples: medical health centres (doctors, practices), architects, barristers, consultancy, training firms

2.1.3 Task culture

Task culture (often described as a **net**): a matrix structure exists to support focus on the job; the organisation is task-oriented. Power tends to be based on expert power. Teams form and re-form to complete specific projects and perform specific tasks. This ability to adapt and change makes the organisation very flexible and therefore suitable for rapidly changing market conditions. This culture tends to encourage innovation and creativity and people are judged by results. Respect for people is based on their knowledge and expertise rather than status and position. There is high job satisfaction with an emphasis on group work. There is often no single individual in authority and power often lies in areas where the 'net' is stronger and points cross.

Figure 9.4   Task (net) culture

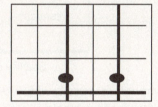

It is difficult to achieve economies of scale or day-to-day control because of the flexibility and changing internal conditions.

Examples: TV/film studios, research and development, advertising teams, management consultancies, airlines.

2.1.4 Role culture

Role culture is all about bureaucracy and being risk averse, and rewards people for standard performance, and not deviating from the norm. A role culture can succeed in stable environmental conditions and where economies of scale are more important than flexibility. Stability is rare, making flexibility essential, and economies of scale are easier to achieve with technological advances. The focus on maintaining conformity usually results in the organisation losing the purpose for which it was formed. Systems, procedures, policies, rules and regulations have evolved over time and dominate the activities of this type of organisation. Systems etc, help achieve highly valued predictability of performance. There is a logical, rational arrangement to everything. Tasks are more important than people, which can dehumanise. Personal development is formalised.

Figure 9.5   Role culture

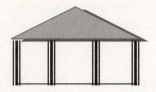

Examples: a role culture often exists in large organisations, particularly the Civil Service.

2.1.5 Cultures as competing values

Quinn *et al* (1983) described organisation cultures in terms of competing values that result in tensions and conflicts as follows:

- **The market:** a rational culture where the boss is in control. Leadership style is directive and focused on goals achieved through productivity and efficiency.

- **The adhocracy:** an ideological culture with charismatic leaders who are risk-takers. Leadership style encourages conformity to organisation values.

- **The clan:** a consensual culture where relationships are important. Leadership style is supportive and encourages participation of employees.

- **The hierarchy:** a hierarchical culture where leaders are risk-avoiders and control through formalised evaluation of performance. Leadership style is formal adherence to regulations and maintaining stability.

Figure 9.6   Competing values framework

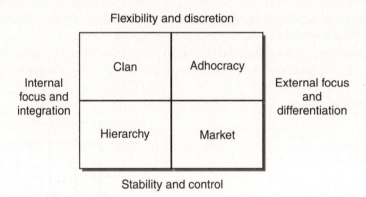

The competing values framework assesses to what extent the organisation focuses internally on, for example, people or operations or externally, for example on customers and competitors.

It also assesses who makes decisions. At the lower-end management make decisions and at the upper-end employees have the power to make decisions.

2.2 Culture as rites and rituals

Corporate cultures include rites and rituals.

Deal and Kennedy (1982) identified four types of culture based on two factors in the marketplace – the degree of risk associated with organisation activities and the speed at which organisations received feedback on success of decisions or strategies. They described their four cultures as:

(a)   **Tough guy, macho:** individualists who frequently take high risks, receive quick feedback. Examples cited include police, surgeons, construction, cosmetics, management consulting, entertainment industry.

The Chartered
Institute of Marketing

(b) **Work hard/play hard:** fun, action, employees take few risks, quick feedback. High level of relatively low risk activity. Highly dynamic, primary value centres on customers and their needs. Teams produce volume, culture encourages games, meetings, promotions, conventions to help maintain motivation. Volume can be at expense of quality. Examples include sales organisations eg estate agents, computer companies, mass consumer companies eg McDonald's, office equipment manufacturers, retail stores.

(c) **Bet your company:** large stake decisions, high risk but slow feedback. Focus on the future and importance of investing in it. Deliberateness is typified by the ritual of the business meeting. There is a hierarchical system of authority and decision making is top-down. High quality inventions, breakthroughs, slow and vulnerable to short-term fluctuations. Examples include oil companies, investment banks, architecture firms, military.

(d) **Process:** low risk, slow feedback, employees find it difficult to measure what they do and get very little feedback on effectiveness so focus on how they do things not what they do. Individual financial stakes low. Memos, reports disappear into void. Cover your back mentality. Bureaucracy results in attention to trivia, detail, formality and technical perfection. Examples include banks, insurance, financial services, Civil Service.

Figure 9.7   Organisation culture

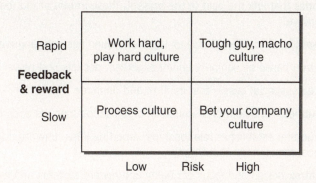

Deal and Kennedy (1982)

2.3 Cultural web

Johnson and Scholes (2002) developed a framework for how cultures are created. This culture web represents the 'taken-for-granted' assumptions or paradigm of an organisation and the physical manifestations of organisation culture.

Figure 9.8   Cultural web

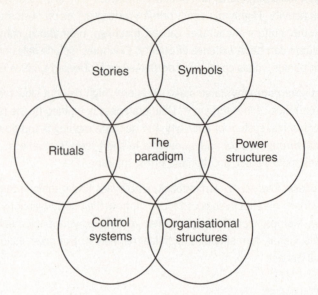

- **Stories** that link the past to the present, those immortalised, confer 'status' on individuals (positive or negative)

- **Symbols:** physical evidence eg logos and buildings and language and titles

- **Power:** based on seniority and/or expertise, pockets real power, most influence

- **Rituals:** special events that confirm and reinforce

- **Routines:** behaviour of members of organisation towards each other and external stakeholders

- **Structure:** establishes relationships, reporting lines, unwritten lines of power, types of structures in place, formal lines of authority

- **Control:** design and focus of quality and reward systems and measurement

- **The paradigm:** sum of the other elements of cultural web, the concept and principles of the culture

ACTIVITY 9.1

Critically evaluate the culture of your organisation. Can you identify aspects of cultures described and does one culture or do different cultures exist? What are the positive and negative aspects of your culture? How does this organisational culture impact the decisions made, as well as meeting the organisation's vision and mission?

3 Functional orientations and cultural drivers

The industry an organisation belongs to, the technology it uses, or products and services it produces influence the organisation's culture. Functional orientations are common. The following are some examples and while we are looking at extremes, which can be found in organisations, more typically an organisation will have one or more of these orientations that reflect this behaviour to some degree. The descriptions therefore provide some clues to what is influencing your organisation's behaviour.

These functional orientations are typically woven into the organisation cultures described above.

3.1 Product orientation

A technical (product/service expertise) oriented organisation believes its products or services speak for themselves and therefore there is no need to worry about focusing on customers: they will inevitably beat a path to your door. Initially, a gap in the market or a unique product sells itself in the early days so little or no effort is needed to market or sell the product providing you alert customers in some way. As markets become more competitive selling the product becomes more challenging. The response is to focus on the product and see how much better we can make it. More quality, more reliability etc are all possibilities regardless of what customers want. The core values of a technical orientation might include:

- Technical ability/expert
- Innovative, quality and precision
- Idiosyncratic, quirky and eccentric

They see the development of ideas as their purpose, not customers' needs, wants and preferences. The prevailing values and attitudes affect their approach to a number of key issues:

(a) **People** (management and staff): senior management will probably be technicians and there will be an emphasis on technical skills and expertise. Other skills, for example finance, HR or marketing, will be seen as either a necessary evil or unnecessary. They will find it difficult to trust those who do not understand technical expertise or engineering to run any aspect of the business.

(b) **Planning of activities:** allocation of resources will favour research and development and be internally focused on producing the product. Measurement focuses on product value and quality control checks. There will be an emphasis on efficiency and they will probably be good at sourcing quality materials. They can reassure themselves they are right because they have generated the ideas in the first place without help from customers or marketing.

(c) **Communications** will be 'features' led and one way; customers need to be informed on technical detail, imparting information rather than engaging customers or stakeholders through communication. There is no integrated marketing communications and the product is the brand.

(d) **Customer service:** technical back-up and service will be good and after-sales service seen as an essential element, not that their perfect product will need much attention; it is more about technical back-up and expertise.

Among the key challenges and concerns for marketing leadership when changing the culture from a technical to a marketing/customer orientation are:

- The reduced power in new product development: marketing co-ordinates using information from customers.

- Quality goals maintenance: quality will be from the customers' perspective not an internally driven decision.

- Investment in research and development will be competing with investment in marketing research and communications, not previously seen as important.

Reassurance and removing perceived threats, improving customer knowledge as the driver of the creation and production of products and services should be the focus of managing the champions of technical orientation.

3.2 Sales orientation

A sales orientation believes that markets are highly competitive and the only way to succeed is to persuade, subtly or forcefully, customers to buy products and services. Good sales people can sell anything so product quality is not necessarily a high priority. In some organisations acquiring new customers is given more prominence than retaining existing customers. The core values of a sales orientation include:

- Winning, competitive, successful
- Aggressive
- Loyal
- Determined and persistent

It is difficult to succeed in this environment without these values. The prevailing values and attitudes affect their approach to a number of key issues:

(a)   **People** (management and staff): senior management will probably be sales people who have worked their way up through the organisation. There will be an emphasis on 'charm' and personality and success comes from effective sales people.

(b)   **Planning of activities:** allocation of resources will favour anything that supports the sales effort. Planning and measurement will be focused on short-term targets and volumes. Personal promises to customers, lack of long-term integrated planning and sales power means production targets will be shifted according to each sales person's 'priority' and promise. Price is used as a tactical tool and has nothing to do with positioning.

(c)   **Communications:** there is no need for integrated marketing communications. Communications will be *ad hoc*, tactical and purely a support function for sales. There will be no plan or targeting as sales people are the main form of communications.

(d)   **Customer service** is about personal friendships and it can be very good at problem-solving and building relationships. Customer service will be sales activated and driven and therefore have a very personal interpretation. The result is *ad hoc* and tactical and the relationship is not built with the organisation.

Among the key challenges and concerns for marketing leadership when changing the culture from a sales to a marketing/customer orientation are:

- Reduced power in customer selection and targeting
- Reduced power in customer management and value creation
- Reduced power and influence in promotional activities

Customer management is shared and educating, and persuading sales of the value of marketing and how it helps sales and the role of sales in marketing should be the focus of managing the champions of sales orientation.

3.3 Financial orientation

A financial orientation has become common as financial people rose to the top of organisations, often as a necessity because of poor financial management. Once there, they do a good job of turning a financial crisis around. However, without either an innate understanding or experience of customers they continue to focus exclusively on the bottom line. The core values of a financial orientation might include:

- Certainty and prudence
- Meticulous and consistent
- Formulaic

The Chartered Institute of Marketing

The prevailing values and attitudes affect their approach to a number of key issues:

(a) **People** (management and staff): the CEO will probably be an accountant. They see people as an 'overhead cost' and there is an emphasis on supervision and control. They are held accountable for mistakes so have a fear of losing control.

(b) **Planning of activities:** planning activities are actually budgeting periods and cycles and internal short-term focus is on the 'bottom line'. Cost plus pricing will be amongst the methods used to set price. Cost control is where their power base lies, as is controlling budgets.

(c) **Communications:** will be one way and thought of as 'if we must haves' brochures etc. There will be little planning or targeting.

(d) **Customer service:** is seen as luxury and a cost. Negotiations, eg returns, can be seen as part of customer service. Some aspects of service are seen as unnecessary eg courtesy calls.

Among the key challenges and concerns for marketing leadership when changing the culture from a financial to a marketing/customer orientation are:

- Reduced power in control with the introduction of a more comprehensive approach, for example the balanced scorecard
- Long-term goals are not sacrificed for short-term gains
- Budget decisions reflect customer goals and objectives

Redefining and designing control and encouraging co-operation should be the focus of managing the champions of financial orientation.

3.4 Technological orientation

There is increasingly a **technology orientation** emerging (regardless of whether or not it is a technology organisation) where the solution to all problems is to buy more technology. It tends to be implemented without proper evaluation of the specification needed by all functions and the impact from a customer perspective, and the people who suffer most from this are customers. We have seen this most obviously in customer relationship management initiatives where technology is seen as the solution to getting closer to customers, but the database remains exactly that: a database that does not facilitate transferring data into knowledge.

An example of an organisation that has avoided this mistake is Tesco; they gather, analyse, interpret data and use the resulting knowledge to tailor marketing communication messages at targeted customers.

Some influences within these orientations are good and managers must protect anything that is a strength.

No organisation culture or orientation is exactly as described above and while we have explored the excesses of functional orientations it is not unusual to find some symptoms of a particular orientation. This can provide managers with valuable insights into the implications on management style in the organisation.

Organisations, even small ones, do not conveniently have just one culture or orientation. Often a number of cultures can co-exist and the larger the organisation the more likely it is that a number of cultures and orientations will exist.

When we understand our current culture and orientation we can assess the extent of change needed to achieve a marketing orientation. Marketing orientation is evolving and increasingly including a more societal orientation, a focus on corporate social responsibility.

▶ **Assessment tip**

Best practice/marketing concepts: you will always be expected to describe, explain and/or review marketing theory relevant to the subject and usually evaluate and compare your performance against best practice. Start the 'critical observation' habit of anything around you in the workplace that is relevant to the subject and your assignment. This critical observation can then be used to help you critically evaluate the organisation in a number of different aspects.

4 Creating a marketing-oriented culture

4.1 What is a marketing orientation?

▶ **Key term**

'**Market orientation** is a business philosophy which finally ensures superior value creation for the customer'.

(Narver and Slater, 1990)

'We can say that a firm is market orientated when a firm's culture is governed by values which systematically ensure superior value creation for customers. Practically, this mean gathering the information about customers and competitors and using this information for building superior value for the customers'.

(Narver and Slater, 1994)

Market orientation is the implementation of the marketing concept. It is important to note that being marketing orientated is more that just being customer-focused. It requires the organisation as a whole to fully support it in the long term and it could mean a change in the organisation's culture.

To ensure that an organisation can remain marketing orientated in the long term it needs to consider the ever-changing environment within which it operates. It needs to take account of the:

■ Business and social changes (globalisation, relaxation of governmental controls over businesses, global competition, consumer behaviour)

■ Customer related changes (increased consumer awareness, buying behaviour, information requirements)

■ Changes in manufacturing and marketing organisations (market research requirements, product development processes, advanced information technologies, levels of communication)

If we think about what marketing should be doing for the organisation and its customers it helps us focus on what a marketing-oriented culture should be. Marketing is broadly responsible for:

(a) **Intelligence and knowledge:** through marketing research and knowledge management marketing can ensure the organisation is aware of macro changes and their possible impact, current and future trends, patterns and possible scenarios, is knowledgeable about and understands customers, is alert to competitor behaviour and possible consequences, and is informed in its decision making and cognisant of the consequences of various decisions and actions.

(b) **Value creation:** from this knowledge marketing can guide the organisation in its strategy development and value creation, avoiding or reducing costly new product/service failures and increasing the potential success of new product/service launches. It can create points of differentiation that match organisation design and customer needs and influence changes in organisation design if needs are not met or are changing.

(c) **Communication:** through marketing communication, marketing can **strategically** create, build and maintain corporate reputation and the brand and support competitive positioning, **operationally** create, build and maintain product/service range brands and build relationships with key stakeholders, and **tactically** create and stimulate demand for products and services and build relationships with customers. Marketing can also reinforce external messages with internal communications that align and behaviour with desired corporate and brand values, inform people of external market expectations and their role in meeting those expectations.

A marketing orientation ensures management's key tasks are focused on the needs and wants of selected target markets which result in a profitable exchange. The core values of a marketing orientation might include:

■ Integrity, trust and respect
■ Creativity, originality

The Chartered Institute of Marketing

- Quality
- Service
- Learning

4.2 A marketing orientation matrix

Marketing orientation Heiens (2000) developed a market-orientation matrix to emphasise that firms can decide to focus primarily on **either competitors or consumers**. The proposed matrix includes four different approaches (degrees) to market orientation:

- Customer focused
- Marketing warriors
- Strategically integrated
- Strategically inept

Firms which put the customer first are considered 'customer focused'. Firms that focus on competitors in their market analysis are considered 'marketing warriors'. These 'warriors' identify the target rivals, identify their own strengths and weaknesses and finally decide how to compete in the market.

Heiens uses 'strategically integrated' as a term for those firms which focus upon the collection, dissemination, and use of both customer and competitor intelligence. Firms should probably seek to remain sufficiently flexible to be able to shift resources between a customer and a competitor emphasis as market conditions change in the short run.

'Strategically inept' is applied to firms which fail to orient their strategic decision making to their market environment.

4.3 People, integrity, trust and respect

The discussion on organisation culture covered many examples of the sort of values an organisation and its people might hold and how this affects the way people behave towards and treat each other. If a marketing orientation is going to be achieved a review of values is a good starting point. As discussed earlier, an organisation might make statements about its desired (or actual) values but if the behaviour that customers experience is poor and incompetent and does not match the stated values customers will not, and should not, believe in those stated values.

Customers expect, and are increasingly demanding, that organisations behave with integrity, ethically and at the very least treat them with respect. If we want customer loyalty we must gain their trust and respect and behave with integrity. These are inescapable facts if we genuinely want to be perceived favourably by customers, employees and other key stakeholders.

Marketing will be taken seriously by and represented at board level either by a CEO who understands and practises a marketing philosophy and/or by qualified marketing professionals. Senior management have a broad grasp of business.

People are valued and trusted by managers and this is reflected in internal policies and procedures, and management attitudes and behaviour to employees. It is recognised that people are key to success and a source of advantage.

The values of the organisation are reflected in how responsive the organisation is to the local community and the responsibility assumed for social and environmental concerns. Customers are the responsibility of everyone in the organisation. Each employee understands their role and contribution in delivering benefits to customers and knows who their customers are and what is important to them.

4.4 Marketing information

Knowledge is recognised as highly valuable and a source of advantage in a marketing-oriented organisation. There is a formalised marketing information system (MKIS) feeding into a management information system (MIS) and primary marketing research is regarded as an essential activity. Management decisions are based on the results of marketing research activities and reflect business strengths and competitive positioning. Managers know what is going on in the environment and know how they compare with competitors; they understand customer behaviour and the values customers attribute to the organisation's brand/s.

Technology does not dictate marketing intelligence or knowledge management processes or design; it is a tool. Leaders, managers and employees discuss, negotiate and agree what technology is required and how it is used and the focus is on converting gathered **data into useful intelligence**. Technology supports the use of knowledge in building relationships with customers and stakeholders.

4.5 Value creation, creativity and innovation

Creativity and innovation are encouraged and valued. The development of new products or services is undertaken with customer input either directly or through marketing intelligence. However, marketing also collaborates with others in the organisation to develop ideas.

Organisation culture can stifle or suppress creativity. We often hear of organisations that have a 'blame' culture and the very negative impact this has on creativity and taking initiative. A blame culture is typified by accusations, threats, criticism and destructive feedback. An approval culture encourages experimentation and is forgiving of mistakes. It is typified by consent, praise and constructive feedback.

Leaders and managers in a marketing orientation create a climate for creativity through freedom, time, space and a willingness to allow people to explore, challenge the status quo, think differently and be different. However, this creative climate is not designed to encourage creativity for its own sake; it has purpose and usually the objective of a clear commercial outcome.

The difference between creativity and innovation is understood and for innovation there is a process for evaluating and testing ideas for their commercial viability. The way this works is for different people with different characteristics and skills to form teams for different parts of the creativity and innovation process.

Quality and customer service are seen as integral to product/service development, not an after thought or add on. The clear objective is to create and maintain competitive advantage in order to acquire and retain customers through enhanced value. This value is represented in relevant and meaningful quality, customer service and brand values which customers can relate to.

THE REAL WORLD

Nestlé

Nestlé is one of the world's biggest food and beverage companies. One of its guiding principles is that it wants to be known as a 'Respected, Trustworthy, Food, Nutrition, Health and Wellness Company'; its actions are then guided by the latter principles.

Nestlé found that customers showed a genuine and growing interest in information about its brands. This information is linked to knowing more about what they eat and drink; customers are almost expecting this as an inherent part of the product. Nestlé has used market research to promote healthy living. A fundamental part of this is the development of 'guideline daily amounts' (GDAs). These were developed by the Institute of Grocery Distribution (IGD); however, Nestlé was actively involved in this development. This information on the packaging has meant that consumers make more informed decisions and it facilitates their understanding on food consumption. So what are the implications of this labelling? It has helped Nestlé with its approach to corporate responsibility. This is a fundamental part of its 'Creating shared value'. This looks at meeting different stakeholders' needs and making the organisation marketing orientated, from sourcing products and manufacturing to the distribution of goods to the middleman and the end consumer.

The Chartered Institute of Marketing

This concept of 'Creating shared value' extends to internal and external stakeholders; it focuses on empowering its customers as well as influencing its employees internally. The key principles of Nestlé are clearly communicated to its employees so they too can make choices that fit in with the overall ethos of the organisation. This 'Creating shared value' concept provides a clear framework within which Nestlé operates, sending out clear messages to all its stakeholders, both internally and externally. The concept is organisation wide, rather than just being one part of the organisation or function led; these principles guide Nestlé and its decision making and so results in creating shared value amongst all it interacts with.

4.6 Strategies and planning

Senior management focus on the future and long-term direction of the organisation. In a marketing orientation, strategies are developed around customers and reflect the reality of the marketplace. Marketing plays an influential role in determining what product/service market opportunities the organisation might pursue. Financial resource allocation for marketing is determined by the objectives to be achieved not spare cash left over.

Planning is ongoing, methodical but flexible and realistic and the long-term goals are not sacrificed for short-term gain. Planning and control are recognised as the most efficient and effective way to use limited resources and to organise activities.

A feature of marketing planning is the **co-ordination and integration** of organisation activities to deliver value to customers and stakeholders. Co-ordination ensures consistency of delivery and takes advantage of maximising value added opportunities. Planning is designed around customer needs so segmentation, positioning and targeting are important. The marketing mix is integrated, co-ordinated and designed to meet needs.

Departments understand each other's problems and needs and work in partnership to solve these and accomplish overall departmental and corporate objectives. Suppliers, distribution channels and other stakeholders are included in the planning process and their activities assimilated into the organisation's plans.

Changing the measures is an important step in supporting a change to a marketing orientation. Measuring marketing orientation will be discussed in more detail later. The most important point to make is that employees have customer satisfaction performance targets and leaders and managers are also accountable to customers and key stakeholders and for more than just financial goals.

4.7 Learning

Learning from experiences is important and informs future decisions and actions. Informal and formal learning are encouraged. Training and development of employees are recognised as key to business success and marketing and customer service training are not confined to marketing personnel. Appraisals form part of continual improvement and development and motivation of employees are seen as a significant management task. Training and development are also seen as the most effective way of ensuring employees are prepared and able to accept and implement change in response to market conditions.

Not learning the lessons and repeating the same old mistakes

A review by CIPD (April 2009) reveals that leaders' responses to the recession have fallen back on old internally focused methods of reacting to a crisis and in doing so are putting the long-term future of the organisation at risk. Leaders admit regretting the cost-cutting measures taken during the last recession but are reacting the same way this time. This will lead, as last time, to skills shortages, low employee morale and customer dissatisfaction and attrition.

Executives were asked which cost-cutting measures worked during the last recession and admitted that cutting back on training, incentives and marketing events had hampered employee commitment and seen their markets shrinking and not necessarily because of the recession.

Employers who hired high performing employees from competitors had the most positive impact on employee engagement and organisation performance during the last recession, but this is one of the least popular actions.

4.8 Communications

Communications both internally and externally with employees, customers and all stakeholders incorporate values and positioning and reflect the needs of different target groups. Two-way communications are important and there are mechanisms for listening as well as talking.

Marketing communications make promises and a marketing orientation ensures the promises are kept. Integration marketing communications influence all forms of communications with internal and external markets to keep those promises and the brand and position are built based on genuine values and behaviour.

ACTIVITY 9.2

Critically evaluate the extent of marketing orientation in your organisation. What values exist and to what extent are these shared effectively? Recommend a new or revised strategy that focuses on making the organisation more marketing orientated.

5 Shared values

As we have said values are central to any organisation and having the right values that everyone shares can be the difference between success and failure. How to encourage everyone to share values is not particularly easy.

Values, rather than beliefs and underlying assumptions, are what tend to be discussed most in organisations today and it has become increasingly popular to make declarations about what corporate values the organisation holds.

5.1 Corporate values and brand values

Stated values will always be positive but often some are aspirations rather than actual values that exist in the organisation. It is an interesting exercise to take the stated corporate values of an organisation you know and see if the experiences you have of that organisation match the stated corporate values. What are often not acknowledged or dealt with are the negative values that inevitably exist in many organisations. It is not enough to make a statement on corporate values. Positive stated values that exist must be protected and reinforced and those that are aspirations must be explained, interpreted and encouraged through various examples, behaviours and programmes.

The Chartered
Institute of Marketing

Internal marketing communication is a key means of encouraging leaders, managers and employees to share and live the values.

First, we must decide what the right values are. Visit a dozen websites where corporate values are recorded and you will find familiar words and phrases being repeated, for example:

- Innovation
- Integrity
- Responsibility

Organisations do not have a monopoly on these values but the winners will be the organisations that can encourage employees to share the values and exhibit the desired behaviours consistently. Phrases such as 'living the values' and 'internalising values' are common but achieving them is not. However, it can be done.

Recruiting like-minded people might be a good start and certainly has some merit. However, there are advantages and disadvantages. Amongst the **advantages** is the obvious one of people already sharing common values and, quite likely, similar beliefs and underlying assumptions. This makes the job of achieving a homogeneous culture much easier; in fact it should just evolve providing the organisation environment, policies and infrastructure support these values. However, all sorts of factors can infect culture, particularly outside forces that might threaten the organisation, so some proactive strategy to maintain the culture is still required.

Among the disadvantages is that everyone being of similar mind can lead to a narrow perspective, and possibly a lack of creativity and innovation, such as an unwillingness to challenge when it is important to do so or to deliberately take an opposing view to stimulate a discussion or debate issues.

5.2 Encouraging people to share values

A better starting point than stating values is to first establish what the real values are. This is an activity that organisations are increasingly engaging in. This requires surveying internal employees, customers and other key stakeholders. All have different interactions with the organisation so will have valuable different perspectives. From this the organisation can establish commonalities, differences, positive and negative values. Leaders may have clear ideas on what values they want the organisation to have but it is more productive to consult with employees and others to find out what they want. Apart from getting a better perspective on what is possible, it starts the process of engaging employees in particular in the task of getting them to share values. From this exercise it is then possible to announce the stated values, being honest about what currently exists that is positive and to be protected, what is negative and needs attention and what is new to be adopted.

5.3 Making the link between corporate values, brand values and the customer

Marketers in particular have a responsibility for ensuring that there is a link between the customer, the value proposition, the brand values and organisation values.

Figure 9.9   Relationship between customer, brand values and organisation cultural values

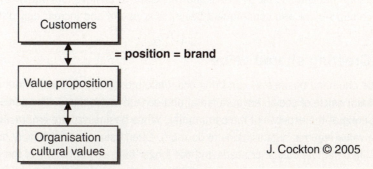

Employees understanding what corporate values mean in their job does not automatically follow statements. Marketing managers are responsible for interpreting and translating corporate values into brand values and brand values into job activities, what it means and what is acceptable and unacceptable behaviour. Managers need to describe and illustrate what values mean for employees to be able to understand and act on delivering them.

Making the connection between brand values and what employees do is essential in matching customer experiences with expectations. For employees and customers, brands need to be:

- Relevant
- Believable
- Unambiguous

Relevant to customers are meeting needs and wants, solving their problems and providing solutions. Relevant to employees is how the brand value is interpreted in their work and execution of tasks. It is also how they are treated and managed by the organisation. If one of our brand values is that we are 'responsible' then employees will be able to take responsibility and expect to be accountable. Examples of what this means will be demonstrated by leaders and managers being held accountable for actions and outcomes. If a value states we are 'reliable' then employees will always deliver on promises. Examples of what this means will be found in leaders and managers keeping promises.

Some employees will get this quicker than others and will be leading examples of the brand values. Marketing managers should identify and 'recruit' these people to help reinforce and embed desirable behaviour and practice.

If we want employees to live the brand we must engage them and we cannot do that if they do not understand or believe in the values. Managers:

- Explain the **meaning of the brand:** values, reflection, imagery
- Make an **emotional connection:** commitment
- Engender an **enthusiasm to deliver:** creativity, service, problem-solving
- Ensure people are **competent to deliver:** training and development

Ideally, leaders are examples of what the values mean who people can emulate. However, if stated corporate brand values are in stark contrast to what is experienced daily by employees, the values will quickly lose meaning and conviction and employees will lose interest.

If leaders are not actively committed and never get beyond lip service marketers can attempt to influence a change. They can draw attention to examples of excellent leadership on corporate and brand values and how this has led to strong reputations and customer loyalty. They can also point out the consequences of failing to commit to corporate and brand values.

Subtlety and patience will be important, and timing and opportunity part of a deliberate campaign to change hearts and minds. Marketers can also be examples of good leadership in creating, building and maintaining values and behaviour that support brand values. As others see repeated and consistent behaviour and leadership that is reflective of values and this leads to positive real outcomes that match stated values, the gap between lip service and commitment becomes apparent and increasingly difficult to ignore.

5.4 Creating shared value

On the one hand businesses can bring economic prosperity; however, more recently they have been regarded as the major cause of social, environmental and economic problems. The perception is that businesses are prospering at the expense of the community. While businesses are embracing corporate responsibility, creating share value requires organisations to do more. Often value creation is very narrow, looking at profit rather than focusing on actual customer needs and the longer-term sustainability of the organisation. There is a divide between the organisation and society and the creation of shared value should aim to bridge this divide. Shared value requires leaders and managers of the organisation to have a greater appreciation of wider societal needs,

greater collaboration with the third sector along with policy influencers. In essence the focus needs to go beyond just meeting internal targets, or reaching certain profit levels. It is this outlook that will then encourage greater innovation, social improvement and inevitably economic success, where businesses are working with their wider society as well as their principal stakeholders.

(a) The need for companies to engage in morally appropriate behaviour, and be socially responsible is an ongoing concern, a concern that is getting more and more exposure

(b) CSR and ethical behaviour is not only important but also expected by the public and stakeholders

---

THE REAL WORLD

The Metropolitan Police in the UK have taken their fair share of criticism including having a poor track record on diversity, being a 'closed shop' to many ethic minority staff and having a lack of people focus. There were plenty of 'stated values' but no real work was done to engage with employees and embed the values. Leadership decided it was time to tackle the problem head on.

After a period of staff consultation and evaluation they developed a set of values, put them on the internet and asked staff for opinions again; this time the feedback was anonymous. From this they established four final values underpinned by 46 supporting behaviours.

The values were:

- Pride in delivering quality policing
- Build trust by listening and responding
- Respect and support each other and work as a team
- Learn from experience and find ways to be even better

Defining behaviours that support these values goes beyond making statements and lays the foundation of how work is done and how people behave towards each other. Examples of what this means start with leadership behaviour, run through management of people and are now part of learning that takes place at the training academy in Hendon. For the first time, civilian staff, representing some 20,000 of the workforce, are being trained alongside police officers.

Rather than adopting positive discrimination programmes the values and behaviours reflect the diversity of the organisation and the communities it serves, leading to a 'positive action programme'.

The goal is to stimulate leadership at every level and in particular for leadership to be more representative of the community it serves. They are trying to develop a leadership style that is more situational.

---

6 Measuring marketing orientation

> **Key term**
>
> The **balanced scorecard** takes a broader and more comprehensive approach to measurement and informing strategic development and embraces strategic as well as tactical performance.

Having established what we need to do to achieve a marketing orientation we now need to put in place measures that will maintain a marketing orientation. If the right measures are not in place our desired orientation will not be sustainable.

6.1 Changing the measures

Too often we measure the wrong things; for example leadership is often only measured on the value of its share price which has more to do with the vagaries of the stock market than what the organisation is doing or how efficiently and effectively. Worse, leaders have little if any control over the stock market but they do have control over the organisation.

Measures need to be comprehensive and include qualitative as well as quantitative measures.

When embarking on a strategy to change to a marketing orientation there are three aspects to this to consider:

(a) Evaluating to see to what extent the organisation has a marketing orientation or not
(b) Measuring to see if the organisation has achieved a marketing orientation following change
(c) Changing the measures to maintain a marketing orientation

The first stage will be part of an organisation audit that might have been triggered by the usual planning process or might have been driven by a goal for marketing orientation.

Measuring to see if a marketing orientation has been achieved following change will be covered in the next chapter.

The third will be undertaken at regular intervals as an organisation widens activity to ensure the orientation is maintained. This is supported by the marketing metrics that become common practice.

6.2 Balanced scorecard and adaptation

One approach to changing measures to maintain a marketing orientation might be to adopt the **balance scorecard** which overcame the problems of traditional measures that tended to focus on finances and volumes and draw on historical data to enable measurement to take place.

The balanced scorecard goes beyond purely financial measures and attempts to evaluate, anticipate and inform the measurement process on current and future drivers of performance.

Figure 9.10   Balanced scorecard (1)

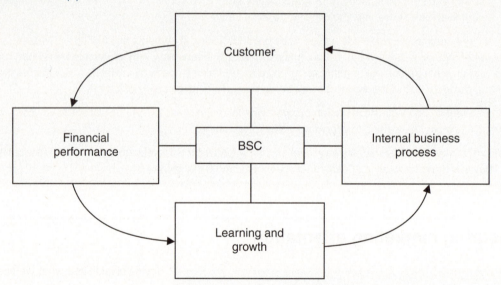

- **Customer:** measure customer/segment performance, satisfaction, loyalty, value/profitability, retention, referrals, complaints, repeat purchases, acquisition, market share (and measures of value proposition – customer needs, wants, preferences).

- **Financial performance:** the well-known measures including profitability, ROCE etc.

- **Internal business process:** systems and processes in which the organisation must excel, operations and value chain. Management of people in delivering value. Innovation across operations.

- **Learning and growth:** infrastructure needed to build long-term growth, people, systems and procedures. People and their role in innovation/idea generation and NPD success, transference into success, re-skilling, new technology. Employee satisfaction, retention, training, skills.

The balanced scorecard is intended to link measurement to strategic direction and is a fundamental part of the strategy planning process.

The Chartered
Institute of Marketing

Figure 9.11   Balanced scorecard (2)

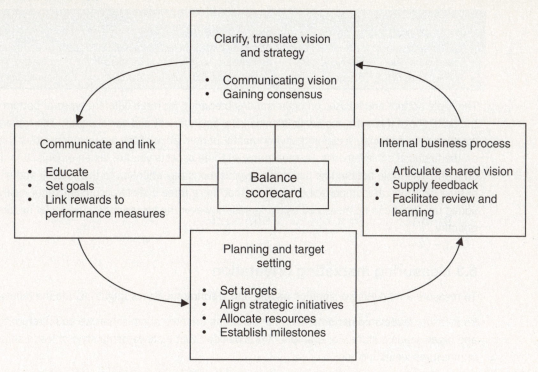

This approach requires effective information systems, which are essential to measurement. People throughout the organisation need to understand the full consequences of their decisions and actions on the organisation, its performance and its markets, and information flow and its access is essential.

The balance scorecard objectives are derived from a top-down process driven by the mission, vision, corporate objectives and strategies, which are translated into tangible objectives and measures. The measures represent a balance between external measures for shareholders and customers, and internal measures of critical business processes, innovation, learning and growth. The measures are balanced between the outcome measures (past performance) and measures that drive future performance. The scorecard is balanced between objectives, easily quantified outcome measures and subjective, somewhat judgemental performance drivers of the outcome measures.

It could be argued that a truly balanced approach requires bottom-up as well as top-down drivers, information direct from front-line staff, effective communication systems and effective knowledge management.

Some organisations have implemented the balanced scorecard very successfully and can provide evidence of the positive difference it has made. Others have been disappointed and described it as a box ticking exercise that has made no difference at all. Success is dependent on how the technique is implemented. A box ticking approach is doomed to fail but if the organisation first establishes what the objective is for implementing the scorecard, particularly if marketing orientation is the goal and then is prepared to adapt, modify and tailor the scorecard to meet the specific requirements of the organisation, it is more likely to succeed. Again consultation with employees is essential if we want them to adopt new measurement practices.

The balanced scorecard, as with any model or technique evolves and adapts to suit your needs. It can incorporate new thinking; for example many organisations now have corporate responsibility as a goal and this requires a **triple bottom line** approach to measuring performance, the simultaneous pursuit of economic/financial prosperity, environmental and social equity, not just a single financial bottom line. The balanced scorecard will therefore incorporate any measures not already included.

Table 9.1   Triple Bottom Line

Triple bottom line		
Economic/financial	Environmental	Social equity
Shareholder value, profitability, cash flow, ROCE, ROI etc	Renewable, sustainable materials and resources balanced against cost	Health, safety, well being, sustainability balanced against cost

The triple bottom line focuses on organisations preparing for three different types of bottom line. As stated in the table above these are economic/financial, the environment and social equity. The triple bottom line measures the financial, social and environmental performance of the organisation rather than purely focusing on the financial achievements. By measuring all three aspects you are, as an organisation, more likely to focus on them. The triple bottom line has made organisations pay attention to the societal and environmental impact of their decisions. It is important to consider that these three distinct accounts cannot easily be compared or added up. Profit can be measured using figures, however the environment and social factors are not so easy to quantify.

6.3 Measuring marketing orientation

To measure a marketing orientation **people and learning** measures might include the following.

To measure **leadership performance** in a marketing-oriented organisation we could return to leadership styles and organisation culture. For example, if it is decided that a stewardship style of leadership is required the sort of measures would include:

- Evidence of learning, development and growth of employees (eg adoption of new skills, changes in behaviour)

- Harmony of relationships and cohesiveness (eg networking and cross-function support, morale)

- Interpersonal skills (eg improvements in listening, verbal communications, briefings)

- Evidence of shared values (eg consistency in behaviour, approaches to work, customers' view of the brand)

Measuring **management performance** in a marketing-oriented organisation might include:

- Employee morale (eg willingness/enthusiasm to/for work, absenteeism)
- Employee productivity (eg quantity of work, quality of work, speed, accuracy)
- Operations (eg efficient use of resources, effectiveness of planning)
- Value of customer relationships (long-term profitability, referrals)

Measuring **employee performance** in a marketing-oriented organisation might include:

- Customer satisfaction (customer perceptions of helpfulness, competence, reliability)

- Contribution to innovation (number of new ideas, regularity, commercialisation)

- Personal learning and development (personal initiatives to learn, improvements in specific tasks)

- Team working (eg supportiveness to each other, collaboration, learning from each other, effectiveness of team task outcomes)

Creativity, innovation and value creation might include:

- **Sources of innovation: who** (individuals), **where** (departments/sections), **what** (technology, processes, people etc), what promotes innovation? What acts as a barrier?

- **Innovation frequency:** a one-off wonder or a regular occurrence. Has there been a period that was particularly innovative – when and why?

- **Innovation success rate:** how many ideas became commercially viable?

- **Innovation payback:** costs, sales volumes, profits, customer satisfaction

The Chartered Institute of Marketing

- **Innovation spin offs:** other ideas generated as a result, new/improved customer/supplier/distributor relationships

- **Innovation distribution:** narrow focus on product or process or broader with a number of areas across the business benefiting

- **Innovation as a source of competitive advantage:** uniqueness, meeting real need, ability to copy, time benefits, contribution to building power of brand/position

Examples of **marketing measures** would include:

Marketing metrics – micro (marketing activities performance):

- Competitors: who, what products, size, markets, strategy, advantage, performance

- Suppliers: who, what products/service/added value, size, markets, strategy and performance

- Distributors: who, what products/service/added value, size, markets, strategy and performance

- **Return on relationships (ROR):** 'Long-term net financial outcome resulting from establishment, maintenance of firm's network of relationships'

Customer measures (put in the context of **market share**):

- **Customer acquisition:** how many new customers attracted, their value and the cost of attracting these customers (eg promotional campaigns, referrals, word of mouth etc)

- **Customer repeat purchase:** repeat purchase behaviour, frequency and value

- **Customer profitability:** net profit of a customer

- **Customer experience satisfaction:** perceptions, service, compare with other organisations

- **Customer retention:** longevity, lifetime value, costs

- **Customer loyalty status:** passive or active, good referral, value of loyalty and referral markets

Measuring effectiveness of marketing strategy:

- **Segmentation** (value/growth of segments)

- **Positioning** (clear, differentiated)

- **Targeting** (effectiveness and return on marketing investment)

- **Planning and control process** (efficient use of resources and effectiveness in delivering marketing activities)

Integrated marketing communications

- **Brand:** perceptions, positive values/associations, awareness. Also brand valuation techniques such as Interbrand seven component criteria, Young & Rubicam Brand asset valuator (BAV)

- **Competitive position:** comparisons between competitors and organisation value

- **Internal marketing:** eg shared values, understanding of corporate goals and strategy

- **Promotions:** eg advertising (queries generated and conversion rates, attitude change – pre-, during and post-testing), PR (column inches), sales promotion (sales volume and sustainability)

Marketing information and research measures might include:

- Methods used
- Accuracy of information
- Utilisation of information
- Accuracy in determining future information needs
- Analysis of usefulness in decision making

When in 2007 the merger of Canada's Thomson Corporate, one of the largest international information companies, and Reuters, the leading news and market data provider, took place the leadership of the newly formed Thomson Reuters saw this as an opportunity to transform the marketing organisation rather than integrate two legacy marketing departments.

The leaders started by defining and clarifying the goal for its new marketing organisation – to provide strategic vision and leadership for the Thomson Reuters business. This signals a very clear message to everyone in the organisation of the role of marketing.

The leadership was not leaving anything to chance. A thorough research project internally and externally preceded decisions on detail and revealed the challenges of achieving its goal.

Among the challenges were the need to align resources with business priorities, build a common view of marketing's role, raise the profile and visibility of marketing, adopt common planning practices, clarify required competence and create progression plans for marketing staff.

The re-orientation was seen as significant and while it was only given eight months it was a full-time project for a small leadership team. To secure marketing's strategic role a newly established Chief Marketing Officer was appointed with a 'seat at the top table'. Among the changes were changes to measures of performance reflecting both customer and strategic marketing performance.

ACTIVITY 9.3

Develop a marketing orientation measurement tool. Compare and contrast it to the current tools for measuring marketing orientation. What are the gaps in the current tools?

Once a measure framework is established it must continually evolve to keep up with the changing organisation and environment. The results of the right measures provide management with information to incorporate back into the planning process with the intention of improving planning next time around.

▶ **Assessment tip**

It is a good idea to start drafting your report sooner rather than later. Gather together information and evidence and organise it into logical groups. From these draft findings, identify presentation formats, eg graphs, charts, tables (sometimes useful when presenting advantages and disadvantages or issues and implications) and so on.

The Chartered Institute of Marketing

> **Assessment tip**

Marketing orientation is a key part of the marketing leadership and planning syllabus. It is important that when discussing marketing orientation there is more than just a description of it, but rather a critical analysis of it. What are the key features of marketing orientation? How can it help the organisation? Marketing orientation must also be a central feature of an organisation rather than just something that can be considered in the short term. The June/September 2010 assessment focused on developing marketing orientated strategies, as follows:

'You have been given strategic responsibility to review the marketing strategy for your organisation and recommend the changes required to ensure its increased competitiveness and long term sustainability. In particular, you will need to focus on developing a market-oriented culture. For an organisation that is already market-oriented, the focus should be on looking at how more market-oriented the organisation can become.'

Candidates need to focus on how the organisation, rather than the marketing department, can become more marketing-orientated and in particular how this will impact the organisation as a whole, with regards to the strategic development, the resource implications and the organisation's long-term sustainability. Candidates need to think about the implications of developing a more marketing orientated strategy, rather than making recommendations without the appropriate evaluation and justifications. The role of leadership in creating a more marketing oriented culture needs to be understood and recommendations need to implemented; this cannot always happen if there is a gap in the leadership skills required to create a marketing oriented strategy.

- There are different organisational culture types: power culture, person culture, task culture, role culture.

- The cultural web is a framework for how cultures are created.

- Functional orientations are woven into the organisation culture, including product orientation, sales orientation, financial orientation and technological orientation.

- Market-orientation is a business philosophy which helps to create superior value creation for the customer; it is not functional but needs to be understood at an organisational level.

- Shared values in an organisation can include corporate and brand values and then need to be linked to the customer.

- Measuring marketing-orientation is as important as developing marketing orientation. Measurement can focus on leadership performance, management performance and employee performance.

FURTHER READING

Anon (2008) Market orientation. *Brazil business forecast report, 4th quarter*. Vol43, p40.

Austin, J. and Currie, B. (2003) Changing organisations for a knowledge economy: the theory and practice of change management. *Journal of Facilities Management*, Vol2(3) pp229-43.

Barksdale, H.R. and Darden, B. (1971) Marketer's attitudes toward the marketing concept. *Journal of Marketing,* Vol35(4), p29.

Bartunek, J.M. (1984) Changing interpretive schemes and organizational restructuring: the example of a religious order. *Administrative Science Quarterly*, Vol29(3), pp355-72.

Beer, M. (1990) Why change programs don't produce change. *Harvard Business Review*, Vol68(6), pp158-66.

Bruch, H. (2005) Strategic change decisions: doing the right change right. *Journal of Change Management,* Vol5(1), pp97-106.

Dunn, M.G. Norburn, D. and Birley, S. (1994) The impact of organizational values, goals and climate on marketing effectiveness. *Journal of Business Research*, Vol30(2), p131.

Elkington J. (1997) Cannibals with Forks: the triple bottom line of 21st century business. Oxford, Capstone Publishing Limited.

Kasper, H. (2002) Culture and leadership in market-oriented service organisations. *European Journal of Marketing,* Vol36(9/10), p104.

Narver J.C. & Slater S.F. (1990) The effect of a market orientation on business profitability. *Journal of Marketing*, October 54(4) pp20-34.

Osarenkhoe, A. (2008) What characterises the culture of a market-oriented organisation applying a customer-intimacy philosophy? *Journal of Database Marketing & Customer Strategy Management*, Jun, Vol15(3), pp169-190.

Sarros, J.C., Cooper, B.K. and Santora, J.C. (2008) Building a climate for innovation through transformational leadership and organizational culture. *Journal of Leadership & Organizational Studies*, Vol15(2), pp145-158.

Saritz, A. W. & Weberk (2006) *The triple bottom line: How today's best-run companies are achieving economic social and environmental success-and how you can too.* San Francisco, Jossey-Bass

The Chartered Institute of Marketing

Slater S.F. and Narver J.C. (1994) "Does competitive environment moderate the market orientation-performance relationship?" *Journal of Marketing*, January pp46-55.

Tien-Shang Lee, L. (2008) The influences of leadership style and market orientation on export performance: an empirical study of small and medium enterprises in Taiwan. *International Journal of Technology Management*, Vol43(4), pp404-424.

REFERENCES

Deal, T.E. and Kennedy, A.A. (1982) *Corporate cultures: the rites and rituals of corporate life*. London, Penguin.

Fairchild, H.P. (1970) *Dictionary of sociology*. Totowa, N.J., Littlefield, Adams and Co.

Handy, C. (2000) *Gods of management: the changing work of organization*. Oxford, Oxford University Press.

Heiens, R.A. Market orientation: toward an integrated framework. *Academy of Marketing Science Review*, www.amsreview.org/articles/heiens 01-2000.pdf.

Johnson, G. and Scholes, K. (2002) *Exploring corporate strategy*. Oxford, Prentice Hall.

Kaplan, R. and Norton D. (1996) The balanced scorecard. Harvard, *Harvard Business School Press*.

Quinn, R.E. and Rohrbaugh, J. (1983) A spatial model of effectiveness criteria: towards a competing values approach to organizational analysis. *Management Science*, 29, pp363-377.

Schein, E. (1985) *Organisational culture and leadership*. San Francisco, Jossey Bass.

Wallendorf, M. and Reilly, M. (1983) Ethnic migration, assimilation and consumption. *Journal of Consumer Research*, 10(3), pp292-302.

QUICK QUIZ

1   Give three examples of organisational cultures and explain briefly how these cultures would impact on customer service.

2   What knowledge management problems might be encountered in a power culture?

3   What knowledge management problems might be encountered in a role culture?

4   How might organisation culture affect teams and team building?

5   What two key factors affect an organisation's ability to develop good standards of customer service?

6   What is the relationship between the customer and corporate values?

7   How would you encourage employees to share values?

8   What measures would you recommend to sustain a marketing orientation?

Activity 9.1

A useful starting point is to check what stated corporate values exist and then use this to test whether or not people's attitudes and behaviours reflect the stated values. Are there differences, are there negative values? It is not untypical for organisations to reflect the sort of cultures described in this chapter and the larger the organisation the more likely they are to be exhibiting a range of cultures. Sometimes this can work well, for example parts of the organisation where precision, method and order are important and other parts of the organisation where creativity is important. However, sometimes it is the result of different and strong leadership styles and it may have an overall negative impact.

Activity 9.2

You can use both the principles of marketing orientation described and the measures to test to what extent you have a marketing orientation. There are diagnostic tests online that you may get access to. Sometimes they are free and sometimes a fee is involved. In particular are values shared? What is actively done by the organisation's leadership and management to communicate the desired values and to explain what it means in terms of jobs and activities? Are measures in place to reinforce a marketing orientation?

Activity 9.3

As marketers a very useful starting point can be to review measures. It is often the best clue to whether or not there is a marketing orientation. It is usually obvious for customer-facing staff to make the connection between what they do and customer value. Important for marketers is making the connection for everyone else in the organisation between what they do and what the customer gets. Too often other functions and even people in marketing not customer-facing do not realise the impact they have on customer value. Their contribution may be indirect but it none the less has value. It's hard fact – if everyone in the organisation is not either directly or indirectly contributing to customer value they should not be there.

QUICK QUIZ ANSWERS

1   You might have selected from a number of typologies including:

- **Power culture** – the entrepreneurial spirit and focus on the market would probably be an advantage and result in good customer service. However, there is unlikely to be a customer service policy or formalised customer service standards of performance, which might result in patchy performance.

- **Role culture** – there may be a problem in acknowledging customers need service in this culture. It is not a concept that would come easily to them. If they did attempt to address customer service it would probably suffer from overemphasis on formal processes and procedures for everything, resulting in no-one taking responsibility (or action when things go wrong) for service. It would be high on procedural quality and low on personal quality.

- **Task culture** – people in this organisation are focused on the task and where the technical aspects of task meet with customer service needs the quality of service would be good.

The Chartered
Institute of Marketing

However, anything outside technical needs is unlikely to be seen as important and there would be no understanding or effort put into meeting other service needs such as courtesy, helpfulness, convenience and so on.

–   Person culture – customer service in this culture would be down to each individual and so service quality would be patchy and vary from person to person. The service is likely to be high on technical needs but personal service would depend on the individuals involved.

Competing values framework (Quinn *et al, 1983*):

–   **The market** – a rational culture where the boss is in control. Leadership style is directive and focused on goals achieved through productivity and efficiency.

–   **The adhocracy** – an ideological culture with charismatic leaders who are risk-takers. Leadership style encourages conformity to organisation values.

–   **The clan** – a consensual culture where relationships are important. Leadership style is supportive and encourages participation of employees.

–   **The hierarchy** – a hierarchical culture where leaders control through formalised evaluation of performance. Leadership style is formal adherence to regulations, risk-avoiders and maintaining stability.

Deal and Kennedy (1982):

–   The **tough-guy macho culture** – individualists, risk-taking, speed, short-term outlook

–   The **work hard/play hard culture** – achievement, low risk-taking, dynamic

–   The **bet your company culture** – hierarchical, top-down management, co-operative, innovative but slow

–   The **process culture** – preoccupied with how they do things rather than what they do, processes and procedures dominate, formal and hierarchical

2   –   Information gathering processes are unlikely to be formalised and the informality may result in lack of connections between separate pieces of information being made.

–   There is unlikely to be formalised analysis of information allowing interpretation and objective evaluation.

–   There may be selectivity and filtering of information by those closest to the central figure if this information does not fit with desired ambitions regardless of outcomes.

3   Bureaucratic processes and systems would result in a lack of selectivity in information gathering.

Information gathered would tend to be over complicated and may involve many unnecessary procedures.

Information gathering would be a slow process and may result in information being out of date before its significance is recognised.

4   Examples might include:

–   In a role culture they would not actively encourage team building. In such a culture it might be assumed that by bringing people together they automatically become a team.

–   In a task culture it would be much easier as team building would be a feature of the organisation. Work routines would be organised around teams.

–   In a power culture team building might not be formalised. There may be a preference for informal team development and any team building might focus on socialising.

–   In a person culture people would resist being formed into teams, preferring to operate on their own. It would be difficult to encourage teamwork.

5   –   Organisation culture – its values, beliefs and attitudes to people
        –   People – their attitudes to customers and what represents good customer service

You may also have included eg training, management skills, which are relevant and important, but customer service cannot be developed without the right culture and people.

6   Customer needs lead to value proposition; value proposition is determined by corporate values; brand values are the desired corporate reputation based on corporate values and value proposition.

7   –   Define values and explain what they mean
        –   Describe how values are interpreted in behaviour and the execution of tasks, what they look like
        –   Change measures and rewards to reflect desired values
        –   Learning and development to translate into behaviour and work
        –   Communications to inform, remind, re-enforce, differentiate (from other values, compare and contrast)

8   –   People measures – leadership, management and employees measured on their contribution to customer value and satisfaction, morale, motivation, creativity

        –   Operations measures – value delivery systems (rather than product), efficient and effective and from a customer/stakeholder perspective

        –   Learning and innovation – new/changes in behaviour, performance that leads to improvements and advantage, implementation/launch of innovation that is commercially viable, adds value and differentiates

        –   Corporate responsibility and the triple bottom line

        –   Marketing activities eg information, strategy, brand, communications, marketing mix

The Chartered Institute of Marketing

CHAPTER 10

Organisational strategies for change

Introduction

Change for most organisations is now a fact of life although the reasons might vary. Change is usually met with apprehension or 'Oh no, not again' and neither of these responses is likely to lead to employees enthusiastically embracing change. The change itself is not really the problem, particularly today in many cultures where change is common; the problem is how change is announced and managed.

Typically the 'announcement' starts with rumours which begin a negative spiral before anything is officially said and managing the truth and the gossip is left to chance, to be fitted in at the manager's discretion.

Change is not without pain but it can be managed with integrity. In this chapter we will review what triggers change, how we can develop a process for effective change and how we plan change, never losing sight of customers in the process.

Topic list

Globalisation ①

Drivers of change ②

The magnitude of change and the impact on marketing strategy ③

Methods of change ④

Designing a process for change ⑤

Preparing a plan for change ⑥

3.3.1	Assess the key drivers and pressures on organisations to change in today's dynamic marketing environment: ■ Environmental audit ■ Contemporary issues ■ Global challenges
3.3.2	Critically evaluate barriers to organisational change, making recommendations of how best to overcome them: ■ Cultural barriers to change ■ Competency inadequacies ■ Community barriers ■ Personal barriers
3.3.3	Critically evaluate why organisations often avoid corporate led change, including: ■ Public scrutiny of large corporate organisations ■ Political/legislative reasons ■ Union intervention ■ Prior strategic commitments ■ Inertia
3.3.4	Critically evaluate the different methods of change available to organisations: ■ Incremental ■ Discontinuous ■ Re-engineering
3.3.5	Design a process for change, to provide insight into the level of involvement and interaction stakeholders will have in the transformation of an organisation and its market orientation, including consideration of constraints and contingencies: ■ Surface/profound change management ■ Organisation wide change – strategic change management ■ Stakeholder mapping – power versus support or resistance ■ Stakeholder personal analysis (getting inside an individual's head) ■ The nature of opposition (knowing your 'enemies' in change) ■ The nature of support (knowing your allies in change) ■ Measuring the impact of change
3.3.6	Prepare a change plan for an organisation, taking into account the need for appropriate resources, capabilities, skills and motivations for its execution: ■ HR policy – recruitment, training, job definition and roles, rewards and incentives, relationships and hierarchies ■ Customer/competitor relations ■ Cross-function and inter-departmental relations ■ Innovation ■ Integrating internal and external pressures ■ Monitoring and measuring success

1 Globalisation

The marketing environment is dynamic and constantly changing. Understanding the forces impacting on our domestic markets is challenge enough, but with global markets this is magnified. Organisations will face both controllable and uncontrollable elements. Controllable elements of the marketing mix may need to be adapted to different environments (and include things that the marketer is responsible for such as the marketing mix). Uncontrollable elements may vary on a country by country basis. These could include aspects such as the

economic environment (unemployment or consumer confidence), new technologies or competitors, government regulations and changing consumer preferences. Natural and man-made disasters can also cause an enormous impact. All these aspects can impact on existing plans and strategies.

The marketing of goods and services across national borders is becoming easier. However, when organisations are looking for markets to enter, they should consider market accessibility and tariff and non-tariff barriers to trade. Tariffs are taxes on products crossing a frontier. These are set up to protect local industry from overseas competition. The World Trade Organisation provides a world-wide forum for discussion in an attempt to avoid tariffs. Non-tariff barriers are other forms of government action to restrict imports, eg quotas. These are specific limits, by volume or value, on the amount of goods exported to specific markets and may be applied to a nation or a group of nations. Other barriers may be exchange rate policies, customs procedures, administrative and technical regulations, geographic and climate barriers.

Additionally, organisations must appreciate the differences between countries in relation to social and marketing practices, political and commercial institutions and language. A product that succeeds in one country may fail in another even if they seem similar in shared customs, language and lifestyles. Even in one country, regional variations on marketing strategies may be required. Customs, tastes, likes and dislikes can be very different.

Once the market has been chosen, the method of entry has to be chosen from indirect export through to export houses, international trading companies, customers' UK buying offices or co-operative exporting. Direct export can be achieved through selling direct, trading companies, agents, distributors, branch offices or marketing subsidiaries.

1.1 Multinationals

Multinational organisations with bases in several countries have a global outlook. They may have their origins in a particular country but their operations span the globe. Manufacturing may be in a number of countries and goods are sold world-wide. There may be influence or control of the company's marketing activities from outside the country in which it is selling or producing.

Lancaster *et al* (2002) highlight a number of advantages for multinationals:

- **Programme transfers:** multinationals can draw upon strategies, products, advertising campaigns, sales practices and promotional ideas that have been tested in comparable markets.

- **Systems transfer:** the successful implementation of systems can be rolled out to new markets, such as planning, budgeting, new product introduction and other processes and software packages.

- **People transfer:** skilled members of staff can be deployed across national boundaries. Many multinationals introduce successor strategies (the future of senior management) and expect staff to work across functions, cultures and geographic borders during their apprenticeship.

- **Scale economies in manufacturing:** components manufactured on scale-efficient plants in different countries can be brought together into the finalised product.

- **Economies of centralisation of functional activities:** activities by functional teams can be concentrated on single locations in order to develop greater competence and reduce costs, eg marketing or the market research department. A disadvantage is that they may not appreciate the complexities of distant markets and may not design appropriate strategies or projects for them. This is particularly true as multinationals cut budgets for foreign travel.

- **Resource utilisation:** the globe can be scanned to identify sources of manpower, money and materials so the organisation can compete effectively in world markets.

- **Global strategy:** the world can be scanned for markets that provide opportunities to apply the company's skills, match markets with resources, exploit opportunities, and create and shift resources to tap identified opportunities.

1.2 Marketing products globally

Economies of scale may be possible if companies could market standard products globally. Unfortunately, in practice, markets often require legal, technical or climatic modifications. Local tastes and culture may also influence product changes.

Keegan developed a useful framework for international marketing strategies (1969, quoted by Lancaster *et al*, 2002, p438):

- **Straight extension:** the product takes the same form and communications as in the domestic market. No additional manufacturing or marketing costs are required.

- **Communications adaptation:** the promotional theme is modified but the product remains unchanged. Major manufacturing costs are not incurred.

- **Product adaptation:** the product is modified but the communications theme is retained.

- **Dual adaptation:** both the product and communications are modified to meet the needs of specific markets.

The following diagram summarises this framework.

Figure 10.1   Framework for international marketing strategies

		Products		
		No change	Adapted	New product
Marketing communications	No change	Straight extension	Product adaptation	
	Adapt	Communication adaptation	Dual adaptation	Product invention

Once product decisions have been made, pricing strategies can be fixed. These will depend on the needs and requirements of the market. They could be similar to the price paid in the domestic market. Terms of payment on how the goods are sold to the export market could also help determine the price. Currency issues are also a factor.

Globalisation is set to continue as we see faster communications, and better transportation and financial flows. Competition is intense. Globalisation is important to governments and economies so measures are likely to be introduced to encourage more activity. The collapse of communism and the rise of Eastern Europe has also brought new opportunities. Countries like Singapore, Malaysia and South Korea are becoming industrialised and will see new competitors bringing technological capabilities, as well as lower labour costs, to global markets. Despite the rise of the anti-globalisation movement, bank loan problems and low-paid sweat shop workers, the process of globalisation is progressing at a rapid pace.

The Chartered Institute of Marketing

2 Drivers of change

The need for change can be triggered by either internal or external triggers.

Phase 1 – Trigger for change and improvement

2.1 External triggers of change

External changes occur in seven broad areas all of which are linked either tentatively or strongly. These ripples in a pool mean a change in one area may have an immediate and direct influence over a change in another, or the change or influence may be almost imperceptible and oblique.

Figure 10.2   Change drivers

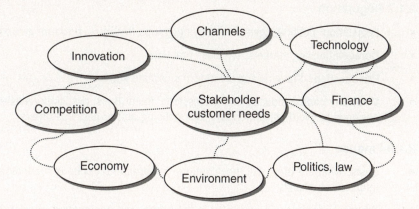

Any one of these factors, at different times, will lead in changing events and marketing is responsible for identifying trends and the potential for change.

2.1.1 Customers

- **Basic needs:** how will these change, what will change them, with what are they disenchanted, what are their expectations etc?

- **Demographics:** what changes are taking place, what groupings can we expect, what are the trends etc?

- **Life stages:** what are they (characteristics), how are they changing etc?

- **Habits and usage:** where and when are products used, why, how?

- **Attitudes:** towards industry, environment, society?

2.1.2 Politics and the law

- **Policy:** for example a change in public spending
- **Legislation:** for example new employment laws

2.1.3 Economy

- **Boom:** employment high, disposable income high, spending high
- **Recession:** employment, disposable income and spending low

2.1.4 Environment

- **Climate:** global warming and changes in customer behaviour
- **Natural disasters:** increase in flooding or drought

2.1.5 Channels

- **Current channels:** which are evolving, working well, which are not?

- **Future channels:** what developments suggest new opportunities, how easy will these be to exploit/implement?

2.1.6 Technology

- **Technology as a product/service:** what products and services are/can be used to exploit opportunities and meet needs, what advances are or are likely to be made?

- **Technology as a means of delivery:** what developments might change the way in which we deliver our products or services, how will this affect the business?

- **Technology as a means of production:** both in terms of manufacturing capability and business operations, what developments might change the way we do things?

2.1.7 Regulation

- **Legislation:** political agendas, lobbying groups (industry, pressure groups)

- **Deregulation:** eg markets, business practices

- **Privatisation:** changing society in terms of state support

- **Voluntary codes:** industry and professional institutions, associations establishing codes of practice designed to avoid legislation and over policing and protect customers

2.1.8 Finance

- **Costs:** what are they, will they continue to escalate (in spite of technology), what will be the impact of inflation, taxation?

- **Pricing:** what role will price play in the future, will pricing wars escalate?

- **Profit:** where will profits be made in the future (opportunities), how will profits be protected (business operations)?

- **Funding:** increasing influence of financial markets, likely convergence of financial markets

2.1.9 Competition

- **Performance:** extent of strategic activities and effectiveness of marketing programmes
- **Nature of:** likelihood of new entrants and their affect on the industry/markets

2.1.10 Innovation

- **Who are the innovators:** are there particular industries driving innovation, particular professions, people?

- **Where are the innovations:** is it mainly technology and in what industries, geographic areas, institutions (eg universities, business schools)?

- **What are the innovations:** is it likely to be the products and services sold, business processes, is it in the way we think and behave?

Bloomberg Businessweek highlighted the top 10 drivers of change in 2010 and beyond:

1   Consumers' preferences will remain 'reset' based on values, not price.
2   Energy costs will continue to increase in the medium term.
3   US tax policy could erode the competitive positioning of US companies (relative to emerging markets).
4   Innovation happens for emerging market consumers, not in emerging markets.
5   A new return to vertical integration gains traction.
6   Industry shifts create competitive shifts.
7   Increases in information require more judgement from decision-makers.
8   Markets reward long-term strategic focus.

The Chartered Institute of Marketing

9   Economic recovery won't mean recovery for everyone.

10   A new war in talent commences.

Further details on these drivers of change can be found at http://www.businessweek.com [accessed March 2012].

2.2 Internal triggers of change

As discussed in previous chapters, we can use the McKinsey S Model (Waterman *et al*, 1980) to identify what might trigger change internally

- **Shared values:** for example if we want to change to a marketing orientation we might want to change values and behaviour.

- **Strategy:** a change in strategic direction can require a change in, eg competitive position.

- **Structure:** a marketing orientation putting customers at the centre of the business might require a change in structure.

- **Systems:** changing to a marketing orientation means changing from a product delivery system to a value delivery system.

- **Style:** leadership and management styles may need to change to reflect different values.

- **Staff:** learning and development will be important to enable staff to adopt new ways of thinking and behaviour to focus on customer value.

- **Skills:** training will be required to equip employees with new or different skills, particularly focused on the customer experience.

Figure 10.3   McKinsey's Model

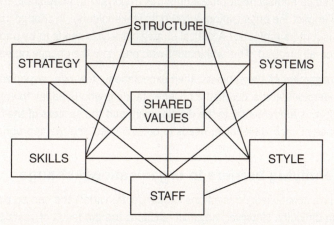

As with external drivers, internal drivers are linked and a change in one area affects what is happening in other areas. Leaders need to understand these connections and while they devolve responsibility for managing and implementing change to management, leaders must co-ordinate and integrate what is going on across the organisation. If there is a lack of integration this can impact how change is accepted by people within and external to the organisation. The need for change must be understood by the internal stakeholders for it to be accepted and implemented.

2.3 The change kaleidoscope

The change kaleidoscope was developed by Hope Hailey & Balogun (2002) to pull together and codify the wide range of contextual features and implementation options that require consideration during change. The change kaleidoscope should be used as more of a model than a method in helping to conceptualise the nature of change.

Understanding the contextual features enables those undertaking change to use the appropriate approach in implementing change.

The eight contextual features of the change kaleidoscope are described in the table below.

Table 10.1   The change kaleidoscope

Time	How quickly is change needed? Is the organisation in crisis or is it concerned with longer-term strategic development?
Scope	What degree of change is needed? Does the change affect the whole organisation or only part of it?
Preservation	What organisational assets, characteristics and practices need to be maintained and protected during change?
Diversity	Are the different staff / professional groups and divisions within the organisation relatively homogeneous or more diverse in terms of values, norms and attitudes?
Capability	What is the level of organisational, managerial and personal capability to implement change? Is there a need to improve this capability before the change process can be started?
Capacity	How much resource can the organisation invest in the proposed change in terms of cash, people and time?
Readiness for change	How ready for change are the employees within the organisation? Are they aware of the need for change and motivated to deliver change?
Power	Where is the power vested within the organisation? How much latitude of discretion does the unit needing to change and the change leader possess?

In any change management programme it is important to understand that the level and speed of change will not only impact the organisation but also its stakeholders. Is change impacting the organisation at a superficial level or is it more profound? A critical strategic analysis needs to be undertaken to determine the impact of change on all involved. This will impact who and how the change managed at corporate level.

The management of stakeholders, their expectations, feelings, responses and recommendations they make need to be understood and accounted for. Understanding who is happy to engage with change, as well as those opposing it, is fundamental to the development and the success of the change management plan. The importance of each stakeholder needs to be evaluated and the appropriate communication developed.

2.4 Identifying barriers to organisational change

As we have acknowledged reactions to change are varied and can be positive particularly if the organisation is clearly in difficulty. However, negative reactions are the result of years of poor change management and of unnecessary change. There is no question that in some industries continuous change is essential, for example the technology industry. However, that is not true of all industries and organisations. The unnecessary change seems to be a result of a knee jerk reaction to the external environment. The marketplace is inevitably always changing. The skill of leaders is to recognise when it is appropriate to change the organisation in response to external changes and when it is not.

Continuous improvement is desirable and it could be argued this leads to continuous change. Continuous improvement is often small and very localised and may not require change beyond a person undertaking a task. There may even be lots of these across the organisation but they do not usually cause negative reactions or

The Chartered Institute of Marketing

meet with resistance unless there is a problem with the employee, the manager or between them both. When the scope of improvements is larger and widespread this will lead to more momentous change.

Among barriers to change are:

- Legacy of previous change programmes if they were poorly managed and did not lead to obvious improvements

- Existing leadership and management styles and relations with employees. If these are not healthy change will be difficult.

- Leadership and management skills if they have no experience of change or have handled change badly

De Wit and Meyer (2005) describe leadership activities broadly in three ways:

(a) Strategic thinking: conceptualising to develop strategic direction
(b) Strategy formation: creating the right environment for strategy development
(c) Strategic change: what needs to be done to change the organisation to deliver the strategy

Leadership naturally is focused on the future, developing a vision for that future and anticipating and scoping strategies to deliver successful outcomes. It can be difficult at this level to understand the practicalities of change but leaders should not be preoccupied with this. They work in collaboration with management who work with employees to design and implement change successfully. Leaders and managers have different roles but together change the organisation.

There can be a number of reasons why there is a resistance to change:

- Change is not understood. This can be for a number of reasons; it is not clearly communicated or there is no clear direction or vision as to why the change is needed or required.

- Leadership fails to take control of the change situation; there is a lack of project management of the whole change process.

- There is a lack of buy in from key stakeholders, which then promotes negativity.

- People's issues, such as reluctance to change, have not been appropriately identified, which in turn means they cannot be resolved and so linger within the organisation and influence others.

- Progress with change is not recognised and this can lead to strategic drift, and the objectives of change not being met.

- A lack of preparation to manage and lead change.

- None or little involvement of employees in designing change.

- Lack of management control in positively motivating employees to engage in change.

There are a number of factors that can prevent/hinder change; however, it can also be as a result of the individual involved in the change. There can be personal barriers that can prevent/slow down change including:

- Fear of the unknown or of future uncertainty
- Lack of trust of those implementing change, bad experiences of change in the past
- Need for security
- Lack of experience of change in the past
- Lack of tolerance of change

If it is essential to continually change, managers cannot assume it is not stressful and de-motivating and have a duty to reduce stress. In our discussion on motivation achievement is a typical motivator so at some point there needs to be a sense of achieving something, arriving somewhere or continuous change can become like a treadmill.

It is important therefore that managers check the validity of 'continuous':

- Is it relevant to us?
- Is it a priority?
- How much needs to change if it is relevant and is a priority?

In addition, managers must provide a sense of achievement and arrival by:

- Acknowledging completion, an end to a particular project
- Recognising and rewarding success
- Learning from the experience

This can help stakeholders to recognise and manage change appropriately. If it is not made clear as to how change is progressing or developing this can take away the focus required for change to actually progress.

Engagement with all stakeholders is required to ensure the success of change. The external community can impact change as well as change that be under public scrutiny. The power of the public or local community can impact the success or otherwise of change

ACTIVITY 10.1

Critically evaluate what changes have taken place in your organisation in recent years and why. Can you identify the purpose or objective of these changes? Evaluate the success or otherwise of the changes that have taken place.

3 The magnitude of change and the impact on marketing strategy

The implementation of a marketing strategy will attempt to bring about strategic change. Sometimes in order to respond to environmental change and maintain a competitive advantage a number of strategic changes need to be executed in a variety of areas to keep the organisation aligned with market demands.

Where this occurs this may be referred to as strategic renewal (De Wit and Meyer, 2005). This process might consist of a few large steps or numerous small ones. The size of the change is referred to as the magnitude of change. This can be divided into two component parts: scope and amplitude.

3.1 Scope of change

- This can vary from broad to narrow. Change is broad when many aspects and parts of the firm are altered at the same time.

- In most extreme cases this will result in entire organisational processes, culture and people being changed in unison.

- Change can also be much more narrowly focused on a specific organisational aspect or department.

- If many changes are narrowly targeted the total result will be a more piecemeal change process.

3.2 Amplitude of organisational changes

- This can vary from high to low.
- It is high when the change deployed is a radical departure from what went before.
- It is low when the step proposed is a moderate adjustment.

3.2.1 The pace of change

Strategic renewal takes time.

Strategic change measures can be evenly spread out over an extended period, allowing the organisation to follow a relatively steady pace of strategic renewal. It is also possible to cluster all changes into a few short irregular bursts, giving the renewal process an unsteady, stop-and-go pace.

The Chartered
Institute of Marketing

The pace of organisational change can be split into two related parts:

3.2.2 Timing of change

- Pace of change depends on the moment at which change is initiated.

- Change can vary from intermittent to constant.

- When change is intermittent it is important to determine the right moment to launch a new initiative.

- The need to wait for the 'right time' is often a reason for spreading change activities unevenly over time.

- On the other hand change can be constant so that the exact moment for implementing a new measure such as the marketing strategy is less important.

3.2.3 Speed of change

- Pace of change also depends on the time span within which change takes place.

- Speed of change can vary from high to low.

- Where a major change needs to be implemented within a short period of time the speed of change must be high.

- A short burst of action can bring about the intended changes.

- Alternatively, where the change measures are less formidable and the time span for implementation is longer, the speed of change can be lower.

Organisations, therefore, have many different ways of bringing about strategic change and this brings about the question of whether to achieve revolutionary (disruptive) or evolutionary (gradual) change.

3.2.4 The demand for revolutionary change

Revolution is a process whereby an abrupt and radical change takes place within a short period of time. Such processes do not build on the status quo – they overthrow it.

Such an approach may be required when 'organisational rigidity' is so deep-rooted that smaller pushes do not bring the required movement. Typical sources of rigidity are shown in the table below.

Table 10.2   Source of rigidity

Source	Comment
Psychological resistance to change	■ Many people resist change because of the uncertainties associated with it. ■ It can be necessary to break through this by imposing a new business system on people.
Cultural resistance to change	■ People can become immune to the signals that they are out-of-touch. ■ Can break through this by exposing the organisation to a shocking crisis or imposing a new organisational system.
Political resistance to change	■ Each organisational change invariably results in winners and losers. ■ Can break through this resistance through a management restructure.

Source	Comment
Investment lock-in	■ Investment in a new product. Technology or activity can result in fixing the organisation to this even if it is not working. ■ Can be necessary to break through this lock-in by radically restructuring or disposing of the investment.
Competence lock-in	■ When an organisation builds a competitive advantage based on a particular set of competences it is natural for that organisation to favour external opportunities based on those competences. ■ This can lead to an organisation becoming out-dated. ■ Changing the core competence of the organisation in a comprehensive and radical manner may be the only way to migrate from one set of competences to another.
System lock-in	■ Organisations can become locked-in to a particular standard or system. ■ Lock-in can only be overcome by a 'big bang' transition to another system.
Stakeholder lock-in	■ Restrictive long-term commitments can be made to stakeholders (ie long-term contracts with suppliers, long-term warranties with buyers etc). ■ It might be necessary to aim for a radical restructuring of the organisation's relationships.

Besides the use of revolutionary change to overcome rigidity there may be other triggers that are necessary for revolutionary change:

■ **Competitive pressure**

When an organisation is under intense pressure and its market position is eroding quickly a rapid and dramatic response might be the only response possible.

■ **Regulatory pressure**

Organisations can be put under pressure by government or regulatory agencies to push through major changes within a short period of time.

■ **First mover advantage**

A more proactive reason to implement a revolutionary change is to be the first to introduce a new product, service or technology and to build up barriers to entry for late movers.

Most managers recognise that their organisations are prone to inertia and acknowledge that is often necessary to move quickly in response to external pressures or to take advantage of first mover advantage. Most would like their organisation to have the ability to successfully implement revolutionary strategic changes.

3.3 The demand for evolutionary change processes

Evolutionary change processes take the current state as a starting point and constantly modify aspects through extension and adaptation. A new system or strategy can evolve out of the old, as if an organisation is 'shedding its skin'.

This is approach is more important where the strategic renewal process hinges on widespread organisational learning. Learning is a relatively slow process and time will be needed to experiment, reflect, discuss, test and internalise the changes.

A more evolutionary approach may be the only option when no one person has enough sway to push through radical changes.

To some extent managers recognise that their organisations need to continuously learn and adapt and acknowledge that they do not have enough absolute power to impose revolutionary change.

Once managers choose to adopt revolutionary or evolutionary change they will find it very difficult to simultaneously or subsequently use the other.

3.4 Discontinuous versus continuous renewal perspective

Some commentators feel that revolutionary change is seen to be at the heart of renewal while evolutionary change can only play a supporting role. This is often referred to as the 'discontinuous renewal perspective'.

Others feel that real strategic renewal must grow out of the existing organisation with a steady stream of adjustments and that, while difficult to sustain, evolutionary change is at the heart of renewal while revolutionary changes are a fall-back alternative. This point of view is referred to as the continuous renewal perspective.

3.5 The discontinuous renewal perspective

- Proponents of this perspective argue that people and organisations exhibit a natural reluctance to change.

- Once general policy is determined organisations are inclined to settle into a fixed way of working.

- This is further cemented after a sustained period of success.

- Advocates therefore argue that long periods of stability are necessary for the proper functioning of firms. However, this leads to rigidity.

- The way to overcome this is to implement co-ordinated, radical and comprehensive measures.

- Some proponents of this view argue that episodes of revolutionary change are generally not chosen freely but are triggered by crises (eg introduction of a new technology, novel market entrant etc).

- However, often a misalignment between the organisation and its environment grows over a longer period of time causing a mounting sense of crisis.

- As tension increases people become more receptive to submitting to the changes that are necessary.

- As long as there is pressure revolutionary change is possible. Managers will therefore induce a crisis to create the sense of urgency and determination that may be required to get people to change.

Others argue that revolutionary change can be proactively pursued to gain a competitive advantage such as using a break through technology, creating a new business model and so on. Old methods must be discarded before new methods, strategies and so on can be adopted.

This process is not orderly or protracted but can be disruptive and intense. Therefore organisations must learn to master the skill of ongoing revolutionary change. So, for example, rapid implementation of new strategy is an essential organisational capability.

Such change management requires strong, consistent leadership to rapidly push through any stress that may be related to it. Battling against rigidity and turning crisis into opportunity become key qualities required by managers. Those responsible for developing and implementing strategic change need to be aware of the timing of such events.

3.6 The continuous renewal perspective

(a) Proponents of this view argue that if organisations 'shift by earthquake' then it is usually their own fault and that such change creates a 'boom-and-bust' cycle.

(b)   Those organisations that maintain a steady stream of change will win in the end.

(c)   Revolutionary change causes unnecessary disruption and dysfunctional crises and only has short-term impact.

(d)   Continuous renewal has a more long-term orientation and is constantly maintained over a longer period of time.

(e)   Three organisational characteristics are important for keeping up a steady pace of change:

    (i)   Employees within the organisation are committed to continuously improve.

    (ii)   Everyone in the organisation is motivated to continuously learn.

    (iii)   Everyone in the organisation must be motivated to continuously adapt.

Managers should strive to create flexible structures and processes, an open and tolerant culture and provide sufficient job and career security for employees to accept other forms of ambiguity and uncertainty.

By pursuing this approach everyone in the organisation is involved and managers recognise that although change can be led from the top it cannot simply be imposed from the top.

4 Methods of change

4.1 Managing evolution

▶ **Key term**

Change management is the deliberate strategy to minimise the negative impact of change thereby reducing resistance and maximising participation to achieve successful design and implementation of change.

As we saw in the previous section change can be managed as an evolutionary process where the change is gentle or almost imperceptible. In these circumstances as long as there are markers of success at appropriate points even continuous change can be rewarding and motivating.

Evolution is less disruptive and expensive so has the advantage of creating little resistance; it becomes a way of life. It is also more likely to encourage learning. If evolution is causing high levels of disruption it is more likely to be caused by the way it is being managed.

4.2 Managing a revolution

Some change is the result of management wanting to 'shake things up' – no bad thing in itself sometimes. However, if that is the only goal the risk is that you shake things up for the worse not better. There has to be a goal, a clear statement on desired outcomes.

Sometimes it is necessary to manage a revolution because externally some dramatic and unexpected change is forcing a fast and dramatic response. Sometimes a revolution is the result of management complacency or failure to identify trends leading to change. Revolutions are only beneficial in particular circumstances, when you have no choice. Managing continuous change as a revolution is a recipe for change fatigue and possibly losing good people and customers.

We are going to focus on changing to a marketing orientation or customer focus. Many of the same principles apply in managing other change.

It is important to remember that evolutionary change is always happening. This involves changes in the way business is done rather than changes in the actual business. This can include changes in the HR policy. Evolutionary change can mean a change in the way things are done. Contrastingly, revolutionary change involves a change in the actual business; this can include changes to the products or services being offered or even new product development.

Apple 1990s to 2012

It is clear that Apple has been able to change its position in the marketplace over the last 20 years. A key person within Apple that helped to facilitate this change was Steve Jobs. He made 'change' the key word and a key part of the organisation. However, this change was not just a small part of the organisation, but rather was organisation wide, impacting all departments, all employees and really getting to the heart of the organisation. Central to this change was Steve Jobs' vision of what he wanted Apple to become; it impacted the computing, music and communications industry. Apple's success has been attributed to its openness to change. Increasingly Apple has been able to change things, from having a Genius Bar in its stores to help customers with problems, to developing products that are user friendly as well as contemporary and arguably fashionable.

Examples of change include the following:

- Originally the Genius Bar did not have appointments but rather a hard copy waiting list. To ensure the process ran smoothly they then migrated this to an electronic waiting list and implemented appointment times.

- The Genius Bar used to do all training within the stores; eventually this was changed to include some one-to-one training and some group training depending on the purchase made.

- Store layouts were also changed to ensure that queuing was easy and payment was prompt.

There have been a number of ongoing changes within Apple; a fundamental part of Apple is knowing that change is ongoing and that as stakeholders as well as customers change, so must the organisation. 'Think different' was an advertising slogan for Apple, which is at the heart of Apple's philosophy. Steve Jobs was at the heart of these changes and developments as he stated:

'You can't just ask customers what they want and then try to give that to them. By the time you get it built, they'll want something new.'

Apple has made and continues to make changes, but more importantly manages these changes; this is a fundamental part of its ethos and philosophy. Making and managing change are as important as one another, as well as having an inspirational leader to ensure this philosophy remains in the heart of the organisation.

5 Designing a process for change

So how do you make the transformation from whatever orientation exists currently to a marketing orientation? A process for change management can help keep managers on track and help employees understand the journey.

Figure 10.4 Managing change journey

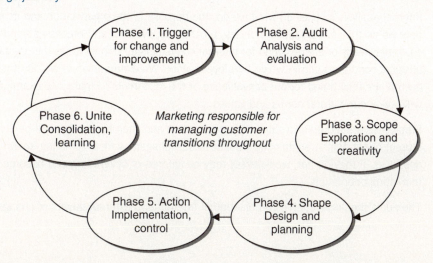

The challenge for the manager is to pull together the process of managing change with managing people through change. It is easy to focus on operations and tasks during change as there is a sense of urgency about getting things right. However, we can only get things right if we manage people.

Crucially, for the marketing department, managing the customer transitions throughout change is essential. Hopefully they will not be aware most of the time unless the change is important to them. Where change may impact on them marketing managers need to develop a strategy for managing relationships, these need to critically assess the organisation's approach, management and execution of change.

5.1 Phase 2 – Audit: analysis and evaluation

A key phase in the management of change is Phase 2 – and specifically how employees become aware of impending change.

5.1.1 Announcement (employee concerns and support)

Employees should not become aware of plans for change via the grapevine, gossip and rumour. They should also not become aware of the intention to change after decisions have been made. Once the need for change has been established there is a timely announcement as part of a planned communication that reduces the potential for shock. The first stage of communications is designed to present the requirement for change and invite employees to become involved in the process.

Communications during Phase 2 are designed to help understand the need for change, create dissatisfaction with the current set-up and a desire for, or at least understanding of, change. The task is to interpret new cultural values and the purpose and mission as something meaningful and personal to all individuals at all levels. Focus on:

(a)   Benefits from the employees' perspective, eg new skills, development and their role and the value of their contribution

(b)   Their association with the organisation's image and reputation

Provide support by encouraging discussion, feedback and airing of concerns.

5.1.2 Analysis and evaluation

External analysis focuses on customers: who they are, what they buy, where, how and when they buy, and why they buy? This analysis includes customer behaviour and their motives and needs. We need to be aware of other environmental factors, for example the nature of industry and competitive situation. Our goal here is to make sure we have a comprehensive understanding of our customers so we understand how we need to respond internally.

Internal analysis focuses on what we do, the purpose of the organisation and its strategic goals. We also review how we do things, operations, policies, procedures, systems and processes and to what extent they meet customer needs or are designed for internal convenience. This includes the organisation environment and the physical conditions within which employees work. We examine when we do things, and timing of activities and events: are they timed for our convenience or the customers'? Finally, we examine why we do things and this will reveal our cultural norms and values.

Employees are required to gather this information and their knowledge will be invaluable in establishing the current orientation strengths and weaknesses. Managers work on creating an atmosphere of honesty and openness. If they do not, weaknesses may be ignored or covered up and become an obstacle to achieving a marketing orientation.

The audit should reveal the combination of internal and external drivers of change and restraining forces.

The Chartered Institute of Marketing

5.1.3 Force field analysis

Lewin (1951) explained that change occurs when change drivers collectively overcome restraining forces. Managers can identify possible drivers and restraining forces and apply weighting to provide an assessment of the change task and likelihood of success or failure.

Figure 10.5 Force field analysis

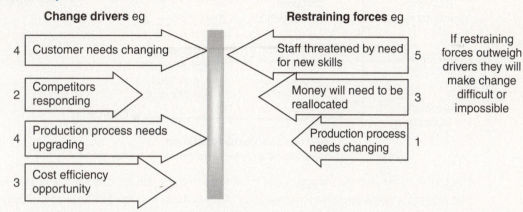

This process encourages managers to think through the issues and problems and plan the change accordingly.

THE REAL WORLD

E.ON, the power company, decided to confront the issue of emissions that pollute the atmosphere. Being an energy company this was never going to be easy. However, the leaders recognised that this is about identifying where you can make a difference and working towards clearly stated goals.

Among the many initiatives is to reduce emissions from all business travel including all staff travelling to and from work and during work etc; and technology is providing opportunities to reduce their carbon footprint, for example changing to 'greener' cars and using GPS and video conferencing.

Leadership recognised that to change behaviour they needed to establish four 'enablers' to support the change. These are:

- Leadership excellence
- Skills and behaviour
- Operational excellence
- Living the brand

For example, one of the leadership initiatives has been to invite leading environmental thinkers to challenge the board and stimulate debate on the development of 'green' initiatives. Learning and development activities were shaped around the changing energy principles with the aims of getting employees to promote and live the changing E.ON brand in their dealings with customers and encouraging behaviours that supported the strategy. 360 degree feedback tools are being changed to incorporate new values and behaviours. Their approach to performance management and reward is also changing with, for example, a system to tie objectives to the strategy. The balanced scorecard has been introduced in support of this. By linking objectives, targets and rewards employees have tangible evidence of what is expected and required and what behaviour fulfils these expectations. E.ON also recognise this change in culture will take time but by communicating, educating, putting in place the right systems and process and leading by example they are already achieving the desired results.

5.1.4 Leadership, management and cultural differences

Good practices do not just focus on employees. Leadership and management respond to change in different ways. If change is taking place across cultures this will affect the approach to change and way in which it will be managed. Lasserre and Schutte (2006) suggest that unless we understand the differences in thinking and behaviour and contextual differences we can make little progress.

Figure 10.6   Transforming management practices in different cultures

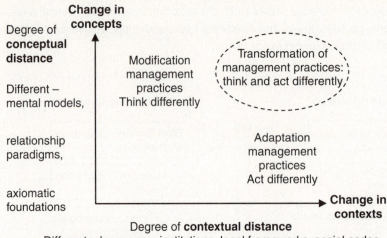

The goal is to get leaders, managers and employees to think and act differently and as discussed in Chapter 9, that requires a comprehensive understanding of the culture. Managing change across cultures adds another dimension to change management. If the culture is risk-averse change will be difficult; if the emphasis is on past glories rather than the future the task is to relate the future to the past. If culture dictates employees defer to managers and do not expect to be consulted on change, adjustments will need to be made to change management.

5.1.5 Understanding employees

Change means different things for different levels of the organisation. Leaders are often the **initiators** of change (but not exclusively) to pursue their vision and future strategic direction and are rarely interested in the detail of implementation. Managers are responsible for managing change and will either be **campaigners** or **opponents**. Either way they are the mediators between initiators and those who implement change. Employees are the implementers of change and will either be campaigners or opponents.

During Phase 2 we established how employees are likely to react to change. This requires that we understand the effect change will have on people including uncertainty, a lack of control over personal performance and increasing frustration, a possible loss of responsibility, possible loss of social networks, lack of security, a sense of abandonment and feeling incompetent as the realisation of newly defined roles emerges.

When change starts employees embark on a journey that runs parallel to daily work routines. It is unsettling if this journey is not understood and people are not properly prepared or managed. It becomes threatening as the journey increasingly impacts on the daily work routines and the social climate. The personal journey involves phases people may go through during the change process. Different people will react in different ways and go through different phases.

People are likely to undergo these phases, or something similar, even if change is managed well. The difference is if change is managed properly they will go through these phases quickly and resistance will be minimal, and they may even avoid some of the more negative phases. However, if change is not properly managed people may get stuck in the more unproductive phases and may never accept the new order. Quiet resistance then becomes a way of life.

Another essential we must deal with is one of the less comfortable aspects of change: the necessity to make people redundant. Sometimes it is unavoidable and as well as the distress for those who will be made redundant it is upsetting and unsettling for those who remain.

For those who have to be made redundant some will deal with the experience better than others but all need support. In large organisations there are often very comprehensive programmes for getting people into new jobs in other organisations. Even for small organisations helping people with CVs, practising interviews and helping

them set up a network of contacts is manageable. This helps those who have to go but also signals to those who remain that managers care and will do what they can to help.

The influence of unions and their level of input will also impact the change plan and process and will need to be considered across different industries.

5.1.6 Internal segments

When embarking on a programme of change employees should be segmented according to their attitude and likely response.

For example:

- **Initiators:** those who have identified the need for change and are driving and/or encouraging change to happen.

- **Opponents:** people who see the change as threatening and will resist. They either cannot see any justification for change or are simply not convinced. They may just want things to remain as they are.

- **Campaigners:** people who can see the benefits or gain in some way and are therefore enthusiastic about the change. They will be keen to help drive the change through.

- **Neutrals:** people who are yet to be convinced one way or the other. They do not feel strongly about the change and have not made up their mind whether the change is for the better or not.

This is useful for understanding internal segments. Marketing directors in particular should be able to identify the needs and motives of campaigners, neutrals and opponents. If we understand the change journey and the very different perspectives we can understand better how we need to segment internal markets. For opponents the journey can be a roller coaster of emotions and will appear more threatening and uncertain than for campaigners.

Also refer to communication and change management, Chapter 5.

Figure 10.7   Managing change journey of opponent

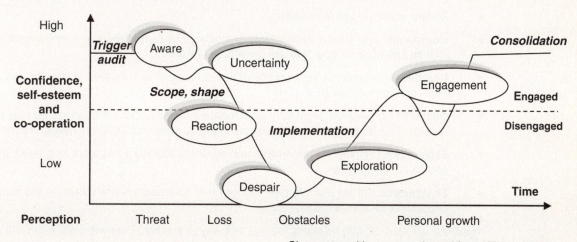

Change transition curve adapted from Wilson (1993)

The opponents' perception of change tends to be negative and viewed as 'problems and trouble '.

- **Aware:** acknowledges information

- **Uncertainty:** apprehension is experienced by opponents as they see threats emerging and try to make sense of what is happening and interpreting messages. They will look for reassurance and hope that the status quo can be maintained.

- **Reaction:** rejection is the response of the opponent as change plans begin to be implemented and hope of maintaining the status quo diminishes. They withdraw and refuse to acknowledge what is happening.

- **Despair:** by this stage opponents may completely withdraw or may actively resist. Whether or not opponents move on from this point depends on either how events are being managed and/or personal opportunities and threats.

- **Exploration:** beginning to come to terms with change, redefining new role and tasks and their confidence and co-operation is growing and they begin to surface from disengagement.

- **Engagement:** settling down to task and new role. For opponents in particular and for change to take hold and be a success a period of consolidation is essential. It is a time for reflection and learning.

The journey for campaigners is not all plain sailing. Their enthusiasm and belief in the change reduces perceptions of threat and they are happy to challenge the status quo. However, during some periods of the journey as the full implications are realised there will be periods of uncertainty and doubt. The journey for campaigners usually causes less emotional turmoil.

Figure 10.8   Stages in employee consultations and negotiations (PACT)

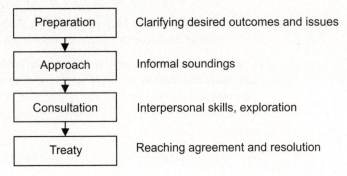

J. Cockton (2005)

The campaigners' perception of change tends to be positive and they see possibilities and progression.

- **Aware:** acknowledges information.

- **Uncertainty:** hesitation is momentarily experienced by campaigners as they interpret information on change and work out how they are going to deal with it.

- **Reaction:** enthusiasm is the response of the campaigner as they see the benefits and opportunities and they embrace the change.

- **Doubt:** as campaigners begin to understand the full implications of change they may question some aspects. This is short lived as campaigners quickly move into exploring how to resolve issues.

- **Exploration:** campaigners are driving and redefining new roles and tasks and their continued confidence and co-operation grows.

- **Engagement:** settling down to task and new role. Campaigners use reflection and learning as an opportunity for consolidation.

'**Neutrals**' will start off with no strong feelings one way or another. They will wait, listen and observe and be swayed either by opponents or by campaigners depending on their own susceptibility to seeing opportunities or threats and the persuasiveness of arguments from both sides. They will then start their journey, either as an opponent or campaigner.

 The Chartered Institute of Marketing

Set objectives for levels of confidence, self-esteem and co-operation. If the starting point is medium to low a higher level of confidence, self-esteem and co-operation is required for the change to improve motivation, loyalty and commitment for employees. Managing motivation must be at the centre of managing change or some worthwhile efforts can be wasted.

From the above, needs and motives emerge that can help us understand the segments we have identified for our internal market and manage their concerns and responses. Who needs convincing, holding back or guiding, who needs pulling or gently pushing? All will need support at different stages but what sort of support and when?

Reasons for resisting or supporting change are complex and varied. Some people gain more power, territory or status as a result of change so will be campaigners. Others lose power, territory or perhaps a social network and so are more likely to oppose.

In your own organisation different segments are likely to emerge and you can segment accordingly to your own specific conditions.

As we have identified **neutrals** may become either campaigners or opponents (and therefore fall into one of the above segments) depending on the circumstances. However, some neutrals can remain just that, neither being convinced nor persuaded of the benefits of change until the end or very near the end. The issue here is that if they remain neutral they are vulnerable to becoming opponents at a time when everyone else has worked their way through the change journey and could set back progress. If they remain neutral there is a chance they are non-participants and increasingly become disengaged as others move forward. It is impossible for them to consolidate something they are not taking part in.

The focus and effort can so easily be on the opponents as the perceived 'trouble makers', and/or possibly the campaigners as the willing drivers of change, that those who remain neutral can be neglected or missed altogether. However, we need to identify and manage those who are neutral and make sure they complete the journey with everyone else, achieving personal growth, a sense of achievement and consolidation.

5.1.7 Uncertainty (employee concerns and support)

As the implications of what we are about to do emerge, but the detail of what that means has not yet been established, people will experience uncertainty as each interprets what they do understand and know and begins to formulate the future.

Again communications has a vital role in reducing perceptions of threat by informing, explaining and reassuring. **Hesitation,** for campaigners, often only requires information from which campaigners can learn and define the job that needs to be done. The methods can therefore be simple and straightforward, for example information sheets and team briefings. The **apprehension** of opponents requires reassurance so a very different type of communication is needed. As well as information any concerns opponents have must be addressed. Providing support through personal or group discussions gives an opportunity for open debate of the issues and is a good way to deal with apprehension.

5.2 Change project teams

The last act of Phase 2 is to set up change project teams. We want to establish change teams that can minimise negative responses and behaviour and maximise positive. However, this might not be as easy as it sounds. Having juggled the functional and team skills (and avoided putting A and B, who cannot stand being in the same room together, in the same team) you now have this added dimension of change segments. We cannot pretend it is going to be easy. However, the goal is to combine expertise and use the opportunity to design a team that will facilitate change.

It goes without saying it will not work if we try to avoid problems by putting all the campaigners of change together and all the opponents in a different group (or in the car park if they are really being a pain!). Quite apart from the potential imbalance of essential skills we need our campaigners championing the cause and

persuading opponents of the benefits with their enthusiasm. We also need opponents to challenge and force debate and discussion around contentious issues. This helps to ensure all implications and consequences are explored.

Establishing a climate of co-operation and recognising the value of all contributions can help alleviate explosive situations or withdrawal. Managers need to pay more attention to teams and work harder at managing them during change.

▶ **Assessment tip**

When you are ready to draft your report, a technique to help organise material logically, verify your decisions and check the flow of your presentation is to work backwards. For example, from control (if used or recommendations if not), check measures will evaluate objectives set and the recommendations made and that recommendations flow from conclusions, which are backed-up by evaluation of analysis.

5.3 Phase 3 – Scope: exploration and creativity

Analysis and evaluation do much to inform managers about the shape and design of the organisation for the future. However, this is an opportunity to explore alternatives and look for creative and innovative solutions. This is important as changing to a marketing orientation requires a better understanding of customers and stakeholders and delivering value that is excellent and/or differentiated.

An evaluation of skills of the change teams will establish which teams/people will be better at this than others. The focus of creativity is on differentiation so ideas about systems, operations, value creation, people management etc should be to identify new ways of doing things and new added-value possibilities that will lead to stronger competitive advantage and opportunities to differentiate.

5.4 Phase 4 – Shape: design and planning

When we have established the current conditions and have a clear understanding of our orientation and approach to customers and the gaps that exist, we can begin to design change. What we want to avoid at this stage is some of the failures we discussed earlier. This requires an **integrated** and thorough approach that looks at the entire organisation and indirect implications as well as direct. We want our initiative to be the result of joined-up thinking, design and action.

The design stage is as much about learning as it is about creating a new order. Sometimes it is difficult to anticipate outcomes until something tangible emerges from the design and only then can sensible judgements be made about the suitability of design. Therefore, it is important to be flexible, willing to learn and if necessary change the design.

5.4.1 Design and integration

There should be goals that determine the desired cultural values. It is important at this stage that leaders and managers demonstrate their commitment to marketing orientation through word and deed. Actions are more important than words: do what you say you believe.

The intention is to design cultural values into what people do and how they do it. This requires focusing on operations, people, process and task and success will only be possible if all employees are involved. These values will be reflected in:

(a) **Design of structure and physical work environment**

- Organised around customers instead of products
- Centralised v decentralised control
- Office space and decor

The Chartered Institute of Marketing

- Equipment and facilities to do the job
- Additional facilities such as rest rooms, car parking

(b) **Design processes, systems and procedures**

- Marketing information and communications
- Efficient and effective from customers' as well as the organisation's perspective
- Ease of use for people delivering value or stakeholders using process
- Health and safety

(c) **Leadership and management practices**

- Professional expertise and practice
- The way work is designed and organised
- The rewards and recognition
- The authority and involvement of employees not just managers
- The type of people recruited
- The approach to learning and development

Employee preparation: the greater part of employee preparation is the identification of learning, training and development needs. Communications also plays a role. The design of blended learning solutions including transfers and secondments should be completed before moving on to Phase 5.

Training precedes implementation and moving into new roles and taking on new tasks. In some cases this may take place on the job but if so experienced coaches or mentors need to be identified before implementation and available during that time. There may be aspects of personal development that are more likely to evolve with implementation. If so this also needs a structure and planning.

Creativity and problem-solving will play a central role throughout design and planning.

Having invited employees to become involved during Phase 2 and 3, in Phase 4 employee communications become a central feature of designing and planning change. There are two aspects to employee communications:

(a) Employee consultations: we consult with them on aspects of design and change.
(b) Employee negotiations: we negotiate for agreement on change.

5.4.2 Managing employee consultations and negotiations: inclusion versus exclusion

The following guidelines are useful for managing change or other situations where consultations and negotiations are required. In changing to a marketing orientation, marketing and other managers need to work in consultation with employees to achieve the goal.

One of the most difficult jobs a manager can become involved in is employee negotiations. Unlike individual interviews such as grievance or discipline, employee negotiations are usually with a group of people, for example between management and unions over changes in the workplace. Whatever the reason, negotiations can often result in emotionally charged situations that can quickly spiral out of control if not handled properly. Employee consultations require skilful communications and careful preparation and follow through.

5.4.3 Preparation

(a) **Outcomes:** focus on and clarify what you want to achieve. This should not be a 'I want my way' goal as it is short sighted and usually requires *'no matter what'*. It results in unhappy, uncooperative employees. Being clear about the outcome allows you to explore the different options open to you.

(b) **Issues:** examine the issues that can help bring into focus the main points to be discussed and dependent factors that are likely to arise. This examination requires two points of view: your own and the employees involved. Trying to see things as others see them can help clarify the problems and concerns.

(c) **Information:** any good negotiator gathers all the facts, not just what has or will happen but also the implications and who will be involved both directly and indirectly. Investigate the various options open and identify common ground.

(d) **Initial possible solutions:** it is worth considering possible solutions and compromises that might have to be made. Begin to think this through before negotiations start when you can think clearly, identify alternative options and assess the impact of compromise. Be prepared for ideas on possible solutions to change during the negotiations in response to the exchange between interested parties.

5.4.4 Approach

Effective negotiators know the secret to success is **persuasion:** take the initiative by engaging the people you need to consult with before any formal consultation meeting. Persuasion takes time and is often more effective in small groups or one to one. Look for opportunities to talk through issues, present consequences of courses of action etc. Marketing managers know the importance of managing expectations and the same is true in consultations. Presenting your case and listening to the other side in a less formal atmosphere can be very productive.

5.4.5 Consultation

- **Build rapport:** even if the consultations have arisen due to conflict it is important to build rapport with all parties. Hopefully some of this will have taken place during pre-negotiations. Respect and trust are vital if negotiations are to have successful outcomes and respect and trust are not built through hostile behaviour.

- **Positions:** it is important not to waste time arguing over positions and falling into the trap of defending a position, no matter how irrelevant or unrealistic. The danger is you become entrenched in a position from which you cannot move. Focus on the issues and concerns and look for areas of mutual interest.

- **Question and listen:** you cannot understand the other point of view without asking questions, often probing questions that reveal all the concerns and facts. Questions indicate you are interested, particularly if you listen to the answers. They also establish exactly what is being asked for.

- **Exploring the options:** you are unlikely to find yourself in a situation where there are only two answers – yours and theirs. There are usually alternative solutions and these need to be discussed and evaluated for their suitability to both sides. Exploring options avoids getting stuck in one place and keeps the negotiations moving forward towards a resolution.

- **Timing:** rather as a comedian's success depends on their timing, so does a negotiator's. Pace the negotiations and make sure you are not presenting alternative solutions before people are ready or persuaded of the benefits.

- **Personalities:** avoid negotiations becoming 'hostilities' because of the personalities involved. Focusing on emotions, eg anger and aggression, risks issues being sidetracked. Try to understand things from different points of view; use active listening skills and avoid barriers to listening; use simple language and avoid being misinterpreted through ill concealed resentment.

- **Agreeing solutions:** before going into negotiations it is important to establish authority for solutions: does it rest with you or will you have to get approval from a higher authority? Conclude the negotiations summarising the concerns and issues and the agreed solutions.

5.4.6 Treaty

A written report of the consultations with agreed solutions must be circulated as soon as possible. Allow time for response and then ensure any agreed actions are implemented. These actions may require support in various forms, for example training or counselling, and arrangements must be made for any support needed.

(a) **Reaction** (employee concerns and support)

As during Phase 2, as people come to terms with the implications of change they will form their own opinions on whether or not they support the change. Rejection may be unavoidable for some people. You are dealing with emotions and feelings and sensitivity and tact are vital. Provide support for those rejecting by allowing them to articulate their concerns and help them translate threats into opportunities. For the enthusiasts allow freedom to examine and define new roles and guide and support where required.

(b) **Despair or doubt** (employee concerns and support)

Despair for opponents or doubt for campaigners may begin to set in at this stage or during implementation. This is a low point when they will or may become disengaged. Underlying concerns will begin to emerge and they may suffer feelings of low self-esteem and confidence. Their doubts or despair may result in them becoming less co-operative. Provide support by encouraging them to explore the positive aspects of change and opportunities that exist and get threats into perspective. Help them see how their strengths fit and the contribution they can make. Reassure them that this is a journey of discovery for all and that others will have similar feelings. We are all learning during this process. Individual discussions are likely to feature more often in communications.

ACTIVITY 10.2

Assessing your own leadership skills, identify what skills you possess to help with change management. Critically evaluate what skills you need to develop to be able to better manage change within your organisation.

---

6 Preparing a plan for change

To ensure that any change programme progresses the choice of communication methods should be agreed between senior managers. Some managers display a preference for face to face meetings while others want information via email or formal methods of communication (reports) or informal briefs. This is also determined by the number of people involved, how dispersed they are and the complexity, timescales and costs involved. In addition to this there needs to be agreement of key timescales for the implementation of change as well as mutual agreement on feedback mechanisms across different areas and departments of the organisation.

6.1 Phase 5 – Action: implementation and control

Once agreement has been reached on all aspects of change and design completed, plans for implementing change begin. There will still be the need for consultations and negotiations during this stage but the focus of communications changes to updates on progress.

Setting new objectives signals a marketing orientation and objectives can include customer satisfaction and loyalty, employee performance (particularly customer service) and morale.

6.1.1 Implementation and control

It is now time to transfer strategy into tactical action plans, a new way of doing things.

Each section, department, and team incorporates the new values as an integral part of their work.

- The way in which they co-operate and collaborate
- Taking a pride in their work
- Meeting quality targets
- Meeting or exceeding targets
- Taking initiatives to improve and solve problems

Action (or project) plans determine who is doing what, when, where and how. Objectives, budgets, schedules and measures are all part of the action plans. Personal targets and performance standards are agreed with individuals and teams. Authority is delegated with responsibility. Pay attention to the scheduling of events.

Control of the change process requires measurements that link back to the objectives, setting-up feedback mechanisms for monitoring and evaluating progress and appraisals, possibly more regularly than usual.

The feedback mechanisms and appraisals allow managers and employees to learn during the change and make any necessary adjustments and modifications. Creativity and problem-solving skills will continue to be needed at this stage.

During implementation continue to communicate and keep the momentum going. For example, you can use visual effects to show how things are progressing towards success, eg:

- Moving graph of reduced complaints
- Moving graph of improving organisation image
- Changing from current position to desired position
- Improving sales/profits

This should be linked back to team and individual performance to be meaningful.

(a) **Exploration (employee concerns and support)**

Allow exploration, experimentation and focus on priorities. Employees need to feel in control of events and that they are genuinely being given responsibility for shaping the changes and improvements. Provide support by giving feedback, guiding and coaching or mentoring where required.

(b) **Engagement (employee concerns and support)**

Some employees will become engaged earlier than others and for some during implementation. For others they may not be fully engaged until there is time to consolidate and assess where you have arrived. Longer-term goals can now be established. Provide support through recognition and reward for progress and success. Controls and supervision change at this stage from controlling the change to the usual controls on performance. Employees can take more responsibility for moving forward.

6.2 Phase 6 – Unite: consolidation and learning

Even if you work in an organisation where continuous change and improvement is a way of life managers have a duty to provide a sense of achievement and a period of consolidation.

Allow time for employees to become familiar with new work routines and practices. There may still be some training, coaching or mentoring required. Employees will either be re-enforcing old social networks or building new and these networks should be encouraging behaviour that reflects the desired values of a marketing orientation. This is a time to embed new ways of doing things.

People are still adapting to a different way of doing things and exploration of what works and what needs adjusting may still be required.

Provide opportunities for review and learning from the process of change, the experiences and activities. Humour will be helpful during this review. Be prepared to laugh (together), if appropriate, at the things that went wrong, the ridiculous and even each other if you are all strong enough post-change. Confront the scary things that happened; share the doubts and concerns in an open and supportive way.

This learning is not just a therapeutic session; the learning is captured to inform any further change and improvement initiatives so that problems and mistakes can be minimised or avoided and successes can be repeated.

Staples, the retail stationers, is an example of an organisation that recognises the direct link between leadership and high organisation performance. Its HR Director spends a lot of time thinking and talking to leaders about how to achieve high performance. He does not believe it is an HR issue but rather a leadership challenge and the challenge is how to negotiate a balance between the organisation (its structure, culture, systems and leadership style) and its people (attitudes, behaviour, skills and output).

The HR Director argues that too often in response to changing trends and the increasing sophistication and demands of customers leaders focus on changing structures and processes rather than attitudes and behaviour where a real valuable difference can be achieved. For leaders who focus on changing operations the usual result is people being able to take less initiative. Leaders need to focus on how they get people to take responsibility for changes that can make a positive and relevant difference.

The leadership challenge is how to create the right environment where people are motivated and willing to take responsibility for developing appropriate attitudes and behaviour and given freedom to innovate. How do leaders move from managing this initiative to leading?

Staples is in the process of creating such an environment. It has started by helping leaders across the organisation understand more about the results they have been getting and how they are directly linked to beliefs and assumptions they hold about themselves or the organisation. This new understanding helps them to make positive choices about work and their lives. The results have been excellent with an observable change in behaviour and Staples can see managers developing into leaders who motivate.

6.3 Managing customer transitions

During change it is easy to become wrapped up in the detail of internal activities and events and there is no question these need extra attention. However, the marketing manager has an additional responsibility. Throughout the entire change project marketing managers are responsible for making sure the focus on customers or stakeholders is not lost. For minor changes and adjustments this is not usually a problem but for major changes it can be.

6.3.1 Integrated marketing communications

Integrated marketing communications are the marketing leader's means to ensure customer transitions are managed. For example, if the organisation is merging with another or changing position customers need to understand what is happening if they are not to be lost. If we take merging brands as an example the marketing communications plan needs to take customers on a journey. First, what does the merger mean for customers: different quality products, different quality service or different people?

In this example there may be two distinct and different customer groups served by each organisation. The decision may be to focus on one segment. In this case communications will be designed to inform, reassure and persuade customers of additional advantages and benefits that arise from the merger. If the desire is to maintain all customer groups communications over time will reflect the best of both brands and again inform, reassure and persuade customers that the separate brands will become one and enhance the customer experience not damage it. Of course, actions speak louder than words and if change does not enhance the customer experience it is back to the drawing board before you start losing customers.

During mergers as employees struggle to come to terms with a complex mix of organisation values and try to sort out what it means for them, customers will be trying to make sense of what the new brand values represent.

Communications need to be careful they do not over promise during change. There can be a danger of communicating the vision long before it is achieved. There is nothing wrong with communicating the vision but

keep in it perspective and ensure promises are honest and achievable: what can realistically be expected during periods of change? Depending on the length of time the change will take different slogans reflecting different stages of progress may be appropriate to signal to customers where you are and where you are going.

6.3.2 Customer service and relationship management

Customer service will be the other area where customers can be lost or retained depending on how change is managed. During a merger there may be differences in approach or in technology used. The experience for customers at worst needs to remain the same and for some may need to improve. Managers and employees need to focus their attention on customer service first, even if it is a short-term solution, so that customers do not become the innocent victims of internal struggles and differences.

During the audit, particularly with a change to a marketing orientation, the market will have been segmented to establish customer groups the organisation wants to focus on. This refocusing of business activities means the organisation will now prioritise customers and these customers are the customers the organisation wants to build long-term relationships with. This is through enhancing customer value and experiences, so as change takes place the marketers in the organisation need to ensure the change is focused on customer value and improving experiences to retain customers.

Even when a marketing orientation has been achieved marketing directors cannot sit back and assume 'the end'. A marketing orientation will come under threat over time for a variety of reasons. Economic downturns and periods of change, eg customer trends, technology, new or different competitive threats, can result in an inward focus or focus on competitors rather than customers and the orientation slips into something else.

Ways to avoid this include ongoing internal communications, delivering results that are linked to success and supporting with evidence of what a marketing orientation can achieve.

ACTIVITY 10.3

Using your own experience critically evaluate how well customers have been managed during a change initiative. What worked well and what did not? What improvements could you recommend and why?

ACTIVITY 10.4

Identify the skills you feel are required to manage and implement change in your organisation. Use examples from different industries of individuals you feel have managed change well.

6.4 Future digital marketing considerations

With the growth of digital communicatons, marketers at corporate level will need to take into account the influence of digital communications from a number of different perspectives. Forms of communication in marketing terms, from on-line, website development, the creation of word of mouth blogs, chat rooms and the influence of social media.

Leaders and leadership teams will need to understand the impact of digital communications both internally within the organisation and externally from different stakeholder perspectives. The influence of social media as an internal form of communication will also need to be incorporated at planning and leadership level to ensure organisations both small and large are developing and evolving with market changes.

CHAPTER ROUNDUP

- Globalisation is a fundamental of doing business in today's world; the impact of globalisation on businesses needs to be understood.

- There are many drivers for change, both internal and external.

- Ignoring the need for change has implications. These implications must be understood by management; ignoring these could be dangerous to the organisation.

- Understanding the barriers to change is the first step in overcoming the barriers and managing change.

- Change can be evolutionary and revolutionary.

- Leadership, management and the organisational culture are a fundamental part of change management.

- Change can be planned, but the execution is as important as the plan.

FURTHER READING

Conner, D.R. (2006) *Managing at the speed of change*. New York, Villard Books.

Coulson-Thomas, C. (2004) *Shaping things to come, strategies for creating alternative enterprises*. Dublin, Blackhall Publishing.

Coulson-Thomas, C. (2004) *Transforming the company, manage change, compete & win*. London, Kogan Page.

De Wit, B. and Meyer, R. (2005) *Strategy synthesis: resolving strategy paradoxes to create competitive advantage, test and readings*. 2nd edition. London, Thomson.

Doyle, P. and Stern, P. (2006) *Marketing management and strategy.* 4th edition. Harlow, Prentice Hall.

Hooley, G. *et al* (2007) *Marketing strategy and competitive positioning*. 4th edition. Harlow, Prentice Hall.

Johnson, S. (1998) *Who moved my cheese?: an amazing way to deal with change in your work and in your life*. London, Vermilion.

Vecchio, R.P. (2007) *Leadership, understanding the dynamics of power and influence in organisations.* 2nd revised edition. University of Notre Dame.

Lancaster, G, Massingham L & Ashford R (2002) *Essentials of Marketing*. McGraw-Hill Education, Berkshire.

The Chartered Institute of Marketing

REFERENCES

Adam, J., Hayes J. and Hopkins B. (1976) *Transition understanding and managing personal change*. London, Martin Robertson & Co.

De Wit, B. and Meyer R. (2005) *Strategy synthesis: resolving strategy paradoxes to create competitive advantage*. London, Thomson.

Hope Hailey V. and Balogun, J. (2002) Devising context sensitive approaches to change: the example of Glaxo Wellcome. *Long Range Planning*, 35(2), pp153–178.

Lasserre, P. and Schutte, H. (2006) *Strategies for Asia Pacific: meeting new challenges*. 3rd edition. Basingstoke, Palgrave Macmillan.

Lewin, K. (1951) *Field theory in social science: selected theoretical papers*. New York, Harper.

Waterman, R.H., Peters, T.J. and Phillips, J.R. (1980) Structure is not organisation. *McKinsey Quarterly* in-house Journal, New York, McKinsey & Co.

Wilson, D. (1993) *A strategy of change: concepts and controversies in the management of change*. London, Routledge.

QUICK QUIZ

1   Provide examples of external and internal drivers of change.

2   Broadly what two methods are there for change?

3   What organisation cultural values will facilitate change and what will inhibit change?

4   Who are the key people involved in change in organisations and what broadly is their role?

5   What are the clues to whether or not an organisation is marketing-oriented?

6   What are the stages people might go through during periods of change?

7   Why would you segment your internal market during management of change and what might these segments be?

8   What are the key factors in effective management of change?

ACTIVITY DEBRIEFS

Activity 10.1

This will very much depend on your organisation but the sort of things you will be looking for are, for example, technology, operational or system changes that lead to increased efficiency or customer value changes that lead to increased differentiation and customer demand and loyalty. Was it obvious to all why the change was taking place and the consequences of not changing? Were people involved and motivated? Did the change achieve the objectives?

Activity 10.2

This requires an analysis of one's own leadership skills generally and in the context of the change required. A critical rather than descriptive evaluation is required of how the changes can be better managed, and how it will advantage the whole organisation.

Activity 10.3

Hopefully customers will not even notice change most of the time but where it is inevitable they will be affected it is essential to keep them on board. Your evaluation might reveal customers were ignored as the focus moved internally; they were confused or lost, even hostile and engaged in a campaign of 'bad mouthing' the organisation. Alternatively, you may find customers were impressed and only noticed the benefits. Improvements might include a carefully constructed communications programme and relationship building activities.

Activity 10.4

This requires the key skills to be identified that will help to not only manage, but also implement, change in your own organisation. To develop this the use of illustrative examples will help to question, consider and understand the skills required. Using other examples can help you think about your own leadership and management skills.

QUICK QUIZ ANSWERS

1. – Macro factors eg political, legal, economic, social, technological, environmental
   – Micro factors eg competitors, supply, channels to market
   – Internal factors eg strategic direction, systems, skills

2. – Evolution – gradual and often continuous small changes
   – Revolution – intermittent large scale change usually in response to some crisis

3. – Culture for change – eg willing to take risks, trust and respect, supportive, creative, curious
   – Culture blocking change – eg blame mentality, risk averse, controlling, traditional

4. – Leadership scope and vision change.
   – Management shape and manage change.
   – Employees implement change.
   – Customers and other stakeholders (eg shareholders) may influence change.
   – Distributors and suppliers may also indirectly influence change and should not be forgotten in the change process.

The Chartered Institute of Marketing

5   – People – valued, marketing education, training and qualifications represented at board level.

  – Culture and structure – values focus on people and their needs and structures are designed to improve employee performance to meet customer needs.

  – Value creation and innovation – business activities are designed to meet customer needs not in spite of customer needs. Customer input into design of product and services is important.

  – Information is seen as vital to planning and the information gathering process is selective, formalised and information is used.

  – Co-ordination and integration are a feature of business operations ensuring the customer receives added value.

  – Good communications and will be open and honest.

  – Learning and development are planned for and focuses on improving relative to customer needs.

  – Measuring effectiveness includes customer satisfaction measures.

6   – Shock and denial – difficulty in coming to terms with changes and refusal to accept what is happening

  – There can be a danger of hopelessness and a feeling of being out of control

  – Acceptance – providing they are supported

  – Experimentation – to allow understanding and to build confidence

  – Commitment – engaging in work routines again and focusing on goals

7 Internal markets need to be understood if resistance to change and perceptions of threats are to be minimised. Change can only be successful if the people responsible for managing and implementing change accept the change.

To understand these internal markets we need to understand how people perceive the intended changes and what effect it will have on them. Different people will be affected in different ways and if we know how they are affected we can set up support systems and training programmes that will help them come to terms with the change and take on their new tasks and responsibilities.

Internal markets will typically be segmented as drivers of change, resistors and neutrals.

8   – Clear objective of the purpose of change
  – Planning for change
  – Communications – internal marketing
  – Segmenting internal market
  – Involving people – project and design teams
  – Learning and development
  – Support systems
  – Evaluation

Index

Index

The Chartered
Institute of Marketing

The Chartered
Institute of Marketing

The Chartered
Institute of Marketing

The Chartered
Institute of Marketing

The Chartered
Institute of Marketing

Review form

Please help us to ensure that the CIM learning materials we produce remain as accurate and user-friendly as possible. We cannot promise to answer every submission we receive, but we do promise that it will be read and taken into account when we update this Study Text.

Name: _____   Address: _____

_____

_____

1. How have you used this Text?
(Tick one box only)

☐ Self study (book only)

☐ On a course: college_____

☐ Other _____

3. Why did you decide to purchase this Text?
(Tick one box only)

☐ Have used companion Assessment workbook

☐ Have used BPP Texts in the past

☐ Recommendation by friend/colleague

☐ Recommendation by a lecturer at college

☐ Saw advertising in journals

☐ Saw information on BPP website

☐ Other _____

2. During the past six months do you recall seeing/receiving any of the following?
(Tick as many boxes as are relevant)

☐ Our advertisement in *The Marketer*

☐ Our brochure with a letter through the post

☐ Our website www.bpp.com

4. Which (if any) aspects of our advertising do you find useful?
(Tick as many boxes as are relevant)

☐ Prices and publication dates of new editions

☐ Information on product content

☐ Facility to order books off-the-page

☐ None of the above

5. Have you used the companion Assessment Workbook?   Yes ☐   No ☐

6. Have you used the companion Passcards?   Yes ☐   No ☐

7. Your ratings, comments and suggestions would be appreciated on the following areas.

	Very useful	Useful	Not useful
Introductory section (How to use this text, study checklist, etc)	☐	☐	☐
Chapter introductions	☐	☐	☐
Syllabus learning outcomes	☐	☐	☐
Activities	☐	☐	☐
The Real World examples	☐	☐	☐
Quick quizzes	☐	☐	☐
Quality of explanations			
Index	☐	☐	☐
Structure and presentation	☐	☐	☐

	Excellent	Good	Adequate	Poor
Overall opinion of this Text	☐	☐	☐	☐

8. Do you intend to continue using BPP CIM products?   ☐ Yes   ☐ No

On the reverse of this page is space for you to write your comments about our Study Text. We welcome your feedback.

Please return to: CIM Publishing Manager, BPP Learning Media, FREEPOST, London, W12 8BR.

Marketing Leadership and Planning

TELL US WHAT YOU THINK

Please note any further comments and suggestions/errors below. For example, was the text accurate, readable, concise, user-friendly and comprehensive?

TQ